Breaking Protocol

Breaking Protocol

America's First Female Ambassadors, 1933–1964

Philip Nash

UNIVERSITY PRESS OF KENTUCKY

Scholarly publisher for the Commonwealth,
serving Bellarmine University, Berea College, Centre
College of Kentucky, Eastern Kentucky University,
The Filson Historical Society, Georgetown College,
Kentucky Historical Society, Kentucky State University,
Morehead State University, Murray State University,
Northern Kentucky University, Transylvania University,
University of Kentucky, University of Louisville,
and Western Kentucky University.
All rights reserved.

Editorial and Sales Offices: The University Press of Kentucky
663 South Limestone Street, Lexington, Kentucky 40508-4008
www.kentuckypress.com

Library of Congress Cataloging-in-Publication Data

Names: Nash, Philip, 1963– author.
Title: Breaking protocol : America's first female ambassadors, 1933–1964 /
    Philip Nash.
Other titles: America's first female ambassadors, 1933–1964
Description: Lexington, Kentucky : University Press of Kentucky, [2020] |
    Series: Studies in conflict, diplomacy, and peace | Includes
    bibliographical references and index.
Identifiers: LCCN 2019037381 | ISBN 9780813178394 (hardcover) | ISBN
    9780813178400 (pdf) | ISBN 9780813178417 (epub)
Subjects: LCSH: Women diplomats—United States—History—20th century. |
    Ambassadors—United States—Biography. | Diplomatic and consular
    service, American. | Women ambassadors—United States—Biography. |
    United States. Foreign Service—Biography.
Classification: LCC E747 .N37 2020 | DDC 327.73009252 [B]—dc23
LC record available at https://lccn.loc.gov/2019037381

This book is printed on acid-free paper meeting
the requirements of the American National Standard
for Permanence in Paper for Printed Library Materials.

Manufactured in the United States of America.

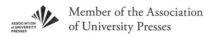

To the memory of
Gerald C. Nash (1932–2001)
and Caroline J. Nash (1935–2017)

History is a slow growth; great events do not happen every day, but are the culmination of quiet years during which there is apparently nothing going on.

—Emily Bax, *Miss Bax of the Embassy*, 1939

Contents

Prologue

Who should represent the United States overseas? Especially day after day, on the ground, where the crucial but seldom-noticed routine business of foreign relations is conducted? Should our diplomats more or less reflect the diversity of the American people? That is, should our representatives be *representative?* For much of our history, they have not been, neither in terms of class, nor race—nor sex. "It used to be," soon-to-be secretary of state Madeleine K. Albright said in 1996, "that the only way a woman could truly make her foreign policy views felt was by marrying a diplomat and then pouring tea on an offending ambassador's lap." We now live in a very different age, when women enjoy myriad opportunities to influence foreign relations in many countries, including the United States. But they also still have quite a ways to go before they enjoy equal influence in this diplomatic world. For both reasons, we should learn more about the pioneers, the first women to enter the world of formal American diplomacy. This book is an attempt to help us do so.[1]

It tells the story of the first half-dozen female US ambassadors, who served between 1933 and 1964. "Shirley Temple Black?" I am sometimes asked when I tell people what I have been working on. No, not Shirley Temple Black, ambassador to Ghana (1974–1976) and the Czech Republic (1989–1992), a far more recent envoy who, despite the grip she obviously retains on the popular imagination, lies beyond the scope of this study. Rather, they include the generally less well known Ruth Bryan Owen, Florence "Daisy" Harriman, Perle Mesta, Eugenie Anderson, Clare Boothe Luce, and Frances Willis. The history of these "Big Six," as they were once called, has never been told. When these women have been written about, the works are usually individual biographies, autobiographies, or narrower articles on particular aspects of their lives or careers. Alternatively, some are quite dated or based on limited evidence. This is the first work to examine the Big Six in a group biography, one that places them in a broader historical context based on deep and broad research in archival sources, some of them only recently made available. Researching women in foreign relations can be challenging, partly because we often lack the sources available in some other fields of history. In this case, the more prosaic difficulties seen in all fields also arose, especially the fact that neither Ruth Owen nor Perle Mesta left accessible papers behind, necessitating reliance on other sources to fill those sizeable evidentiary gaps.[2]

This is largely an act of historical recovery, capturing the experiences of these women, restoring them to their rightful places in the history of women in foreign relations. It contributes to the larger project of rendering women in international history visible. As Glenda Sluga and Carolyn James have noted, "one can study gender in these political settings where men remain dominant and women are rarely to be seen, on the understanding that women are just not there." This has meant that despite the evidence of women's agency in the world of diplomacy, they remain absent from many if not most histories of international relations. This omission itself, of course, reflects the power of patriarchy: even when masculinity and femininity are studied, the men get attention and the women get lost, as if to reinforce the assumption we are trying to question.[3]

To be sure, until very recently, diplomatic women were indeed the exception. The "exceptional women" approach to this history, which seeks to recognize those few unsung women who have played roles in US foreign relations, is one of four ways scholars have incorporated women and gender into the history of American foreign relations, as Emily Rosenberg noted in 1990. The other three are the "women's work" approach, which studies women who have worked internationally in gender-typed capacities, such as missionaries, nurses, and peace activists; the gender ideology approach, which explores how gendered concepts and imagery in such areas as popular culture have affected US foreign relations; and the "Women in Development" approach, which emerges from the world systems literature to reformulate fundamentally the study of international relations along gender lines. The first of these does suffer from certain limitations. Rosenberg expressed concern that "by reinforcing women's roles as outsiders," this focus may "actually perpetuate exclusion." Or, worse still, if only atypical women appear in the history of foreign relations, then "the analysis may implicitly suggest that the problem with women lies in their being women and not men," thus in effect blaming women for their own marginality.[4]

These are legitimate concerns. The problem is, we do not yet understand nearly enough about those exceptional women's stories. Most of the scholars working in this subfield have moved beyond Rosenberg's first approach to pursue the others. Restoring women to history has been a much more "primitive phase" in the growth of gender history, as Sluga and James argue, but that makes it no less crucial, and it has made few appearances even as international history has thrived in recent years. In turning to gender, many historians have missed the importance of looking for women's agency. Historian Molly Wood agrees, urging US foreign relations historians to "'drill down' into lives of long-forgotten individual women and men."[5]

Moreover, much of the scholarship that has focused on exceptional women has neglected an important subgroup: female ambassadors. With very few exceptions, they were the most influential women in US foreign relations until the 1980s, and they were part of the important, larger process of change. More specifically, the suggestion Joan Hoff made twenty-five years ago, sadly, remains true: we cannot yet even begin to generalize properly about the history of women in foreign relations without the biographies of these ambassadors.[6]

Thus, this study occupies the intersection of foreign relations history and women's history, an exercise nevertheless vital to the writing of gender history. Writing several years ago, Alice Kessler-Harris wanted to fight for a history of women and gender—both equally important—"where gender constitutes the relational category, and the history of women the arena that we have yet to excavate." It is still the case, as she wrote, that "we have not yet fished out" that latter "pond." She added, "Unless gender history challenges the normative view of the world through the eyes of men, unless it continues to build on a growing knowledge of how women thought and acted, it could kill the goose that laid the golden egg." I agree, and I have written this book in the spirit that Sluga and James, Wood, Hoff, and Kessler-Harris evoke.[7]

It will begin by establishing the historical context, the male-dominated world of American diplomacy in the first half of the twentieth century. It will then devote one chapter each to the six female ambassadors, describing their backgrounds, explaining their motivations and how they came to be appointed, and analyzing the issues they faced and experiences they had. These will include the complications of diplomatic protocol; in light of the crucial importance of the traditional diplomatic spouse, how they coped without one; the media coverage they received, which was paradoxically overwhelmingly favorable and yet deeply sexist; and their sometimes fraught relationships with the State Department and career Foreign Service. Along the way, the reader should get some sense of what an ambassador's job was like in the mid-twentieth century. The book will also examine how others perceived these women and, in part drawing on these perceptions, evaluate their performances. And it will argue that, to a remarkable degree, these women proved themselves far ahead of their time for their practice of "people's diplomacy," establishing connections to their host countries' broader societies, and not just to their elite or official circles. It will end by drawing some conclusions about the Big Six as a group, assessing their importance, and outlining the history of women in American diplomacy since the mid-1960s. I hope that "Uncle Sam's Diplomatic Nieces" afterward will have reaffirmed that a woman's place is in the embassy.[8]

1

The Patriarchs

American Diplomats in the Early Twentieth Century

Ambassador: A man, just a little below God.
—Lillie de Hegermann-Lindencrone,
"The Alphabet of a Diplomat," 1914

In June 1896, the humor magazine *Life* featured a cartoon titled *An Ambassador's Ball in the Days to Come.* Assembled in their finery, diplomatic decorations prominently displayed, almost a dozen envoys filled the space. It was a scene unexceptional apart from what it lacked: men.[1]

This vision of a diplomatic world not only breached but hijacked by women belonged to Charles Dana Gibson, creator of the Gibson Girl, and, consistent with Gibson's own ambivalence toward what his progeny represented, the cartoon can be read in at least two ways. In one interpretation, the picture is playful and positive. For this was one of a series of illustrations in which the Gibson Girl appeared in a variety of exclusively male roles, including those of lawyer, general, minister, and athlete. That is, the Gibson Girl symbolized the "New Woman," strong, independent, breaking boundaries. In *An Ambassador's Ball,* the center of attention is in fact the archetypal Gibson Girl, the youngest, prettiest, tallest woman in the group, beheld warily by some of the other women, but standing there erect, confident, more than holding her own.[2]

From another angle, *An Ambassador's Ball* captures the gender anxiety of the late nineteenth and early twentieth centuries in America. Native-born, middle-class American men especially sensed a multipronged challenge to their manhood from immigrants, the working class, and, by no means least, women. Perhaps Gibson knew his male-free gala would touch a nerve and he

AN AMBASSADOR'S BALL IN THE DAYS TO COME.

Charles Dana Gibson, *An Ambassador's Ball in Days to Come* (1896). This image depicts the "Gibson Girl" or "New Woman" (*right*) not only breaking into a traditionally male profession, but joining other women in taking it over. Gibson may have been playing on male fears about what might result from the movement for women's equality. (Charles Dana Gibson, *Pictures of People* [New York: Russell, 1896])

was aiming to provoke as well as amuse. Because as the New Woman staked her claims and the women's suffrage movement gained strength, many men feared that a sweeping inversion of gender roles lay ahead. Women might not only break into the men's worlds of politics, breadwinning, or the professions, they might seize complete control of them—thus forcing men into women's roles. One can imagine many of *Life*'s male readers enjoying Gibson's work for its humor, even its absurdity, but also becoming a tad uneasy at the prospect of all portions of the public sphere, even the crucial business of international relations, falling into the hands of their mothers, sisters, or daughters.[3]

A Man's World

Those who dreaded even the slightest step in this direction, however, need not have worried—and not for a very long time. That is because the American diplomatic world of the early twentieth century was one made up—with a tiny handful of exceptions, and among chiefs of mission with no exceptions whatsoever, until 1933—of men. For the time being, their stranglehold was secure. In "days to come," ambassadors' parties would remain completely stag.

The most important shapers of this overwhelmingly male world overseas were the chiefs of mission—whether ministers running legations or ambassadors in charge of embassies, depending on the level of representation between the foreign and host countries (I will use *ambassador* and *chief* as shorthand). What were ambassadors expected to do? In one sense, an ambassador's job was, and is, straightforward: stay out of trouble. Do not embarrass one's country. In the late nineteenth century, before America's international commitments and diplomatic seriousness grew in tandem, more than a few US ambassadors simply disgraced the flag on a routine basis. For example, Robert Beisner writes of Minister to Japan Charles E. DeLong, "who sent ungrammatical and misspelled dispatches" home and "astonished the Japanese by careening through Tokyo streets at full speed in his carriage, his whip cracking at startled pedestrians and a pistol stuck prominently in his belt." Mercifully, such appointments dwindled in number. And in our own time, most have been able to avoid the fate, say, of the Israeli ambassador to El Salvador who, in 2007, was recalled after having been found by police in the yard of his residence drunk, tied up, gagged with a ball and wearing a sex bondage outfit.[4]

But that is setting the bar a little low; much more was expected of a chief of mission. The list of an ambassador's basic responsibilities provided by Cordell Hull, President Franklin D. Roosevelt's secretary of state, is as good as any. An envoy's first task was reporting, "to keep us informed, speedily, accurately, and with absolute impartiality." Second was representation, "to interpret our ideals, explain our policies, make friends, and facilitate . . . the transaction of our Government's business." Third came negotiation, which of course entailed following Washington's instructions and often, in the case of technical issues, "detailed study." Fourth and finally, ambassadors had to protect American lives and property.[5]

These all seem straightforward enough. But beyond them, endless tasks arose to keep chiefs of mission, certainly at the larger posts, constantly busy. According to Walter Hines Page, America's ambassador to Britain during World War I, these included "American marriages which they always want the ambassador to attend; getting them out of jail when they are jugged; looking after the American insane, helping Americans move the bones of their ancestors; interpreting the income tax law; receiving medals from Americans; hear[ing] American fiddlers, pianists, players; sitting for American sculptors and photographers, writing letters of introduction, getting tickets to the House gallery . . . and art galleries . . . ; people who are going to have a fair here; lunch for returning and outgoing diplomats, people who present books, women who wish to go to court."[6]

The diversity of these chores and responsibilities was not matched by the diversity of the diplomats themselves. Decades into the twentieth century, American diplomatic circles were highly exclusive, on the basis of race, class, education—and sex. The old saw that diplomats were "pale, male, and Yale" was inaccurate only insofar as they typically had graduated from several elite universities (and before that, boarding schools), not just Yale. The diplomats believed, Hugh Wilson commented in 1927, that "they belonged to a pretty good club." This sentiment was widely shared among those who, like Wilson, dominated US diplomacy and founded the modern Foreign Service, known as the "Old Hands." Indeed, George F. Kennan, with a non-elite, midwestern background but rather strong elitist sensibilities, may have seen the Foreign Service as an opportunity to join an exclusive club, an opportunity he had missed when he was enrolled at Princeton.[7]

This "club" was elite—and elitist. The Old Hands overwhelmingly saw their role, as the standard guide at the time put it, as "the application of intelligence and tact to the conduct of official relations between governments of independent states." Even to those of the younger generation, such as Kennan, this was the very definition of diplomacy. And so, diplomats spent the lion's share of their time, both during business hours and afterward, cultivating relations with their diplomatic counterparts and other members of the host capital's upper crust. As understandable as this tendency was, it fostered considerable insularity.[8]

Occasionally one of the Old Hands would see a need to burst the bubble. Diplomats should concern themselves with "all of those relationships carried on by the people of one country with the people of another," Hugh Wilson wrote in 1941. They must learn the host country's ways, language, and developments through a variety of sources and people. Some outside observers argued similarly. A chief of mission "quickly discovers that his duties are not limited to brushing off his silk hat and going to tea every day," Bertram Hulen wrote in 1939. He "must keep in touch with diverse interests so that he may interpret the country in every aspect to his government."[9]

And at times, ambassadors took this advice. For example, Harry Truman's ambassador to Iran, Henry Grady, and his senior staff helped perform the manual labor necessary to complete the construction of a public park in Tehran (a project launched and led by his wife, Lucretia). This act came as a shock to some of Grady's allied counterparts in the city, and British newspapers decried the loss of ambassadorial dignity involved. But Grady was proud about what his participation suggested about American values. As FDR's envoy to Britain during World War II, another ambassador, John Winant, sent far more powerful signals. Arriving during the Blitz, he was immediately embraced by his hosts, and not only because he was someone other than Joseph P. Kennedy, his defeatist predecessor who had taken up residence outside of London to avoid the bombs. Soon after his arrival, Winant was seen everywhere, both during and after visits from the Luftwaffe and heedless of his own safety, touring ruins, comforting the newly homeless, offering assistance—in short, leaving the office and bolstering British morale by personifying American concern for its future ally during the Empire's darkest time.[10]

The contrast between the widely and narrowly exposed envoys was something Ellis Briggs saw firsthand as a newly minted Foreign Service Officer in Peru in the late 1920s. Briggs's first chief of mission in Lima, Miles Poindexter, often traveled the country and got to know it. He told Briggs that the gravest issue facing Peru was the one of Native Americans, especially the virtual serfdom under which they toiled. Poindexter's successor, Alexander Moore, was perhaps an extreme case but still closer to representative in that era. About the indigenous people, Briggs noted, Moore "knew little and cared less." Their fate was none of the United States' business. More generally, Moore wondered, why travel in Peru, "when Lima was the only comfortable place in the country?" Briggs, to his credit, seems to have learned more from Poindexter. During World War II, by which time he had become ambassador to the Dominican Republic, Briggs wandered much of the Dominican countryside and, under the guise of bird shooting, conversed with many local farmers.[11]

But in the first half of the century, this expansive definition of a chief's proper circle of familiarity was not widely shared. Closer to the norm was the quintessential Old Hand, Joseph Grew. He formed elitist habits right away; as second secretary at the Berlin embassy before the First World War, while professing attachment to the American democratic ideal, Grew nevertheless happily immersed himself in the aristocratic society of Wilhelmine Germany. Looking back, he had to admit that diplomats constituted almost all of his good friends in Berlin. As minister to Denmark in the 1920s, Grew similarly became quite intimate with the Copenhagen "blue book," its official diplomatic list. He knew he must get out more, and he met a few business leaders and learned enough Danish to read the local newspapers. But he made no friends with the businessmen, and he seldom spoke Danish (probably because most prominent Danes spoke English). He considered public speaking a painful chore, and his exposure to common Danes was more labored still. Family outings to the beach or the fair often ended early on account of "the dirty, smelly crowd of all the rabble of Copenhagen." He once hosted a group of Danish American singers who were listed as tradesmen; he noted in his diary, "They look it."[12]

In 1932, Grew moved on to the most important post of his career: ambassador to Japan in the crucial years leading up to Pearl Harbor. Ordinary Japanese people only appeared in his later-published diary excerpts when he quoted as amusing asides the broken English in their letters to the embassy. Rather, Grew continued to maintain a rather limited circle of acquaintance: apart from other diplomats, this consisted almost entirely of businessmen, naval officers, and members of the court set. And, because the relative moderates on whom Grew pinned his hopes for preserving a peaceful US–Japanese relationship were heavily overrepresented among his contacts, his isolation in this context may have led him to overestimate their importance and thus seriously warped his reporting.[13]

This insularity among many chiefs of mission had not changed very much by mid-century. In 1953, with the Cold War well underway, former US high commissioner for Germany John J. McCloy argued that to compete with the Communists, the United States needed effective representation "at the level of the people themselves." As high commissioner, he had found meetings with farmers, labor, journalists, academics, and youth leaders far more useful than any diplomatic reception. And yet, at this late date, McCloy still had to state that with few exceptions, envoys still viewed any nongovernmental interactions as "imprudent or as intervention in the domestic affairs of other sovereign states." He then wondered, with considerable understatement, "whether this meets the modern need." Eight years later, incoming president John F. Kennedy wrote, in his general instructions to new ambassadors, "The practice of modern diplomacy requires a close understanding not only of governments but also of people, their cultures, and institutions. Therefore, I hope that you will plan your work so that you may have the time to travel extensively outside the nation's capital. Only in this way can you develop the close, personal associations that go beyond official diplomatic circles and maintain a sympathetic and accurate understanding of all segments of the country." That Kennedy felt the need to ask this of his envoys suggests that as late as 1961, many ambassadors simply did not get out much or, at the very least, were widely perceived as not doing so.[14]

Protocol

"Protocol and striped pants," Harry Truman once wrote, "give me a pain in the neck." Considering how arcane or unnecessary many of diplomacy's formal conventions seem to outsiders, one can understand Truman's impatience. But at its root, protocol is entirely justified, and ambassadors and their staffs devoted considerable attention to it for good reason. Protocol had emerged alongside formal diplomacy centuries earlier as a means of imposing order on a profoundly chaotic, even violent enterprise. "Protocol is the art of manners," wrote Old Hand William Phillips, "primarily intended to simplify and formalize the social relationship between peoples of different countries."[15]

Protocol also established the recognition of precedence and prestige among diplomats who, after all, were extensions of sovereign nations for which recognition counted greatly. The longest-serving foreign ambassador in a capital's diplomatic corps became known as its dean or doyen, a prestigious post whose occupant served as spokesperson for all members regarding their rights and privileges. "Every curlicue in protocol," Waldo Heinrichs notes, "had as its objective the preservation of unruffled national dignity." The principle of precedence, or seniority, for example, established by the Congress of Vienna in 1815, settled the nightmarish disputes over seating arrangements at state dinners. Such rules were eminently practical as well. Without those for seating precedence, a British protocol chief argued, people would not know where to sit. "Apart from everything else," he added, "the damned soup would get cold." Other curlicues included a new ambassador's presentation of credentials and calls made upon all the other ambassadors, how to entertain (excessive opulence and frugality were equally to be avoided), and how to dress for official functions. Treatment of another country's representatives within the rules of protocol, moreover, was an extremely useful means of signaling favor or disfavor; this only served to increase its political salience. Some of the particulars of protocol may have been arbitrary, but all its facets were well-established by the early twentieth century and diplomats had no choice but to take them seriously.[16]

But how seriously? One American hostess so angered her most important guests by seating them according to her fancy rather than to protocol that they left the dinner early. She thought they were acting like "overgrown babies," but her husband, apparently, soon found himself seeking another line of work. Protocol was an important part of the diplomatic world, and one did not violate or alter it willy-nilly.[17]

Spouses

One large group of women did inhabit this man's world: diplomatic spouses. It is difficult to overstate the importance of the wives of Foreign Service Officers (FSOs) and, especially, wives of ambassadors. Their significance has usually received little public notice, but plenty within the diplomatic corps. Veteran diplomat Willard Beaulac knew of no field "in which a wife can be more helpful." The Foreign Service Personnel Board explicitly considered the performance of an officer's wife when evaluating his performance, a policy in place until the early 1970s.[18]

This recognition is not surprising, considering the list of the wife's responsibilities. She was every bit her husband's partner in cultivating the social bonds with other diplomats and host-country officials that were indispensable in furthering the official relationships. William Phillips argued that only through social contacts could a chief of mission learn about a country itself and judge its views toward the United States. The wife also oversaw the logistics of her family's transfers from post to post. She similarly managed the family's home, a key symbol of American status in the host country. This included supervision of the domestic help, a surprisingly complex task. She engaged in volunteer work, an important form of public diplomacy. In all her dealings, she of course had to be "diplomatic"; a discourteous wife could easily undo her husband's professional relationships. She had to build and then maintain her public persona, as Harriet Bunker did in Buenos Aires when she regularly attended the American church there—even though she was not a churchgoer. The ambassador's wife, moreover, was responsible for the wives of the lower-ranking diplomats, a role that often came to resemble mothering. Marshalling of the other women could extend into crisis situations as well. Jane Thompson, wife of Llewellyn Thompson, US ambassador to

Austria, was later praised for doing "a man-sized job" organizing the women to aid refugees from the 1956 Hungarian uprising. The spouse also frequently had to stand in for her husband at events he was unable to attend.[19]

In many cases, wives compensated for their husbands' insularity. Their many activities took them all over the host countries, and they often came to know the locals and their environments better than did their husbands, who, after all, spent much of the day in the embassy. Ambassadors' wives thus often served as their husbands' "public faces," role models for the local population, and conduits between the embassy and the host country all at the same time. In Tokyo the isolation of Joseph Grew, who could not speak Japanese, was somewhat mitigated by the presence of his wife, Alice Perry Grew, who had spent some of her youth in Japan and could.[20]

Most wives, of course, also served as critics, confidants, and sources of ideas for their husbands. This is not to reinforce the pernicious stereotype of the all-powerful woman behind the scenes, as the title character in Gilbert and Sullivan's opera *Princess Ida* did while addressing the students of her college for women:

> Diplomacy? The wiliest diplomat
> Is absolutely helpless in our hands,
> *He* wheedles monarchs—woman wheedles him!

It is, rather, to acknowledge often crucial influence—over diplomacy, informally, and over their husbands' careers, formally, because of the aforementioned role a wife's "performance" played in a diplomat's evaluation. For example, Elise Henderson, born into a wealthy landowning family in pre–World War I Latvia, clearly helped shape the anti-Soviet views of her husband Loy, one of the key State Department experts on the Soviet Union after establishment of formal bilateral relations in 1933. Such influence could assume various forms, of course; Mrs. Henderson was so enraged when the Soviet Union annexed her native land in 1940 that she verbally attacked, and nearly came to blows with, the wife of the Soviet ambassador at a Washington, DC, dinner party. Toward the end of Henderson's career (1954), an assistant secretary's two-paragraph evaluation of him declared him an "outstanding" ambassador in the first, but in the second, longer paragraph, described his wife as being "unbalanced," meddling in political issues beyond her comprehension, and causing trouble for staff and their wives. This did not outweigh the ambassador's strengths, it concluded, but it did warrant assigning Henderson next to a large city, "where Mrs. Henderson will not stand out conspicuously."[21]

Yet for every unfortunate incident, several occurred in which wives helped rather than hindered. Jane Thompson even turned around a sexist quip to retrieve one awkward situation. A few months after the U-2 spy plane was shot down, Soviet premier Nikita Khrushchev trampled on the foot of her husband, now the ambassador to the Soviet Union, at a Kremlin reception. "If I do that to you, I ought to apologize," Khrushchev said. "Your government ought to have apologized." Thompson shot back, "the Soviet Union spied without apology on the United States." As others gathered around the escalating exchange, Khrushchev's colleague Anastas Mikoyan intervened by lamely joking that perhaps Mrs. Thompson was to blame—"women are always starting something." "Yes it was all my fault," Ms. Thompson agreed, "and let's not talk about it anymore." With all their roles and responsibilities, many a diplomatic wife understandably believed she had a "career." But this career was uncompensated—a "bargain" for the taxpayer who, wrote a retired ambassador in 1965, got "two for the price of one" when hiring a diplomat. And this uncompensated career, when done right, was an arduous one: in the 1950s, one ambassador's wife measured her own typical work-week—again, uncompensated—at seventy hours. During these long hours, women played vital roles in diplomacy and often demonstrated on a daily basis their possession of all the basic skills necessary for diplomatic work. They were just refused the positions, the pay, and the prestige in that field, on which the men had a complete lock.[22]

Hunting and Male Insecurity

Leisure activities were the means by which diplomats developed the social ties and friendships that allowed them to do their jobs effectively, and their choices in this area suggest their relatively pronounced male insecurity in the decades bracketing the turn of the twentieth century. Generally, they tended to embrace the same pastimes as other upper-class men throughout the western world, such as golf, bridge, tennis, and polo. But one of the most important leisure pursuits for diplomats was hunting, which began to enjoy renewed popularity among American men around 1900. Few in the service were as fanatical about stalking animals as was Theodore Roosevelt, a man who would eagerly show guests the cougar fang marks on the butt of the Winchester he had used in the North Dakota Badlands. But many doubtless shared his view that hunting, second perhaps only to war or life on the frontier generally, was key to preserving masculinity—or recovering primitive masculinity—in an increasingly "soft" and "overcivilized" society. "The chase is among the best of all national pastimes," Roosevelt had written in 1893; "it cultivates that vigorous manliness for the lack of which in a nation, as in an individual, the possession of no other qualities can possibly atone."[23]

When someone like Minister to Persia Lloyd Griscom pursued ibex and mouflon in the Elburz Mountains, he was not only developing vital social ties with counterparts and host-country officials—other diversions accomplished that goal as well—but also proving his toughness. And as generations of ambitious men would learn, as with other professionally useful diversions such as golf, being good at it was less important than was simply taking part, although of course stray bullets posed risks that shanked golf balls did not. "I have spent the better part of several diplomatic shoots," Charles Thayer recalled, "flat on my face in a ditch while bullets whistled above me."[24]

Hunting prowess certainly could help, though, as a young Joseph Grew learned. Partly inspired by President Roosevelt, a fellow Harvard alumnus, Grew traveled the world seeking adventure after graduating in 1902. In China, he stalked the Amoy tiger, which Roosevelt had called one of the greatest challenges for a sportsman. After tracking a ten-footer to a dark cave, Grew managed to crawl inside and shoot it dead from just a few feet away. He returned to America and accepted an appointment in the Consular Service, but he really wanted to be a diplomat. His request for a transfer was denied by Roosevelt, who had never heard of Grew. But then, in 1906, a mutual acquaintance asked the president on Grew's behalf, this time adding the story of Grew's tiger kill. Roosevelt generally considered diplomats to be "stuffed dolls" and "pink-tea" types, but he was impressed by this hunter, as he later said, "the sort of man we want in our foreign service." And so he found Grew a secretaryship, thus launching the career of one of the most distinguished Old Hands. Twenty years later, as chief of the Foreign Service Board of Examiners, Grew delighted in telling the candidates, "You gentlemen have a very easy time entering the Service. All you have to do is to answer a few questions. I had to shoot a tiger."[25]

Few owed their careers to hunting, of course. But for many, hunting was a true passion. It helped that the envoys' worldwide travel offered them a stunning variety of game. Ambassador Ellis Briggs was such an avid sportsman that he published an entire book on the subject, *Shots Heard Round the World* (1957). The popularity of hunting among diplomats, again, is no coincidence. They found it a fun, exciting means by which to blend two types of bonding they considered crucial to successful diplomacy: social and male. One could measure oneself against a physical challenge, perhaps even a mortal threat, and, if successful, strengthen one's reputation among other diplomats and dignitaries. One might even hope, as Theodore Roosevelt had done, to transform oneself in the eyes of others from a cloistered dandy into a roughneck adventurer. And unfortunately for the diplomats, as we will see, they had good reason to fear for their reputations.[26]

The male insecurity reflected in this love of hunting also appears in how frequently diplomats likened themselves to soldiers. Typically, the diplomatic corps contrasts itself with the military. That is, diplomacy exists to settle disputes peacefully, warfare violently. Indeed, diplomats might say that soldiers are only necessary when the diplomats fail—unless of course that handoff is part of the plan, in the sense meant by that anonymous wag who wrote, "Diplomacy is the art of saying 'nice doggie' until you can find a rock." Or, diplomats see themselves as complementing soldiers, providing half of a nation's international one-two punch. In this light, it is striking how often in this period diplomats resorted to militarized self-descriptions, such as America's "first line of defense" or, as one book later labeled President Dwight Eisenhower's secretary of state, John Foster Dulles, a "soldier for peace" (one would never, of course, hear generals or admirals describe themselves as "America's first line of negotiation" or "diplomats for war"). This may in part reflect an overall national militarism; it may also have comingled with the resentment produced by the double standard: generals and admirals were routinely considered good, even superior choices as ambassadors, but the reverse was out of the question. "Do you suppose," one diplomat asked after several such appointments were announced, "that one day they will appoint Ambassador Smith to take command of the Sixth Fleet or Counselor of Embassy Jones to head the 45th Fighter Squadron?" Still, the effort to adorn the pinstripes with a bit of khaki suggests a certain insecurity on the diplomats' part, a concern about a weak image that led them to adopt a vocabulary of martial toughness.[27]

A Reputation for Elitism, Effeteness, and Homosexuality

When it came to American diplomacy, male insecurity long went hand in hand with concerns about elitism. Suspicion of elitism was a major reason Americans, especially at first, lacked enthusiasm about formal diplomacy. From time to time they did not even consider ambassadors necessary. In 1783, John Adams expressed his belief that before too long, perhaps the United States ought to recall its ministers from Europe and dispatch them "only on special occasions." Many in the young republic observed the formalities, rituals, and high living of diplomacy and concluded there was something suspiciously elitist and European about the very institution. Thus while the United States had no choice but to participate in it, many Americans only grudgingly came to accept that fact. As late as 1889, the *New York Sun* declared that the diplomatic service was a "costly humbug and sham"; Congress ought to fold up this "nurse of snobs." The United States did not bestow the rank of ambassador until 1893; previously the title had seemed out of sync with the country's democratic ethos (even though it appears in the Constitution).[28]

Truth was, most American diplomats were indeed unrepresentative, and not just because they were all men. In the nineteenth and early twentieth centuries, before professionalization, diplomats were paid little or nothing, and only wealthy, elite men—many interested primarily in the social life of Europe—could afford to serve. Many chose a few years in the diplomatic or consular corps not in order to live Teddy Roosevelt's "strenuous life" but to avoid it. Thus, some of the men attracted to the profession only reinforced the pampered, elitist stereotype that already existed. In 1923, one diplomat wrote in the *Saturday Evening Post* of the "pleasurable excitement" he felt in the presence of royalty. Similarly, a senior diplomat in the mid-1920s was the Old Hand J. Butler Wright—rumor had it that some called him "Butsy." He was described in 1931 as strolling to Washington's Union Station "attired in Bond Street topper, cutaway, tailored in Saville Row, cream-colored gloves and malacca stick." Later, career diplomat George Platt Waller, famed for his heroic service in Nazi-occupied Luxembourg, expressed his belief in "government by the wise, the wealthy, and the gentle born."[29]

Although professionalization after the 1924 Rogers Act did succeed in shifting the average socioeconomic profile of diplomats downward, some elitists remained, as did an outsized stereotype. State Department officials of the 1930s, according to Arthur Schlesinger Jr., constituted the "croquet-playing set . . . who adored countesses, pushed cookies and wore handkerchiefs in their sleeves." Most seemed to strive, journalist I. F. Stone wrote in 1943, to resemble "their own ancestral portraits." In their environment, the diplomats too often lost sight of their values, the *Washington Post* claimed in 1947. That is, "they are so busy being diplomats that they have no time to be Americans."[30]

Just how widely held was this negative stereotype? One could always find anecdotal contempt for diplomats among the general public. Shortly after America entered World War II, one West Virginian, a pulp magazine vendor interviewed by Alistair Cooke, refused to differentiate between interned Axis diplomats and their free Allied counterparts. "They oughta poison the whole breed," the man said. "It's the diplomats that start the wars anyway." Better evidence actually suggests mixed but slightly favorable popular views of diplomats. A poll conducted confidentially for the State Department in December 1945 revealed that, when respondents were asked to free-associate about American diplomats, 37 percent gave favorable comments, 28 percent unfavorable, and 35 percent neutral. Thus, public attitudes were more positive than negative, although diplomats received a less favorable response than did admirals or Supreme Court justices. Among negative responses that pegged diplomats as "upper-class, society men," respondents did generate the stereotypical terms "caviar . . . high hat, Gray striped trousers, stuffed shirt, waxed mustache, cane and spats, fancy pants, tea parties, [and] corporation counsel," but only 4 percent of respondents produced such adjectives. A significantly greater number of pejorative responses had diplomats as "grafters" or "fast-talkers."[31]

Still, the negative stereotype of the pampered elitist persisted and, because it still contained some truth, State Department officials and FSOs remained extremely sensitive to it. The inevitable denials found frequent expression. In 1950, one twelve-year veteran of the Foreign Service indignantly denied even owning a pair of striped trousers. These denials were matched with positive claims about the overseas emissaries' toughness. American diplomats "have more experience of malaria than of spats," Secretary of State Hull said in 1938. And then came assertions, such as the one in an unconvinced journalist's 1952 article, "Cookie Pushers Resent the Tag, One of 'Em Says," that the stereotype hampered the diplomats in their important work. "Horse and buggy prejudices" against diplomats, one department official told a group of educators, are "a hazard to all of us."[32]

Elitism and effeteness readily shaded into effeminacy. This was equally true whether one considers the accusations or the denials. For many critics, epithets such as *cookie-pusher* and *striped-pants boy* stood as code words that had long meant not merely patrician or Anglophile, but also weak and effeminate (or, as we shall see, gay). These, in turn, compounded existing male insecurity among the diplomats. Even advertisers soon realized that appeals to this insecurity could help them hawk products. "There's no place in the Service," read a 1941 Royal Typewriter advertisement in the *American Foreign Service Journal,* "for either men or machines that can't stand the gaff." The boldfaced heading: No Sissies Wanted.[33]

At times, the State Department had to worry about accusations of effeminacy from within the government itself. In a confidential 1954 evaluation, for example, the department declared Ambassador to Greece Cavendish Cannon more than satisfactory. Yet elsewhere in the government, he was seen as a "hag ridden Miss Nancy with no gumption." One wonders whether the evaluators were at all self-conscious about these differing perceptions.[34]

Such reports surprise even less in the context of the Cold War, which, once it began in the late 1940s, fostered yet another intensification of gender anxiety. The threat of Communism from abroad seemed to demand the strength of the he-man or the rugged individualist, while Communist subversion at home was explicitly linked to homosexuality. Morally, Communism and homosexuality were alleged to be similarly degenerate, seductive cabals that threatened American manhood and society alike, while, practically, closeted gay officials could supposedly be turned into Communist agents through blackmail. Beginning especially in early 1950, these fears sparked a Lavender Scare, a witch hunt for alleged gays in government generally and the State Department in particular, that was intertwined with the more prominent Red Scare now led by Senator Joseph McCarthy (R-WI). McCarthy's infamous Wheeling, West Virginia, speech of February 1950 smearing the State Department was anti-Communist and anti-patrician. But before too long, the senator was publicly threatening to expose the "egg-sucking phony liberals" and the "Communists and queers" of Foggy Bottom. In the same vein, a 1951 potboiler, *Washington Confidential,* passed along "a gag around Washington [that] you had to speak with a British accent, wear a homburg hat, or have a queer quirk if you wanted to get by the guards" at the

Royal Typewriter Co. advertisement, *American Foreign Service Journal,* 1941. This ad provides a glimpse of male diplomats' sensitivity to the stereotype: they were seen as effete, effeminate, even gay "cookie pushers" and "striped-pants boys." This contributed to an environment in the diplomatic world hostile to the admission of women. (Royal Consumer Information Products, Inc., 1941)

State Department entrance. As John Foster Dulles was leaving a congressional hearing in 1953, the committee chair remarked, "it must be terrible to have to work among all those homosexuals" (Dulles did not respond). The gay-baiting of diplomats was hardly new, but now homophobia morphed into a formal purge, the nation's capital a busy site of innuendo, investigations, ruined careers, and even a few suicides. Between 1947 and 1953, more than four hundred State Department and Foreign Service employees were fired or forced to resign for alleged homosexuality.[35]

It did not help the diplomats in this regard that, as the world plunged into the years of deepest Cold War in 1949, their new boss was Secretary of State Dean Gooderham Acheson. Product of Groton, Yale, and Harvard Law, sporting tweed suit, homburg, and waxed mustache, Acheson quickly became a potent symbol for those who saw his department as a den of effete, effeminate appeasers. "I watch his smart-aleck manner and his British clothes and that New Dealism," Senator Hugh Butler of Nebraska groused, "and I want to shout, Get out, Get out. You stand for everything that has been wrong with the United States for years." In one political cartoon, Acheson was shown in tails and spats, handkerchief protruding below limp wrist, the hand having just lofted a cream puff at Josef Stalin. President Truman rebuffed the many calls for Acheson's resignation, but the secretary remained a lightning rod for his last two-and-a-half years in office, "proof" that the "lavender lads" had seized the commanding heights of foreign policymaking when the nation was most vulnerable.[36]

The Lavender Scare and the male insecurity it intensified matters here because they embodied not merely homophobia but misogyny. One of the most vicious scaremongers was the Hearst newspaper columnist Westbrook Pegler, who published the following bit of red- and lavender-baiting doggerel in 1950:

How could [Truman] help it if par-
ties both unusual and queer
Got into the State Department
which true patriots hold dear?
To hear the dastards tell it
They are true to Uncle Joey
And call each other female
names like Bessie, Maud and Chloe.

And write each other poetry
and confidential notes so tender
Like they was not he-men at all
but belonged to the opposing gender.

State Department officials fled as quickly as they could from such smears and became keener still to demonstrate their manly virtues. George Kennan, ever reliably bolstering the ramparts of masculinity, even called in early 1953 for "a special manliness and fortitude" among civil servants to face the anticommunist witch hunts themselves. Manliness, in short, was a key currency of domestic debate, which both sides readily spent as a remedy for many problems related to the Cold War. Thus for all the advances American women had made by 1950, a point at which four women had served or were serving abroad as chiefs of mission, the male insecurity and related abhorrence of femininity in official circles helped create a diplomatic environment no more conducive to the inclusion of women than it had been fifty years earlier. Why welcome women when one's manliness was already under suspicion?[37]

Exclusion of Women

When the legendary French foreign minister Talleyrand said that in "critical situations, let women run things," he of course was joking (although he relied heavily on women to conduct his diplomacy). While over the centuries women served as formal envoys in several instances, and more commonly they played informal diplomatic roles (although no less important for that), by the nineteenth century both phenomena became rarer, with the emerging professionalization of diplomacy—and so the men believed it should be. British diplomat Grenville Murray spoke for most men in 1855 when he wrote that only men should conduct diplomacy. He likened women's diplomacy to that of eunuchs: "It is false and dangerous; ultimate good seldom comes of it."[38]

In the nineteenth and early twentieth centuries, women did continue to play other important roles in foreign relations despite their exclusion. In the United States, these included at least three in the antebellum period: Lydia Maria Child, opponent of pro-slavery expansionism; pro-expansionist Jane Cazneau, an informal diplomat; and the equally pro-expansion Anna Ella Carroll, foreign policy critic and lobbyist. In the early twentieth century, Lucia

True Ames Mead worked tirelessly as a leading peace activist, while Vira Whitehouse served as a de facto diplomat as Woodrow Wilson's director of the Committee on Public Information for Switzerland during World War I.[39]

Beginning in the late nineteenth century and especially in the early twentieth, more importantly, women organized tirelessly and transnationally as advocates for women's rights and international peace. Through such groups as the International Council of Women, the International Alliance of Women, and the Women's International League of Peace and Freedom, European and American women in particular established extensive networks that produced a collective identity and an unprecedented women's internationalism. By bringing new issues to the fore, playing important roles in the League of Nations, and promoting peace and women's rights around the globe, this movement gave activist women an international voice they never had before.[40]

Throughout this period, however, women remained excluded from formal diplomacy, though not for want of trying, at least on the part of a few brave souls. In 1897, New Hampshire lawyer and feminist—the word used in this book to denote one who or that which supports women's equality or rights—Marilla Ricker sought to become minister to Colombia. She frankly stated that her goal was to open the diplomatic service to women, because "there is no gender in the brain." Indeed, she considered herself far more qualified than the incumbent in Bogota, Luther McKinney. If he "can fill the place," she told a reporter, "I can overflow it." The new Republican president William McKinley shared neither her confidence nor her feminism, and he turned her down.[41]

Why Women Were Excluded

Why did men scoff at the idea of female diplomats? The most important and obvious reason is the pervasive misogyny and sex discrimination of the modern era, which blended with the gender anxiety seen above and only intensified in the early twentieth century. Especially among the increasingly large and powerful American middle class, gender anxiety fundamentally reordered male mindsets and behavior, including such changes as the enthusiastic promotion of vigorous sport, war, and hunting (seen above); the emergence of a starker straight identity (and resulting homophobia); and the switching of the basis of that identity from the opposition man versus boy to that of man versus woman. This last change in particular led many men increasingly to stigmatize anything feminine, use new or popularize old pejorative terms such as *sissy* and *pussy-foot* and *mollycoddle,* and develop rituals of mutual reassurance at women's expense, such as sexual objectification. That is, as some women threatened to dissolve men's and women's perceived "separate spheres," many men sought to reinforce them. None of this would have made men more likely to welcome women into the professions in general, or diplomacy in particular—quite the contrary.[42]

Exactly how these intensified gender considerations affected diplomats is difficult to determine. One we do know about is George F. Kennan. Kennan, who joined the Foreign Service in 1926 and would go on to gain considerable fame as intellectual architect of the policy of containment was probably more sensitive than most. But hints of gender anxiety appear early in his memoirs; he confessed to having once shed "unmanly tears" and to having considered himself "something of a sissy in personal relations" during his time as a student at Princeton University. Gendered expressions recur in his writings thereafter, for example, his call for "political manliness" in standing up to Soviet expansionism as World War II drew to a close.[43]

Nor did Kennan have much regard for women. In an unpublished but now-infamous 1938 manifesto, "The Prerequisites," he argued that American women, "delicate, high-strung, unsatisfied, flat-chested and flat-voiced," already presiding over "a matriarchy," should lose their right to vote. Their re-confinement to family and church events, he wrote, "would take an enormous strain off the country." After World War II, when he directed the State Department's Policy Planning Staff, he did recruit one woman to assist him, Dorothy Fosdick (to work on United Nations affairs). She recalled that, even though he (correctly) noted that women historically had served monarchs as confidential advisors, their "role was to listen sympathetically, to provide comfort, to give private counsel." That is about as much as Kennan, and no doubt most other male diplomats, was willing to concede.[44]

Rather, women were considered inherently lacking in skills and attributes fundamental to diplomacy. Old Hand and Director of the Consular Service Wilbur Carr spoke for many when in 1923 he described the ideal university product to be molded into a Foreign Service Officer: "hearty, personable, manly, shrewd, business-like, observant, and well-informed, with a good knowledge of human nature," as well as having "the instincts of a gentleman in the finer sense." It is difficult to imagine Carr conceiving of *homo diplomaticus* in a more gendered way; small wonder that women were found to be decisively wanting.[45]

Some of women's supposed drawbacks stemmed not from their sex but rather sexism; however, they were considered no less disqualifying because of that. Numerous Old Hands noted that because they were excluded from men's clubs, women would be unable to cultivate the social contacts vital to success in the field. A woman was likewise considered unsuited for the many countries (even) less gender-progressive than the United States was; she would not be received with the necessary respect, and the host nation might take her assignment there as an insult. "Everything for them in this country," William Castle, Division of Western European Affairs chief, wrote in his diary in 1925, "but if we cannot respect the prejudices of other lands we at least should not offend them." This carried with it the bonus of shifting responsibility for exclusion to less enlightened foreigners. In the case of both exclusive clubs and hostile lands, women were essentially to be punished for having been punished.[46]

But other alleged weaknesses were inherent, for example, lack of discretion. Perhaps the greatest obstacle to hiring female diplomats, one department official wrote in 1909, was their "well-known inability to keep a secret."[47]

Another fear was that women were neither up to nor could properly be exposed to the physical or even deadly risks that could arise overseas. After all, while it was rare, it was not unheard of for an FSO to end up like the US consul general in Beirut, Theodore Marriner, whom a disappointed visa applicant gunned down in 1937. And consuls routinely bore responsibility for Americans abroad who got drunk or otherwise into serious trouble, and many of the men believed female consuls could not handle them. As late as 1961, one former diplomat, E. Wilder Spaulding, staunchly defended sending the few female chiefs who had served by then only to western Europe. "There is a rough and tumble quality about the ambassador's work elsewhere," he wrote, such as confronting anti-American demonstrations or harboring prominent asylum-seekers, "that a woman cannot be called upon to face." Emphasizing the rigors of the profession thus served two purposes: demonstrating the toughness of the men, and justifying the exclusion of the women.[48]

Another objection was that women would let their emotions interfere with the task of diplomacy. Perhaps the most famous advice ever given to diplomats comes from Talleyrand—*Et surtout pas trop de zèle*—"And above all, not too much zeal." This edict alone would have led men to disqualify women. Wilbur Carr, now assistant secretary of state, described in his diary a Foreign Service interview in June 1925: "Another girl to-day. Frightened badly. The thumping of her jugular vein was so visible that I took out my watch and counted. 120 per minute! And notwithstanding all this emotion she answered questions well." Similarly, he interviewed another female candidate the following year and found her "very feminine and lacking in power to argue or negotiate, and in practical judgment." In reality, of course, the men of the Foreign Service were not immune to exhibiting emotion or allowing it to affect their behavior; witness, for example, the emotional framing of, and emotional appeals in, George Kennan's arguments for ending cooperation with the Soviet Union after World War II. Nevertheless, emotionality was considered a major disqualifying characteristic for women. This was especially true in light of the premium the Old Hands placed on "soundness of judgment" when they recruited junior diplomats.[49]

A related belief, finally, was that women were too "soft," unable to stand up to adversaries in tough negotiations. Again, this concern would only have intensified when the men were at pains to demonstrate their own toughness in periods of gender anxiety. The first women in the field were particularly aware of this stereotype, and if anything they overcompensated in an effort to immunize themselves against the accusation.

The First Female Envoys

Despite all of these objections in the late-modern era, women first began entering formal diplomatic work in the early twentieth century. But the change came very slowly, and other countries preceded the United States in naming women as diplomats, at both junior and ambassadorial ranks. The first female chief of mission was Rosika Schwimmer (aka Róza Bédy-Schwimmer). Born in Hungary in 1877, Schwimmer gained international renown as a leading suffragist and pacifist. In November 1918, Mihály Károlyi's short-lived republican regime in Budapest, which emerged from the ruins of the Austro-Hungarian empire, named Schwimmer minister to Switzerland. One can see why Károlyi, a fellow pacifist, chose her: she spoke nine languages and knew some heads of state personally. She had also met twice with President Woodrow Wilson, whose Fourteen Points included the call for national self-determination upon which the Hungarians were counting so heavily.[50]

Yet Schwimmer turned out to be an unfortunate choice, for several reasons. Having misrepresented Wilson's views to the press after their first meeting, and then berating him for his inaction during the second, she actually enjoyed little popularity in the White House; she was overconfident; and because of her pacifism, she was quickly (and falsely) accused of being a Bolshevik, at a time when such a charge immediately closed almost all doors. Moreover, most of Károlyi's own government objected to her appointment; she was Jewish, which alienated the anti-Semitic US minister in Switzerland in particular; and, of course, she was a woman, headed to one of the least gender-progressive countries in Europe. The president of Switzerland said that he was "very reluctant to break with the tradition under which diplomatists are of the male sex."[51]

But even if one disregards her formidable baggage, her task, to gain diplomatic recognition for the Károlyi government, was impossible. That regime lacked stability from the start, its security threatened from abroad and its legitimacy contested at home. As a result, Schwimmer had to compete in Bern with fellow Hungarians representing, or claiming to represent, competing domestic factions. What is more, with the war either still underway or not yet formally ended, the Allies considered Hungary an enemy state. The Allies thus refused to grant the Károlyi regime diplomatic recognition, and Schwimmer's mission was a complete nonstarter. Within six weeks of her arrival, she had become totally isolated from the US delegation, and she resigned in January 1919. Despite Schwimmer's obvious courage and the historical breakthrough she represents, her mission was doomed, and one can scarcely conceive of a less auspicious beginning for female chiefs of mission.

Schwimmer was no Bolshevik, but the first enduring female ambassador in the twentieth century certainly was. Born in 1872, Alexandra Kollontai was a longtime socialist sent in 1922 to represent the young Soviet Russia in Norway. Kollontai had risen to become the most prominent female Bolshevik, certainly the leading Bolshevik feminist, and was named people's commissar for social welfare immediately after the Revolution of October 1917. She also had significant international experience, including as head of an unofficial delegation to Britain and France in early 1918. She accepted a foreign appointment in part because she wanted to put some distance between herself and her failed second marriage and in part because, as a leading member of the Worker's Opposition, she had tired of clashing with the regime's increasingly authoritarian leadership.[52]

The Commissariat of Foreign Affairs first proposed Kollontai as envoy to Canada, but the British (still in control of Canadian foreign relations) rejected her on account of her rabble-rousing past and her sex. Norway, the commissariat's next choice, accepted her in 1922 as head of a trade delegation, and then as ambassador when the two countries formally recognized each other, in 1924. Transfers to Mexico (1926–1927) and again Norway (1927–1930) followed. In 1930, Kollontai was named minister to Sweden (ambassador in 1943), where she would remain long enough to become dean of the diplomatic corps.

Kollontai had mixed feelings about her diplomatic career, suffered bouts of despair, and several times wanted to resign. She also feared that she would fall victim, as did many other Soviet diplomats and all other original Bolshevik leaders still alive in 1937, to Josef Stalin's bloody purges. But miraculously, she was spared, and she served in Stockholm until poor health forced her resignation in 1945.

Kollontai was, by all accounts, a success. True, not everyone thought highly of her; her British counterpart in Norway in the 1920s wrote that she gave the impression that "butter would not melt in her mouth," and he especially objected to her sex. "I should much prefer," he reported, "a masculine blackguard of the usual Bolshevik type." But later, Sir Archibald Clark Kerr, British minister in Stockholm, found her effective and marked by a "gentle and pleasing" humanity as well as "uncommon" intelligence. She successfully negotiated several trade treaties and played a major role in helping to end the two Russo-Finnish wars, in 1940 and 1944, repeatedly violating her instructions—an extremely bold habit, considering her boss's proclivities—to help reach agreement. She also became extremely popular in her host countries, despite having to represent a murderous, totalitarian police state engaged in reprehensible international behavior (e.g., the Nazi–Soviet Pact of 1939). Early in her career, she claimed that in diplomatic service, she never considered herself a woman: "The work I had to carry out was too serious." Later, she told Clark Kerr that at all her postings she had "been treated as a man and [had] never been conscious of any disability on account of her sex." And yet, she derived great pride from the role she played in achieving progress for women.[53]

Female American Diplomats

American women had made first, limited inroads into the professions before 1920, but with the exception of clerks, they remained locked out of the diplomatic field. The process of change, by no means a smooth one, began shortly after the end of World War I as the women's rights movement peaked in strength and secured women's suffrage with ratification of the Nineteenth Amendment in 1920. In this heady atmosphere, feminist organizations and the deans of women's colleges pressured the State Department to admit women. And, because women's suffrage bestowed full citizenship on women, they were now eligible to take the Foreign Service entrance examinations. In the period 1921–1923, ten women took either the diplomatic or consular examinations, but only one passed both the written and the oral: Lucile Atcherson. The handling of her case tells us much about State Department attitudes toward women at that time.[54]

Born in Ohio in 1894, Atcherson graduated from Smith College and worked tirelessly as a women's suffragist before World War I. Work in France with the American Fund for the French Wounded and the American Committee for Devastated France piqued her interest in service abroad. Atcherson passed the diplomatic entrance examination in July 1922 and in December of that year was appointed secretary in the Diplomatic Service and assigned to the department in Washington, DC. Of course she was, however, interested in an overseas posting.[55]

The executive order implementing the 1924 Rogers Act did not address the question of who was eligible to take the entrance examinations. Thus, before they considered Atcherson's case, top department officials, especially J. Butler Wright, Joseph Grew, and Wilbur Carr, had to grapple with overall policy. One official made the suggestion—the only one at all favorable to the admission of women—that the department create a separate branch just for women. Others sought a formal executive order barring women from taking the test. Still others considered that unlikely and argued that the solution was to "defeat them at the examination" or even dissuade them individually from taking it in the first place. They were all overruled, however, by Secretary of State Charles Evans Hughes, who insisted that women (as well as African Americans and naturalized citizens) be eligible to take the examinations.[56]

Suffering this setback, the Old Hands on the new Foreign Service Personnel Board now turned to consider the question of Atcherson's overseas assignment; the "short period of service" at the department in Washington promised her at the time of her appointment had now lasted over two years. Finally, in April 1925 the board decided to send her to Bern, Switzerland, where, they concluded, she "might attract no particular notice."[57]

Lucile Atcherson, the first American woman to enter the US Foreign Service, 1922. Provoking considerable controversy and resentment among senior diplomats, she suffered sustained discrimination and then resigned when she married (1927). A de facto marriage ban for female diplomats remained in place until 1971. (National Photo Company Collection, Library of Congress, Prints and Photographs Division)

Yet, sending Atcherson abroad settled little. From the time of her assignment through 1927, senior officials continued to resist and wring their hands. Her new boss in Bern was veteran diplomat Hugh Gibson, who lamented in a lengthy letter to Grew all the difficulties, especially those of protocol, Atcherson's assignment would cause among the Swiss; he signed it "Michael J. O'Prune" (Grew signed his reply "Wee Willie Winkie"). He also tried to contain the damage, asking William Castle (now assistant secretary) whether it might not be wiser to admit no additional women until those who had been allowed to take the exam could be evaluated. Subsequently, some officials worried about treating her harshly, for fear of provoking charges of sexism; others wanted to transfer her to a "tougher post," where she would demonstrate her lack of ability and thus justify her dismissal while minimizing grounds for charges of discrimination. Still others simply considered her "totally unfit for the Service," fretting over Swiss dissatisfaction with a female officer and dreading the prospect of Atcherson assuming charge of the Bern Consulate when her superior was away.[58]

Atcherson initially received favorable performance reviews, but these progressively worsened, especially because Gibson believed that because of their inability to form the essential social ties with male colleagues, neither Atcherson nor any other female diplomat could ever be effective. Unlike the men in her Foreign Service class, she received no promotions, and the personnel board worried that this would cause a public relations problem. But finally, her transfer to Panama, a post she found disagreeable, together with her impending marriage to physician George Curtis, led her to resign in the fall of 1927.

For years thereafter, the Old Hands of the department continued to direct the same hostility toward women in diplomacy generally. One member of the personnel board wrote in 1932 that in the department's view, "the Foreign Service is not a suitable place for women. No one says this publicly, but it is a fact." Perhaps then it was no coincidence that the subsequent flow of women into the Foreign Service was not even a trickle, leaving aside the rate of attrition. Six women had entered the service by 1930, but only two remained in 1931, the average tenure of the four departees amounting to only three and a half years. And then, while an average of seventeen women applied every year between 1931 and 1939, not a single one made it in. Six were then admitted in the latter year, but only through lateral movement from the Department of Commerce permitted by the Reorganization Act of 1939.[59]

Thus, by the early 1930s, the men of the State Department were accommodating themselves to the presence of female Foreign Service Officers, but only technically. They admitted not even a handful of women, and they were adjusting to the female presence only grudgingly, responding with resistance, if not outright sabotage. And from their standpoint, this was entirely justified. After all, like almost all men, they considered women inferior and their presence an embarrassing comment on their own masculinity. They deemed women woefully lacking in the skills necessary for diplomacy, such as discretion; the ability to form the necessary social contacts; the respect of foreign diplomats and possibly insulted host nations; the wherewithal to survive the physical risks of the job; the detachment necessary to pursue US interests based on rational calculation; and the toughness required for negotiations. Happily for the men, the pace of change was so glacial that they could expect to contain the damage for the foreseeable future. Certainly, they would not have to worry about a woman running an embassy or legation—that was preposterous. Neither a "Gibson" nor any other type of "Girl" would conceivably be attending any real *Ambassador's Ball in the Days to Come*, except perhaps as an ambassador's wife.

2

Ruth Bryan Owen

Denmark, 1933–1936

What a marvelous diplomat's wife she would make.

—a journalist, circa 1927

On the evening of May 9, 1933, eight hundred people gathered in the ballroom of the Hotel Commodore in New York City for a dinner sponsored by the Scandinavian-American Foundation. They were there to give a proper send-off to Ruth Bryan Owen, forty-seven, whom President Franklin D. Roosevelt had recently named US minister to Denmark. The guests included such luminaries as First Lady Eleanor Roosevelt and arctic explorer Vihjalmur Stefansson, who, on this occasion, probably withheld one of his favorite sayings: "Adventure is a sign of incompetence." After a meal consisting of grapefruit cocktail Florida (a nod to Owen's home state), potage ambassadeur, lemon sherbet, sautéed chicken, frozen pudding, and petit fours, several guests sang Owen's praises. Eleanor Roosevelt declared that she was qualified because of not only her adaptability and diplomatic qualities but also her "good, hard, common sense, the spirit of adventure, trust in other human beings and the courage to do new things." Danish minister to the US Otto Wadsted said that the Danes were used to seeing women in prominent positions—having extended the vote to women five years before the Americans did—and that they had met Owen's appointment with "great enthusiasm." Aviator Amelia Earhart congratulated Owen for having the courage to enter a new field at a time when the "world does not yet regard women as persons" (in the audio recording of the event, chuckling is audible in the background after Earhart said this). In a similar vein, finally, the novelist Fannie Hurst likened Owen's "blazing a trail in diplomacy" to the brave frontierswomen who "in covered-wagon days had blazed a trail in geography."[1]

Then Owen spoke, with great humility and many thanks, and noting the multiple bonds that joined the two countries across the Atlantic. Yet she dwelled on neither matters of policy nor the ties between governments. Rather, she personalized the relationship by recalling an idyllic scene in a Danish church when she had toured the country in 1931, a woman and her son, praying. Now, she imagined the boy making the journey to the New World and then, many years later, she conjured an old man returning to Denmark, prosperous. Although she had told the president that she was proud to be his personal representative, she concluded her remarks by addressing the guests, "I go forth from you, as America's envoy, and if I may say, yours." In light of the occasion and her sentimentality, Owen's listeners could have been forgiven if they did not take seriously her stated intent to set a populist tenor for her mission to Denmark. But they should have.[2]

Owen's Background

Ruth Baird Bryan was born in Illinois in 1885 but grew up in Nebraska. She was the oldest child of William Jennings Bryan, famed populist firebrand, three-time Democratic nominee for president, and Woodrow Wilson's first secretary of state. Her mother, Mary Elizabeth Baird, was highly educated and one of the first women to pass the Nebraska bar exam. Although Mary set aside her own ambitions to support those of her husband, she advocated women's liberation and encouraged Ruth to pursue a career, despite the obstacles. "The work which a woman can do as well or better than a man," Ruth remembered her mother telling her, "is her work." Perhaps young Ruth needed little encouragement. As a child, she was a rebel. She was the sole girl in a neighborhood "company" of "soldiers"—all the boys were captains, and Ruth the only private. They unanimously promoted her to "sharpshooter," however, after she drilled the annoying captain of the band in the eye with a large peach. Family legend had it that Ruth, captivated by the Capitol dome after four years in Washington during her father's stint in Congress, pledged herself to public service at the age of nine.[3]

Ruth Bryan studied at the University of Nebraska for two years, was married, had two children, and then was divorced. But she was also extremely active outside the home, for example, working at Hull House in Chicago, perhaps under Jane Addams, and speaking on her father's behalf during his final presidential bid, in 1908. In 1910, she married a Briton, Reginald Owen, a Royal Army officer with whom she had two additional children. During World War I, Ruth Owen worked in war relief and then as a volunteer nurse with the Royal Army in the Egypt and Palestine campaigns. After the war, she settled in Florida and became a pioneer woman filmmaker, independently producing, writing, and directing *Once Upon a Time/Scheherazade* (1922, now lost). Then, her husband's chronic illness forced Owen to support the family, and she did as her father had done, entering the Chautauqua and lyceum circuits as a lecturer and demonstrating that she had inherited his oratorical gifts. Many of her speeches dealt with the issues of war and peace and civic duty but also included such titles as "This Business of Diplomacy" and "Denmark's Right to Survival."[4]

In 1926, Owen sought the Democratic nomination for Congress in Florida's Fourth District, a five-hundred-mile strip spanning the state's entire Atlantic coast. But she lost narrowly, and the following year her husband died. She recovered from the blow in part by throwing herself into another quest for the same House seat in 1928. This time, she logged thousands of miles and hundreds of speeches as she tirelessly blanketed the district. She won the primary easily, the general election in a landslide. Florida, which had voted against the women's suffrage amendment, was now the first southern state to send a woman to Congress. Representative Owen joined only six other women in the House. Yet her ambitions knew few bounds in this period; she apparently envisioned herself becoming the first female vice president.[5]

Owen's famous lineage led her colleagues to create an additional seat for her on the prestigious House Foreign Affairs Committee, on which her father had served, again a first for women. Yet Owen devoted most of her time to domestic and home-state efforts, such as flood relief, aid to citrus farmers, creation of a US Department of Home and Child, and establishment of the Everglades National Park. To help protect Florida's economy, she supported high tariffs and even voted for the infamous Smoot-Hawley Tariff of 1930. Jokes circulated about her father, a staunch free-trader, spinning in his grave. Owen was reelected unopposed in 1930, but in 1932 she faced a stiff challenge: repeal of prohibition emerged as the key issue in her district, which was increasingly "wet," whereas she had been "dry"—in public, at least—and now equivocated. The Women's Organization for National Prohibition Reform recruited a staunch "wet" to challenge Owen in the primary, and she was defeated by a twelve-point margin. As a lame duck, Owen dutifully voted for legalization of beer, but more importantly, she also stumped vigorously for Franklin Roosevelt's presidential campaign, delivering hundreds of speeches on his behalf. She was one of the top speakers employed by Molly Dewson, head of the Women's Division of the Democratic National Committee.[6]

Owen's Appointment

Franklin Roosevelt had long been relatively open to the idea of women in government. As a young New York state legislator during the Progressive Era, he had initially opposed women's suffrage, but he then changed his mind (and thus championed the cause even before his wife, Eleanor, did). After 1920, Roosevelt understood, perhaps more quickly than many others, the importance of women's votes to his and his party's fortunes, especially in New York State. There, most clearly as governor (1929–1933), Roosevelt had positive experiences working with women. Perhaps most crucial, Eleanor steadily pushed him in this direction, recruiting numerous women for government service under him. These factors, combined with the landmark expansion of the public sector resulting from the New Deal, explain President Roosevelt's creation of unprecedented opportunities for women in public life, what the press called "a New Deal for Women."[7]

Even before his decisive election to the presidency in November 1932, Roosevelt had already considered making history by appointing a woman to the cabinet. His first choice was Ruth Owen, although he ended up naming Frances Perkins his secretary of labor. As governor, he had appreciated Perkins's work as his labor commissioner, and that was far more relevant experience than Owen had. But Owen was the only other woman he considered, and he still wanted to place her somewhere. Roosevelt assured her she would get a good post, one in the United States (so she would retain some of her domestic political utility), probably assistant secretary of state, although chief of the Civil Service Commission and assistant secretary of interior were also discussed. But her would-be superiors in State and Interior, Cordell Hull and Harold Ickes, respectively, objected. So ultimately, Roosevelt settled on a less prominent but still path-breaking appointment for her: minister to Denmark. State Department Old Hands, undoubtedly horrified by the prospect of a woman serving as either assistant secretary or minister, reportedly talked her into taking the ministership as what they considered the lesser evil. Pushing

Ruth Bryan Owen, minister to Denmark (1933–1936, *right*) and first female US chief of mission, with First Lady Eleanor Roosevelt, 1934. Owen had also served as the first US congresswoman from the South (Florida, 1929–1933). Roosevelt played a key role in lobbying her husband, President Franklin D. Roosevelt, to open positions in government to women, including Owen. (Franklin D. Roosevelt Library Public Domain Photographs)

hard from the other direction, perhaps decisive in securing the Denmark appointment, were First Lady Eleanor Roosevelt, tireless force behind placing women in government, and Molly Dewson.[8]

Although Owen had no diplomatic experience, like most noncareer chiefs of mission, the appointment made considerable sense: not only had Owen accrued several years' international experience (especially during World War I) and four years on the House Foreign Affairs Committee, she had also toured Denmark extensively by car for two months in 1931 and knew the country relatively well. Finally, naming Owen was also a way to pay homage to her late father, still revered among many Democrats.[9]

For her part, Owen had eagerly sought a post in the new administration. In September 1932, she noticed the buzz around the Roosevelt campaign that a Democratic victory might result in a woman receiving a cabinet appointment for the first time, and she wanted to be considered. She sought the support and advice of several influential people, including newspaper magnate William Randolph Hearst and "Colonel" Edward House. House, Woodrow Wilson's famous chief adviser, had known Owen since childhood. Now he was one of the elder statesmen of the Democratic Party and an early supporter of Roosevelt's candidacy. He was not part of FDR's inner circle, but he was probably one of the most influential figures Owen knew, and so she approached him. In letters to him, she cited as rationale her congressional experience, the wide exposure she had gained from Chautauqua, and her popularity among women. House was most encouraging, promised to help, and advised her not to speak publicly about her wishes. Owen complied.[10]

When the consolation prize came in the form of the Denmark post, Colonel House advised her to accept. Owen, even if disappointed by the step down, found the offer attractive right away. She acknowledged the great responsibility that came with being the first female chief of mission, as well as the heightened scrutiny this status would entail. Her only serious doubt, however, was a practical one: whether she could bear the financial burden. This was cleared up when she learned that the exchange rate was favorable and that the Danish press was reporting that her hosts would not misconstrue "a standard of simplicity in the conduct of legation affairs." The president's insistence and the favorable Danish response also helped her overcome her misgivings. Perhaps she was also right for the job if it was true that, as assistant secretary of state and prominent Brain Truster Raymond Moley concluded after a long interview with Owen, that she had the "soul of a troubadour."[11]

The appointment was a major development by any standard. As we have seen, Owen was not the first female chief of mission anywhere; Rosika Schwimmer and Alexandra Kollontai had preceded her. But Owen was the first female envoy from the United States. One can then perhaps understand why the outgoing minister to Denmark, Frederick Coleman, noted in his diary simply, "Mrs. Owen to be my successor!" Yet despite the novelty, the US Senate unanimously approved her appointment; again, her lineage and political ties undoubtedly smoothed her path, as did the plain reality that Denmark was a small country of little note in Washington. Moreover, another factor mitigating the appointment's importance as the Roosevelt administration unfolded was the simple fact that, compared to other presidents before and since, FDR placed less faith in his chiefs of mission and often circumvented them (and the State Department) on important matters by dispatching personal representatives. Had Roosevelt sent a woman rather than Harry Hopkins to meet with Winston Churchill or Josef Stalin in 1941, that would have represented a truly momentous step for gender progress.[12]

Danish officialdom, including the king, seems to have taken the selection in stride. Most reactions were favorable. One Copenhagen predecessor, Joseph Grew, took the trouble to congratulate Owen, adding, "It is a splendid step to create the precedent of sending distinguished American women to such positions" (although note he said "such positions," rather than, say, "ambassadorships"). Among the Old Hands, it probably helped that she was not following a tough act. Chief of the State Department's Division of Western European Affairs J. Pierrepont Moffat had recently reported that Minister Coleman "has been a near invalid most of the time and has taken little active part in the work of the Legation."[13]

Owen's friends were of course ecstatic, as were many women on both sides of the Atlantic. A female member of the Danish parliament called Roosevelt's move a "great triumph for feminism." Owen was alive to the feminist implications as well. In an interview she gave toward the beginning of her tenure, she was asked what her objective in Denmark was. "Not to let down my country," she replied without hesitation, "or women all over the world."[14]

Danish press opinion was most favorable. The appointment was a first for American diplomacy, the *Extrabladet* wrote in a typical comment, "and Denmark is the happy country upon which the honor has been bestowed." The *Berlingske Tidende* reacted to Owen's arrival by noticing how much she contrasted with her counterparts: "It was not a Minister with striped trousers, with a monocle and hard-set mouth. It was not a meeting between nervous Danish press representatives and serious steel and iron men from the great Dollar land. The picture was quite different. President Roosevelt's new lady Minister disembarked with her associates smiling and laughing, with arms full of roses, small Danish and American flags and a beautiful grandchild with yellow curls."[15]

Owen in Denmark

Minister Owen arrived on the American Scantic Line steamer *Scanstates* in late May 1933. Denmark, a traditionally neutral kingdom, sitting atop Germany with a little over 3.5 million people and occupying about a third more space than the state of Maryland, immediately enchanted her. She later wrote that it was as if she "were stepping into the pages of my Hans Christian Andersen book!" She was especially taken with the pomp surrounding the monarchy, the presentation of her credentials to King Christian X in particular. If anything, like many Americans and even professional diplomats, she may have been too impressed. After she attended a court ball wearing an opal tiara and a yard-long train, this daughter of "The Great Commoner" wrote, "There are some things which Republics have lost perhaps, like white powdered wigs and lace in formal coat sleeves." She lauded "the old world's grace and beauty" and felt as though she were "moving around inside the frame of a picture." Usually, however, Owen remained a staunch convert to the egalitarianism of Roosevelt's New Deal and espoused its values at every opportunity.[16]

Protocol

As the first female chief of mission ever accredited to Denmark, Owen by definition sailed uncharted territory in the world of protocol. Newly arrived envoys were to have called on all their counterparts, beginning with the dean of the corps, while the ambassador's wife called on the dean's and then the other ambassadors' wives. Owen, of course, had no spouse; she solved the problem by visiting each wife as well. This would be neither the last issue of spouses to face the female ambassadors nor the last issue of protocol. Owen broke a centuries-old tradition when she became the first woman to attend the king's New Year levee for diplomats and cabinet members. Protocol suggested that as the most junior member of the diplomatic corps, she should have stood at the back of the line to greet the King, but instead, she led it. "She let the men diplomats consider courtesy to her sex," wrote *Newsweek,* "more important than seniority." Other situations, and solutions to them, could prove awkward. Owen solved the difficulty of a woman entering a room alone by appropriating the legation counselor as her escort, which unfortunately then left his wife trailing behind them, alone.[17]

Press Coverage

Owen had to contend with press coverage that, although far more extensive than what most male ambassadors received and indeed generally quite favorable, nevertheless reflected the sexism prevalent in the 1930s. Denmark was the "ideal country" for a woman envoy, the *New York Times* editorialized, "a very neat, very hardworking, very thrifty housekeeping nation." An otherwise glowing *Times* portrait of early 1934 observed that Owen had, "in the best sense of the phrase—a man's grasp of affairs." One survey of America's envoys (titled "Men of State") presented Owen as "a delightful, strikingly handsome, and attractive lady." The men, of course, were neither described in such terms nor judged for their relative "hospitality" as she was. One pundit congratulated the United States for "having the most beautiful envoy." Positive yet patronizing treatment could be found in the Danish press as well; one newspaper called her "Denmark's girlfriend." Other commentary obviously took neither Owen nor her new post seriously. *Literary Digest* wrote that she was "expected to reflect credit on her country and have an excellent time." Again, the press Owen received, both in Denmark and the United States, was overwhelmingly flattering. Some of its substance and much of its tone, however, imposed on her a tinge of frivolousness with which her male counterparts did not have to cope.[18]

People's Diplomacy

One of the first issues to concern Owen was the harm that exchange rates inflicted on the incomes of Foreign Service Officers, despite her earlier expectations to the contrary. In late July 1933, she complained to FDR in a personal letter about the failure of a House bill that would have ameliorated what effectively had been a 42 percent pay cut over the previous eighteen months. The administration's solution, instituted that summer, was to pay US diplomats in gold. But in November, Owen pointed out to him that this brought no improvement to those serving in countries that, like Denmark, were not on the gold standard. Her staff continued to suffer, and she stayed on the case, even enlisting the help of her counterpart in Madrid, Claude Bowers, who wrote to FDR at her urging. A solution finally appeared in early 1934 in the form of an equalized fund for embassies. It is clear from her handling of this issue that Owen did not hesitate to use her personal connection with the president, with some persistence, to promote her own interests and those of the Foreign Service.[19]

The United States enjoyed cordial relations with Denmark in the interwar period, as it did with all Scandinavia, but the interactions were limited, consistent with Washington's relative political isolation from Europe and its belief in Denmark's peripheral importance. The major issue in US–Danish relations in the mid-1930s was trade. Especially in 1934, Owen repeatedly pressed her superiors to begin negotiating a reciprocal trade agreement, as provided for under the Reciprocal Trade Agreements Act, passed that same year. The act authorized the president to reduce tariffs sharply on goods from individual trading partners, provided those countries did not discriminate against American goods. The State Department's response to Owen's requests was essentially that because Denmark did discriminate, it could not expect such negotiations to occur. Thus did Owen fail to sway the department on the trade issue. The cables suggest that this was one of many cases in which the US envoy expressed the interests of the country to which she or he was accredited with perhaps excessive enthusiasm. With their immersion in host-country issues and opinions, envoys often risk succumbing to this "localitis." Owen's view, however, was that a trade agreement would head off even steeper Danish tariffs and that it would benefit both countries. This attitude meshed with her broader belief that the growing interdependence of nations ought to guide diplomacy, indeed, that a successful diplomat was one who promoted the interests of home and host countries alike.[20]

Despite her amateur status, Owen also did not refrain from innovating as chief of mission. For example, she was one of the first to be concerned about the image of the US foreigners gathered from American popular culture, especially motion pictures. She told an American audience that one prison film, presumably *I Am a Fugitive from a Georgia Chain Gang* (1932), "resulted in prayers in the Copenhagen churches" among Danes who assumed the conditions depicted on screen were representative. She collaborated with the US minister in Stockholm, Laurence Steinhardt, on a collection of Swedish and Danish newspaper clippings about the United States; these included numerous lurid distortions, for example, of the extent of American gangsterism. She claimed that 75 percent of the news they sampled from a typical period concerned crime. Secretary of State Hull and his colleagues were so impressed by it that they passed it along to the president and commissioned their own study of American news in foreign newspapers. Nor was Owen content merely to observe this trend. One Danish newspaper editor, noting the friendly relationship the Danish press enjoyed with Owen, added that it was at pains to avoid reporting inaccurate statistics about the United States, because the US minister would call immediately, demanding a retraction.[21]

More important was Owen's new practice, what Eugenie Anderson would later call "people's diplomacy." This involved moving beyond representing official Washington in official Copenhagen, as was the very definition of diplomacy at the time, to representing the American people and the Danish people to each other as well. People's diplomacy predated, although it was narrower in scope than, the "public diplomacy" that would emerge as an official, integrated policy after World War II. Most definitions of public diplomacy center on crafting the image of one's country abroad and influencing foreign public opinion to one's own advantage. People's diplomacy shared the interest in communicating with groups beyond government elites, but it was neither as manipulative nor as self-interested. This is equally true, more specifically, if one accepts Nicholas Cull's taxonomy of public diplomacy as encompassing listening, advocacy, cultural diplomacy, exchange, and international broadcasting; people's diplomacy clearly overlaps only with listening and, to a lesser extent, with exchange. And as Cull points out, in public diplomacy listening is in large part placed self-interestedly at the service of the other four. Owen and, as we will see, her female successors were interested mainly in getting to know the entirety of their host countries and thereby strengthening bilateral ties at multiple levels. A systematic study of ambassadorial behavior awaits its author, but it seems clear that few male political appointees, and certainly few if any male career envoys, emphasized people's diplomacy until the Cold War, when it was subsumed under a systematic public diplomacy that became required of all ambassadors.[22]

Before leaving for her new post, Owen suggested her keenness on mutual learning when she declared her interest "in the progressive development in Denmark which I hope to study for my country." Owen further set this tone for her ministry soon after arriving in Denmark. She shocked a seventy-eight-year-old woman by personally appearing at her small house to convey greetings from the woman's son, who had emigrated to the United States twenty-four years before and with whom Owen was acquainted. The woman expressed her gratitude, and the Danish press took note. One newspaper wrote that the episode illustrated how Minister Owen had gained popularity with "her charming personality and her democratic manners."[23]

Owen's people's diplomacy, or "interpreting countries to each other," as she put it, also encompassed an attempt to learn at least some Danish, an act extremely rare for foreign diplomats and greatly appreciated by the Danes. Her Danish was good enough to enable her, for example, to tell a fairytale in

Danish at a benefit for National Children's Help Day, which generated "demonstrative applause," according to the Danish press, which in turn showed "how popular this Minister is amongst us." Other, more symbolic acts followed, such as adopting the Danish custom of bicycle riding.[24]

People's diplomacy also entailed traveling to understand more deeply all of Denmark—and its possessions. Owen may have been inspired by what she had done as a congresswoman: spending several weeks and considerable effort each year visiting every county in her sprawling district. In July 1934, she joined a Danish official party aboard the MS *Disko* for a seven-week expedition to Greenland, which no US minister, and perhaps no foreign ambassador at all, had yet visited. The trip was certainly exotic; few diplomats could have garnered such newspaper headlines as "RUTH B. OWEN VISITS ESKIMOS, EATS CARIBOU." Owen noted Danish pleasure that she had taken the time. Locals erected a cairn at Upernivik to honor her as the "diplomat who had gone the farthest north" (five degrees north of the Arctic Circle), and she became an Eskimo baby's godmother. The following year, she published the daily journal she had kept during the trip as *Leaves From a Greenland Diary*.[25]

Finally, people's diplomacy involved working on both sides of the Atlantic. That same year, 1934, the minister delivered seventy-two lectures during her annual leave in the United States, thus introducing Denmark to the American public. A Milwaukee resident attended one of these "wonderful" speeches, and he wrote in appreciation to Secretary Hull, "Mrs. Owen sold Denmark to everyone in the audience."[26]

Owen certainly suffered her share of the infringements on her time and bizarre requests from Americans that Walter Hines Page had griped about earlier, perhaps more so because of her sex. One rancher asked her to travel to a distant Danish island and photograph a particular breed of cattle. Many philatelists sent "orders" for particular Danish stamps, one asking that she "just keep my letter by you, and send me any peculiar kinds that you happen to see." American schoolteachers, finally, often had entire classes of students write her asking for information. Then again, with her people's diplomacy and the priority she assigned to introducing Denmark to Americans, she probably brought many of these intrusions on herself. When a reporter asked her whether she found tourists' visits at all hours inconvenient, she replied, "Not at all! I wish there were twice as many!"[27]

Owen's people's diplomacy meant great exposure and together with her sex and the novelty of her appointment made her immensely popular among the Danes. In contrast to Minister Grew, she formed her closest acquaintances not with members of the Danish Court but with those outside it. Everyday Danes liked her manner, elegant attire, speaking ability, and winning smile. "This is not the American Minister," a prominent Copenhagen lawyer reportedly said to himself, "—it is the American Empress." An American reporter solicited random Danes on street for their opinions. "*Fru* Owen?" a cabdriver responded. "*Ja,* she just fine!" A Danish mother added in even better English, "We Danes feel highly complimented by your President, who has sent us such a distinguished representative. We are especially glad to be the first country so honored." From the available evidence, one can see why an American traveler was moved to write to Secretary Hull, "It is universally conceded" that Owen "is the 'most popular woman in Denmark.'"[28]

Owen's Resignation and Later Years

"The hypothetical case of women in the foreign service whose marriage to a national of another country would introduce an embarrassing and troublesome element," Owen wrote in early 1935, "deserves to be considered." She hastened to add that a woman who could handle the job's other duties could probably, as men with foreign wives had, "combine marriage and a career without detriment to either." She would soon have the opportunity to test her proposition—personally.[29]

In the early summer of 1936, Owen caused a major stir by announcing her engagement to Borge Rohde, a captain in King Christian's Life Guards. Owen and Kammerjunker Rohde, eight years her junior, had been seeing each other at least since the beginning of the year. The president's immediate reaction when Owen broke the news is unknown. The two were married on July 11, 1936, in the president's church in Hyde Park, New York, with the First Couple on hand, although apparently it was Owen who chose the site and a date on which she knew the Roosevelts would be in town, thus practically compelling them to appear as guests and host a wedding luncheon. But with this marriage, Owen achieved another first: she became the first US envoy to marry a member of the court to which he or she was accredited. Eleanor Roosevelt paid her the ultimate backhanded compliment later when she wrote, "[Owen] identified herself to such an extent with the interests of the country to which she was accredited that she returned to us married to a Dane."[30]

Tired from work and very much in love, Owen (now Ruth Bryan Owen Rohde) would return to a calmer life and concentrate on writing, but only after Roosevelt was reelected and her successor chosen. She planned to campaign extensively for Roosevelt in the fall, but she hoped to keep her ministership, in part because it was her only source of income. She thought she would be able to retain her post, because US law allowed her to keep her citizenship. However, under Danish law she became a Dane, which of course was an unacceptable status for a US minister. Stumping for FDR, moreover, might raise some eyebrows, both because of her position as minister and her questionable citizenship.[31]

Perhaps understandably, State Department officials had something of a fit, not least of all because they first learned of Owen's impending nuptials only from the newspaper, just days in advance, like everyone else did. Carefully measuring press reaction in both Denmark and Washington, they quickly decided that she must step down. William Castle, though no longer with the department, probably spoke for many when he wrote in his diary that "it would be a crime if she remained." The First Lady urged Hull to keep her on, but he too was adamant. It did not help Owen's cause that public and press opinion, on one or more grounds, was decidedly negative.[32]

Under mounting pressure, Owen asked Roosevelt what she should do; her "usefulness" in the campaign, she wired him, was her "only consideration." No doubt wanting to avoid election-year controversy, Roosevelt concluded she should resign. Either Owen's commitment to campaign for him for weeks on end or her marriage to a Dane and the doubt it cast on her citizenship might, in isolation, have compelled her resignation. But the two factors in concert made Roosevelt's decision easy: she had to go. Owen quickly went along, tendering her resignation to the president on August 29, 1936.[33]

One of Owen's few consolations was the heartburn she had caused her superiors. "You were right!" she wrote to one of the few female FSOs at the time—Frances E. Willis. "It was an experience to see the ruffled feathers in the State Department!" The double standard Owen had encountered—male US diplomats routinely married foreign nationals without the slightest repercussion—was lost on neither her nor the *New York Times*, which editorialized that absent a ban on all diplomatic marriages to foreigners, women would never achieve equality in international relations. Roosevelt would indeed issue an executive order prohibiting all such unions without special permission, in November 1936.[34]

Molly Dewson and other Democrats welcomed the return of Owen and her formidable voice to the campaign trail. Eleanor Roosevelt remained in her corner, now asking whether the State Department might be able to pay her salary for two or three more months; Hull refused. But a few leading women did worry that perhaps she had been away for too long. Dewson passed along to the First Lady a suggestion that she talk with Owen before she set off, because "Ruth is living in the romantic age of kings and courts and has no idea of what is going on in the USA." Such fears appear to have been unfounded, however, as Owen campaigned diligently and effectively, towing a trailer from state to state, FDR's image on the back and "100% FOR ROOSEVELT" banners on the sides. She delivered between two and five speeches per day—that is, until late September, when she suffered a broken leg in a trailer accident and was forced to leave the campaign. *Time*'s characteristically glib account of the "matronly woman" having to curtail her "honeymoon-campaign tour" could not have salved her disappointment.[35]

Over the next few years, Owen traveled, lectured widely, and sought another post. In 1938, she may have been discussed as a candidate for the ambassadorship to the Soviet Union. Owen thought it impossible for the time being, seeing as her husband's naturalization would not come through until 1940, and she remained painfully sensitive to the spousal policies of "our rather conventionally minded friends in the State Department." Apparently a leading candidate for the position in 1938 was another woman, Cecil Norton Broy, forty-seven, a Foreign Service Officer's wife and Mississippi congressman's widow. Broy knew Secretary Hull personally and enjoyed the support of many influential members of Congress, but she lacked any relevant experience. "I had no doubt that she was a charming and estimable woman," George Kennan wrote, his disdain for both women and political appointees doubtless merging into outright scorn. "But the question was: what possible connection [did] all this [have] with Russia?" He need not have worried. The dispatch of Owen or Broy or any other woman to Moscow in 1938 would have rocked the diplomatic world and was highly unlikely. Owen's earlier collaborator, career diplomat Laurence Steinhardt, was ultimately sent instead.[36]

In 1939, Owen was a candidate to become archivist of the United States and then to head a proposed US tourist bureau, but these opportunities likewise bore no fruit. By now, Owen had little clout in the White House, the Democratic Party, and least of all the State Department, and it showed in her hard luck in finding another position. She was not even asked to campaign for Roosevelt in 1940.[37]

During the Second World War, Owen became active in the internationalist cause. In 1942, she published *Look Forward, Warrior,* one of the first calls for an international organization to preserve the peace in the postwar era. In it, she went so far as to propose a "Constitution of the Union of Nations" based on the US Constitution, which one reviewer, a fellow former diplomat, dismissed as having "little relevance to reality." Owen's record and activism led President Roosevelt to send her to the founding conference of the United Nations in San Francisco in the spring of 1945 as a public liaison to nongovernmental organizations (NGOs).[38]

In the postwar years, Owen remained a staunch advocate for the fledgling United Nations. In speeches, she urged public education about, and engagement and patience with, the new world body. In 1949, President Harry Truman named her an alternate US delegate to the United Nations General Assembly, where her primary responsibility was the work of NGOs recognized by the United Nations. Instrumental in this appointment was the indefatigable India Edwards, cochair of the Democratic National Committee and one of Molly Dewson's successors as chief of the Women's Division. Owen was also active in related unofficial efforts, for example, serving as acting president of the Institute for International Government, a predecessor of today's World Policy Institute.[39]

She sought another ambassadorship in the early 1950s, perhaps in India, to end her career "on a high note," as she wrote in a letter. But it was not to be; as we shall see, Truman had already appointed two female chiefs of mission. After several more years of writing, activism, and travel, Owen died in 1954 at age sixty-eight—in Denmark.[40]

Assessments

Owen's robust popularity among the Danes is clear from how genuinely they regretted her resignation in 1936. "A great many of us undoubtedly hoped to see this charming woman Minister return to her post," wrote *Extrabladet,* but, with her marriage to a Dane, "few of us believed that she would." *Børsen* applauded her for having cemented "the mutually good relations between the two countries." In 1946, the Danes presented Owen with the Pro Dania (Medal of Liberty) for her support of occupied Denmark during World War II and in 1949, the gold Fortjenstmedaljen (Medal of Merit), their highest decoration. Owen was in Denmark to receive yet another award when she died.[41]

Some observers of Minister Owen came away impressed. For instance, a visiting James McDonald, the League of Nations high commissioner for refugees and a man who encountered hundreds of diplomats, noted in his diary that she "from all accounts has been brilliantly successful. Nor was this surprising in view of her personality and exceptional intelligence." The US naval attaché assigned to Copenhagen and Berlin returned to the latter "enthusiastic" about the minister; the military attaché thought her a "wonderful woman."[42]

Other views were more complex. She possessed "much charm of manner and character," wrote Hugh Gurney, Owen's British counterpart in Copenhagen, but the Danes liked neither having a female minister nor all the publicity she attracted. He noted her Greenland journey and US lecture tour, adding dryly, "all of which have been more than adequately reported." An insider's view unique for its depth and candor is that of Garret Ackerson Jr., a young vice consul posted to the Copenhagen legation for about one year (1934–1935). His first impression was of the minister's gravitas, charm, and popularity among the Danes. He believed she made "a good representative," but he objected to her entourage of relatives and secretaries, a "side show" he found "rather cheap and bawdy," lacking a "ring of true breeding and unaffected simplicity." She was a politician at heart, always playing to the crowd, although he allowed that this was typical of political appointees, and that she probably did it "with more finesse than most."[43]

After paying his official respects to Owen, Ackerson reported to his parents that the minister was sharp and pleasant and had "mastered her job quickly" but that as a good politician, she focused mainly on networking. Similarly, he reported over the ensuing days and weeks that he liked her but not her love of publicity, praise from her entourage, and being photographed, the last of which he claimed provoked snickering among the Danes. Ackerson also noted "signs that Ruth hasn't made a hit with the Department and with certain other people," presumably excluding himself, "who are out to get her if they can."[44]

One of those "certain other people" was probably her deputy chief of mission, North Winship, whom Ackerson said never did like Owen. Winship reported to Assistant Secretary of State Wilbur Carr that Owen read neither any of her instructions nor any of the cable traffic. In addition, Winship claimed that she was overly ambitious (striving to be named ambassador to Great Britain—which was indeed a naive ambition at least at one point) and too feminine, was interested in her job only as a means of self-promotion and gaining lecture material, and hated the State Department.[45]

As with Ackerson's, Winship's objections to Owen bore a distinct class aspect. He reported that she lacked good taste and consorted indiscriminately, going so far as to entertain the prime minister and his mistress at her residence, even though other members of the Diplomatic Corps refused to do so because they considered it improper.[46]

Winship also clearly worked behind Owen's back. At the end of a memo to Division Chief Pierrepont Moffat, in which he disputed Owen's portrayal of the Danish press as having exaggerated unflattering news about America, he added a handwritten note: "P.S. Don't put this in the file as I might get Hell," as had happened when Owen read an earlier dispatch of his. "So I can't put what I think or know on paper officially again." Winship probably felt justified in doing this because, as he reported to Carr, Owen had brought several proposals (which received only "cool responses") directly to the White House, bypassing Secretary Hull. In May 1935, however, Winship reported to William Phillips that matters had improved, as she had become more careful in word and deed.[47]

How much of Winship's criticism was based on Owen's merits, and how much stemmed from elitism, contempt for political appointees, or misogyny— Carr, for one, was a frank opponent of women in diplomacy—is unknowable. After all, the professionals could also look down their noses at, resent the White House connections of, and attempt to undermine male political appointees. Such was the case with FDR's first ambassador to Hitler's Germany, William E. Dodd; department officials considered Dodd excessively anti-Nazi, and they treated him far more shabbily than they did Owen. However, in a misogynist age, one would have expected the most intense hostility directed toward the first woman to have invaded the men's exclusive club. Whatever the source of Winship's views, the charge that Owen read no dispatches is almost certainly false, considering her obvious personal engagement in the issue of bilateral trade, among others. Nevertheless, if Owen was even half as detached, lackadaisical, and self-promoting as Winship (and Ackerson) claimed, then her performance must be found wanting.[48]

Winship's tales out of school and the reaction to her marriage notwithstanding, Owen seems to have enjoyed a decent day-to-day working relationship with the State Department and the Foreign Service. She repeatedly praised both the reception and cooperation she enjoyed from her subordinates at the Copenhagen legation. In one of her first comments on the subject, she wrote that her staff consisted of "men of admirable ability who are accepting the innovation of a woman as minister with good grace and fine cooperation." She even tried to arrange a promotion for Winship (an attempt rebuffed as the violation of procedure that it was). If she "hated the Department," as Winship claimed, she kept her hatred well hidden. In public, Winship was kind enough to confirm how busy the minister was. She probably did not know how he really felt or that he was informing on her in Washington. But even if he or Carr or others were "out to get her," their efforts were insufficient, that is, until she gave them the gift of her Danish marriage.[49]

In February 1934, not quite one year into her ministership, Owen addressed her experiences as a woman in a letter to British MP Nancy Astor, and she denied having ever felt handicapped by her sex. To be sure, Astor was heavily involved in the effort to open the British Diplomatic Service to women and later submitted Owen's letter to the key investigating committee as supporting evidence, so it is possible that Owen chose encouragement rather than complete honesty as her approach. Still, there is little reason to doubt that Owen's direct experiences with male counterparts were mostly positive.[50]

Did Owen's tenure help launch the slow process of changing men's attitudes toward female diplomats? Direct evidence is spotty, and mixed. For the affirmative, consider the diary of Undersecretary William Phillips. In it, in 1934–1935, he demonstrated his obvious disdain for her people's diplomacy, her publicity-seeking, and her boastfulness. "Mrs. Owen, our Minister to Denmark," reads the entire description of one meeting he had with her, "spent some time telling me about her success in Copenhagen." And yet in April 1936, after a meeting with Winship, he wrote that the Danes' perception of Owen's value as a "propaganda agent" meant that they were affording her "every consideration." Most diplomats did not share this conception of a minister's job, but it had its uses. He concluded, "On the whole she may be considered highly successful." Thus, Phillips managed to combine an insightful critique of people's diplomacy with a modicum of open-mindedness to gain some grudging respect for Owen—rather than just the earlier dismissals.[51]

However, others' attitudes did not change at all. In November 1934, Assistant Secretary Carr spoke publicly on the issue of women in diplomacy and was privately offended afterward when the press portrayed him as favorably inclined. He claimed the newspapers had distorted his views; he had never approved of women in the Foreign Service and still did not, except in those few extraordinary tasks at which they could equal a man's performance.[52]

Owen was not always the savviest minister. Soon after arriving in Denmark, for example, she suggested to Fannie Hurst that she organize prominent women to mark the appointment of the first female envoy by raising money to purchase the US legation building in Copenhagen (which the US government only rented at the time, and only part of the building). The purchase price, $35,000, was a considerable sum at that time (and over $600,000 today), especially for that purpose in the midst of economic depression. Such a project would undoubtedly have triggered a public outcry, and Hurst wisely steered Owen away from the idea.[53]

Owen cannot be declared one of the great chiefs of mission in US history, not nearly. In any case, she enjoyed neither the prestige posting nor the long and varied career to belong in that circle. However, President Roosevelt certainly seems to have approved of Owen; she kept her post for over three years, and had she not married a Dane, she would have kept it longer. It is hard to believe Roosevelt did not share the sentiment when he wrote to her in August 1933 that he had "heard from many people of the splendid reception you have had in Denmark and the excellent way in which you have undertaken your task." Moreover, had she not married, her resignation (which she had intended to submit shortly after the 1936 election) would undoubtedly have been her decision, not Roosevelt's. In addition, Secretary Hull, not in the habit of praising subordinates, least of all political appointees, apparently believed Owen was competent and had compiled a fine record in Copenhagen. The prestige press agreed. According to the *New York Times,* Owen had demonstrated that "a woman diplomat can serve her country as ably and acceptably as a man" and had successfully promoted Danish attitudes toward the United States. In short, she may not have satisfied the Foreign Service or State Department, but she certainly earned approval where it counted most. Similarly, she may not have excelled in the nuts and bolts of traditional diplomacy, but by means of her version of people's diplomacy, she indisputably increased the less tangible but nevertheless vital goodwill in Danish–American relations.[54]

"She is certain to feel that an unusual responsibility rests upon her," one observer had written in early 1933 at the time of her appointment, "since the success or failure of her ministry will have much to do with the question of whether or not other women will be entrusted with the delicate and often trying tasks of diplomacy." To the extent that this was true, Owen succeeded. More to the point, she succeeded publicly, which was crucial because it meant that Roosevelt—and his successors—remained free to experiment further with the appointment of female envoys.[55]

3

Florence Jaffray Harriman

Norway, 1937–1941

Isn't Mrs. Harriman being splendid?
—President Franklin D. Roosevelt,
White House meeting, circa April 13, 1940

At three in the morning on April 9, 1940, Florence Jaffray Harriman, US minister to Norway, was awakened by the phone ringing. It was the British minister, Sir Cecil Dormer, calling with word that German warships were steaming up Oslo Fjord toward the capital. When the hastily assembled Norwegian government rejected the German ultimatum at 4:30 A.M., war, however lopsided, was underway, and Minister Harriman was caught right in the middle of it. Later that same day, back in the United States, her sister attended a small dinner party in New York. The hostess announced, "Oh, I've been in such misery all day. If only we had a *man* who knew what he was doing in Norway tonight." Her worries about the situation in Norway were legitimate; those about the American chief of mission on the scene were not. US interests in Norway at this crucial moment, it turned out, were in pretty good hands.[1]

Harriman's Background

Florence Jaffray Hurst was born in July 1870 in New York City, the daughter of Francis W. J. Hurst and Caroline E. Jaffray. The latter died when Florence was only three years old, so "Daisy," as she would always be called, was raised by her grandparents and her father, a former Civil War blockade runner and prominent owner of a steamship company. Although Florence received what she later called "a very sketchy education," she enjoyed a privileged, society upbringing; meeting such figures as Mark Twain and Woodrow Wilson while vacationing in Bermuda was not unusual. She made her debut in 1888, and the following year she married J. Borden Harriman, the ceremony attended by the likes of Grover Cleveland, Cornelius Vanderbilt, and J. P. Morgan. Borden Harriman, a Wall Street financier and a first cousin of railroad tycoon E. H. Harriman, and his new wife had one daughter. They led lives of affluence and social prominence, which created the space for Florence to engage in political activism, which Borden encouraged.[2]

While in her thirties, Harriman began the transition, as she titled her first memoir, "from pinafores to politics." She followed the path taken by many other upper-class women in the Progressive Era, through "womanly" pursuits toward public activism. First, she was the driving force behind the founding of the Colony Club, the first woman's social club in New York City, and served as its first and longest serving president (1904–1917). Particularly through the club, Harriman got involved in the women's suffrage debate, made important contacts, and got her feet wet organizing and speaking in public. Then she accepted an appointment to the board of managers of the New York State Reformatory for Women (1906–1918).[3]

Harriman entered politics in 1912, when she devoted herself to Woodrow Wilson's presidential campaign. She founded and led the Women's National Wilson and Marshall Organization, which represented a new level of female political engagement. Harriman declared that women now "have more to do than just to sit around a bridge table or sewing basket. . . . We must get out and make the world better." Although she supported women's suffrage, Harriman and the organization avoided the issue in the campaign because they sought to appeal to anti-suffrage women as well (and probably because their candidate was not yet on board either). Her reward after Wilson's victory was a seat on the Federal Industrial Relations Commission (1913–1916), created to look into the causes of labor strife, which made Harriman the first woman ever to serve on a federal commission. She and her husband relocated to Washington, DC, although he died shortly thereafter, at age fifty, in 1914. During his prolonged illness, most of their wealth evaporated, and Florence, now a forty-four-year-old widow, would experience recurring financial difficulties the rest of her long life.[4]

Harriman declined to remarry. She would have her share of suitors over the years, including General John J. Pershing and US senator Thomas J. Walsh (D-MT). At one Democratic National Convention, a rebuffed pursuer lashed out at her: "What are you in politics for? The only reason women go into politics is to meet men." But Harriman rejected all proposals. She thus joined a group of early-twentieth-century women who became publicly involved for economic and personal as well as political reasons after their husbands' deaths. When the time came, widowhood would also free Harriman to become a chief of mission.[5]

During World War I, Harriman worked more directly on behalf of women's suffrage, but that was only one pursuit among many. As chair of the Committee on Women in Industry for the Council of National Defense, she reported on munitions factory safety for women. Although she had only driven twice in her life, she was also called on to organize the American Red Cross Motor Corps, which soon deployed three hundred female drivers aiding the Allies in France. Harriman had barely returned home after the Armistice when President Wilson named her to the Inter-Allied Women's Council, which consulted with the committees of the Versailles Peace Conference on women's and children's issues. A fitting culmination of these first steps into the international realm occurred in 1920. A devoted Wilsonian, Harriman agreed to stump nationwide, at the request of the Democratic nominee for vice president, Franklin Roosevelt, on behalf of US membership in the League of Nations.[6]

Harriman did not slow down during the Democrats' wilderness years, from 1921 to 1933, far from it. In addition to publishing her first memoir, she headed the campaign committee of the National Consumers League, which opposed the Equal Rights Amendment (as did many of the more conservative feminists, who tended to oppose complete equality if, for example in the form of the ERA, it threatened protective legislation for women). In 1922, she helped establish the Women's National Democratic Club and served intermittently as its president (1923–1926, 1929–1931, and 1947–1949). In 1924, Harriman began what would be a thirty-two-year stint as Democratic National Committeewoman from the District of Columbia. Perhaps most important, she began hosting Sunday suppers at her Washington home, Uplands, attended by prominent figures from government, journalism, and the intelligentsia, women and men alike. With what Arthur Schlesinger Jr. would later describe as "imperious charm," Harriman carefully managed the conversations; Arthur Krock once complained that he found the dinners "a great bore; you had to sit there and listen to other people talk." But the likes of Felix Frankfurter and Winston Churchill kept coming, and Harriman's "teacup chancellery" would be the capital's foremost salon for many years. Moreover, although ostensibly bipartisan, it helped Democrats by facilitating their networking and buoying their spirits during their years out of power. It also kept Harriman, who naturally enjoyed "living at the center where the wheels go round," connected to all the right people.[7]

Finally, Harriman kept a hand in international issues, embracing pacifism from a perspective that was clearly gender essentialist, that is, positing the existence of inherent, essential differences between men and women. "American women have a special call to work for world peace," she wrote in 1923, and she worked to promote the League of Nations and the outlawing of war. She did believe in maintaining strong armed forces until the latter was achieved, a pretty stark contradiction of pacifism. But her opposition to war, and belief in women's key role in preventing it, were inseparable. "If war is to be stopped," she told a radio audience in 1931, "we women must help to stop it. . . . If every mother will implant the seeds of peace in the minds of her sons and daughters, we may end war."[8]

At the 1932 Democratic National Convention, delegate Harriman made the mistake of backing Newton D. Baker, Woodrow Wilson's secretary of war, for the presidential nomination. This, of course, the Roosevelt people noticed. Harriman sought a government position, and although she would meet with President Roosevelt, for example, to discuss governance of the District of Columbia, she was frozen out of the administration in his first term. This may have been because Roosevelt mistakenly believed Harriman had actively campaigned against his nomination, which she had not. She also later claimed that other Democrats who had actively opposed him managed immediately to mend fences, whereas she had to spend a few years in political exile. Rumors in 1934 that she was to be named a minister, perhaps to the Irish Free State, were completely idle.[9]

In any case, Harriman would make up for having bet on the wrong horse. She continued her Sunday salon, solidified her ties with influential figures such as Secretary of Labor Frances Perkins, and then took advantage of the opening provided by the 1936 campaign. She hopped aboard the Roosevelt bandwagon, taking her car "grass tramping" and delivering eight speeches a day. After Roosevelt's resounding reelection victory, she even put up a vigorous public defense of his disastrous "court-packing" scheme.[10]

Minister to Norway

In April 1937, Harriman was visiting New York City when a *Times* reporter called her in the middle of the night, asking for a statement on her appointment as US minister to Norway. It was the first she had heard of it. "Interesting, if true," she replied in astonishment. Clearly, her new allegiance to Roosevelt had paid off. Moreover, with Ruth Bryan Owen's departure, no woman ran any embassy or legation, and Roosevelt may have felt the need to appoint another. Undersecretary of State Sumner Welles, closer to Roosevelt than Secretary Hull was, had encouraged Harriman to seek such a post.[11]

"More Women" Molly Dewson had applied pressure on Harriman's behalf; if anything, she played an even larger role in this case than she had in Owen's. When Harriman's name was floated, FDR told Dewson that the post could not be in Europe—because of the risk of war, already thinkable in early 1937—except perhaps the Scandinavian countries, which, as Dewson noted, lay "outside of the turmoil!" Whether this stemmed from a paternalistic desire to keep a woman out of harm's way or because another post would be too important or difficult for a woman is unknown. It is worth noting that like Denmark, Norway did not rank very high on Washington's list of important countries. Roosevelt had appointed the incumbent minister in Oslo, Anthony J. Drexel Biddle Jr., in 1935 only as a temporary measure until he could find him a more important post. For her part, Harriman harbored no illusions and likewise suspected she was chosen for Norway mainly because it "was a small country and in a quiet corner of the world where a woman minister couldn't do any very great mischief."[12]

Norway deserved its pacific reputation. In 1937, it was a country of fewer than 3 million people but with territory stretching eleven hundred miles from the North Sea to northern Russia, almost half of that length above the Arctic Circle. After becoming an independent kingdom upon splitting from Sweden in 1905, it avoided war by scrupulously maintaining its neutrality, which worked during World War I and thus seemed a formula worth keeping. In 1939, with Europe clearly facing the prospect of war, Oslo would decline a guarantee by the Western powers, clinging to its neutrality in denial and complacency. As Conservative leader Carl Hambro would recall, "Were not tourists still flocking to Norway, now often advertised as 'the peaceful corner of Europe,' a land which in 1939 could look back upon one-and-a-quarter centuries of undisturbed tranquility?"[13]

US–Norwegian relations had always been relatively warm, which is not surprising, considering the hundreds of thousands of Norwegians who had immigrated to the United States. The two governments were in even greater harmony after the onset of the Great Depression, which ravaged both economies. The Roosevelt administration and successive governments in Oslo all relied on organized labor for political support and stressed the development of modern welfare states. Norwegians of many stripes, including Hambro and Labor's foreign minister after 1935, Halvdan Koht, adopted an increasingly optimistic view of the United States, seeing Roosevelt as not only a leading source of enlightened domestic policies but also a moderate potential savior from the growing twin threats of German Fascism and Soviet Communism. The problem, of course, was US isolationism, which would disappoint Norwegians (and many others) before too long. But 1937 saw two governments facing similar economic problems, embracing similar philosophies and policies, and adopting similar views of global issues. This, combined with the two countries' historic ties, helped ensure a friendly relationship in the late 1930s. Tensions and disagreements did exist, on such issues as Norwegian claims regarding US expropriation of ships under construction in the United States during World War I and high US tariffs on Norwegian whale oil. But these problems did not prevent an essentially cordial and constructive relationship from enduring through the end of the decade.[14]

Thus it could have been a far worse relationship in which Harriman was invited to play a key role. But at first she was unsure whether to accept, doubting her courage and ability. Her daughter told her to think carefully before refusing, because few women were granted an opportunity for "real adventure," much less at the age of sixty-six. And she was an energetic sixty-six. A magazine had described her as "incorrigibly young" when she was fifty-seven, and she would live for another thirty years after having been sent to Oslo. In the end, the "real adventure" proved irresistible, and her misgivings insufficiently grave. Nor were the reservations serious among members of the US Senate Foreign Relations Committee, nor indeed the whole Senate, which confirmed Harriman with little debate. Powerful political backers, who apparently included US Senate majority leader Joseph T. Robinson (D-AR), no doubt sped things along.[15]

Norway did not officially object to Harriman's appointment. Perhaps this is understandable; Norway, one of the first countries to grant women the vote (1913), was, like the rest of Scandinavia, well-known for its high level of gender equality. "These northern countries," the *New York Times* wryly observed, "did not have to wait for a World War to demonstrate woman's right and capacity in the matter of the franchise—like some bigger nations one could mention." Norway had also already received the Soviet Union's

Florence Jaffray "Daisy" Harriman, minister to Norway (1937–1941), with the Norwegian minister to the United States, Wilhelm Morgenstierne, 1937. President Roosevelt insisted that Harriman be sent to a country unlikely to take part in a European war—which meant she was caught in the middle of the Nazi invasion in April 1940. (Harris and Ewing Collection, Library of Congress, Prints and Photographs Division)

Alexandra Kollontai, in the 1920s. Resistance was not unknown; the king's wife, Queen Maud—by no means alone among women—apparently was opposed to having female ministers (although even she would end up treating Harriman most kindly).[16]

Reactions in the United States were mixed. The news was celebrated by Harriman's influential friends, who included Old Hands such as Hugh Gibson and William Phillips, which immediately gave her an advantage over the far less connected Ruth Owen. Indeed, Harriman's membership in their social class removed one additional barrier for her. But the warm congratulations were tempered with a patronizing attitude (Gibson: "I know you'll have a tremendous time & bring cheer into the frozen north") or faint praise (Phillips: "You will represent us as few are able to do."). Those sexist acquaintances who honestly shared their objections with Harriman earned her appreciation. Not so those "who gushed a little to my face," she would later recall, "and whose voices I overheard running on about 'the absurd appointment.'"[17]

Harriman took a bit of time to adjust to her new status. Her period of State Department orientation featured many diplomatic dinners in Washington, DC. "At first, when the butler announced, 'Her Excellency, the Minister,'" she later recalled, "I quickly stepped aside thinking I was blocking the way of some much more important personage."[18]

Harriman's Reception

Harriman disembarked in Bergen on June 28, 1937, with her secretary, her German shepherd, and her cocker spaniel in tow. Before departing America, Harriman had expressed the hope that she would be "as much a credit in my country as was Mrs. Ruth Bryan Owen," who, Harriman later acknowledged, had made her job easier by going first and doing so well. She presented her credentials at the Royal Palace in Oslo two days after arriving. She was impressed by King Haakon, who noted her interest in social welfare. Harriman responded that she understood that Norway was at least twenty-five years ahead of the United States in such matters. "Oh no, not twenty-five years," he replied, laughing heartily, "at least one hundred." She reported that both Norwegian officials and other diplomats had created "an atmosphere of friendliness" for her mission.[19]

Candid and insightful reactions to Harriman's ministry by a well-placed career diplomat appear in the private letters of Jefferson Patterson, her Deputy Chief of Mission (DCM) during the first half of her tenure. Although the two were acquainted from their days in Washington, Patterson initially reacted warily. Before the new minister's arrival, he feared chaos and wondered whether it would all work out. When the outgoing minister's wife had heard nothing from Harriman about her arrival plans, Patterson stereotypically noted Harriman's welcome ability to keep a secret. "She will have to work . . . to be taken seriously," he added a few weeks later, giving a sense of the Norwegian scuttlebutt. Although he defended her when others made jokes at her expense, he still marveled at the nerve required to enter a new profession at her age. But he does not seem to have objected to her sex.[20]

Although Patterson then received a kind letter from Harriman en route, which inclined him favorably toward her, once they began collaborating, he sometimes responded snidely. For example, he supposed that the minister would regret the resignation of British foreign minister Anthony Eden because he was good-looking. Overall, Patterson bore two substantive complaints. One was that the minister was away from her post too often, traveling in Norway or Europe or visiting the United States. His other criticism, far more serious, was that she did not sufficiently apply herself to the position's day-to-day work. In response to indications of her boredom, he wrote, "I could recommend that she interest herself more in her work, in which case time would not hang so dully on her hands." The same would result were she to read or write some dispatches. One can imagine, if Patterson was shouldering much of her load, why Harriman valued his assistance so highly.[21]

Yet Patterson also admitted that he had actually taken a shine to Harriman; her foibles were mostly harmless. He often qualified or downplayed his criticisms and he found much about her to admire beyond the fact that she was "amusing company." On one occasion, after again decrying her absences, he allowed that Harriman's attendance was actually not that bad, compared to other political appointees, and that was true. She was certainly no Joe Kennedy, US ambassador to Britain at roughly the same time, who was away from London fully ten months out of his thirty-three-month tenure. Patterson also had to admit that when Harriman faced visiting Americans with staunch political views at odds with her own, she skillfully kept things cordial. Finally, he sensed the minister's unflappability. She found herself in Paris during the 1938 Munich crisis and had reported to him that in the French capital only Americans were panicky. Patterson assured his mother that the minister was not among them, since she enjoyed all types of excitement, "no matter how lethal it may prove. I can't imagine her being terrified." In the peaceful, neutral Norway of 1938, he also could not have imagined how well this quality would serve her one year later. Overall, and to his credit, Patterson assessed his boss with considerable evenhandedness. He was clearly no vicious misogynist, and several of his criticisms he probably would have leveled at a male political appointee as well. But as was typical of even more enlightened men in this period, enough sexist barbs litter his commentary to remind us that a female minister in the late 1930s would never be treated equally.[22]

Harriman's Obstacles

Apart from her strengths and weaknesses that Patterson identified, Harriman of course had to work with the career Foreign Service, and overall her experience was better than Owen's had been. Harriman gave Patterson a glowing Annual Efficiency Report, crediting him with "perfect" cooperation, assistance, and encouragement from the moment of her arrival. Whatever his misgivings, she claimed that she worked with him in "complete harmony," and to his credit he gave no sign, even privately, of resenting having to serve under a woman. Moreover, she experienced relatively little trouble with other American diplomats.[23]

The major personnel problem she faced was her consul general, William Beck, especially when it seemed he might be named interim DCM after Patterson was transferred away in late 1938. She saw Beck as a tactless, socially ambitious motormouth who had "no brains" and was unqualified for the promotion because he lacked knowledge, convictions, and foreign language ability. His subordinates, according to Harriman, did his work for him. Beck was not named DCM, but he remained a problem as consul general. Eight months later, she complained to Hugh Cumming of the State Department's Division of European Affairs: Beck had only gotten worse, and what of the increased workload if war came? As it was, one clerk's time would be devoted to writing Beck's personal correspondence and doing his child's homework. Finally, news of Beck's transfer to Bermuda came on Thanksgiving Day 1939, which, Harriman wrote, "made the day a true Thanksgiving for all of us." The permanent DCM replacement, Raymond Cox, struck the minister as "a complete prima donna!"—but she collaborated well with him, as she did with most everyone else. Beck was the glaring exception.[24]

Some of the mutual resentments that existed between Harriman and the Foreign Service stemmed from the clash of political appointees and career diplomats, irrespective of sex, as seen with Patterson. The minister grew impatient, for example, with the wordiness of the diplomats' prose. Some political distance, seen often during the New Deal years, also separated Democrat Harriman from the typically conservative diplomats. This would explain Patterson's reference to the minister's "parlor pinkishness." But all female chiefs in the mid-twentieth century should have had such minor worries, especially considering the difficulties some of her successors would experience with FSOs. Harriman, finally, would ultimately defend FSOs against the charge of snobbery.[25]

Gender inequalities and double standards posed more significant obstacles. As the Old Hands had feared, for example, Harriman came to regret her exclusion from men's clubs, which hampered her ability to gather intelligence, build networks, and forge bonds of trust with her colleagues. As countless women have found across the professions, to earn access to a certain field but to be barred from attendant realms, clubs, and other institutions and activities amounts to a cruel drag on one's potential—especially since the breakthrough garners all the attention, and the unchanged informal context, a set-up for failure, no attention at all.[26]

Equally important was the spouse issue. Although Norway's bracing climate often made her feel as though she were "growing younger," Harriman recalled, she found it tiring to be, "as it were, both the Minister and his wife." Moreover, a bachelor chief could always call on the wife of a subordinate, "but a woman Minister remains her own hostess." It did not help that the Biddles, her predecessor, Anthony, and his wife, Margaret, had left formidable social shoes to fill. In this light, Jeff Patterson's complaints about Harriman's inattention to cable-writing suddenly appear somewhat unfair: she unavoidably spent hours every week on such tasks as official entertaining that male diplomats took for granted.[27]

Other instances of sexism appeared, most of which were minor but did have a cumulative weight that Harriman had to carry while her male counterparts did not. This included press coverage which, as in the cases of other female diplomats, generally praised Harriman but often overlooked her extensive political experience, placed heavy emphasis on such things as her appearance, or treated her ministry as a mere transatlantic extension of her Sunday salon. References to the "busy grandmother" keeping her "womanly eye on small detail" were, of course, typical of the age. An otherwise glowing portrait in the *Saturday Evening Post* (1940), probably the most in-depth treatment she received during her life and written by a woman, had it that Harriman "thinks chiefly with her emotions," has "no capacity for concentrated attention to detail," and is "often incapable of comprehending the broad economic or sociological or philosophical implications" of issues that sparked her interest. This may have contained elements of truth, but of course these attributes in a male colleague were seldom if ever noted.[28]

Like Owen before her, Harriman inevitably faced issues of protocol, similarly complicated by monarchy. Her account of her first diplomatic dinner at the Royal Palace is worth quoting in full:

At the dinner before the Foriningen Ball, the King . . . skols each head of Mission. He lifts his glass, and the diplomat stands, sweeps a deep bow, and drinks. My turn was bound to come. The King lifted his glass, I started to rise, but he motioned me to be seated. I compromised by bending my knees which got me half way back in my chair but not quite. At the Palace dinner, I did the same, not quite up, not quite down. The Finnish Minister, who had a sort of anti-talent for diplomatic remarks, gave one look at me, and called across the table to the Queen and to his colleagues that it was ridiculous for me to be treated differently from the rest. Was she a Minister or was she not? If she was, she should stand up. . . . I had a moment of embarrassment, but their Majesties, by their tact and kindness, tempered it later. It was explained to me that, of course, the King would not let a woman stand without standing himself; that if he stood for the American Minister he would have had to stand for all. It seems I had "played ball" in just the right way after all. When the meal was over, we went into the ballroom and His Majesty came to me, and addressed the "Minister," "Are you ready for your cigar?" and then laughed that hearty, characteristic laugh when the "Woman" managed to say, "Not yet, thanks!"[29]

On other occasions, Harriman or others acting on her behalf had to go out of their way in an attempt to gain her equal treatment. US ambassador to France William Bullitt, hosting Harriman on her way to Oslo, felt the need to introduce her as "the American Minister to Norway, *not* the wife of the American Minister, but *the* Minister in her own right." Or, consider what happened when Harriman and other envoys attended the opening session of the Storting, Norway's parliament: the Polish minister, dean of the diplomatic corps, said to her, "I dislike having you relegated to a back seat." Harriman believed it necessary to remind him that "at such times," she was "one of the men."[30]

How serious a handicap such incidents represented is difficult to gauge. In the end, the obstacles Harriman faced do not seem to have been as serious as those other early female chiefs did. They certainly did not prevent Harriman from more than adequately fulfilling her duties, even in trying circumstances. Indeed, from the day of her arrival in Norway, she believed the foreign minister never treated her any differently because she was a woman.[31]

Although, as we have seen, Harriman was an essentialist when it came to women and international affairs, she otherwise tended to downplay gender differences when asked. This is seen in the direction in which she took a Norwegian reporter's question—"Is it thanks to Roosevelt that the women in America have achieved so much?"—shortly after her arrival in 1937. "Yes, absolutely," Harriman replied. "President Roosevelt regards us not as women, but first of all as human beings." If one is qualified, he makes no distinctions. Far more hopeful than accurate, this response says much more about Harriman's views than Roosevelt's. She maintained this stance when the reporter suggested that a female minister might have an advantage, for instance, "womanly charm." "We won't talk about that," Harriman interrupted. "Naturally, that will always play its role—but it does also for a man who is a politician. President Roosevelt, for example, is the most charming person I know—and he is a man."[32]

Harriman's Success

Harriman was widely considered a successful minister. This is seen in all available assessments of her performance, from the highest leadership circles in both the United States and Norway to the accounts of visiting dignitaries and tourists. Both Eleanor Roosevelt and Ruth Owen, perhaps not surprisingly, effusively praised her work.[33]

Numerous factors might be cited to explain her success. One was simply the substantive work she performed, again, Patterson's criticisms notwithstanding. For example, Harriman constantly brainstormed ideas that might benefit both the United States and Norway, such as her suggestion in December 1939 that the United States give, sell, or lend aging destroyers to bolster Norway's miniscule navy. FDR rejected the idea; he had no vessels to spare, and selling them was illegal anyway (of course, in September 1940 he would find a way to trade fifty destroyers to Great Britain—some of which would take part in the North Atlantic convoys during World War II, ironically, with Norwegian crews). Her reports on Norwegian trade talks with third parties, moreover, won high praise from the State Department; they were the most detailed it had received from any mission, and the confidential data they contained spoke well of the close ties she must have had with the Norwegian Foreign Office. She modestly credited Foreign Minister Koht, and her access may in part merely reflect the close relationship the two countries enjoyed. Nevertheless, her energy, inquisitiveness, and ability to develop contacts (despite her exclusion from male-only venues) served her and the State Department well.[34]

Perhaps Harriman's most notable approach was to follow Ruth Owen in practicing "people's diplomacy." The Foreign Service's goal is to help with the "eventual democratization of all diplomacy," she argued after leaving Norway. The US mission must be to convince others of how democracy had benefitted the United States and to make connections not only with governments but with all democratic elements. More simply, she would act as though she were the accredited representative to all Norwegians.[35]

One way Harriman sought to realize this ideal was by attempting to learn Norwegian. She did not become fluent, not nearly. She later rued the many times she wished she could have said exactly what she wanted to say, in Norwegian. But like Owen, to the extent that she learned the local language—an act few foreign diplomats attempted—she not only allowed herself to better understand the country but also won her hosts' enthusiastic approval. Some manifestations of her people's diplomacy were largely symbolic; for example, she purchased and learned to weave with a loom, widely used by Norwegian women, in part to suggest how Norwegians and Americans could learn from each other. Similarly, the sixty-seven-year-old minister learned how to ski. "Her physical prowess," one American newspaper claimed, "pleases the sons of the Vikings." A few years later, this would rate inclusion in the Sunday comic *Private Lives* (similar to *Ripley's Believe It or Not!*) under the caption "AGE OF DESCENT!"[36]

More substantively, Harriman traveled extensively throughout Norway, getting to know people from all walks of life. She even donned oilskins and joined twenty-five thousand Norwegian fishermen in their annual cod-fishing expedition to the Lofoten Islands, above the Arctic Circle. She was probably the first foreign chief of mission to take part. Afterward, she sampled cod tongues for the first time. "Ah, so you are the one who went to Lofoten," Norwegians would later greet her. In short, much of the travel that so rankled her subordinate was actually her deliberate effort to meet, understand, and establish close ties with the Norwegian people. Whether spending more of her time drafting cables—work which, after all, did somehow get done—would have been preferable is at minimum open to question. Patterson criticized her travel because, as a traditional FSO who conceived of diplomacy as taking place on the official level only, he did not appreciate what she was up to.[37]

A similar incident occurred in the fall of 1939, after the Second World War broke out. In neutral Norway, women of the Oslo Red Cross had normally made layettes for the wives of northern fishermen, but now, with the war imposing other demands, they could no longer fulfill this function. Minister Harriman helped organize a Red Cross committee, consisting of American diplomats' wives, refugees, and American wives of Norwegians, which picked up the slack. State Department officials back in Washington apparently pooh-poohed this "teacup diplomacy in Norway," but the Norwegian press and public expressed profound gratitude for how these American women had helped in a difficult time. Again we see a clear illustration of people's diplomacy and of the traditionalists' reaction to it.[38]

Such actions on Harriman's part were not magical; they did not transform US–Norwegian relations, which had already been friendly for years. Nor did they represent a complete break with past practice; Anthony Biddle had also traveled widely and enjoyed immense popularity in Norway, though his efforts along these lines paled next to hers. Obviously this does not make Harriman a better envoy than Biddle; she just placed incomparably greater emphasis on people's diplomacy. But on its terms, she clearly succeeded. One Norwegian reporter visited with Harriman and, as was typical, came away satisfied with having a female minister who understood Norway so well and wishing her tenure would last a long time. More important, in a bilateral relationship already enjoying a firm footing, a focus on people's diplomacy to further enhance that relationship made sense because it involved two democracies. Harriman understood this and thus succeeded in breaking from the traditional role of chief of mission as well as in reaching out to Norwegians of all regions and social levels.[39]

The *City of Flint*

The most important aspect of Harriman's ministry, however, was her performance in crisis situations caused by the war. The first of these involved the SS *City of Flint,* a US Merchant Marine freighter bound for Great Britain in early October 1939. Off Newfoundland, it was intercepted by the marauding German pocket battleship *Deutschland.* The German boarding party determined that the *Flint*'s cargo—food, oil, lumber, and farm equipment, which the British Admiralty declared an urgent necessity—was contraband, making the vessel subject to seizure. With apparently perfect legality, a German prize crew took control of the ship, still nominally skippered by Captain Joseph Gainard, and headed toward Germany via neutral Norwegian waters. Coming during a lull in the global conflict, according to J. Garry Clifford, the *Flint* affair "would capture the world's headlines, create a diplomatic controversy involving five countries, and nearly give ulcers to the American Secretary of State."[40]

The Americans mainly worried about the safety of the *Flint*'s crew. But as the vessel sailed about, unable to send messages (the Americans had sabotaged the radio) and diverted by weather, fear of the Royal Navy, and a battle of wits between Gainard and the Germans, simply finding it proved difficult enough. At one point, it ended up in Murmansk, and the Soviets provided frustratingly little information. Harriman suddenly found herself at the center of all this. "How foolish I was," she later admitted. Asked to locate the *City of Flint,* she replied that she thought it was in Michigan. But, as she would write, she quickly began obsessing along with everyone else: "Where *was* the beastly ship?"[41]

She found out on Friday afternoon, November 3, when she was the only person in the legation on Nobelsgaade, doing her leisure reading and needlework. A reporter in Copenhagen shared the rumor that the *Flint* was in Bergen. For the next ten hours, the minister furiously worked the phones, like a "cub reporter," supervising the equally busy American consul in Bergen and badgering Norwegian officials. Only at 3:45 A.M. on Saturday, after somehow locating a code clerk, could she cable Washington the happy news: the Norwegian navy had captured the German prize crew and released the *Flint*. The German officer in charge had made the mistake of allowing the ship to drop anchor, at Haugesund; under international law, docking in a neutral port absent an emergency obligated the neutral power to intern the prize crew and set the ship free. The assertive Norwegians had managed this in the middle of the night by boarding the craft and capturing the prize crew without a struggle. But the episode was not yet over, for the following week saw German protest and heightened international tension. This demanded a deft touch, and the Americans decided to keep the American crew on board, away from the press, to avoid upsetting the Germans. Harriman arrived on the scene and, after outtalking the German minister, personally spoke with each member of the crew, all of them restless, a few of them rebellious, calming them and convincing them all to sign a uniform statement about their ordeal. Tempers cooled, and the ship's odyssey finally ended, after ten thousand miles and 116 days, when it made it back to the United States in late January 1940. *City of Flint*'s luck did not last forever; a German U-boat would sink it three years later.[42]

The United States had preserved its neutrality and avoided loss of life, with some sense of triumph and relief replacing the earlier humiliation and anxiety. Harriman's role had been a supporting and somewhat fortuitous one, but she played it with great skill and vigor. She was, as Clifford notes, one of the diplomats who performed "yeoman service" in this event. Captain Gainard, awarded the first Navy Cross of World War II for his performance, in turn enthusiastically praised the job Harriman did. One US senator cited the affair as part of her "fine record," which seemed to remove all doubt as to whether a woman could perform as well as a man could as a diplomat.[43]

The Nazi Invasion

Far more excitement and peril were shortly in store as the minister approached her seventieth birthday. Just a few months after the *City of Flint* episode, the German Blitzkrieg came to Denmark and Norway. Very early on the morning of April 9, 1940, Harriman was awakened with news of the invasion, which she was the first to cable to Washington. She then began preparations to fulfill the requests of the British and French ministers to take over responsibility for their legations, since they were at war with Germany and the United States was neutral.

The invasion, unfortunately, caught the Norwegians ill-prepared and woefully overmatched. They might have known something was up four days earlier, when the German minister invited officials from the Norwegian Foreign Office to view a "peace film"—which turned out to be harrowing newsreel footage of the aerial destruction of Warsaw from the previous fall. Now it was Norway's turn to experience the Wehrmacht's power. The Germans seized Oslo and most of southern Norway with little effort. Mere hours after her initial report, while trying to reach Washington Harriman noticed that the telephone operator had an unmistakable German accent. The only good news that sad day was that the antiquated guns and torpedoes of Oscarsborg fortress had sunk the lead German cruiser *Blücher* in Oslo Fjord and with it the Germans' hopes of seizing King Haakon, His Majesty's government, and the Storting, and thus paralyzing Norway's response and using the captured leadership as legitimizing cover for Nazi rule. Instead, they all gained precious hours with which to escape north by train (other officials made an even more spectacular escape, right under the Germans' noses, with Norway's $54 million in gold reserves). With Norway at war, Harriman's concerns had now mushroomed, for example, to include the fate of more than a thousand Americans trapped inside the country. But for the moment, her key instructions were to remain in contact with the Norwegian government, wherever it might go. Unfortunately, she could not get her staff and their families ready in time for the train, so they had to follow by automobile.[44]

Unlike chasing the *Flint,* pursuing the Norwegian royals and government entailed considerable danger, mainly because German ground reconnaissance units and bomber aircraft were also in the hunt—literally—trying to capture or kill the Norwegian leadership. Harriman's mobile legation—her "trusty Ford," large American flag covering the roof, staff and luggage packed within, her huge code book never out of her sight—struggled to keep up. Harriman kept Washington informed via Frederick Sterling, US minister in Stockholm. Encountering roadblocks, sleeping in farmhouses, leading a lengthening column of American refugees, Harriman and her staff were often in great jeopardy. In frantic pursuit, the Luftwaffe destroyed buildings and entire towns, such as Elverum; immediately after leaving it, Harriman watched from a hillside as it burned to the ground. At another town the German bombs fell only thirty minutes after the government had escaped. After the party crossed into Sweden—delayed because the Swedish border guard refused to believe that a woman was US minister in Oslo—and then back into Norway, the US assistant air attaché for Scandinavia, Captain Robert Losey, was killed in Dombås by a German bomb splinter, making him the first American death in the war. Only because he had insisted she stay behind was Harriman not by his side at that moment. During this period, Minister Sterling asked Harriman about her health, because rumors had been circulating that she was not well. No doubt exhilarated by events and offended by the gossip, Harriman replied that she had "never been better in her life."[45]

After a few days, Harriman agreed with her British and French counterparts that further efforts to keep up with the government were futile. By early June, with the campaign in the north lost as well, King Haakon and the government would flee into British exile anyway. The only thing left for Harriman to do was to head to Stockholm, complete her paperwork, and supervise collection of American officials, their families, and refugees; to these were added responsibility for escorting back to the United States Crown Princess Marta and her children, who had also been marooned in Stockholm.

Harriman was disappointed that she could not accompany the Norwegian government to Britain, but she believed she was of greater use seeing to the refugees in Stockholm anyway. To be sure, Harriman did not endear herself to the US legation staff in Stockholm. Winthrop Greene, secretary of the legation, confided to a colleague that Minister Sterling ought to have received a medal for keeping his sanity after two months contending with Harriman, who kept "dashing in and out with utter disregard for everything except herself and her ridiculous problems." Harriman was, Greene concluded, "a lot of fun at a dinner party but an incredible complication in an office." Her "ridiculous problems," of course, may have included the care and organization of hundreds of refugees understandably worried about their safe transit home, the importance of which Greene may have unjustly slighted. Also, Harriman tried to make no significant decisions without first consulting Sterling, which may have fueled the impression that she was a pest.[46]

After hitting numerous snags, Harriman and refugees of several nationalities, common and royal, finally managed to reach the remote port of Petsamo in northern Finland (today Pechenga, in Russia). There, nearly nine hundred people—including American veterans of the Russo–Finnish War as well as hundreds of women and children—crammed aboard the US Army transport *American Legion*, refitted to accommodate so many people. They included pro-Nazi German Americans, who provoked heated arguments with some Norwegian passengers and American crewmen. This led the cruise commander to issue an order stating that he would allow "no propaganda, no political discussion, and no strong language aboard." The ship set sail on August 16, through the official war zone. This meant that in addition to some rough weather, it had to pass through uncharted Soviet, German, and British minefields. Both anxious officials in Foggy Bottom and journalists, some of whom privately suspected Roosevelt of deliberately using the vessel as a means of getting the USA drawn into the war, tracked its progress. Despite the dangers, it managed to reach New York harbor safely on August 28. Newsreel cameras were there to greet the passengers and, as movie audiences would learn, "America's heroic Ambassador to Norway."[47]

Harriman received widespread notice and applause for her performance. "'DAISY' HARRIMAN OUTRUNS BOMBS" was the headline of *Life* magazine's photo spread. Foreign Minister Koht used the "most complimentary terms" to describe her conduct, and her friend (but opponent of female diplomats) Old Hand William Castle noted in his diary that Harriman "had made no mistakes at all." Even the resentful Winthrop Greene managed to praise her. Secretary of State Hull had been impressed immediately, cabling her five days after the German invasion,

> To her excellency, Mrs. Harriman
> Somewhere in Norway
> I am greatly relieved to learn that you and your party are safe and in good health. I congratulate you on the courage energy and efficiency with which you are performing your duties under such trying and dangerous conditions. It is in the best traditions of our diplomatic service.

The same was true of President Roosevelt, who asked his advisors shortly after the German attack, "Isn't Mrs. Harriman being splendid?" Equally pleased, Molly Dewson, to whom Roosevelt said, "Daisy did a great job," could not resist reminding the president of his earlier lack of confidence in his female envoy. With every expression of satisfaction from Roosevelt, Hull, and other men, the stereotype of women's lack of reliability in the breach was undermined just a little bit more.[48]

Aftermath

Safely home, Harriman delivered a few speeches in support of FDR's 1940 reelection bid, and with his victory she, along with all other chiefs of mission, submitted her resignation, expressing her gratitude for having been given the opportunity. Roosevelt accepted her resignation in February 1941.[49]

Within a year of returning from Scandinavia, Harriman published her account of her ministry, *Mission to the North*. It was a modest success, enjoying favorable reviews and steady sales throughout the war. At the same time, clearly moved by Norway's ordeal, she plunged back into her career as a private citizen activist, an ardent internationalist devoted to defeating the Third Reich. In January 1941, Harriman testified before Congress on behalf of the Lend-Lease Bill. Asked if the United States should enter the war, she disavowed her earlier pacifism. War was a last resort, but "with a Hitler loose in the world . . . we have to change our tactics." Yet, she continued to base her stance on what she claimed was women's unique perspective, as seen in a speech she delivered later that year defending increased aid to Great Britain.

American women hated war, she argued, but they hated slavery more. They wanted to keep their husbands and sons out of combat, but more so they wanted their children to grow up free. Pacifism had yielded to the need to risk or wage war, but the gendered explanation remained.[50]

Harriman became vice chair and chair of the Women's Committee of the Committee to Defend America by Aiding the Allies, a key pressure group (which, truth be told, had lost much of its importance by the time Harriman joined, in April 1941). The former minister also exerted herself on behalf of her occupied host country, helping to found and chairing the American Friends of Norway. The Norwegians did not forget her either; in 1942, King Haakon awarded her the Grand Cross of the Order of St. Olav, which only one other woman had ever earned. Finally, especially in the latter half of the war, Harriman diligently promoted the creation of the United Nations, through such organizations as the American Free World Association and Americans United for World Organization. Yet her efforts were not entirely Wilsonian; she also served on the Board of the Society for the Prevention of World War III, a group advocating imposition of a harsh peace on Germany. The only trouble for Harriman during the war was that she was no longer collecting her annual $10,000 minister's salary. In early 1941, she may have been under consideration as chief of mission in New Zealand, but that came to naught. Roosevelt's repeated efforts to find her another government position failed, and Harriman's financial troubles returned.[51]

Harriman remained active, especially in Democratic Party politics, through the 1950s. She was prominent enough to appear in an advertisement in the October 1950 issue of *Ladies Home Journal,* readers of which learned that she chose "a Contemporary Georgian Philco model 1875 television for her living room." In 1955, at age eighty-four, she led a march for District of Columbia representation. In 1963, President John F. Kennedy awarded Harriman the very first Citation of Merit for Distinguished Service as well as the Presidential Medal of Freedom. She died in 1967, after suffering a stroke, at the age of ninety-seven.[52]

Harriman's Importance

Among Harrimans in the history of US foreign relations, Daisy was not nearly as famous or influential as Averell, her husband's first cousin once removed, ambassador, diplomatic troubleshooter, cabinet secretary, and governor of New

York. Nor can she be declared one of the great chiefs of mission in US history. Like Ruth Owen, she enjoyed neither the high-profile post nor the lengthy résumé to belong in that circle (although of course that begs the question—women could not be "great" because they were not allowed the opportunity to be great). Moreover, Harriman's relative lack of diligence and time away from the legation cannot be entirely justified. From another angle, her roles in domestic politics left a bigger mark than her Oslo ministry did in foreign affairs—although arguably her earlier roles as political activist, government official, and political *salonnière* by definition produced greater opportunities for wielding influence than did a minor ministership.

Nevertheless, Daisy Harriman's brief diplomatic career deserves recognition for at least two reasons. First, as a woman, who faced additional burdens because of her sex, and as an amateur who was unencumbered by the elitist norms of the diplomatic corps, she challenged the traditional role of chief of mission and suggested its redefinition. By having to devote considerable time and effort to duties a diplomatic spouse would normally handle and by concentrating on people's diplomacy as a means of winning the confidence of the Norwegians and improving bilateral relations, Harriman earned the disdain or incomprehension of the career diplomats around her. But there is no evidence that she or her legation failed to do their jobs—quite the contrary. That Norway was not a major power and thus not a top priority in US foreign policy, of course, afforded Harriman some slack she would not have enjoyed at a more prominent post. Still, she demonstrated that innovation and improvisation as a chief of mission could be good things. To the extent that she successfully coped with obstacles emplaced by others (sexism) and anticipated the growing representational responsibilities of the chief of mission (people's diplomacy), Harriman incrementally aided the development of modern diplomatic practice. In this sense, her experiences and her contributions mirrored those of Ruth Bryan Owen.

Second, and more important, are the feminist implications of Harriman's ministry, both in general and regarding her wartime performance in particular. Harriman, although in many ways a conservative feminist, recognized these implications. After eighteen months in Oslo, she was under consideration to become chair of the Washington, DC, District Commission. Among the reasons she declined were her received assurances that she had seriously undermined opposition to female diplomats among Oslo's ruling elites, and she wanted to sustain this progress.[53]

This opposition more broadly is not to be underestimated. Indeed, the chauvinism Harriman faced was strong enough that it resurfaced twenty years later. Her involvement in the *City of Flint* affair, diplomat E. Wilder Spaulding wrote in his 1961 study of ambassadors, was "more strenuous than appropriate for lady diplomats" (one wonders how he viewed her role in the German invasion six months later). Before such sentiment could receive the ridicule it deserves, individuals like Harriman had to help demolish it on the ground. For the parts she played as both an envoy and a subverter of the male stranglehold on foreign affairs, Florence Harriman was an "exceptional woman" in both senses of that term.[54]

The changing assessments of her British counterpart, Cecil Dormer, also suggest Harriman's impact. In early 1938, Dormer reported that Harriman's charm had failed to win over members of Norwegian society, who considered a female minister beneath their dignity. "She is not credited with any profound political instincts," he concluded, but, happily, "her work here cannot be very exacting." Then, after observing her for another eighteen months, Dormer had a very different view. Despite, in Norwegian eyes, the burden of her sex, Harriman had become nearly as popular as the Biddles. She had made the most of her opportunities, traveled extensively, and always demonstrated her admiration for all things Norwegian. She still was "not credited with profound knowledge"—but now the final clause was different: she "seems to be an admirable representative of her country."[55]

Leading women, moreover, including women's suffrage giant Carrie Chapman Catt, had pleaded with her at the time of her appointment not to harm the cause of women by leaving her post before the president finished his term. Harriman shared their view that "if I left now those who disapprove of women in diplomacy would have a fine time saying: 'Another who couldn't make a go of it'"—an obvious reference to the nature and timing of Owen's departure. She also listed Norway's resentment of frequent ministerial changes and her own general desire to see a job through to completion, but the cause of women was paramount. She had not wanted to disappoint the American people, she recalled in 1940, but especially not women. If she failed, it might be some time before another woman was sent abroad.[56]

Others understood her importance as well. That a woman did so well in a crisis, as *Independent Woman* argued in naming Harriman its "Woman of the Month" for May 1940, would ease the path of women who followed her. Agreement came from the *Spectator* of London, which editorialized that whatever might be said in favor of admitting women to the British Diplomatic Service—an event under discussion but destined to occur only in 1946—should be greatly strengthened by Harriman's record. It added, casting considerable shade toward the King's male diplomats, that "women might even bring to our diplomacy a habit of liking the country to which they were accredited and . . . being intelligent, sympathetic and unprejudiced."[57]

In short, Harriman had confirmed the wisdom of the precedent; Ruth Bryan Owen's success in Denmark had been no isolated incident. Indeed, Harriman had not only served with at least equal merit, but she had succeeded in situations and under duress that most male ambassadors had seldom to face. (In fairness, Owen never had the opportunities created by war—as unfortunate, stressful, or risky as they were—that Harriman had with which to prove herself.) One woman's success might have been aberrant; two women's successes, the latter with the added dimension of performance in wartime, left more than twice the impression. It would also make it that much more difficult to oppose a similar move when Roosevelt's successor, Harry Truman, was ready to name another female chief some years later.

4

Perle S. Mesta

Luxembourg, 1949–1953

No country in the world can be more productive of colourful legends
than the Grand Duchy of Luxembourg.
    —W. J. Taylor-Whitehead, *Luxembourg: Land of Legends,* 1951

On October 25, 1950, US minister to Luxembourg Perle Mesta, First Lady
Bess Truman, her daughter, Margaret, and a newspaper columnist settled
into their fifth-row orchestra seats at the Imperial Theatre on Broadway. To
avoid being noticed, they had stolen in just as the lights were dimming. Pre-
miering not two weeks previously, Howard Lindsay, Russell Crouse, and
Irving Berlin's musical comedy *Call Me Madam* starred Ethel Merman as
Sally Adams, a Washington, DC, society hostess sent by her friend President
Harry Truman to the small European Duchy of "Lichtenberg" (the name fic-
tionalized, apparently at the request of Luxembourgian officials). "Neither
the character of Mrs. Sally Adams nor Miss Ethel Merman," the program
announced, tongue firmly in cheek, "resembles any person alive or dead."
But there she was, Perle Mesta, the show's obvious inspiration, sitting down
to watch a parody of herself on stage.[1]

Mesta had originally intended to see the premiere, but Undersecretary of
State James Webb instructed her not to attend; she should to come to Washington instead. Upon arriving, she had to press before learning the reason
behind the denial. "Your presence," one unnamed functionary explained in
her retelling, "would tend to dignify a burlesque on a State Department official." Now even more determined, Mesta went over her bosses' heads and
received the president's permission to see the production. So, with her prominent companions, she returned to New York and took in the matinee.

Although the First Lady disliked how "it made far too much fun of her
friend," Mesta enjoyed the show, despite afterward being somewhat

overeager to refute its many distortions. She did not, for example, fall for Luxembourg's foreign minister the way Sally Adams did for Lichtenberg's. Many others enjoyed it too: it was a smash hit, running for 644 shows, grossing over $4 million, and going on to be adapted for the big screen by 20th Century Fox in 1953. Its popularity meant that it played a major role in reinforcing Mesta's image as a party-giver par excellence—she, and not just Sally Adams, became known as "the Hostess with the Mostes'." Indeed, *Call Me Madam* perfectly captured, and continues to capture, the ease with which many have dismissed Mesta's real-life ministry. But Mesta deserves, at the very least, to be retrieved from the realm of caricature.

Mesta's encounter with *Call Me Madam*, rather than the musical itself, does embody many aspects of her stint in Luxembourg. These include Mesta's difficulty in being taken seriously; her clashes with professional diplomats, and her use of her personal ties to the president to defy them; and Luxembourgers' ambivalence about being "put on the map," not necessarily in the way they would have chosen. More broadly, reality and fiction merged to reflect how Mesta was hamstrung by her party-giving background but also how she ended up becoming, like Sally Adams, a better chief of mission than most would have expected—and, of all things, a more progressive and feminist one.

Background

Pearl (she changed the spelling later) Reid Skirvin was born in Sturgis, Michigan, in 1889. Her father, William B. Skirvin, was a hotel and oil tycoon in Oklahoma City, where Pearl enjoyed a comfortable upbringing and attended private schools. After high school, she studied music in Chicago, and her dreams of a singing career took her to New York City. There she met and fell in love with George Mesta, a Pittsburgh machine-tool magnate. They were married in 1917. George served on government boards as a "dollar-a-year man" during World War I, which brought the Mestas to Washington, DC. After the war, George became a major contributor and good friend to such leading Republicans as Calvin Coolidge, and the Mestas were soon frequent guests at the White House. By the time George died in 1925, Perle had made substantial inroads into Washington society.

She inherited fortunes from her husband and then later her father, totaling more than $16 million in in today's dollars, but rather than remain an heiress and socialite, she became an active businesswoman and committed feminist. She continued to sit on the Board of Directors of Mesta Machine Company for years after her husband's death and learned a great deal about the business. She managed her inheritances well, even supplementing them by profitably running a thirty-thousand-acre cattle ranch in Arizona during World War II. And in the 1930s on top of the Republican party-giving and fundraising one might expect, Mesta became active in feminist politics. In 1938, after overcoming her admitted ignorance about women's inequality, she joined the National Woman's Party (NWP), with its well-to-do but relatively militant membership, quickly becoming its best-known member, rising to one of its leadership positions and serving as a major contributor of both funding and influence. In this capacity, she also lobbied Congress on behalf of the Equal Rights Amendment and helped pressure the two parties into adopting women's equality planks in their party platforms for the first time—first the Republicans (1940) and then the Democrats (1944, as a member of their Platform Committee, see below). With her bipartisan connections, Mesta played a key role in keeping the amendment's planks in place in both parties' platforms in 1948. Moreover, in keeping with the international activism of the NWP, Mesta participated in organizing the World Woman's Party in 1938, becoming its international publicity chair. Years later she would dream of owning a radio station, staffing it entirely with women, and using it to promote women's rights.[2]

Mesta remained a staunch Republican through 1940, when she supported Wendell Willkie's presidential candidacy. But she soon concluded that the GOP had failed to unite behind him, and more important, she was now beginning to acknowledge her own progressive beliefs. Although obviously not a New Dealer, Mesta applauded its housing and pro-labor programs. Moreover, she had come to believe the Democrats more firmly supported women's rights. For all these reasons, she switched parties. Beginning around 1942, "Two-Party Perle" formed a close friendship with US senator Harry Truman (D-MO) before he had gained prominence on Capitol Hill. After Vice President Truman succeeded to the presidency, upon Franklin Roosevelt's death in April 1945, Mesta remained a good friend of his; his wife, Bess; and their daughter, Margaret. On average, she attended an event at the Truman White House almost every other month.[3]

Mesta soon earned a reputation for throwing successful parties of all sorts, especially those that brought together interesting combinations of people, even political enemies. She was part of a new generation of celebrity hostesses who openly promoted themselves and cultivated journalists. Although now a staunch Democrat, Mesta maintained close ties to prominent Republicans, for example, House minority leader Joe Martin. Hers was no salon like Harriman's; serious or controversial topics were to be avoided, which some guests appreciated, although political bridges might be built nevertheless. Hosting such events, enjoying the president's friendship, and fearing no competition from a First Lady uninterested in dominating the Washington social scene (or even residing in Washington), Mesta had by 1946 established herself as the capital city's No. 1 hostess. She did this despite fierce opposition from rivals such as Eleanor "Cissy" Patterson, editor and publisher of the *Washington Times-Herald,* who forbade any mention of Mesta in her paper's society columns (Mesta responded by attempting literally to buy herself favorable references from their authors). Perhaps because of her rising prominence and ties to Truman, Mesta resigned from the NWP at the end of 1946.[4]

She further solidified her relationship with the president during his famous 1948 election bid. Mesta stuck with Truman despite the conventional wisdom that he would lose badly; more tangibly, she played an important role in raising funds for Truman's cash-strapped campaign (and then helping the party retire its substantial debt after the election). According to his daughter, Truman admired Mesta's fundraising far more than her parties. These, of course, did not really constitute separate activities. In fact, although Mesta exaggerated her roles—she later saw herself as a "politician, diplomat and hostess, in that order," and her party-giving as the best thing she could "do to render service to my President and my country"—many underestimated her influence. By early 1949, she had certainly become one of the most prominent women politically tied to President Truman, even warranting a cover story in *Time* magazine.[5]

Mesta's Appointment

The president named Mesta to a diplomatic post, though, largely due to the efforts of India Edwards, vice chair of the DNC and executive director of its Women's Division. A loyal operative whom Truman greatly respected, Edwards tirelessly pressured him to name women to a variety of government posts. She later admitted to having felt "ghoulish" when, after reading of one official's death, she rushed to the White House to see if Truman would consider a woman as a replacement. Edwards set her sights on posts in foreign relations as well.[6]

It probably helped that Eleanor Roosevelt weighed in at this same time. News that the administration was planning to create a pool of negotiators for overseas conferences provoked Roosevelt to ask the new secretary of state, Dean Acheson, why no women appeared on the list of candidates. She suggested to him that recognizing women, "particularly in the field of foreign affairs," would help the administration. One reason for the omission may have been that Acheson was not fond of the idea of female diplomats. India's ambassador in Washington and the first female chief sent to the United States, Madame Vijaya Lakshmi Pandit, recalled that Acheson had difficulty accepting her as India's envoy. He asked her, "Why do pretty women want to be like men?" Acheson replied to Roosevelt defensively, making the astonishing claims that the department always tried to hire women and that its goal was to hire without discrimination. He then added a list of women serving in the field, using it to demolish the straw man that no women had been slotted into "responsible positions." But the list was short, and only a couple of the women on it occupied posts that were even arguably mid-level, let alone the significantly more senior level Roosevelt clearly had in mind. And Roosevelt's urging was something neither Acheson nor Truman could easily ignore.[7]

Truman needed cajoling, even more so than his predecessor. No women had served as chiefs of mission from 1941 to 1945, despite what one might expect in light of the opportunities opened to many American women during World War II. While completing Roosevelt's fourth term after the war, Truman saw no need to fill the existing void. He would offer India Edwards a cabinet post or ambassadorship in 1948 (which Edwards declined), but she was clearly an exception. Regarding women in government generally, Truman initially represented a step backward. He shared neither FDR's background with women nor his disposition to hire them, nor of course did Eleanor Roosevelt wield the same influence she had before, her bit of lobbying notwithstanding. Women's access to the president declined markedly, and signs of the new climate readily appeared. At a February 1947 press conference, Truman joked about naming a "gentleman"—"or lady"—ambassador to Great Britain; when pressed, he replied that women were candidates for many positions, "but not that one." Nor can one imagine Franklin Roosevelt responding to Emma Guffey Miller's request for consideration of the Equal Rights Amendment with Truman's flippancy. Truman privately described Miller's presentation as "a lot of hooey" and said directly to her that in his experience, "there is no equality—men are just slaves and I suppose they will always continue to be."[8]

With fading direction from the top, women gained scant additional access to government employment in the 1940s. Of course, after World War II, the hiring of female diplomats could only improve over the doldrums of the 1930s. Indeed, female FSOs became significantly more common, jumping from 1 percent of the total in 1947 (10 officers), to 5 percent (118 officers) in 1953, to 9 percent (336 officers) in 1960. As we shall see, this was a fluke (stemming from reorganization and reclassification of personnel), and virtually none of these women rose above the middle levels. As in other countries, moreover, American attitudes toward such women changed only slowly. As late as 1942, the *American Foreign Service Journal,* the readers of which, after all, now included some women and the men who served with them, reprinted a British article that completely rejected the fitness of women to serve. Even relatively progressive voices continued to promote an essentialist and constricted view of a woman's place in the diplomatic world. In June 1946, for example, US ambassador to Turkey Edwin C. Wilson encouraged the graduates of the American College for Girls to pursue a variety of careers. Some of them, he said, "under the standard of social justice, may enter the lively arena of public affairs." As his example, he chose the United Nations, where women "will carry on their age-long fight for security of home and loved ones in a world of peace." In other words, if to perform international public service women left their separate sphere of home and family, they rightfully belonged in the separate sphere of the United Nations, the young organization already becoming a low-prestige spot useful for padding the number of female appointments. Wilson made no mention of career opportunities in the Foreign Service or Department of State. More blunt was a US senator from Texas, Tom Connally. As a delegate to a UN committee, also in 1946, Connally objected to UN affiliation being granted to the World Federation of Trade Unions. Alternately waving his hands in the air and pounding them on the table, he argued that the body would then have to admit all kinds of other groups, including women's organizations. "Would you like to have women in here," he shouted to a Syrian delegate sitting near him, "dictating to us what to do?" His startled colleague responded, "No."[9]

Moreover, the views of the broader public remained mixed at best. In 1949, the year of Mesta's appointment, 34 percent of Americans polled still

Perle S. Mesta, minister to Luxembourg (1949–1953), speaking at the Cercle de l'Union Interallié, Paris, 1950s. Mesta struggled against her reputation as a mere Washington socialite—she inspired the musical comedy *Call Me Madam* (1950)—as well as State Department hostility to achieve a mixed record as minister. (National Archives)

disapproved of women serving as ambassadors. Female diplomats continued to swim against the current, and that no woman had run an overseas post for almost a decade is not surprising. And yet, this long absence may also have augmented Truman's incentive to name a female envoy.[10]

Lobbied by Edwards, Truman decided to appoint a woman, and to send her to either Denmark or Luxembourg, before he settled on Mesta in particular. In early March 1949, Eleanor Roosevelt was floated as a possible ambassador to France, an appointment which, far more than Ruth Owen going to Moscow, would have stopped the presses. But top State Department officials, including Acheson, "agreed that it would be much better for her to remain doing special representation work for us at the United Nations." For Luxembourg or Denmark, Truman first suggested Eleanor McAdoo, daughter of Woodrow Wilson, before making the offer to Mesta in May 1949.

Secretary Acheson, no doubt ranking allies, chose Luxembourg—in which the United States had maintained no separate representation until this point—over Denmark. Mesta and Luxembourg most likely seemed a good match because of her background in steel, of which Luxembourg was the world's seventh-largest producer, and because Luxembourg was ruled by a woman, the Grand Duchess Charlotte. Most obviously, Luxembourg was a tiny country of limited importance to the United States and yet firmly lodged in its orbit. Washington risked little dispatching a woman, indeed, a famous socialite, to Luxembourg.[11]

Mesta faced a difficult decision in whether to accept the offer. When Edwards broached the idea over lunch, her initial reaction was to reject it as "ridiculous." Thus, Edwards had to lobby her as well as the president. She called Mesta to her office in early May and revealed Luxembourg as the destination. But the president, Edwards reported, "isn't sure you'll take the job. I told him I thought you would. Will you?"[12]

Reasons to decline, on which Mesta and some friends agreed, included her lack of training and language ability, her outspokenness, her importance to the Democratic Party at home, and her fear of failure. However, she recognized it as a great opportunity and challenge, and her experience as a hostess renowned for uniting the fractious might actually come in handy. But the feminist implications loomed largest of all. "I hope that other women will follow me in diplomatic and governmental posts," she would somewhat grandiosely put it to Luxembourg's journalists after her arrival. Women were entitled to official roles because of their equal intelligence, and Mesta especially wanted to succeed, and thereby inspire younger women. Moreover, like many early champions of women in diplomacy, Mesta was an essentialist: "women's intuition . . . fits in well with diplomacy," she said in 1950. In short, as she said at the time of her appointment, "I think this post is an advancement for women and I ought to accept it." And so she did.[13]

Mesta's connections certainly helped after that. The Senate Foreign Relations Committee approved the appointment unanimously without even requiring her to appear. On the Senate floor, Forrest Donnell (R-MO) did seek to block her, but his colleagues rallied to her defense. "She has not come before the committee," explained Charles Tobey (R-NH), "but the Senators have come before Pearl Mesta." Some of her supporters set the bar low. Senator Owen Brewster (R-ME) read into the record an earlier statement to the effect that, as neither dotard nor drunkard, Mesta would represent an improvement over some of our previous envoys. In the end, Donnell's was the lone dissenting vote. For her early July swearing in, the State Department auditorium was needed because of the extraordinary number of attendees, apparently more than had been on hand for Secretary Acheson's own ceremony earlier in the year. US senators, Supreme Court justices, cabinet members, and Vice President Alben Barkley looked on as Mesta accepted her official commission from an uncomfortable-looking Acheson. After the standard three weeks of department briefings, she arrived in Luxembourg, via Paris, in late August 1949.[14]

Mesta's appointment attracted so much attention that it may have overshadowed the other women Truman named to government posts—as he improved his record—a total of eighteen in Senate-confirmed positions, the vast majority after India Edwards took over the Women's Division in 1948. In December 1949, Edwards appeared on *Meet the Press* to tout the president's record, although this was shortly after Truman had selected one other woman, Eugenie Anderson, to run an overseas mission.

> EDWARDS: I think we have already gotten some perfectly wonderful appointments that should inspire women to get into politics.
>
> DORIS FLEESON: Mr. Truman appoints women that he could send as far away from him as possible.
>
> EDWARDS: Oh-h-h!

The venerable Alice Roosevelt Longworth, one of Mesta's fiercest capital city rivals, went Fleeson one better. "The only benefit to Old Perle's new position," she quipped, "is that she's no longer in Washington."[15]

Truman's attitude, now that Mesta was on her way to Luxembourg, is reflected in his request to seasoned diplomat Robert Murphy, then beginning a term as ambassador to neighboring Belgium, that he do everything he could to help Mesta. The president wanted Mesta to succeed but was concerned that her lack of experience and expertise might get her into trouble.[16]

Luxembourg, 1949

The Grand Duchy of Luxembourg is one of the smallest countries in Europe—at 998 square miles, it is smaller than Rhode Island. In 1949, its population was about three hundred thousand, or as one US diplomat would scoff, "one ward in Chicago." The country's own leaders were given to wry comment on the subject of size. "I'll bet," Prime Minister Pierre Dupong remarked, "that if all the baseball diamonds and football fields in the United States were set side by side and dropped over Luxembourg, they'd cover the country entirely—with a few left fields lapping over into France, goal posts jutting into Germany and side lines edging up to Brussels." Its strategic location negated its traditional neutrality, and two World Wars severely tested the Luxembourgers' resilience. They liked to tell the story of a solitary small house alongside a road favored by foreign armies, which was either badly damaged or flattened on four occasions—in 1914, 1940, and twice in 1944–1945—and rebuilt every time. By liberating the country, Americans earned a special place in Luxembourgers' hearts. After Adolf Hitler Strasse in Luxembourg City once again became the Avenue de la Liberté, the nation abandoned its neutrality and became a leading advocate of European integration. It joined as a charter member the North Atlantic Treaty Organization (NATO), founded just months before Mesta's arrival, as the Cold War entered its darkest phase. The nation was relatively progressive on gender issues, women having secured the right to vote in 1919, the same year Grand Duchess Charlotte, constitutional monarch in this stable democracy, ascended her throne.[17]

For Luxembourgers, the path for Mesta's appointment was smoothed by the fact that their country was receiving its own US minister for the first time. Previously, Luxembourg was the responsibility of the US embassy in Brussels, with US interests in Luxembourg being handled only by a chargé d'affaires. Luxembourg certainly welcomed this new, higher level of representation and the recognition it suggested.

At first, when Mesta's appointment was rumored, Luxembourg's minister to the United States, Hugues Le Gallais, sent home a disapproving cable. "I'm afraid," he added with resignation, "we can only say yes." But after the appointment became official, the minister surveyed his foreign colleagues in Washington and discovered their envy. They believed her close White House ties and motivation to succeed would only redound to Luxembourg's benefit. He did pass along gossip that Mesta was a nonreader and would not spend her money in Luxembourg. Nevertheless, her press connections would mean welcome attention for the nation. He concluded that the Mesta pick was not perfect, but still cause for satisfaction.[18]

Back in Luxembourg, Le Gallais's superiors did not necessarily share his attitude. A US diplomat later claimed that when Secretary Acheson informed Luxembourg's esteemed longtime foreign minister, Joseph Bech, of the appointment, Bech's reply was diplomatic: "It is a great honor for so small a country!" But according to the diplomat, all the Americans "knew what he thought."[19]

Mesta's Difficulties

Once on the job, Mesta committed gaffes just as other amateur diplomats did. In fact, her tenure began with one, although through no fault of her own: the chauffeur leading her impressive caravan from Paris, packed with luggage and relatives and trailed by numerous reporters, took a wrong turn and ended up at the Belgian frontier; they thus missed the welcoming party at the intended border and finally arrived in Luxembourg City hours late and unescorted. At times, Mesta lacked subtlety, such as when, for a ceremony for the visiting General Eisenhower, she donned a red hat, white fur wrap, and blue dress. On another occasion, too vain to wear glasses in public, she misread a tribute to visiting representatives of the 4-H Clubs. She thus congratulated "these young people of the 4-F Clubs of America."[20]

She won at least a few skeptics over. After spending some time with her, journalist C. L. Sulzberger noted that she made no pretense of diplomatic mastery but was nevertheless shrewd, amiable, and popular. Eleanor Roosevelt, who visited Luxembourg in June 1950, had her doubts at first. She had "shrugged and smiled a little" after learning of the appointment, wondering how Mesta would occupy herself after quickly running out of entertaining to do. But then, after observing her for three days, Roosevelt came around. Mesta, she wrote, was devoted to duty. America's female diplomats, including the minister, were capable of "serving their country not as women but as able representatives of the United States."[21]

Some commentators found the minister confusing or contradictory. Westbrook Pegler considered her strong but frivolous, "a baffling combination of traits overlaid by extravagant generosity." The young stringer Daniel Schorr was more blunt when he wrote privately that Mesta "always tickles me with her mixture of stupidity and shrewdness."[22]

More common, however, were steadfast dismissals of Mesta as silly and uninformed. According to Ambassador Murphy's memoir, Foreign Minister

Bech told him, "She and I are good friends. . . . Of course, I don't talk with her any more about European politics." Similarly, Bech's Belgian counterpart Paul-Henri Spaak reported to Murphy on a dinner he had with Mesta: "We had a thorough discussion about the weather and all such matters."[23]

And those are the stories that made it into Murphy's published memoir; others he excised from the draft version on advice of counsel. His attempt to discuss with Mesta the Saar region of western Germany foundered on her belief that the Saar was part of Switzerland. He believed apocryphal the story that Mesta had asked to see a "steel mine"—and yet had included it originally anyway. Finally, he has her referring to Foreign Minister Spaak as "that very interesting Mr. Sparks."[24]

Many others commented on her ignorance. Especially at first, afraid of misspeaking or revealing her lack of knowledge, Mesta refused comment or gave vapid answers to substantive questions, which of course only justified suspicions. "We talked and talked," journalist Martha Gellhorn noted, "but it was like flying through a cloud. So dim, so vague." The labor attaché in Brussels seconded to Luxembourg, Eric Kocher, had to work to overcome her horror when he told her that Socialist trade unions would be hosting her visit to an iron mine; like many Americans, she knew of no distinction between "socialist" and "communist," one that was enormous and critical in Europe at the time. Such anecdotes steadily accumulated. Mesta joined many other political appointees in her lack of knowledge, but she certainly confirmed this major objection of such appointments' critics. Her reputation—and thus her effectiveness—suffered accordingly.[25]

Thus, it is not surprising that Danish, Norwegian, and Dutch opinion, both official and public, objected strenuously later when (idle) rumors circulated about Mesta's impending transfer to their respective countries; they considered her unqualified. Such perceptions, even if a bit unfair, were grave. If a chief of mission is not taken seriously by the host country's foreign minister, then his or her ability to function—to report, negotiate, and represent—is profoundly compromised, to say the least.[26]

Two further obstacles stood out: one was press coverage. Newspaper and magazine articles were at times positive or nuanced, certainly; Mesta was too well connected not to enjoy some good press. Early on, for example, one news magazine reported that Luxembourgers found her more diplomatically sensible than other Americans. Also, she won over most of the Luxembourger papers, indeed, from her opening press conference. Perhaps because her reputation so lowered expectations, local reporters were charmed by the new minister. When one asked her whether Americans believed Luxembourgers were pulling their own weight regarding the Marshall Plan, Mesta replied, "My President thinks you are very, very important. You may be a small people but we have a saying in America that precious pearls come in small packages." The journalists, at least on this key occasion, were also impressed by her knowledge of their country (her orientation sessions had obviously not been for naught). Thereafter, they mostly favored her in their coverage; only the Communist press routinely attacked her.[27]

But because she was a famous society hostess, a neophyte, a political appointee, and a woman, American journalists often strained to criticize or belittle her. They snidely described her as "buxom and bustling," a "blue-eyed, chunky little Oklahoman," or as having arrived in Luxembourg "with plump aplomb." Much of this, of course, typified the patronizing, chauvinist attitudes of that era. But Mesta's fame as hostess presented a particularly acute problem. A 1952 *Longines Chronoscope* television interview, for example, began with questions about the food she served and Luxembourg cuisine in general. Presumably few other ministers holding press conferences back in Washington, DC, were asked such questions as "What in the dickens is a flaming ice cream omelette?"[28]

Especially unfair were Henry Luce's publications, *Time* and *Life.* The latter pounced on her lost motorcade, blaming her for the mistake. "MRS. MESTA'S GRAND ENTRY," the title began. "The new U.S. minister has some difficulty in locating Luxembourg." This bias, moreover, outlasted her term as minister; noting Mesta's confusion over whether to place her hand over her heart or salute at a farewell ceremony in 1953, *Life* juxtaposed the two photographs with the large caption, "What's a Woman Do?"[29]

Such treatment presented Mesta to the public as an absurd hostess posing as a diplomat, which sold her rather short. Symbolically, the conflict between image and reality could be striking. In *Collier's,* a skeptical editorial titled "Chafing-Dish Diplomacy" was accompanied by a large Al Hirschfeld caricature—and, with her wide grin and effervescent personality, she lent herself to caricature—which shows Mesta happily ladling soup, dark circles around her eyes and chef's hat prominently perched on her head. It suggests perhaps a demented Julia Child after a fistfight, but it definitely connotes upper-middle class domesticity. Yet, consider this alongside a photograph, found in Mesta's memoir, of Mesta and Dwight Eisenhower in her residence kitchen. Eisenhower, then NATO's military chief, is showing Mesta how to roll steak in dough. Both are wearing aprons, but a more complete gender role-reversal is difficult to imagine. However, it represents reality as accurately as Hirschfeld's cartoon does. Mesta apparently could cook, but she usually did not; with her means, she always maintained a large staff to do such things. Rather, she had invaded the "man's worlds" of first business, then politics, now diplomacy—and here was being shown around the kitchen by a man, indeed, the great hero of the Second World War. Mesta's "baggage" as hostess, in short, served to distort public depictions—and conceal the incremental advance of feminism her appointment represented—even more than was the case with other female diplomats in this period.[30]

Mesta's second major problem was the State Department and Foreign Service. This was not uniformly the case; department officials could at times see domestic political value in Mesta, for example, using her to promote US foreign policy to domestic audiences, and they appreciated this work. But such acknowledgements paled beside the manifold signs of hostility, contempt, and resistance. These appeared from the moment of Mesta's nomination, when unnamed department sources signaled their opposition to the press. One kept repeating to a *Time* reporter, "No comment," and then, when pressed further, snapped, "You know sometimes a 'no comment' can be damned significant." Another was a bit more direct, estimating that running the legation "would leave her about 23 hours of free time each day." Once she was on the job, references to her in department correspondence could be sarcastic, sexist, or both. On one occasion, an official described Mesta having "changed her mind (a lady's privilege)." At least one Old Hand sounded off as well. William Castle wrote in his diary that he was "ashamed to say" that he had attended a Press Club luncheon for the "self advertiser" Mesta; from her "appallingly dull" speech one learned nothing about Luxembourg.[31]

Undersecretary of State David Bruce, in particular, had no use for Mesta, who, after their first couple of meetings, appeared in his diary as "not my favorite person." Before long, he joined in the circumscription of her role: When he informed her of plans to establish US representation with the High Authority of the Schuman Plan in Luxembourg, he found it necessary to admonish her that "she would have no control over the operations." When he refused to approve a trip home at government expense, a privilege he believed she had already abused, she went over his head, secured Truman's approval, and gloated about it afterward. She knew nothing about the proper functioning of diplomacy or government, he fumed in his diary, and seemed, "in her pursuit of personal publicity, lacking in almost all commendable qualities." Almost everyone in the department hated Mesta, Bruce concluded, "as a phoney, an ignoramus and a pretentious bore."[32]

How Mesta's White House access may have pleased the Luxembourgers but offended the State Department is evident from an April 1950 Washington meeting. Acting Assistant Secretary of State for European Affairs Llewellyn Thompson explained to her that both the State Department and the Civil Aeronautics Board had rejected the idea of a civil aviation agreement with Luxembourg. This was in part because such pacts required reciprocity, which, because no American airline sought landing rights in Luxembourg, did not obtain. Mesta responded by citing Luxembourg's strategic importance to the United States. After this point was shot down, according to notes of the meeting, "Mrs. Mesta then inquired as to what reaction might be expected if the White House interested itself in this case." Thompson and his colleague replied that because of the congressional backlash and personal attacks on the president that might result, this would be a mistake. Mesta ended the meeting by asking whether it was alright if she contacted the board directly. On the one hand, one must admire her assertiveness, and had Joseph Bech been able to read these notes, he would have had cause for great satisfaction. On the other hand, this account certainly exposes Mesta to the charge of localitis (a condition she later essentially admitted to having contracted: once, back in Washington and recording a statement for Voice of America, she referred to Bech as *our* Foreign Minister"). The department officials, moreover, must have shared Bruce's resentment at how quickly Mesta threatened to go over their heads to 1600 Pennsylvania Avenue.[33]

Far more serious, however, was Mesta's relationship with her Foreign Service subordinates at the legation. Initially, First Secretary and ranking FSO George West welcomed Mesta's appointment, at least in the same way Le Gallais had; she represented, West wrote, "a good opportunity to sell the Foreign Service to someone close to the President." But the conflict with the FSOs began the moment the minister arrived in Luxembourg City. In their first meeting with her, the three officers assigned to her made it clear that they intended to perform the work of the legation and treat her as a mere figurehead.[34]

For Mesta's second day on the job, Labor Attaché Kocher arranged to have the minister visit an Arbed iron mine and then a steel mill in the town of Esch-sur-Alzette. However, First Secretary West urged her to cancel the trip, citing protocol and the "undignified" nature of the event, no other country's minister nor any female official ever having done such a thing. The new minister defied him and went down in the mine, accompanied by the labor attaché, leaders of the miners' union, and the late minister of labor's widow. Some in the Luxembourg elite shared the first secretary's distaste for the trip: "It's like visiting a house through the servants' entrance," one socialite sneered. Mesta then went on to visit the steel mill.[35]

The fullest account of the visits, other than Mesta's own, is that of Attaché Kocher (who had "smiled, then shuddered" when he learned of her appointment). While clearly bemused by what he reported of Mesta's moodiness, awkwardness, ignorance, vanity, and publicity-seeking, he ended up taking a somewhat nuanced view of the minister, while providing an explanation for Murphy's story about the "steel mine." At her press conference toward the end of the day, Mesta said that she visited a "steel mine" and an "iron mill." After a stunned silence and a request that she repeat herself, she winked at Kocher and uttered the exact same words, emphasizing the words *mill* and *mine*. The attaché believed she "quite purposely committed this malapropism." He thought long and hard about her performance and concluded that Mesta had decided, because she would win no acclaim for her "political wisdom," that she would keep her name in Washington, DC's newspapers by playing the "oddball." There is no corroboration for Kocher's intriguing theory (although the press director of the Luxembourg government later recalled that Mesta knew how to use the media and chose all her gestures deliberately). Kocher gives Mesta more credit than most other FSOs would, but he shares their belief that her interest lay in publicity and little else.[36]

Thereafter, her relationship with the FSOs only worsened, in the words of a Foreign Service Inspector, becoming the "capital feature of the Legation" and "adversely affect[ing] the entire substantive work of the office." For example, the inspector believed Mesta ought to delegate more administrative duties to her subordinates. This may reflect the relatively large amount of free time Mesta's post afforded her, but perhaps also Mesta's mistrust of her FSOs. The British minister, impressed with her "capable staff" of FSOs, noted that "she does not like to hear their praises sung." According to one of her administrative assistants, while discussing some upcoming event with one of them, Mesta said simply, "I hate you. I don't want you to come."[37]

In August 1952, and only because Truman insisted, Mesta drafted a personal account of her clashes with the FSOs. The political officer, who was also the ranking FSO in the legation after George West was transferred away in mid-1950, was Anthony Swezey. Swezey seems to have gradually organized the other officers against Mesta, keeping her in the dark as to legation business and snobbishly resisting her public relations efforts. Ultimately, after learning of his transfer (which both Mesta and the Foreign Service Inspector had urgently recommended), Swezey stormed into the minister's office and launched into a shouted rant about how much he hated Luxembourg and how his talents were being wasted there. Precisely sorting out the FSOs' motives is difficult. They had a narrow, traditional sense of their duties and an expansive sense of their own importance. How much we are to attribute to the location, to these individuals' own characters, to Mesta's status as a controversial political appointee, or to her sex, is unknowable. Whether they would have repeatedly shown such insubordination and disrespect to a male superior, even a political appointee, is worth considering.[38]

President Truman sided with his minister—unsurprisingly, since he had long subscribed to the popular stereotype of the effete, pretentious "cookie pushers" of the diplomatic corps. He once passed along a story about a US chargé d'affaires in Cairo, a Topeka native, who "wore a checked suit, carried a cane, wore a cap and talked with an Oxford accent." If the man had dared return to Topeka in that attire, Truman commented, "he would have lasted about ten minutes in the Kansas Hotel lobby." Mesta's memo angered the president, in part because he had heard similar stories about several other legations and embassies across Europe and Latin America. "Had I known of this situation when it was taking place," he wrote in a memo he passed along with the report to Acheson, "these birds would have been kicked out forthwith." He was sure Acheson would agree "that these people need a first class kick where it will do the most good." This was probably the president releasing steam by memo-writing, as was his habit; there is no evidence that either he or Acheson followed up on the matter.[39]

Mesta deserves a share of the blame for the conflict. She was not merely assertive; she could also be stubborn and even domineering, traits consistent with a life of privilege and the expectation of deference from subordinates that often accompanies it. Moreover, she fully shared Truman's prejudice against the "striped pants boys"—the title of the relevant chapter in her memoir—and this no doubt contributed to the relationship's dysfunction. It is also hard to avoid the conclusion that socioeconomic class played a role here, for the patrician East Coast elite was still overrepresented in the Foreign Service circa 1950, whereas Mesta was clearly a midwestern nouveau riche. And then this clash happened to come, as we have seen, at a particular moment of heightened gender anxiety, Red and Lavender Scares, and a besieged diplomatic corps. It was a mixture more toxic than that seen with any of the other early female chiefs.

Perhaps then we should not be surprised that during the Senate debate in 1949, Texan Tom Connally—now switching his preferred form of prejudice— had cited the very fact that Mesta was not "a man with striped breeches, and a silk hat" as reason to appoint her, the gendered stereotype of the cookie-pusher trumping Mesta's sex. Similarly, FSO George West would later recall Anthony Swezey as having had "exquisite tastes," in contrast to Mesta, who "was the most gauche person you can imagine." Mesta waited not even a year after stepping down to express publicly how badly the FSO's snobbery had stunned her. To her discredit, Mesta even made her own minor contribution to the antigay witch hunt by sharing with the State Department her suspicions of Swezey's "tendencies"—innuendo that could have destroyed his career, and if she was aware of that fact, her comment must be seen as utterly ruthless. Thus did the Mesta–FSO conflict come to exemplify several troubled facets of American diplomacy's social environment in the early postwar period. But the clashes with staff and the legation intrigue also represented by the far the greatest drag on Mesta's ministry.[40]

Mesta's Strengths

In spite of these formidable hindrances, however, Mesta managed fairly well at her post, exhibiting several strengths that, when tallied, render her a qualified success. The press sometimes acknowledged this, often grudgingly or with evident surprise. One asset was her popularity in Luxembourg, which was immense, consistent, and beyond dispute. In a highly critical article published a few weeks after her arrival, Daniel Schorr marveled at her reception. In four days of interviews with all sorts of Luxembourgers, he wrote, "I have not met one who is not happy about her presence."[41]

A second strength stemmed from her fame and high-level American connections: her impact on Luxembourg's status. Luxembourgers, like many citizens of small countries, had long felt ignored. At the time of the Allied liberation in 1944, one native often had Americans to dinner and always made a point of asking them, "Did you know this place was here before you came?" After Mesta's arrival five years later, so many Americans, powerful politicians among them, now included Luxembourg in their European itineraries that her friends took to calling it "Perle Harbor." Luxembourgers did not like to admit it, but Minister Le Gallais had predicted accurately: Mesta's presence raised their country's profile in America and throughout the western alliance.[42]

Third, Mesta was able to adapt to the absence of a spouse. Even though her mission was small and entertaining was second nature, Mesta had much to do but no husband to assist her. Mesta compensated in part by using her wealth to maintain an unusually large personal staff of twelve. But more important, she relied heavily on her sister, Marguerite Tyson, and eventually Tyson's family, who ended up renting a house nearby. Tyson could even remind a distracted Mesta that the butler had announced the service of breakfast. "Come on, Sister, the food's getting cold," Tyson said. Considering all the entertaining Mesta did, finding a substitute spouse was nevertheless crucial to what success she did enjoy.[43]

Fourth, Mesta may also have compensated slightly in the realm of protocol. Her diplomatic dinners followed the rules; she would retire with the ladies while the men enjoyed their after-dinner cigars and drinks. "But that's a lot of nonsense about conducting diplomacy over the brandy," Mesta insisted. "I do mine over the food. Give them a good meal and plenty to drink, and that's all you need." To some extent, this may have represented Mesta again remaining in her safe zone of party-giving, but if true the result was a clever work-around.[44]

Fifth, Mesta had no illusions about her ignorance of diplomacy and world affairs and worked diligently to catch up. She could even poke fun at herself along these lines, as seen in her attendance of *Call Me Madam*. But she was clearly willing and eager to learn; she worked hard, assuming increasing responsibility for the business of the legation, with or without her staff's cooperation, as she gained experience. One journalist noted Mesta's preference to discuss economic conditions in Luxembourg, after less than a year on the job. "Can't we get away from that question about parties?" she said. "I'm trying to do a job over there." The British minister, as we have seen, generally a critic, changed his assessment from "[Mesta] does not attempt any non-representational duties" (1950) to "Mesta does not undertake very many non-representational duties" (1951), a seemingly minor difference but one significant in context. In her 1952 *Longines Chronoscope* interview, Mesta demonstrated some command of political issues and gave decent answers to what substantive questions she was asked. Similarly, for her speaking engagements, she increasingly departed from texts prepared by her Foreign Service Officers. The minister often sought and followed advice from Robert Murphy, and in the otherwise unflattering portrait he drew in his memoir, he even claimed to have learned "a great deal" from her.[45]

Sixth, leveraging her personal connection with the president to prevail bureaucratically, while it aggravated department officials, was shrewd. Not that this always worked, as seen with the civil aviation agreement. Other attempts to throw her weight around, for example, pushing to have her military attaché promoted—contrary to regulations and ahead of fifty-eight hundred more senior officers—also failed. But sometimes the minister succeeded. She got the State Department to renovate the building that housed the US legation. It had been the German Gauleiter's residence during the war; its basement had apparently been used for imprisonment and executions, the bodies disposed of via the coal chute. Afterward, many locals swore the building was haunted, and when the Americans bought it, they had the Roman Catholic bishop in to sprinkle holy water to drive out any evil spirits. Now, it was decrepit but low-priority, and so Mesta pulled strings to get it refurbished.[46]

Seventh, Mesta did not at all play it safe in finding her way as minister, a fact underscored by the public reappearance of her feminism. One of her favorite ways of modifying her speeches was to include a discussion of women's rights. Although she grossly exaggerated the extent of women's equality in the United States, her message was universal and unmistakably feminist. "The woman who lives by the democratic principles," she told club women in Germany, "rises up and lets herself be heard in no meek terms." Scheduled to speak in Switzerland, where women could not yet vote, she was told to stay off the subject of women's rights. This she would not do, and she canceled the speech instead. Mesta was not only no mere hostess, she was also the most outspoken feminist among the early female chiefs of mission.[47]

Eighth and most key, however, were her representational activities. Here, she fell back on her party-giving experience, a move timid because of its familiarity, and yet somewhat bold because it promoted US–Luxembourg relations in new ways and because she persisted along this line despite opposition. It helped that she had such deep pockets and was willing to dip into them: she later reckoned that she spent almost $14,000 of her own money (in today's dollars) per month on entertaining, an amount almost four times her minister's salary.[48]

Some of her initiatives worked indirectly, such as the parties she began throwing for US troops stationed in Europe. She is estimated to have entertained some twenty-five thousand soldiers with these monthly GI parties, after each of which she wrote to many of the soldiers' parents. One soldier spoke for many: "Gee, ain't Mrs. Mesta swell?" Not everyone was impressed; one congressman asked the State Department who paid for these parties (Mesta did, entirely out of pocket). But not only did these events improve relations with the US military. In little ways—keeping visiting GIs out of trouble, having officers and enlisted men mingling as equals, attracting additional payroll dollars and publicity to the country, increasing person-to-person contact—they also benefited Luxembourg and the United States alike.[49]

More directly, in her version of people's diplomacy Mesta reached out to everyday Luxembourgers. Her descent into the mines had set a fittingly populist tone to her efforts. Used differently, the US minister's large black limousine, forty-eight-star chief-of-mission flag flapping in the breeze, might have appeared as a symbol of American hegemony or excess. But while Mesta's was seen everywhere, in towns large and small, the minister would always emerge to meet average citizens. Indeed, within weeks of her arrival she had traveled widely and everywhere was "received with pleasure," as Daniel Schorr noted; "for her predecessors usually did not bother to stir from the capital." One Luxembourger told a newspaper columnist that he knew of no other minister who had taken such a personal interest in the country.[50]

Beyond general outreach, her actions would come to include throwing yearly Christmas parties for hundreds of local orphans; personally arranging the first university student exchanges between the two countries; playing an active role in the Luxembourg Red Cross; and throwing a party for all of Luxembourg's mayors, again, contrary to her FSOs' recommendation. This last event was most striking, for it was only the second time in history when the country's Bürgermeister had all been assembled (120 out of 126 accepted the invitation). Mesta had their local dishes investigated and prepared; musicians played accordions rather than the usual strings. Soon the mayors overcame their initial stiffness and began discussing common problems. The party was such a huge success that the minister made it an annual affair. In

the 1980s, some thirty years later, US ambassador to Luxembourg John Dolibois heard so much about these events that he took it as a hint and hosted one
himself.[51]

Such moves may seem trivial, and they were accomplished with relative
ease in such a small country. Had Luxembourg been a more important US
ally, or the post of US minister more demanding, they would have been far
harder to pull off. Nevertheless, Mesta's record stands out in the context of
the relatively traditional, elite-oriented diplomacy still common in 1950. The
Foreign Service Inspector, well positioned to make the comparison, appended
to his report a separate page to underscore "the unique position" in which the
minister had placed herself through her representational activities. She had
"extended her acquaintance into unofficial circles to an unusual degree," a
record unlikely to be replicated in Luxembourg.[52]

Mesta's people's diplomacy helped build grassroots goodwill and support
for US policy. US–Luxembourg relations were not in need of repair when she
arrived, far from it; Cold War Luxembourg firmly embraced the West both
economically and militarily, while deeply appreciating the Americans' role in
liberating their land just a few short years previously. And in a relationship in
which direct, intergovernmental ties thus required less effort—no major
treaty negotiations were required, for example—the cementing of cultural
relations and international popular support was entirely appropriate. Moreover, to the extent that any chief of mission can shape a bilateral relationship,
especially an amateur operating amid established friendship, Mesta's public
diplomacy clearly created more positive reinforcement than had she just
retreated and let her career subordinates take charge. She, far more than they,
helped raise US–Luxembourg relations to an even higher level.

Despite having been asked a leading question to the contrary, one career
FSO who would go on to serve as US ambassador to Luxembourg in the early
1990s, Edward Rowell, dissented from his colleagues about Mesta. Although
people tended to underestimate her, he considered her a "serious political figure" who "happened to play politics via a social mechanism." While this
innovation in Luxembourg upset the career diplomats, Rowell concluded
that Mesta "should be given a lot of credit for what she accomplished." However, among professionals, Rowell's take places him in a distinct minority.[53]

Finally, President Truman certainly thought Mesta did a fine job. She
held the position for almost four years, significantly longer than many other
envoys. And while she was never offered an ambassadorship, which she was

rumored to have sought, the president did appreciate her performance. "I think you have done more to create good will for us in Occupied Germany, Luxembourg, Belgium and France," Truman wrote her in July 1950, "than anyone who has been in any of those Posts since I have been President." This and other such praise went well beyond the dutiful or pro forma.[54]

Minister Mesta submitted her resignation to Truman on his last day in office, as was routine for all chiefs of mission. But she asked the new president, her friend Dwight Eisenhower, to keep her on, and she sent fawning letters to him and his wife toward this end. This was wishful thinking, though, for so prominent a Democrat, indeed, one who had become a target of considerable ridicule in Republican circles. Yet another State Department official who hated Mesta took great glee in drafting an ice-cold letter, for Ike's signature, denying her request. The drafter himself, however, regretted the dispatch of a final version even more impersonal than his had been. Her term ended in April 1953, two months earlier than she had anticipated.[55]

At the time of her departure, official Luxembourg remained ambivalent at best, after her term of more than three years. In response to a general question about having a woman represent the United States in his country, Minister Le Gallais conceded Mesta's popularity but lamented one's inability to discuss international issues with her. Foreign Minister Bech then instructed him to express a preference for a replacement who was a career diplomat and not a woman, despite Mesta's fluky success. That is, she had made up for her shortcomings in other ways—presumably, her access to President Truman first and foremost—whereas such compensations might be lacking in another amateur or woman. That the Luxembourgers at this juncture specified and yet conflated these two categories suggests that, unlike most of the other female chiefs, Mesta had done little to undermine official sexism.[56]

Her host country did give Mesta a grand send-off, however. This included an unusual tribute by the US Army, in gratitude for her GI parties, and the presentation of Luxembourg's Grand Cross of the Order of the Oak Crown, which apparently had been awarded to neither a woman nor any member of the diplomatic corps. "She does a good job here," another country's minister commented. "You should see the crowd cheering her at official functions. That never happened to any other diplomat accredited here." The country's newspapers expressed profound regrets at her departure. Mesta, one of them typically gushed, "may be considered one of the best friends Luxembourg has abroad."[57]

In the following years, Mesta traveled widely, including a three-month tour of the Soviet Union shortly after she left Luxembourg. Beforehand, she apparently took her trip a tad too seriously, seeing it as a "mission" and provoking concern in the Moscow embassy that she might cause trouble for Soviet–American diplomacy, but it went off without incident. A bit later, in an era when other female diplomats had surprised many with acts of great physical courage amid war and chaos, ex-minister Mesta got her chance to do likewise. While touring Asia in July 1955, she had the misfortune of finding herself in Saigon when a student riot broke out, in protest against the 1954 Geneva Accords and the international observers on hand to monitor them, that left two dead and dozens injured. Trapped with two other women in the Hotel Majestic as it was ransacked by rioters, Mesta confronted the mob when it began attacking the locked door to her suite with axes. She opened the door. "No! We are your friends!" she shouted. "We are Americans!" The ringleader with the large knife was not deterred. Only when she added, "I'm Perle Mesta!" did he remember her as the woman who had addressed his group the previous day. He prevailed upon his confederates to let her and the two others leave the hotel, and they were whisked away in an embassy automobile amid gunfire and tear gas. Mesta's good fortune in part determined the outcome, but perhaps she also demonstrated some diplomatic skill after all. "Perle proved," in the words of the *Daily Oklahoman,* "she can talk her way out of anything."[58]

Of course Mesta also returned to Washington to resume her role as celebrated hostess, and she retained much of her social prominence through the 1950s. For example, when the Army-McCarthy hearings began in April 1954, she received one of the choice seats set aside for VIP observers. Yet she also remained active in women's rights, party politics, and philanthropy. She died in Oklahoma City in March 1975 and today is remembered, if at all, as a party-giver, the "Hostess with the Mostes'." But she correctly insisted that she did more in her life than just that. It is true that she occupied a minor post in the diplomatic sphere, and the names Mesta and Metternich will never be confused. She was probably the least distinguished of the early female chiefs, although to some extent, the combination of her reputation and the hostility she faced denied her the opportunity to demonstrate fully just how competent or incompetent she was. But among the early female ambassadors, she in effect held serve. Had she failed, embarrassed the United States, confirmed the criticisms of her appointment, or somehow damaged relations with Luxembourg, she might have further slowed the already glacial pace with which women were entering the diplomatic field. Instead, she performed better than one would have expected, considering her own obvious limitations, and in the face of stiff resistance in the media and State Department—and did so without stifling her feminist views or motives.[59]

As seen in the embarrassing anecdotes they circulated for years thereafter, most Foreign Service Officers never softened their assessment of Mesta. These included the claim that once she appointed her sister as chargé d'affaires ad interim when she left the country, certainly outrageous if true, but then again perhaps a function of the distrust between her and her subordinates.[60]

Mesta's poor reputation among other officials enjoyed a long afterlife as well. Her immediate successor (and another political appointee) Wiley Buchanan explained that he had accepted the position in part because he knew Luxembourgers had had enough of her and his appointment would demonstrate to them that the Mesta era was over. The Luxembourg post, too, carried a Mesta taint for some people. As late as the Carter administration, a political appointee was offered an ambassadorship in six countries, one of which was Luxembourg. He struck this last from his list, seeking to avoid being "thought of as Perle Mesta."[61]

Shortly after her death in 1975, approval came from a most unlikely source in a most unlikely context: disgraced former president Richard Nixon offering grand jury testimony in the Watergate prosecutions. After perpetuating the gendered stereotype of "career ambassadors" as mostly "a bunch of eunuchs," Nixon defended the appointment of political contributors (especially to smaller countries such as Luxembourg) because of their performance abroad. His example? Perle Mesta: "May I say, she was a very good ambassador in Luxembourg."[62]

Most Luxembourgers, moreover, applauded the minister. True, at least one senior government official saw the downside of her notoriety, since it had transformed his country in American eyes into "a musical-comedy nation," an indignity it did not deserve. But according to the *Historical Dictionary of Luxembourg,* Mesta was the most popular US envoy in the country ever. Again, among chiefs of mission, "popular" does not necessarily equal "good" or "effective." Most other chiefs were not *unpopular,* just unknown, and may have carried out their nonrepresentational responsibilities brilliantly. By contrast, Mesta's success, while tangible, was limited.[63]

Nevertheless, Mesta, with her emphasis on public, grassroots diplomacy, had more in common with—and better represented—the "man of the people" who hired her than did the career diplomats she battled daily. "If relations between countries is the job of diplomacy," she asked in 1951, "should it be done only at the top levels where tradition and conservative protocol turn it into coldly formal and uninspired representation?" This is a stereotype, but, as we have seen, one with considerable merit. More important, she added, was this not plainly the opposite of everything America stood for? With her populist approach, she helped suggest a different way to serve the United States as a chief of mission. For these reasons, perhaps Ethel Merman was unwittingly speaking to us when she said, "Get a load of that Mesta."[64]

5

Eugenie M. Anderson

Denmark, 1949–1953, and Bulgaria, 1962–1964

Now Uncle Sam will be in the background.

Yes, from here on in, it will be Auntie Anderson.

—dialogue in a Danish newspaper cartoon, c. 1951

On July 4, 1950, Eugenie Moore Anderson, US ambassador to Denmark, stepped up to the microphones on the speaker's platform between the Danish and American flags. She was one of several dignitaries, including King Frederick IX, on hand to address a crowd of thirty thousand at the annual American Independence Day event at Rebild National Park on Denmark's Jutland peninsula. But Anderson's speech was special: in a move unheard of for foreign envoys, Anderson would address the crowd in their language, not a word of which she had known seven months earlier, when she arrived at her post.

Despite her terror, which she overcame partly by memorizing the text, Anderson delivered her four-minute remarks on Danish–American interdependence without a hitch. When she finished, there was a brief silence, and the ambassador worried she had not been understood. But then came the thunderous applause that lasted several minutes. "You got more applause than the King," her public affairs officer, William Roll, said to her afterward. "That's not good." Later in the day, as she was leaving the park, people called out to her, "*Tak for deres dejlig Dansk*"—"Thank you for your beautiful Danish." Broadcast live on Danish radio, the speech also received unprecedented coverage in Danish newspapers, some of them reprinting the text in full. *Berlingske Tidende,* Denmark's largest-circulation daily, detected only "a slight trace of accent" in the ambassador's Danish and found it remarkable that a "foreign envoy has taken the trouble to master almost perfectly the difficult language of this little land."[1]

Remarkable too was the career of which the speech was just a small part. For Anderson (1909–1997) combined a prominent career in Minnesota politics with an admirable record of firsts for women in American diplomacy: she was the first woman to hold the rank of ambassador (Owen, Harriman, and Mesta were ministers); later, as minister to Bulgaria, first female chief of mission behind the Iron Curtain; and first woman to sign a treaty for the United States. Anderson's career in diplomacy and politics was repeatedly shaped by the interaction of her personal and public life in Minnesota on the one hand, and international affairs on the other. And Anderson's firm populism—in the sense of siding with ordinary people, which would help lead her, for example, to learn her host country's language—undergirded the domestic and foreign halves of her career.[2]

Anderson's Background

Helen Eugenie Moore was born in May 1909 in Adair, Iowa, the third of five children. Her mother taught school but was also a homemaker who urged her children to take up music. Her father was a Methodist minister, liberal Republican, and internationalist extremely active in the community, although not in partisan politics. Both parents stressed the importance of education, for the girls in the family as well as the boys. Eugenie enjoyed a humble but pleasant prairie upbringing, from which she seems to have learned to value diligence, modesty, egalitarianism, and grassroots democracy. She was bright, curious, poised, and cheerful, traits that prepared her well. "Eugenie has been a diplomat since she was in pigtails," one friend would later recall. A fine student, she studied music at various midwestern institutions, including Carleton College, where she met Minnesotan John Pierce Anderson, an artist and son of the inventor of puffed cereal. They were married in 1930 and settled on the four-hundred-acre Anderson family farm, Tower View, outside the Goodhue County seat of Red Wing. Here, on the banks of the Mississippi, the Andersons raised two children, Johanna and Hans, with John continuing his artwork and Eugenie her piano study. They enjoyed financial security, enough to allow John to become a patron of Eugenie's brother-in-law, abstract artist Charles Biederman, but not great wealth. Apart from being a successful homemaker, she later said, she "wanted to be a Bach expert more than anything else." She did not plan a career. She could not have known it, but by providing foundation, motivation, and broad-mindedness, this combination of Minnesotan domesticity and cosmopolitan interests would set the stage for a fruitful life in politics and diplomacy.[3]

Anderson unwittingly embarked on this journey in the spring of 1937 when, at the age of twenty-seven, she traveled to Europe to visit some of its cultural sites before a war might deny her the opportunity. The big celebration of Adolf Hitler's forty-eighth birthday on board the SS *Bremen* during the crossing might have foreshadowed the import of her tour, for she was welcomed into Germany by the view of a procession of uniformed, goose-stepping five-year-old boys. The sight "of those little tykes being prepared for war" sickened and frightened her, she later recalled, and she worried about the threat Germany posed to her country. Anderson returned to Minnesota painfully aware of how little she knew about both global and domestic issues and resolved to educate herself. To this end, she joined the nonpartisan League of Women Voters in 1938, her first political involvement. Years later, she would remember this as having been "excellent training-ground for my later political work."[4]

A desire to protect her two young children provided much of the initial motivation for Anderson's public activism. Thus, her next public effort was to cofound, in 1940, the first nursery school in Red Wing. But she continued to take part in the League of Women Voters and, like many women, expanded her involvement once the United States entered World War II. Her family planted a victory garden, and she worked for the Red Cross and helped with war bond drives, where she discovered her knack for public speaking. More important, through the league Anderson learned about the emerging United Nations and became an enthusiastic advocate. She viewed the UN and American leadership in it as the best hope for keeping the peace once the war was over. Anderson's politicization mirrored the trend, especially clear in Minnesota, away from isolationism.[5]

The foreign and domestic converged for Anderson again in 1944, when her growing internationalism directly led her into partisan politics. Although she had grown up around Republicans, she had morphed into a New Deal Democrat in the 1930s. Now she believed the isolationism of her congressman, Republican August Andresen, would jeopardize her children's future. "What kind of a world would they have to live in," she asked herself, if America reverted to isolationism after the war? As a complete novice, she sought the advice of a young Democratic Party activist and Macalester College political science instructor named Hubert Humphrey, whom she had heard on the radio. Thus began a political friendship that would influence Anderson's career for years to come.[6]

Humphrey urged Anderson to enter at the bottom, recruiting friends, building support, and seeking election as a party delegate. So few Democrats inhabited Minnesota's GOP-dominated First Congressional District that Anderson was immediately elected Democratic chair for Goodhue County. As the state Democrats merged in April 1944 with the Farmer-Laborites to form the Democratic-Farmer-Labor Party (DFL), Anderson and her First District colleagues agreed they should attempt to unseat the longtime incumbent Andresen, whom she later angrily dismissed as a "fraud" and a "dumbbell." To her great surprise, Anderson was chosen as DFL chair for the First District to manage the upstart campaign, again because she had no opposition, yet "mainly," as she later recalled, "because of my enthusiasm." Unfortunately, enthusiasm alone wins no elections, and her candidate went down to crushing defeat.[7]

Yet as a DFL district chair, Anderson began forging close political ties with other young party activists, especially Humphrey (elected mayor of Minneapolis in 1945), Evron Kirkpatrick, Arthur Naftalin, and Orville Freeman. By the time the new party faced its first major challenge, Anderson had gained significant stature. In parallel with the emerging Cold War with the Soviet Union, the DFL split into rival factions. Through discipline, deception, and ruthlessness, the Communist-influenced, pro-Soviet wing, led by Elmer Benson, seized control of the party from Humphrey and the liberals in 1946. Thus, for the second time, Anderson received an education in the ways of political extremists. The experience so traumatized her that she went home to her family and cried. It was a horrible introduction to Communism, she later remembered, something she had not thought possible in a democratic country. Her anti-Communist beliefs were unshakable from this point on.[8]

After this stunning defeat, Humphrey adopted unabashed anti-Communist liberalism—a move in which Anderson was instrumental—and marshaled his forces to retake the DFL. This would require them to learn, as Anderson later put it, "to outstay and out-organize and out-idea" their opponents. Over the next two years, Anderson joined Humphrey's inner circle and played a key part in the precinct-by-precinct campaign to build decisive anti-Communist strength inside the DFL. To do this, she and her colleagues first needed to regroup outside the party; so in early 1947 they launched a state chapter of Americans for Democratic Action (ADA), the new national organization of anti-Communist liberals. The ensuing struggle at times "got dirty," Humphrey said later. "But we were just as tough as the Commies were—and sometimes just as mean." During the struggle, Anderson's interest in international affairs only grew, because every issue seemed to be a foreign policy issue. The ADA liberals prevailed in 1948, the vanquished Benson wing abandoning the DFL altogether for Henry Wallace's Progressive Party. Left firmly in control, the ADA wing chose Freeman as DFL state chairman, Anderson as national committeewoman, and Humphrey as candidate for the US Senate.[9]

In July 1948, Humphrey led the Minnesota delegation, including Anderson, to the Democratic National Convention in Philadelphia. Humphrey considered cosponsoring a strong ADA civil rights plank for inclusion in the party platform, but he knew that President Truman, not to mention southern and many other Democrats, opposed it. Forging ahead might split the party and threaten Humphrey's own prospects. Until virtually the last minute, Humphrey could not be convinced to take the plunge. Then, Anderson suggested adding a brief line praising the president for his "courageous stand on the issue of civil rights"—which Truman had not taken at the convention. He had previously, but now he supported only a cursory, mealy-mouthed statement and rejected the "crackpot" ADA plank. Yet Anderson's bit of rhetorical finesse would allow Humphrey to promote civil rights without appearing to oppose the president. Humphrey now agreed to go ahead, and his speech, in which he challenged Democrats to "get out of the shadow of states' rights and walk forthrightly into the sunshine of human rights," electrified the convention. After a tumultuous demonstration, the throng voted to adopt his plank. This triggered the southern "Dixiecrat" revolt, transformed Humphrey into a national figure, and helped push the Democratic Party toward its historic role as champion of racial equality. And Eugenie Anderson, unsung, the sole woman in the liberals' smoke-filled room, had made a major contribution.[10]

Anderson spent the fall energetically stumping across Minnesota for both Humphrey and Truman. Humphrey triumphed and launched his storied Senate career, while Truman took the state by a large margin in his celebrated upset victory. Anderson, exhausted from years of intense political work and feeling as though she had neglected her family, looked forward to returning to private life at Tower View, at least until the next campaign, two years later.[11]

Appointment

Then, one day in January 1949, Anderson was just leaving for her father's funeral when the ancient box phone on the kitchen wall rang. It was India Edwards, continuing her personal crusade to land government jobs for women. She wanted to know if Anderson might be interested in an ambassadorship, perhaps in the Netherlands or Scandinavia. Her female predecessors, not coincidentally sent to this same geographic region, had been ministers; Anderson would be the first female ambassador, because the United States shared the highest level of diplomatic representation with the countries in question.

Anderson was at first "astonished" and "hesitant"; she wondered whether she was capable. But then, especially after gaining the keen support of her husband, who, as an artist, was free to accompany her, she became "intrigued by the possibilities." Colleagues voiced their support—even when using a patronizing tone. Arthur Schlesinger Jr. wrote to her that instead of the current US ambassador "pinching Dutch ladies," as was his wont, it would be interesting to have an ambassador who brought out "the same impulses in Dutch men." Her confidence also grew, like Marilla Ricker's had, as she considered another (unnamed) Minnesota Democrat who had been named an ambassador by FDR. "If this man could do it," Anderson believed, "I certainly could do it."[12]

As Denmark emerged as the likely posting, Anderson's interest grew. With a population of only 4.2 million in 1949, Denmark was a progressive democracy with a strong labor movement. Now, having like Luxembourg abandoned its prewar neutrality, it was a western alliance member on the frontline of the Cold War as well. Denmark thus neatly encapsulated Anderson's domestic ADA liberalism and her internationalist anti-Communism.[13]

Anderson was also fully aware of the gender implications of accepting. True, like many progressive women of her era, she considered feminism too aggressive and thus futile. Later, in her proposed autobiography, looking back on her Denmark tenure she considered her sex peripheral to her experience. However, when she praised India Edwards for her efficacy in the nation's capital, she could just as well have been writing about herself: she felt certain that one woman "doing such a big job well" would help erode entrenched sexism. More directly, at the time of her appointment she commented modestly that it was not for her but for all women and what they had achieved in public life. True, she expected some resistance from staff for being a woman (men were "not notably enthusiastic" about having women as peers or superiors), and for being a political appointee. But despite her initial misgivings, Anderson recalled later that she was not scared by the challenge, in part because of her political experience. She had never found male political colleagues uncooperative, and she had never been confined to work on women's issues. In short, she had already succeeded in one "man's world," so entering another did not intimidate her.[14]

But first, Anderson had to secure a nomination, and this required (for her, distasteful) self-promotion. More important, it demanded tireless lobbying on her behalf, performed above all by India Edwards and the now-freshman Senator Hubert Humphrey. This support was especially critical because the process of nailing down a nomination lasted months, held up by the FBI background check—after all, the anti-Communist witch hunts were underway and she had encountered numerous Communists—and by a patronage struggle between Humphrey and his rivals in Minnesota. The delay so frustrated Anderson, and, as she saw it, so jeopardized her reputation, that at one point she threatened to withdraw her candidacy and expose the machinations of Humphrey's enemies. Only President Truman's personal intervention broke the logjam, and when the nomination became official in October, it struck Anderson as an anticlimax. On the Senate floor, Forrest Donnell, who had opposed Perle Mesta's confirmation, questioned Anderson's qualifications. But after vigorous defenses offered by Humphrey and one other senator, Donnell, perhaps chastened by the Mesta episode, defensively explained that he had no objection to Anderson and indeed that he hoped she would prove as successful as Ruth Owen had been. Anderson was then confirmed without objection. The "Pride of Red Wing," as *Time* dubbed her, set sail for Denmark with her family aboard the Danish freighter MS *Jutlandia* in December 1949. She was only forty years old, making her the youngest of America's sixty-eight chiefs of mission at the time.[15]

People's Diplomacy

The same day that Anderson presented her credentials to King Frederik, the Danish daily *Information* published on its front page an open letter to her: "Warning to an Ambassador." The admonition was straightforward: "Do not let yourself get kidnapped by the party-givers"; rather, get to "know the

Denmark that really matters"—not high society "but the people who work with their brains and hands." Anderson was pleasantly surprised, because without knowing anything about her, the author had anticipated her inclination. She had been further pushed in this direction by well-wishing Minnesotans, who so touched and inspired her that, like Ruth Owen before her, she considered herself their personal representative, not just her country's.[16]

Anderson's predecessors practiced it, but she would name it: "people's diplomacy." "The biggest job facing our nation," Anderson told a reporter before she took up her post, "is that of developing human understanding between the people of the United States and the peoples of other countries." In her first interview, before she had even stepped off the boat, she announced her intention to meet people "from all circles" in order to form an accurate impression. Foreign policy success for the Western democracies, she would later elaborate, depended on people understanding and supporting the policies. Thus the ambassador from a democratic country must keep close contact with "the decisive majority," not just "the ruling few."[17]

The new ambassador demonstrated her egalitarian ways almost immediately. Eighty Danish workingmen had swiftly refurbished Rydhave, her fifteen-room official villa, which lay on the island of Zealand, north of the capital (and, like Perle Mesta's residence, had belonged to the German Reich Plenipotentiary during World War II). One would pass it on the coastal road when headed toward Kronborg castle, known to readers of Shakespeare as Elsinore. Now, Anderson planned to show her gratitude by throwing a housewarming party for the workers and their wives, that is, Joseph Grew's "rabble of Copenhagen." According to Anderson, her DCM, Edward Sparks, was horrified. "Oh, Mrs. Anderson, I don't think you want to do that," he said with sadness. He thought, "There are many people that won't understand this at all." But the new ambassador was not deterred. "I would have done the same thing in Minnesota," she remarked later. "Why not do it here?"[18]

The gathering, the first large function she hosted, was a gesture unprecedented in Denmark. All invitees accepted, although some asked whether they should come to the front door when they arrived. After enjoying the smorgasbord, Coca-Cola, and aquavit, singing songs, and watching films until 2:00 A.M., the guests were sent home, each with a pound of Maxwell House coffee, a commodity still rationed in Denmark at the time. They would never forget the evening, and the Danish press covered it thoroughly. "Nothing could have better expressed American democracy to the Danes," remarked Prime Minister Hans Hedtoft. One of the carpenters, who had never expected such an invitation, agreed. "That is the sort of diplomacy we understand."[19]

By the same token, Anderson quickly developed a strong disdain for the endless formalities of diplomatic life. She loathed cocktail parties, and at one of the king and queen's annual state dinners for chiefs of mission, she "felt rather foolish" wearing the opal tiara she borrowed for the occasion from Ruth Owen (who had rather enjoyed sporting it). Anderson also lost patience with what she saw as the pretentiousness of professional diplomats, many of whom struck her as "dried prunes and stuffed shirts." Her homegrown informality even rubbed off on her hosts. "In Minnesota," she told the Danish leadership over for dinner one hot summer evening, "when we feel really at home, the men take off their coats." They joined her husband in doing so, and "shirt-sleeve diplomacy" had arrived in Denmark.[20]

Learning Danish

Anderson reached out in part by learning Danish, or as she later called it, "that fiendish language." She never intended to use it for official business, but people's diplomacy seemed to demand learning it. She recalled Sparks telling her that it was "a waste of effort" and "absolutely unnecessary because everybody who is anybody speaks English." But she was determined—she already knew that neither the prime minister nor most of his colleagues in the ruling Social Democratic Party spoke English. (Sparks's "anybodies" presumably included only those in the foreign ministry.) The language came more easily to her children, who enrolled in Danish public schools, but the regular lessons she took one hour per day soon paid off. On Mother's Day 1950, not five months after arriving, she was able to prerecord a brief speech in Danish that was then broadcast over radio. Then came the July 4 speech in Rebild National Park, where she upstaged His Majesty and caused a sensation.[21]

Apart from the simple fact that she was a female ambassador (and as such a major novelty), nothing made her a household name to average Danes more than her effort to learn the native tongue—which was extremely rare among foreign envoys, at least one of whom regretted it. Anderson's British counterpart was Sir A. W. G. Randall, and as he prepared to leave Copenhagen in 1952, having spent a total of nine years there, the last seven of them as chief of mission, Randall admitted his failure to have gained a full understanding of the Danish character. One of his major reasons: his inability to master the language. He had his excuses: its level of difficulty, the few opportunities to speak it with locals, and their own facility with English, which they were always eager to try out on him. But in the end, he could only wring his hands. "Without a good knowledge of Danish, written and spoken," he wrote, "a fundamental knowledge of the Danish people cannot be acquired."[22]

Travel in Denmark

Anderson's ability in Danish nicely complemented her decision to travel extensively throughout the country. Happily, she ignored the French ambassador when he told her—whether out of ignorance or snobbery, she did not know—that travel was impossible because no hotels existed outside Copenhagen; she always found perfectly suitable lodging. Her French colleague was in good company, for Anderson visited numerous towns and villages that foreign diplomats had never seen, such as Esbjerg, a fishing port on the North Sea. In such places she learned the views of Danes from all walks of life while educating them about America. Being from the Midwest, rather than Atlantic seaboard cities, taught her the importance of leaving Copenhagen. "I enjoy these trips outside of Copenhagen," she wrote to India Edwards, "since they give one quite a different view of the country, just the same as you must need to get away from Washington now and then."[23]

Anderson only bolstered her strong reputation by speaking on a variety of subjects, including sensitive ones. For example, she gave a speech titled "The Negro in America Today," a subject of intense interest among Danes. The ambassador, not surprisingly, emphasized the progress America was making in race relations, but she also admitted her country's shortcomings, which greatly strengthened her credibility.[24]

Danish Reactions

Initial press reaction to Anderson in Denmark was favorable, although the Communist newspaper *Land og Folk* predictably assailed her, tagging her as the American "Gauleiter" and "Mrs. Reichskommissar." Many Danes were unenthusiastic or wary upon learning of Anderson's appointment, especially since many believed they had dodged a bullet regarding Perle Mesta. Copenhagen asked its ambassador in Washington, Henrik Kaufmann, to investigate.

He met Anderson for lunch in New York, and he was immediately impressed. He reported back: "No Perle; a pearl!" One Danish editor confessed his concern, especially considering the Cold War and Denmark's new situation in it; this seemed to demand a seasoned hand coming from America. A little over a year later, he had changed his mind. "We couldn't have made a better selection ourselves," he said.[25]

Despite any official misgivings, Denmark remained a relatively welcoming place for a female ambassador. After all, it too was under popular pressure to appoint women. A female minister served in the cabinet, and just weeks before Anderson's appointment, the Danes too named their first female ambassador: Bodil Begtrup was being sent to Iceland.[26]

Fame

Anderson's identity and activity resulted in a level of fame unheard of for ambassadors in any time or place. Danes selected at random from the phonebook all knew her name, as did most middle school students (few of whom could name any other diplomat). In some cases, her celebrity reached the point of embarrassment; one day, a Danish businessman accosted her on the street, thanked her profusely for "the interest you have shown in getting to know us," kissed her hand—and then essentially repeated the process three times before the ambassador could free herself, her glove "literally damp from his hand-kissing." One American traveler was repeatedly asked to give her regards to "Mrs. Anderson" and then received a scolding from one shopkeeper for not knowing who that was when she finally admitted her ignorance. The Foreign Service Inspector, while marveling at the success of Anderson's extraordinary outreach, which he termed "a new development in diplomacy," worried she might lose some of her effectiveness through overexposure and becoming "public property." Regardless, the ambassador had made herself a household name.[27]

Conventional Success

Anderson also succeeded as a diplomat in the more conventional sense. She worked hard pursuing US objectives, primary among which, especially in the grim days of the Korean War, was moving Denmark away from its traditional neutralism and pacifism and toward a more active role in the infant

NATO. The Danes found this transition difficult; inhabiting a land small and vulnerable, having just suffered invasion and occupation, and needing to build a defense force virtually from scratch, they suffered understandable pessimism. A joke had it that a Danish optimist was someone who believed the Red Army was not coming until the day after tomorrow. One Dane called at the embassy to retrieve the New Year's card he had sent Anderson because he did not want it on file in the event that the Russians invaded. Thus the Danes tried to walk a line between supporting the United Nations action in Korea and appearing too aggressive. So their contribution was to send to the war zone a hospital ship: the *Jutlandia,* the same vessel on which Anderson had arrived to take up her post, now refitted for the purpose. The ambassador recalled that the Danes were rather proud of their first contribution to the war effort, and perhaps even a little smug about its humanitarian form. Still, Denmark was changing course, and Anderson applied a tireless yet light touch in encouraging the redirection. In 1951, she played a major role in negotiating the Greenland Agreement, which granted the United States access to important strategic air bases on the Danish possession. The ambassador likewise helped hammer out a new Danish–American Treaty of Commerce and Friendship, the first in over a hundred years, and thus became the first American woman to sign a treaty.[28]

Press Coverage

Anderson's accomplishments mounted despite American press coverage, which, while extensive for a diplomat and overwhelmingly favorable, was nevertheless typically sexist. Numerous stories marking her appointment played up her role as a "mother" or "housewife" and downplayed or ignored entirely her background as one of Minnesota's leading political figures. Coverage was riddled with such descriptions as "Denmark's American Sweetheart" or the "petticoat diplomat," and endless references to her appearance ("still a pretty brunette as a diplomat"), attire (she had "a preference for Philip Mangone suits"), and homemaking ("Here she puts a favorite dish into the oven"). Other depictions were more subtly gendered. An early 1950 *Minneapolis Tribune* Sunday magazine cover showed Anderson in an evening gown and the aforementioned opal jewelry, with her daughter Johanna looking up at her admiringly—suggesting the girl's stereotypical longing for the fairytale princess life her mother now obviously led in the courts and ballrooms

Eugenie M. Anderson, ambassador to Denmark (1949–1953) and minister to Bulgaria (1962–1964), with her daughter Johanna on the cover of the *Minneapolis Tribune* Sunday magazine, *Picture,* in 1950. Typical of the gendered press coverage all the female ambassadors received, Anderson is shown with the opal tiara that, true to her anti-elitist views, she "felt rather foolish" wearing. She had borrowed it from Ruth Owen, who rather liked such trappings of royalty. (*Minneapolis Star Tribune*)

of Europe. More standard belittlement appeared in a 1951 *Time* magazine overview of US ambassadors, in which only the segment on Anderson claimed that the "more complex diplomatic chores are carried out by her staff of career men." This of course was (and is) true of all ambassadors, career diplomats included, and this ignored the fact that Anderson was, certainly compared to Owen, Harriman, Mesta, and many male political appointees, very much a hands-on chief. At a press conference in Chicago, where she was to speak at the 1952 Democratic National Convention, Anderson was answering questions posed by female reporters about new immigration rulings, conditions in Berlin, and the tariff on blue cheese when another reporter interrupted her. "May a man ask a question? I would like the ambassador to describe the dress she is wearing and tell us where she bought it." While no doubt intended to be humorous, this sort of treatment meant she had to work harder, and perform better, to be taken seriously—a reality women in most professions experienced through the current day.[29]

Relations with the Foreign Service

Sexism may have also figured in a second challenge, the opposition of a few diplomatic colleagues, although, again, this also may have entailed the rather common clash of professional diplomats and political appointees. One incident involved her predecessor, Josiah Marvel Jr. (minister, then ambassador, 1946–1949), who seems to have resented Anderson. He visited Copenhagen in early 1951 and apparently spent his time trying to undermine Anderson with her staff. His first question to FSO Harold Shantz was "How are you getting along with your *master?*" Happily for Anderson, the staff rallied to her side, one even suggesting to her afterward that she protest Marvel's behavior to the State Department (she declined to do so). From across the Skagerrak and Kattegat, US ambassador to Norway Charles Bay used some "frank words" to tell Anderson personally he disapproved of her diplomatic style. We cannot know for certain whether sexism motivated either Marvel or Bay— but as with Anderson's predecessors, one wonders whether a male in precisely the same circumstances would have encountered such opposition.[30]

Certainly, Anderson worked effectively with most embassy staff and department officials in Washington; the only major policy disagreement she recalled later was over a US tariff increase, especially on Danish cheese, and this initiative came not from the administration but from Congress (an effort, featuring the accusation of Anderson having gone native, led at one point by her Red Wing nemesis, August Andresen). Anderson clicked right away with Roll, her public affairs officer. He entirely supported her approach, and she leaned on him heavily. But this reliance also resulted partly from the tense relationship with Sparks. Sparks, a longtime career officer, was a traditionalist, like many in the Foreign Service of 1950. After Anderson indicated her approval of the *Information* letter, he dismissed it as needless and tactless and counseled her to forget about the whole thing. Sparks's more specific advice was nothing if not consistent. Not only did he oppose Anderson's decision to learn Danish, but he also advised against throwing the housewarming party and speaking about American labor at a George Washington Day dinner. In all three cases, however, the enthusiastic Danish response allayed the ambassador's initial doubts. Sparks also kept Anderson uninformed about his handling of personnel issues, and only after some months did she establish her authority in the embassy (Anderson later speculated that, having run it for many months as chargé, he found it difficult to step back down). His transfer in late summer 1950 eased Anderson's staff situation immensely, for his replacement, Harold Shantz, was far more cooperative.[31]

Back in the State Department, views of her tended toward qualified but positive. To a *Time* reporter, "Old pros" acknowledged her success "a trifle grudgingly." They conceded that she was "intelligent, attractive, personable, [and] sweet," but then they would stress that her main strength was representation. That is, they considered her mediocre, but she made a "hell of a lot of friends for the U.S." Some complained that in running the embassy, she delegated too much. "But she's damned attractive, smart and sympathetic. And God, how the Danes love her." Another caught himself being too admiring. "She's the best ambassador we've got in Europe," he said, before adding quickly, "I mean comparatively. She's done a first-class job in Denmark. That does not mean she's ready for Paris or London." Some were so complimentary that she likely helped change some men's minds about women in this role. One assistant secretary of state was "amazed" that the best suggestions for a NATO defense program at a meeting of US ambassadors in Paris "came from a woman." It is worth noting, however, that such praise from male colleagues, while perhaps incrementally breaking down prejudice, was nevertheless often doubly sexist: both because they were surprised a woman could perform so well and because they, including at least one member of her own staff, were impressed that a "housewife" made such a good ambassador—neglecting her years as a politician, which meant the leap she had taken was not nearly so high, and thus the magnitude of their astonishment was unwarranted.[32]

Running the Embassy

In the embassy, Anderson tried to address morale. The Foreign Service Inspector had found in October 1949 that the embassy staff enjoyed "very good morale" before Anderson's arrival (although this same inspector had praised Sparks and written Anderson separately, "to the best of my knowledge, there are no serious defects nor 'problem children' that will cause you any worry"). According to Anderson, however, the embassy she inherited was too hierarchical, too divided between senior and junior officers. Only senior staff, for example, enjoyed the privilege of purchasing duty-free liquor. Moreover, the many Danish nationals on staff had been treated as second-class citizens, never having been invited to embassy social functions, and many staff members had never even laid eyes on Ambassador Marvel, arriving at work as he did via his personal elevator and heading straight into his office. Anderson quickly resolved to change all this, despite, in the case of the Danish staff, at times having to combat Danish government regulations in the process. She began inviting all staff to embassy social gatherings and instituted an open-door policy for personnel who could not resolve issues directly with their immediate superiors. One staffer soon wrote to her, lauding the interest she had taken in all staff and expressing confidence in her fairness.[33]

Gender on the Job

After some time in her position, Anderson retained a mix of views on the gender issue. On the one hand, she was reinforced in her impression that she was contributing to gender progress. She was gratified by the many letters she received from women stating how pleased and inspired they were by her appointment and how well it reflected on all women. But on the other hand, she could downplay her female identity, wanting to be remembered not as America's first female envoy but as a good one. "The important thing for any woman in public life," she said in 1962, "is to forget first that she IS a woman and concentrate on her objectives." She also publicly denied the existence of any downsides to being a female ambassador, which was obviously untrue. And finally, she remained essentialist when it came to women in international affairs. One female Danish journalist asked whether women should be allowed to run things. The ambassador demurred but said that women do have "a special contribution to make to Government." Asked on another occasion whether women made particularly good ambassadors, Anderson replied, "Women are good at human relations," and, ultimately, "diplomacy is human relations."[34]

The Spouse Issue

Unlike the widows Owen, Harriman, and Mesta, Anderson had a spouse, but that does not mean she was free of the "spouse issue." It is true that her husband handled some of the responsibilities of a spouse. For example, her son, Hans, seriously injured his knee in early 1951 and had to recuperate at home for two weeks; Anderson's husband was able to postpone a planned trip to Paris and stay at home. This was an instance, Anderson recalled, "when I felt a conflict between my duties as mother and ambassador." But she was grateful her husband made it possible to continue her embassy work uninterrupted, that he was there as a spouse, at least for this purpose.[35]

For dinner parties, however, Anderson noted how demanding it was, especially at larger functions, to perform the "dual role of diplomat and hostess." That is, as helpful, understanding, and supportive as her husband obviously was, he did not completely fulfill the role played by the traditional ambassador's wife. This reality was mitigated somewhat by the fact that Anderson enjoyed the assistance of a first-rate household staff and an exemplary personal secretary, Vivian Meisen, who worked for Anderson in all her diplomatic assignments.[36]

Protocol

Protocol, or rather, how others handled it, presented a special challenge for Anderson not only because she was a woman, but also, again, because she was accompanied by her husband, John. What would his official rank be? Established practice was that for the purposes of protocol, a male ambassador's wife had the same rank as her husband. The day Anderson arrived, the Danish Foreign Office informed her the reverse would not be true and that her husband's rank would be that of "distinguished foreign visitor," that is, as she later put it, "really no rank at all." Both procedurally (a decision made before her arrival, without her input) and substantively (a discourtesy), the policy did not sit well with the Andersons, but they declined to make an issue of it at this point, in part because, consistent with their populist, outsider's perspective, they did not take protocol very seriously. Nor did Anderson protest some time later when she learned, to her chagrin, that it had not been the Foreign Office's decision but rather that of the dean and vice dean of the Diplomatic Corps (the Norwegian and French ambassadors, respectively) in consultation with her own deputy, Sparks. Apparently the French envoy, in particular, could not bear the idea that he might ever sit "below" Mr. Anderson.[37]

This meant that at formal dinners, Mr. Anderson was not seated anywhere near the ambassador, unlike the situation for all male ambassadors and their wives. Gradually Anderson came to believe that this slighted not only her but also the prestige of the United States. The last straw was a dinner for 140 hosted by the foreign minister at Christiansborg Palace in March 1952. The entire crowd could not be seated in the dining room, and so John Anderson was seated at what was effectively the kids' table, out in the hall with thirteen other guests, mostly unofficial Danes. On top of that, Ambassador Anderson was seated "below" the new French ambassador, that is, a colleague inferior to her in precedence. She took up the issue with the foreign minister and insisted that her rank should be purely a function of her status as an ambassador, not as a woman, and that her husband's rank should derive from that status. By her recollection, he was mortified and pleaded ignorance. After his protocol chief learned that the United States had afforded India's Madame Pandit her status on that basis, his ministry relented. Thereafter, for protocol purposes Anderson was treated like any other ambassador, although her husband now received not the rank of ambassador, as he should have, but rather minister—still not "wholly satisfactory," as she wrote in her official report, but a vast improvement over his previous state of limbo. She derived some satisfaction from her successful protest and hoped that future female ambassadors would not have to suffer all this.[38]

Resignation and Return to Minnesota

Anderson overcame all such obstacles and lasted three years in Copenhagen, tendering her resignation in early 1953 with the change in administrations. King Frederik paid only the finest among many tributes by bestowing upon her the Grand Cross of the Order of the Dannebrog, which no woman of any profession had ever received, in appreciation of her superb service. Anderson's boss was equally pleased. "I'll never forget your wonderful and efficient service," Harry Truman wrote her in 1956. "A Dane came to see me yesterday and all he wanted to talk about was our Ambassador to Denmark!"[39]

In the official, secret report she wrote as she stepped down, Anderson argued that "the basic developments" in Denmark were cause for encouragement. The Danes' economy, defense cooperation in NATO, and morale had all improved markedly. The following year, however, she wrote of her "unfinished mission." The Social Democrats, now in opposition, seemed to be wavering in their support of NATO and had begun to attack the government's foreign policy. The issue of NATO bases in Denmark remained unresolved. Anderson was stressing these developments from the vantage point of 1954, and she implied that Denmark's backsliding was influenced by a post-Stalin Russia and a post-Truman America; the latter may have reflected her partisanship. But overall, she gave herself a mixed review for her policy impact.[40]

Anderson returned to Red Wing and devoted much of her time to the farm and family. But she kept busy in the public realm as well. She was named the first chair of the Minnesota Fair Employment Practices Commission (1955–1960). She also served on the foreign policy advisory committee of the Democratic Advisory Council, advised on foreign policy for Adlai Stevenson's 1956 campaign, sat on the Zellerbach Commission investigating the plight of East European refugees, handled foreign guests for the 1958 Minnesota Centennial, and lectured widely.[41]

The major event for Anderson during these years back in Minnesota, however, was her 1958 bid for the DFL US Senate nomination. She had passed on the opportunity in 1952, largely out of consideration for her family but also because she wanted to finish out her term as ambassador. Six years later, she was ready. At first, two-term incumbent Republican Edward Thye seemed tough to beat, and DFLers urged Anderson to run in part, she believed, because "we can't win so let's let a woman try it." Here, Anderson first perceived the difficulties women faced in politics. She could have sought a House seat, as many friends urged her to do; she surely would have been a strong candidate, even in her conservative home district. Nevertheless, she doubted her prospects, found distasteful the notion of campaigning every two years, and knew the House would offer far fewer opportunities for involvement in foreign affairs than those that had drawn her to the Senate.

So she declined. Once more, her interest in international affairs had helped define her political choices at home.[42]

Anderson conditioned her Senate candidacy on winning the DFL's endorsement at the party convention, scheduled for May in Rochester. But she was up against another DFL rising star, Congressman Eugene McCarthy. She campaigned with her usual vigor in what became a fierce contest. Early on, Anderson fared slightly better against Thye in opinion polls than McCarthy did; but in Rochester, McCarthy prevailed on the second ballot. His decade of congressional experience and his solid support from labor and fellow Catholics certainly contributed to his victory, but Anderson's sex probably did as well. The DFL "unfortunately wasn't quite ready for a woman," Arthur Naftalin later remarked. Anderson believed many assumed the woman could not win in November and so chose the man in May. McCarthy went on to defeat Thye in what turned out to be a banner year for liberal Democrats, making 1958 perhaps the greatest "what if?" of Anderson's life. She returned, as always, to Red Wing, although in 1960 she devoted herself to Humphrey's unsuccessful quest for the Democratic presidential nomination.[43]

Kennedy and Bulgaria

The new president in 1961 was John F. Kennedy. When it came to hiring women, Kennedy's overall numbers were comparable to Eisenhower's and Truman's, but he failed to place women in prominent positions, with no cabinet members, no "firsts," and plenty of trivial posts (although in fairness, "firsts" by definition become more difficult as time progresses). His poor record provoked complaints from prominent women, including Eleanor Roosevelt. Despite what his rather degrading treatment of women in his personal life suggests, Kennedy was probably no more prejudiced against women than his predecessors. Most men at the time shared the sexist cluelessness of his comment to a group of female UN delegates—he never knew whether women in politics wanted "to be talked about as women or as politicians." In fairness, moreover, Kennedy deserves considerable credit for contributing to social change beyond appointments through such initiatives as the President's Commission on the Status of Women and the Equal Pay Act (1963). But in the realm of appointments, his team's talent search focused on drawing the "best and the brightest" from elite universities, corporate boards, and law firms—where virtually no women occupied senior positions to begin with. In addition, no equivalent to Eleanor Roosevelt, Molly Dewson, or India Edwards existed—indeed, the Women's Division of the DNC had been disbanded in 1953—to exert pressure on Kennedy to hire women.[44]

What Robert Dean has identified as an "ideology of masculinity," furthermore, undergirded Kennedy's career and presidency. Kennedy and most of his top advisors shared a background of elite education and World War II military service that led them to style themselves as smart-but-tough "warrior-intellectuals." Gender-insecure, macho, and homophobic, indeed, very much the masculinist heirs of Teddy Roosevelt, they sought to toughen up an America they thought had gone soft, a mindset that helped promote confrontation with the Soviet Union and, ultimately, Americanization of the conflict in Vietnam. Consistent with this, Kennedy subscribed to the gendered stereotype of weak, effeminate career diplomats. "The State Department is a bowl of jelly," he remarked in 1961, its employees "constantly smiling. I think we need to smile less and be tougher." "They're not queer," he allowed on another occasion, "but, well, they're sort of like Adlai"—that is, Adlai Stevenson, now his ambassador to the United Nations and, to the Kennedys, the very embodiment of soft, indecisive pusillanimity. In one conversation, the president successively derided three career diplomats: one was un-American, one was an "Old Lady," and one had no "*cojones*."[45]

The result was a particularly discouraging environment for the hiring of women, but with a Democrat back in the White House, the possibility arose of a second appointment for Anderson. Before taking office, Kennedy and Stevenson had placed Anderson on a list of candidates for the US delegation at the United Nations, but they did not select her. Before too long, though, Humphrey was again touting Anderson for a diplomatic post. Orville Freeman, now Kennedy's secretary of agriculture, lent a hand, but it was Humphrey who badgered the administration for months on Anderson's behalf. Some inside the State Department may have objected; when Freeman went to see White House assistant Ralph Dungan, the latter "mumbled something about the 'striped pants boys' but said 'to hell with 'em'"—suggesting that opposition in Foggy Bottom to female chiefs persisted nearly three decades after Ruth Owen's selection. After considering her for other posts, the administration offered Anderson the ministership to Communist Bulgaria. Kennedy evidently thought the people's diplomacy Anderson practiced in Denmark might be worth repeating, a refreshing alternative to the elitist approach of the career envoys who had run every US mission in postwar Eastern Europe.[46]

Anderson's impeccable anti-Communist credentials undoubtedly helped entice the administration; they also helped attract Anderson to the assignment. Although she wondered whether she was insane to have agreed to such a "daring thing," Anderson welcomed the challenge presented by a Communist host. She saw it as a great chance to draw on her experience battling Communist rivals in Minnesota. However, she departed for Bulgaria with a sense not only of what she opposed but also what she cherished. She was taking with her, she said to two hundred friends gathered in the Red Wing High School cafeteria to send her off, not only a pair of "sturdy Red Wing boots" for hiking Bulgaria's mountains but also her "roots from Minnesota and Iowa." Her native Midwest, she believed, with its agricultural-industrial combination, its "pioneer traditions" and "love of [the] land," represented "The True America"—thus implying that as a midwesterner she felt best suited to represent America as well.[47]

Considering where she was headed, Minister Anderson would need the inspiration of this midwestern vision. With some 8 million people in 1962, the People's Republic of Bulgaria had been thoroughly Sovietized from the late 1940s, and its leader after 1954—through to the collapse of Communism thirty-five years later—was the lamentable Todor Zhivkov. Chosen first secretary of the Communist Party, as one historian puts it, "mostly because of his obvious mediocrity," Zhivkov was a true Stalinist clone and Muscovite lapdog. He presided over one of the most underdeveloped Soviet dependencies. It had to export foodstuffs to earn foreign currency, for example, which meant the best produce was sent to Moscow or to the West, leaving little for its own people. For American diplomats, it was a "dismal, isolated post," in the words of a State Department report, "a communist police state where Mission personnel are subjected to surveillance and the usual attempts at penetration and compromise." These efforts included sexual seduction and, in at least one case, drugged wine at a restaurant.[48]

"I think it's a sin to send you to Bulgaria," President Kennedy said upon welcoming Anderson to a White House dinner before her departure. "But I'm really very grateful to you that you're willing to go there." Anderson later wished she had been quick and bold enough to reply, "Well you're the one who is sending me there, Mr. President." Her encounter with the president's brother Attorney General Robert Kennedy went less well. He greeted her by name, but then confused her with the ambassador to Ceylon, Frances Willis (see chapter 7). He then displayed deeper ignorance about her record, perhaps understandable in the whirl of official dinners and guests, when he asked her about her appointment: "Well, I guess you made quite a few campaign speeches, didn't you?"[49]

When she arrived in Sofia in late July 1962, Anderson was practically driven to tears by the gloomy, dilapidated condition of her official residence, which looked like a fortress or prison on the outside. She could and did redecorate, but the country beyond the walls remained a source of profound dismay. She quickly took a liking to Bulgaria's natural beauty and its citizens, but the latter left her with an "intense feeling of horror and hatred for the inhuman, stupid, cruel system" imposed upon them. And, true to her populist inclinations, Anderson never overcame her guilt over the gross disparity between the lavish lifestyle of the Diplomatic Corps and the squalor and privation of the Bulgars.[50]

Anderson's Bulgarian stint mirrored her first in many ways. Again, she immediately became famous and popular, as the first female chief of mission in the country and a ubiquitous public presence, complete with the effusive street greetings and hand-kissing. Again, she experienced the favorable but often sexist press coverage, with headlines devoted to the "doll" or "grandmother," the "Little Woman from Red Wing" or "Belle of the Balkans." Again she sought to learn the host's language, an effort for which other diplomats chided her. Although her Bulgarian never remotely rivaled her Danish, she learned enough to deliver a Fourth of July address on radio and television—which the authorities had thought they could thwart by requiring its delivery in Bulgarian—becoming the first western diplomat to appear on Bulgarian TV and the first from any foreign country to do so in the host language. Again she clashed with her relatively traditional DCM, Charles Stefan, and relied heavily on the less senior public affairs officer, Alex Bloomfield, more open to her grassroots approach (and thus causing some resentment in the legation political section). And again, she effectively promoted US interests, for example, successfully negotiating a settlement of sticky financial claims outstanding from the Second World War.[51]

Yet the fundamentally different nature of her host, a Stalinist, Cold War adversary, demanded much more of Anderson. This was true in terms of her daily life: the restrictions, the isolation, the constant surveillance all exhausted her and her husband. In the heavily bugged US legation, only the secure room, a giant plastic cube suspended within another room and engulfed in white noise—in the Moscow embassy, they called it "the icebox"—afforded unfettered conversation. Otherwise, communicating freely required trips to the countryside or handwritten notes read, torn up, and flushed down the "security file."[52]

Bulgaria also tried Anderson's diplomatic skills as never before. Minor irritants constantly arose, such as when the minister felt compelled to defend the right of Bulgarian youth to dance the Twist (even though she personally disapproved of it). But the first major incident occurred at the International Trade Fair at Plovdiv in September 1962. Such "spectacles of plenty and consumption," as one historian describes them, became ancillary Cold War battlegrounds. They also afforded Eastern Bloc citizens rare glimpses of the West, and Communist leaders bridled at the enthusiastic responses to western goods they inevitably provoked; in 1958, Zhivkov had complained that his people's "necks have been twisted from looking toward the West." At Plovdiv, the Bulgarian authorities at first withdrew permission they had earlier granted the US Pavilion to distribute exhibit brochures, and they confiscated many of them. Anderson refused to back down in the face of this and other intimidation, even showing up to hand out brochures personally at the pavilion entrance. When Zhivkov himself appeared, she cleverly handed one to him; he had no choice but to take it. At their first chance, members of the public stampeded for their own copies. "You would have thought we were passing out dollar bills," Anderson reported. Bulgarian officials soon stopped resisting, one of them admitting, "We underestimated the determination of your minister. We didn't know the Americans could be so tough." Hundreds of thousands of visitors, eager for even the smallest dose of Americana, were now free to crowd around the hi-fi sets, model Mercury spacecraft, and Ford Thunderbird.[53]

Prefiguring Mr. McGuire's advice to Benjamin Braddock at the beginning of *The Graduate,* the State Department sponsored an exhibition, called "Plastics USA," the following year at the Arts Gallery in downtown Sofia. Bowling pins and bicycles, sailboats and sports car chassis, all the bounty of America's plastics manufacturers was on display, in the first such American event ever mounted in the Bulgarian capital. Official Bulgarian harassment ensued; at one point, sixty thousand exhibit brochures disappeared, as did an equal number of small plastic souvenir calendars and buttons, the latter intended for children. Again, though, the event seems to have succeeded.

Over eighteen days, a quarter of a million visitors waited up to three hours to enter. Anderson was on hand every day, and many visitors responded warmly. "Eugenie, I wish to thank you for the exhibit," said one man, despite the glowering People's Militiaman only a few feet away. "Please convey our best greetings to the American people and to President Kennedy," he continued, before kissing Anderson's hand. Visitors left almost uniformly positive remarks in the exhibit's comment book; several suggest the minister's prominence. One wrote, "I am especially pleased with Mrs. Anderson for bringing about closer ties between our two countries."[54]

During the October 1962 Cuban Missile Crisis, Anderson learned that anti-American demonstrations were being planned for her residence and the US legation. She knew that her predecessor had been trapped in the legation for hours during a rock-throwing protest in response to the 1961 Bay of Pigs invasion. So she headed straight to the foreign ministry where, after a long argument, an official promised to guarantee the Americans' safety. When she asked how he would do this, he answered with remarkable candor, "If we can organize a demonstration, we can call it off just as quickly." Anderson added, "It was." Soon after the crisis, Anderson stormed out of a Soviet-sponsored reception when Bulgarian president Dimiter Ganev denounced the United States for its "piratical actions." Other Western mission chiefs, whose practice it had been to ignore such insults, huddled briefly and then followed her out the door. Her walkout, the result of a snap decision on her part, won Anderson widespread praise, one American newspaper lauding her for "upstaging a vulgar Bulgar."[55]

Perhaps most troublesome, finally, was what one might call the Battle of the Windows. The US legation occupied a former department store, and the new denizens placed blown-up photographs of scenes from American life in the oversized display windows. A constant stream of Bulgarian citizens stopped by for a glimpse of America they were otherwise denied, which of course irked the regime no end. It tried everything to interfere—Militia harassment of visitors, establishment of a Bulgarian photo shop next door, even organization of "spontaneous" riots. The worst of these, in December 1963 (interestingly, coinciding with Anderson's absence from the country), involved a mob of three thousand that roughed up Foreign Service Officers, overturned staff automobiles, and shattered most of the legation windows. But at Anderson's insistence, the glass was always replaced, the displays constantly updated. In standing up to this obnoxious government and in evading it to reach out to average Bulgars, Anderson remained utterly tenacious.[56]

Bulgaria took its toll, however, especially on her husband John, and Anderson decided to submit her resignation to President Lyndon Johnson in November 1964. Despite the many frustrations she encountered, her record once again deserved all the plaudits it received. In March 1963, the State Department noted "unanimously favorable judgment on her performance." No less a figure than the decidedly non-feminist George Kennan, who had won fame as intellectual architect of the Containment policy and who was now US ambassador to neighboring Yugoslavia, took the "improper" step of writing Secretary of State Dean Rusk a letter about his Sofia colleague. Anderson "has shown not only common sense," Kennan wrote, "but exceptional shrewdness and courage in tackling a diplomatic task" that is among the most formidable "faced by any of our Chiefs of Mission anywhere."[57]

Aftermath

Anderson returned to the United States with energy and ambition left over. Further might-have-beens accumulated. Before she stepped down, she was high on the list of candidates to complete the remainder of Humphrey's third US Senate term (1965–1967) after he won election as Lyndon Johnson's vice president, but Walter Mondale was tapped instead. Secretary Rusk considered Anderson for an assistant secretary post (either Educational and Cultural Affairs or Security and Consular Affairs)—which would have been another impressive first for women—but apparently Senator J. William Fulbright, chair of the Senate Foreign Relations Committee, "was not interested in either a woman or a negro." Ambassador to Canada was also a possibility. Instead, in 1965 Anderson was appointed to the US delegation to the United Nations, with the personal rank of ambassador. As Ruth Owen had learned more than three decades earlier, the gap in importance between possible posts and actual posts somehow always seemed widest with the women. Anderson represented the United States on the UN Trusteeship Council and at one point sat on the Security Council, becoming the first woman to do so. She officially retired in 1968, to help, naturally, with Humphrey's presidential campaign, as she would for his senatorial and presidential bids in 1970 and 1972. In retirement, Anderson lectured, served on several boards, and traveled. She died in 1997 at the age of eighty-seven.[58]

Throughout this post-Bulgaria period, Anderson seldom wavered from her militant Cold War views. This included strong support of America's war in Vietnam, which only hardened when she undertook a fact-finding tour of the war zone in late 1967, and thus, perhaps unwittingly, played a role in President Johnson's prowar public relations campaign. Although she believed the United States was overemphasizing the military dimension of the conflict while neglecting the political, her report to the president toed the administration line: the war was winnable and warranted a long-term commitment to a free people struggling "against outside aggression and internal subversion." Although she became more ambivalent about the war in its later stages, Anderson underwent no softening of her overall views. In 1984, the seventy-five-year-old even crossed party lines and endorsed a Republican US Senate candidate, in part because his opponent, Joan Growe, supported a US–Soviet nuclear freeze. "We can never be secure," Anderson was quoted, with "policies of weakness and vacillation."[59]

As a domestic liberal but international hawk, Anderson had much in common with the original neoconservatives, like her friend Max Kampelman. But unlike many of them, her foreign policy views had not really changed between the early and late Cold War. She remained a Wilsonian internationalist and, while newly alive to its limitations, a supporter of the United Nations. Similarly, at no point in her long public career would Anderson have approved any policy, such as the nuclear freeze, that she viewed as detrimental to American security. Yet at the same time, and to her credit, Anderson on occasion criticized and attempted to redirect US policies she viewed as self-defeating because unenlightened, such as America's "backward" approach toward African decolonization or its unfulfilled commitments to its trusteeships in the Pacific. Moreover, she did not at all oppose arms control on principle; she in fact favored "enforceable agreements" that would "control the nuclear Frankenstein."[60]

Nevertheless, it is also clear that Anderson the Cold War liberal sometimes crossed the line separating steadfastly principled from rigidly dogmatic. Most clearly when it came to Vietnam, as author Peggy Lamson saw at the time, Anderson's "consciousness of what happened in the past blind[ed] her somewhat to the realities of the present." Confronting Communism was not always the answer. But her critical formative experience in Minnesota, as well as her successful missions in Denmark and Bulgaria, had been built on battling the Communists; now, toward the end of her career, she had become too inflexibly attached to that formula. As was true of many cold warriors, Anderson's anti-Communism served her well overall, but it was not a loose-fitting garment; nor did the convergence of the domestic and the international always point her in a sensible direction.[61]

In the end, however, Eugenie Anderson should not be judged for her stances on foreign policy issues; neither in American diplomacy nor, for that matter, in Minnesota politics was her role primarily one of formulating policy. Rather, she should be judged for the service she provided her state and her country, and in this regard she excelled. Apart from some career diplomats who disparaged her populism, and of course Bulgarian officials who found her a tough opponent, in the historical record one finds only those offering the highest praise for Anderson's performance. Three presidents, two secretaries of state, countless host country leaders, and fellow diplomats all appreciated her soft-spoken yet straightforward, unpretentious, and effective representation as an envoy.

Anderson's people's diplomacy stands out most, although it should not surprise us. For her career ran the gamut from the local to the global; indeed, she was an amateur who entered public life for personal and international reasons simultaneously. Anderson's subsequent journey was guided by a love of democracy that made her detest both elitism and Communism while connecting with average citizens wherever she went. Overseas, she put her Minnesota concerns and experiences to use and thus represented not just a government, but a people. This made Eugenie Anderson, if not the "ideal ambassador," as Secretary of State Dean Acheson described her, then something awfully close.[62]

6

Clare Boothe Luce

Italy, 1953–1956

[Lincoln] was born in Kentucky, grew up in Illinois, was elected President and was assassinated at Ford's Theater by Clare Boothe Luce.
—from a schoolboy's essay, 1959

On May 28, 1953, US ambassador to Italy Clare Boothe Luce stood to speak before a gathering of six hundred at a dinner at the Hotel Continental in Milan. New to her office, and apparently trying to minimize her glamour, she wore a plain black dress, a simple pearl necklace, and horn-rimmed glasses (upon arriving in Italy she had even selected, she said, her "most schoolmarmish looking picture" for her official photograph). After thanking her host, the American Chamber of Commerce in Italy, she began her remarks by offering the Italians a carrot: $22 million in new US foreign assistance. But then came the stick. National elections were scheduled for early June, and the ambassador was "required in all honesty" to say that if "the Italian people should fall unhappy victim to the wiles of totalitarianism of the right or the left there would follow—logically and tragically—grave consequences for this intimate and warm cooperation we now enjoy." What this might mean for, say, the continued flow of American aid dollars, she did not say. She did not have to.[1]

That this essentially was and had been official US policy—and toward most countries, not just Italy—did not matter. Soon, the Italian far right and far left were decrying Luce's interference in their country's internal affairs. The Monarchist newspaper *Popolo di Roma* commented that "Italians are ready to defend freedom" but not at the price of their independence. The neofascist *Secolo* declared Luce's warning "a new humiliation for Italy" (although laying ultimate blame at the feet of the government in Rome, not Luce).

What would the foreign ministry say, the left-wing *Il Paese* added, if the Soviet ambassador did what Luce had done?[2]

Italians fell unhappy victim to few wiles on election day, but they dealt the ruling centrist coalition, led by the Christian Democracy's (DC) Alcide de Gasperi, a minor defeat, putting it just below the magic 50 percent that under the new electoral law would have yielded it a two-thirds majority in the Chamber of Deputies. Although this outcome would most likely have resulted anyway, some in the United States blamed Luce's interference for the electoral setback. It helped further cement her well-established reputation as excessively frank at best, acid-tongued at worst.

And yet the reality was more complicated. During the drafting of the speech, Luce had sought to excise its controversial portion. Before arriving in Italy, she had declined to predict the outcome of the vote on the grounds that "we don't like people or other nations to interfere in our elections. Why should they?" She had also been instructed to avoid "overt pressures" during the campaign. But her embassy subordinates, including her DCM, Elbridge Durbrow, had argued the necessity of clarifying the US position, as well as perhaps quelling rumors that Washington preferred a victory for the neo-fascist Italian Social Movement. So they restored the original text, and Luce deferred to their expertise. The ambassador, of course, took all the heat for the remark, and to be sure, she largely deserved her long-standing reputation as a firebrand. It also remains odd that the United States had assigned to Rome not only another amateur but one renowned for her caustic wit—a trait that, while instrumental in her ascent, is not normally associated with the diplomatic profession. After all, diplomacy "is to do and say," the author Isaac Goldberg once wrote, "the nastiest things in the nicest way." Neverthe-less, the Milan speech episode nicely captures Luce's historical situation: a tension between her stark image as rhetorical bomb-thrower and the more complex reality of her diplomatic career.[3]

Luce's Early Years

One of the most accomplished American women of the twentieth century came from an unlikely background. Ann Clare Boothe was born in New York City in March 1903. Her youth was marked by parental separation, modest means, and sporadic schooling. It is possible that, being primarily raised by a single mother, Luce was less apt to grow up accepting limits the patriarchy imposed on female ambition. Her education did not include college, which she would always regret, but rather finishing school, which, she later remarked, "sure finished your education!" But the head of the Castle School in Tarrytown, New York, was Cassity Mason, a suffragist who tried to instill in her pupils a level of feminism surprising for such an institution. Mason told Clare she would go far but should remember the two things she would need: "confidence in yourself and confidence in God and *She* will protect you." Still, Clare followed her mother's wish that she marry well, and at age twenty, she wed wealthy New York financier George Brokaw, twenty-four years her senior. Together they had one daughter, Ann. But Brokaw was an abusive alcoholic, and Clare divorced him in 1929, after six years of marriage, receiving a handsome settlement. By then she had discovered her talent as a writer, and she became managing editor of *Vanity Fair* at age thirty. In 1935 she married Henry R. "Harry" Luce, influential publisher of *Time, Fortune,* and soon *Life* (in part Clare's idea), and together they formed a powerful media couple. She then wrote several plays, most of which—namely *The Women* (1936), *Kiss the Boys Goodbye* (1938), and *Margin for Error* (1939)— enjoyed considerable success on Broadway.[4]

In one unpublished play, Luce actually helped conjure a female chief of mission years before she could have imagined becoming one herself. "Madame Minister" (1939), coauthored with journalist Marquis Childs, tells the story of Lila Poole, US minister to the Scandinavian country of Vingland. Poole becomes embroiled in a drama involving a large herring purchase, a female sports star of unclear nationality, a Hollywood mogul, a spy inside her legation, and evil Nazis. The thrust of the play, however, despite some feminist moments, is not what one might expect from the imagination of Clare Luce: in the play's denouement, the hapless, impulsive minister loses her head and is essentially shunted aside; the day is saved not by the title character but by the studio chief. And then, oddly bridging Ruth Owen's experience previously and *Call Me Madam* later, Poole resigns to marry a Vingish opposition politician, Baron Llenguel. Similarly, a supporting character, Helen, is a bright, aspiring diplomat who (it is implied) abandons her own career to marry a male FSO.[5]

Throughout this period, Luce repeatedly relied on the attentions of powerful men to get ahead—not only Henry Luce but also Condé Nast and Bernard Baruch. But she was no mere social climber; she was not only ambitious but assertive, talented, inventive, and intelligent.[6]

Especially with the smashing success of *The Women,* a wicked comedy of manners lampooning upper-class society women, Luce began to earn notice for combining movie-star sex appeal with a wrecking-ball wit. "No good deed goes unpunished" is perhaps the most famous line commonly attributed to her. She once described Secretary of the Interior Harold Ickes as "that prodigious bureaucrat with the soul of a meatax and the mind of a commissar." Some of her bon mots would end up in anthologies, such as *A Woman's Book of Inspiration* (2017)—"The politicians were talking themselves red, white, and blue in the face." But on account of her more biting wit, she and her husband were soon known as "Arsenic and Old Luce." Again, it was not just the poisonous words that drew attention but the fragile beauty as well. Meeting her, someone once said, was like being "dynamited by angel cake."[7]

Luce and World War II, 1939–1942

Like her husband, Luce paid increasing attention to world affairs as war clouds gathered over Europe in 1939. Just as did "Madame Minister" only more so, *Margin for Error,* her play that did debut that year, had an anti-Nazi theme. Her growing curiosity as to what the newly begun war meant for the United States led her to visit western Europe in the spring of 1940 as a correspondent for *Life.* Her husband joined her in London, and they happened to be staying at the US ambassador's residence in Brussels on May 10 when the Blitzkrieg struck. Aerial bombs destroyed buildings across the square. Under these anxious circumstances, Luce met her first female Foreign Service Officer, Frances Willis, second secretary of legation. Luce was impressed with Willis, later describing her as "*une femme serieuse.*" Either would have been surprised, Luce later recalled, "if anybody had come in and said, 'You're both going to be ambassadors'" (and at the same time, no less). Amid the bombing, Luce may have suffered a nervous breakdown. Willis drove the Luces through the refugee-choked roads to Paris, whence they made their way back to America, where later that year Clare published her account of her tour, *Europe in the Spring.* Although heavily anecdotal and famously labeled by Dorothy Parker *All Clare on the Western Front,* the book contained many insights and sold well, taking a prominent place among other works alerting Americans to the Nazi menace.[8]

That same fall, Luce involved herself in partisan politics for the first time. Embracing her husband's conservatism and opposition to a third term for Franklin Roosevelt, she spoke at dozens of events for Republican candidate

Wendell Willkie. She made her biggest splash right away, in her first public speech, trading snide, personal attacks with the Republican but pro-Roosevelt journalist Dorothy Thompson. The press and public loved the spat, but Luce immediately regretted it. She deeply resented the sexist double-standard— men have a debate, women a "catfight"—and vowed never again to engage in a public dispute with another woman. Still, in this period, acquaintances were already warning her about her wicked wit. "Forgive me if I say that seemingly you have some irresistible impulse to tear things down," Hollywood mogul David Selznick wrote her in 1941. "I am fond enough of you, Clare, to wish that you could get some help . . . in curing you of this habit. Believe me, it is going to boomerang on you increasingly."[9]

Luce the Politician, 1942–1952

But for the moment, the boomerang did not return. *Boomerang* may even be the wrong metaphor; *double-edged sword* may be better, for Luce's wit was a major source of her fame, and fame helped a great deal as she set out on yet another career path—not just political activism but public office. In 1941, with her husband she worked to raise money to support beleaguered China. And, into 1942, she attempted some additional war journalism, but this career had essentially fizzled for her. So in that midterm election year, Luce successfully ran for a seat in the US House of Representatives from Connecticut's 4th District. She would serve two terms (1943–1947), sitting on the Military Affairs Committee—the first woman to do so—and touring the European battlefronts, meeting, among other such figures, General Dwight D. Eisenhower. As Helen Lawrenson would write, Luce's "acidic tongue and glistening beauty" were "a diverting novelty" in Congress, where most female members were "on the frowzy side." Luce made her mark with her first address to the House again, due not to substance but style. Her subject, Vice President Henry Wallace's proposal for the internationalization of civil aviation, was important enough to the British that they dispatched intelligence officer and future author Roald Dahl to seduce her in an (apparently unsuccessful) effort to influence her stance on the issue. But few people long remembered it. Congresswoman Luce's term for Wallace's idea—*globaloney*—is what stuck.[10]

In late June 1944, Representative Luce addressed the Republican National Convention in Chicago on its opening day. In her speech, she told the story of "G. I. Joe" and his dead buddy, "G. I. Jim." While perhaps tame by today's standards, the speech attacked President Roosevelt in time of war, impugning his honesty and integrity, something most politicians refrained from doing. Luce accused FDR of having promised, in order to win reelection, economic security and peace. These promises, Luce intoned, "lie quite as dead as young Jim does now. Jim was the heroic heir of the unheroic Roosevelt Decade: a decade of confusion and conflict that ended in war." The speech sparked widespread objections. Offended by Luce's laying of the American war dead at the feet of the majority "who voted wrong," the *New Yorker* wrote that the speech "made it difficult to keep anything on our stomach for twenty-four hours." At minimum, Luce's growing reputation as a partisan fire-breather was secure.[11]

Indeed, her inflammatory RNC speech also inadvertently contributed to the future of female diplomats long before Luce would become one herself. Listening to the address at home on the radio was none other than India Edwards, whose only son, an Army Air Force pilot, had lost his life in a training accident. Edwards was so incensed that a Republican would presume to speak for her son and pin his death on President Roosevelt that she immediately became a Democratic activist. Within a few short years, Edwards had risen to become cochair of the Democratic National Committee and chair of its Women's Division and was positioned to push for the appointment of women such as Perle Mesta and Eugenie Anderson.[12]

In early 1944, Luce was devastated by the death, in a car crash, of daughter Ann, a nineteen-year-old Stanford University undergraduate (who had planned to become a diplomat). This loss, coming not long after her mother's passing, and together with a growing despair over the war, triggered a spiritual crisis that in part explains Luce's conversion to Catholicism in early 1946. All this led her to announce that she would not seek a third term in Congress; her stated reason was her desire to avoid the charge that her religious conversion had been intended to court the many Catholic voters in her district. Thus, in 1947, she returned to private life, although she remained active in Republican politics. In 1948, Luce reprised her earlier role, gleefully serving up more red meat at the Republican National Convention in Philadelphia. In her telling, Roosevelt and Truman had been "troubadours of trouble, crooners of catastrophe"; Progressive Party candidate Henry Wallace was "Red Hank" and "Stalin's Mortimer Snerd" (Snerd was one of ventriloquist Edgar Bergen's dummies). Her appearance merely confirmed her as a prominent polarizing figure. *Time*'s Henry Grunwald recalled thinking her performance insincere, though the crowd "loved her delectable malice."[13]

In 1952, Luce unsuccessfully sought the Republican nomination for US Senate in Connecticut. The Luces then turned their focus to Dwight "Ike" Eisenhower's presidential candidacy, of which they became early and generous supporters. As early as 1949, Clare Luce had begun urging Eisenhower to enter politics. When he did, winning the Republican nomination, Harry lent two of his best writers, and he and Clare contributed over $400,000 (2018 dollars), to the general's campaign. Clare made dozens of radio and television appearances on Ike's behalf, some of them widely seen as extremely effective. And, true to form, Luce did not hold back. On September 30, for example, she stood in for Senator McCarthy in a national television broadcast—both figuratively and literally, echoing his accusations of Communist infiltration in the highest levels of the Truman administration.[14]

Eisenhower and Luce's Appointment

The war hero Eisenhower won handily. He was neither more nor less committed to appointing women than his immediate predecessors had been. However, on the campaign trail candidate Eisenhower had called for more women in public life. And while he was not as personally involved in making appointments as Harry Truman had been, Republican Party officials wanted to do at least as well with women, and Eisenhower agreed. Thus, the new president did appoint the second woman to the cabinet (Oveta Culp Hobby), several other women to high-ranking posts, and two female ambassadors. The first of these was by the far the most famous, perhaps of all time: Clare Boothe Luce.[15]

The president-elect first offered to make Luce his secretary of labor, but she declined. Then he asked what she wanted, and she suggested succeeding Eleanor Roosevelt at the United Nations Commission on Human Rights. He was surprised she aimed so low, and the position was already taken anyway. She believed she would only fit somewhere in foreign affairs, and the London ambassadorship was taken. So she suggested Italy. Luce had had many involvements there, first as a journalist in 1940, then twice as a wartime congresswoman visiting the front, and then receiving an audience with Pope Pius XII. As both a Cold War battleground and a cultural center, it had attracted great interest from both Luces. The ambassadorship in Rome was a great prize, and she wanted it very much.[16]

This was a significant appointment, by any standard. Luce was the first female envoy any country sent to Italy, and the first female American chief

Clare Boothe Luce, ambassador to Italy (1953–1956) with her husband, media mogul Henry R. Luce, 1954. For years, they formed one of the most influential couples in Republican circles. As the first woman ambassador to a major US ally, as well as a journalist, playwright, and two-term congresswoman, Luce was one of the most accomplished American women of the twentieth century. (Phil Stanziola, *New York World-Telegram and Sun,* Library of Congress, Prints and Photographs Division)

assigned to the capital of a "major" ally; indeed, Italy was a key ally in the western alliance, and these were still the critical years of the early Cold War. Luce correctly predicted considerable opposition to the appointment, both in Italy and at home, which delayed her nomination. Many Italians objected to the fact that Luce was too staunch an anti-Communist, an amateur, and, most of all, a woman. Italian women, after all, had only just gained the right to vote, in 1946. "What do you think we are, Luxembourg?" asked one Italian official. The Italian foreign minister complained to DCM Durbrow that sending a woman suggested that Italy was not a second-class power but a third-class power. Although the Italian ambassador in Washington, Alberto Tarchiani, at first reacted favorably and told Luce that the Italians were "delighted at the possibility" of her coming, he was told to obstruct the nomination before it was officially announced; after that, Rome feared, it would have no choice but to go along. His instructions stated that feminism was "an imported plant" that had not yet taken root in Italy, which meant most Italians would not understand the appointment and might take it as an insult. A woman might also cause "uneasiness" among all the Italian officials with whom she would interact. Beyond the foreign ministry, Italy's left-wing press in particular viewed the choice as an affront.[17]

To these complaints, many Americans added her conversion to Catholicism, which they feared would bend her loyalty toward Catholic Italy (or toward the Vatican), and her extreme partisanship in American politics. Discontent inside the US embassy in Rome was loud enough to earn the staff a scolding by the outgoing ambassador. Nevertheless, her nomination also received widespread support. And although the process dragged on long enough to provoke a terse note to Dulles from an angry Harry Luce, whatever informal objections Tarchiani may have raised were obviously insufficient, and the intensity of resistance in the Italian foreign ministry does not seem to have been shared outside of it. The prime minister, Alcide de Gasperi (in office 1945–1953), gave his approval of the appointment, as then did a unanimous US Senate, on March 2, 1953.[18]

Luce, Gender, and Diplomacy

Luce had earlier shown some interest in the subject of women and diplomacy. Because female diplomats were still pioneers, facing an uphill struggle, Luce had supported them at least since World War II. Despite the militant views she formed later, she was a thoroughgoing essentialist, promoting the pacific contributions only women could make. The congresswoman wrote in a 1943 article, "Victory Is a Woman," that the war might not have happened had women been equally represented in diplomatic circles. During the war, she had conducted research on women in the field and concluded that women were serving well in the State Department. She also believed that as the war was drawing to a close, women deserved a seat at the peace conference table.[19]

Thus it comes as no surprise that Luce was acutely aware of the gender implications of her appointment. Shortly after her confirmation, she wrote to Congresswoman Frances Bolton (R-OH) that since women were fated to be more a force for good than for evil, they "must play a vigorous role at every level of national life" in these dangerous times. But her sense of responsibility was even greater than that. She told a reporter that as a woman it was her duty to strive especially hard for success. "If I fail," she said, "no one will say, 'she doesn't have what it takes.' They will say, 'women don't have what it takes.' Success by a woman makes it easier for other able women."[20]

Protocol

Despite the now-substantial history of accommodating female chiefs in the world of protocol, which new host countries could investigate, practices continued to vary somewhat from country to country. The Italian protocol chief suggested Luce be addressed as *Ambasciatore* rather than *Ambasciatrice*, since the latter meant "ambassador's wife." Then came the question of where Luce was to sit at functions. She chose to be seated based on her rank alone and not also her sex, with the one exception of preserving a seating scheme based on alternating sexes. Last came the question of what to do with Mr. Luce, who planned to spend half of each year in Rome, working out of *Time*'s local office. The solution, similar to that ultimately arrived at with the Andersons in Copenhagen, was to give him the honorary rank of minister: this placed him below all real ministers at the table but above the chargés d'affaires. Harry would go along with this. "It's wonderful," he said to Durbrow. "The girls are much better looking and younger at my end of the table."[21]

Luce and US–Italian Relations

Luce arrived with her husband on April 22, 1953, aboard the (ill-fated) SS *Andrea Doria* in Naples, where she was met by a crowd that included 120 photographers and journalists. She made her way to Rome and established herself at the Villa Taverna, the eighteen-thousand square-foot US ambassador's residence, parts of it dating to the sixteenth century. More recent history, however, shaped the present. Italy in 1953 was still recovering from the horrors of Il Duce's fascism and the devastation of war, one that had killed nearly a half-million of its people and, in its effect on per capita income, erased the economic growth of the twentieth century. Atop these ruins, postwar Italians had established a republic (1946) and a fragile multiparty democracy. De Gasperi's DC—with the help of a major Central Intelligence Agency covert operation—had dominated the 1948 elections and formed a centrist coalition with three far smaller parties: Republicans, Liberals, and the Italian Democratic Socialist Party. The Italian Socialist Party and Italian Communist Party (PCI), however, had together received nearly one-third of the vote, and in the depths of the Cold War, this is what attracted the most attention in the Eisenhower administration.[22]

La Luce (literally "The Light" in Italian, fodder for endless puns) settled into the job, and soon Italians formed opinions of her that were diverse, changing, at times ambivalent. On the one hand, many found her to be a heavy-handed, meddlesome presence, because Italy was a major NATO country and wanted to be treated as a partner, not a client. But as a fierce anti-Communist, Luce fully subscribed to the interventionist policy, continued from the Truman administration, of "psychological warfare": as Alessandro Brogi notes, this consisted of "posturing, propaganda, and covert operations," although nothing after 1953 rivaled the intrusion of 1948. The ultimate goal was to get Rome to outlaw the PCI, and in the meantime, Luce merely executed Eisenhower administration policy, spelled out in National Security Council policy statement 5411/2 (April 1954): to use aggressively all levers, including foreign assistance, to attack Communist influence in Italy.[23]

The understandable clash between this policy and the Italians' self-esteem helps explain the negative reaction of some to Luce's May 1953 Milan speech. Similarly, many Italians, especially on the left, objected when Luce froze offshore procurement contracts by which NATO allies could manufacture their own armaments with US aid dollars—until the firms in question, notably FIAT, reduced the PCI's influence in their trade unions. She was (predictably) so reviled among the Communists that her very name became a self-evident insult: "Luce! Luce! Luce!" they chanted in the Chamber of Deputies when Prime Minister Amintore Fanfani (early 1954) said, "Foreign observers have noted an increase in communist ideology in Italy." But her ongoing, overt attempts to steer the DC into a coalition with the Monarchists (the "opening to the right")—or prevent it from sliding to the left—sometimes led Italians to resent her as a ham-fisted proconsul.[24]

On the other hand, Luce came to enjoy immense popularity as an aggressive promoter of Italy's interests. This stemmed most clearly from her greatest diplomatic triumph, the settlement of the dispute over Trieste. Situated at the top of the Adriatic Sea, this historic port city and the bit of territory around it had become, by 1953, object of a full-blown diplomatic crisis between Italy and Yugoslavia. It was certainly a top priority for successive Christian Democratic leaders, who believed their party's fortunes depended heavily on resolving the issue. Luce saw the problem clearly—probably too clearly. Early on, she explained the situation's gravity by updating the old proverb:

> For the want of Trieste, an Issue was lost.
> For the want of an Issue, the Election was lost.
> For the want of the Election, DeGasperi was lost.
> For the want of DeGasperi, his NATO policies were lost.
> For the want of his NATO policies, Italy was lost.
> For the want of Italy, Europe was lost.
> For the want of Europe, America. . . . . . . ?
> And all for the want of a two-penny town.[25]

Although not the main actor in the final negotiations, Luce, on her own initiative, badgered Eisenhower into approving a major diplomatic effort, resorting at one point, according to the president, to pounding on his desk for effect (this may have been one reason another US ambassador described Luce as one of the few envoys who "had the guts to stand up and fight for what is necessary"). After a chance meeting in Washington, she also recruited diplomatic troubleshooter Robert Murphy, who knew Yugoslav president Josip Tito from World War II, to help overcome the last sticking points in the negotiations. The ultimate result was a settlement, in October 1954, acceptable to both sides. Luce received rock-star treatment when she visited Trieste in December, and Eisenhower would later describe her work on the issue as "brilliant." It not only delighted the Italians, who saw one of their worst foreign policy problems solved, but it clarified why they should embrace Luce: her relationship with Eisenhower and Secretary of State John Foster Dulles gave her access and influence of which most other ambassadors could only dream (although Luce privately complained about her *lack* of access to the president and secretary of state). "Mrs. Luce is the most important ambassador you have ever had here," as Gastone Guidotti, a senior official in the Italian foreign ministry, put it to an American journalist, "because she is a member of your Politburo. If there is anything we really want done, we persuade her—she circumvents the State Department and telephones the White House. *Time* and *Life* are more valuable to us than experience." Although Guidotti was inaccurately (and patronizingly) depicting Luce as an Italian errand girl dependent solely on her husband's clout, he was understandably acknowledging her access in Washington and the legitimate grounds for Rome's satisfaction with her performance.[26]

With her zeal—she kept a sign with Talleyrand's warning against it on her desk—for promoting Italy's interests, Luce at times exhibited distinct symptoms of localitis. During the months-long effort on Trieste, in acting as if only Yugoslavia should make any concessions, she frequently seemed in lockstep with Rome. In at least one case, President Eisenhower noticed a similar stance on the foreign aid issue, and he delivered his ambassador a mild rebuke. In addition to knowing what aid Italy sought from Washington, he wrote, "it would also be useful to know what kind of pressure we should put on these governments to do something themselves." But there were also times when Luce could play the heavy. In June 1954, when the United States believed Rome's obstructionism on both Trieste and the proposed European Defense Community had gone on long enough, she warned the foreign ministry of a possible "agonizing reappraisal" (Dulles's famous words) of US assistance programs. Almost a year later, when Premier Mario Scelba considered requesting a Marshall Plan–sized aid package, Assistant Secretary of State Livingston Merchant lauded Luce for "dissuading Premier Scelba from presenting any such unrealistic request."[27]

When judging Luce's view of the Italian political situation, what leaps out of the documents most clearly is her alarmism, especially regarding how failure to address the Trieste crisis would lead to the collapse of the Italian political center, the triumph of the Communists, or worse. Signs of it appeared weeks before she even departed for her post. "We simply *must* win there," she wrote in her diary, "or the jig is up with NATO and all else in Italy." In September 1953, she worried that if Eisenhower failed to settle Trieste shortly, the GOP might lose control of Congress. The following March, she wondered, in a letter to Dulles, whether Italy might become "the powder keg of World War III." Again and again she reported to the State Department that the collapse of the DC-led coalition and thus triumph of the PCI lay right around the corner, and repeatedly she used its prospect to push her recommendations. This vocal fretting was not without its uses—it probably helped get the ball rolling on Trieste—but her warnings soon acquired a boy-who-cried-wolf quality that could not have enhanced their efficacy.[28]

Like Perle Mesta and many Americans at the time, Luce was such an ardent anti-Communist that distinctions among leftist parties were lost on her. She viewed the Italian Socialist Party as little more than a Trojan horse for the PCI, which it simply was not. Similarly, she could not fully appreciate why DC leaders like de Gasperi resisted the "opening to the right." Italy had been wrecked by fascism, and they saw the far right as a bigger threat than the far left. Moreover, even if they embraced only the Monarchists, and not the neo-fascists, they believed that act would drive voters into the arms of the far left. All this rendered Luce's opening to the right anathema to them.[29]

Cajoling Italian leaders was made difficult by the fact that Luce's main leverage over them was diminishing steadily. Gone were the flush days of the Marshall Plan, under which Italy received an average of roughly $400 million per year (1948–1951, almost $4 billion today). Under Luce, annual direct US assistance amounted to $105 million in FY 1954, and then it was roughly halved, and then halved again. Similarly, offshore procurement contracts dropped from $383 million in 1953, to $91 million in 1954, to $39.5 million in 1955. In terms of leverage, the US ambassador had her crowbar replaced by a spatula.[30]

The United States did continue running a large-scale covert operation in support of the centrist political parties. The No. 2 CIA officer in Luce's embassy, future director of Central Intelligence William Colby, was given roughly $30 million per year for this purpose. His deputy recalled that the main problem was transporting the enormous stacks of cash used for bribes. Colby and Luce were in constant conflict, however, over how to use the covert money to gain leverage—she wanted to withhold it, he to spend it—and over their approaches to Italian politics, Colby preferring an "opening to the left."[31]

For all the justified criticism of her hardline approach, Luce became somewhat more flexible toward the end of her ambassadorship. For example, while she continued to prefer connecting with conservative Italian intellectuals, she came to see the value in reaching out to their left-of-center counterparts, even facilitating lecture tours in the USA for some of them. Moreover, Luce had instinctively distrusted those DC leaders who pursued an opening to the left, such as Fanfani; she tarred him as an "Italian Kerensky." But grudgingly accommodating herself to Italy's moderate political reality, she decided in 1956 that she would "do anything" to bolster Giuseppe Saragat, leader of the Italian Democratic Socialist Party, the more moderate socialist party and a DC coalition partner, just to the DC's left. Considering Luce's previous, staunch attachment to the Italian right and her consonance with many of its views, this amounted to a significant departure. Finally, as these actions would suggest, overall the ambassador presided over a gradual softening of the aggressive forms of psychological warfare and cultural policies she helped push at the outset, replacing them with a stronger emphasis on diplomacy.[32]

Luce's Acid Tongue

Moreover, apart from perhaps the 1953 Milan speech, and phrases provocative because they accurately represented some other controversial policy, Ambassador Luce's mouth seems only rarely to have caused her trouble. In Luxembourg in September 1953, she apparently "horrified" guests at a dinner party attended by numerous European dignitaries. She was discussing the Kinsey Report on *Sexual Behavior in the Human Female* and "said in a loud voice that it wouldn't have taken her any 480 pages to prove that all men are dopes." This attracted all the male guests' attention. "After all, she said, women are not interested in sex. All they want is babies and security from men. Men are just too stupid to know it." If this account is accurate, the incident could not have helped her reputation, to put it mildly. However, and while many were put off by the *quantity* of her speech, and by their resulting inability to get a word in edgewise, its quality was seldom so offensive. In official documents, she was snide only when she could clearly get away with it, for example, in her memorandum of a stultifying protocol meeting with her Soviet counterpart. She was waiting for him, "and then the Ambassador's stomach came in, followed at a respectful distance by the Ambassador."[33]

Luce and People's Diplomacy

Luce did not emphasize Anderson's "people's diplomacy" as much as her predecessors had. Considering her responsibilities, including management of one of
the six largest US missions in the world, this would have been difficult. Toward
the end of her tenure, the mission she oversaw encompassed forty-five agencies,
nine consulates, 1200 Americans and 1100 Italian nationals (as of 1939, the
tally had been four agencies, nine consulates, 130 Americans, and 235 Italians).
But as a civilian she had embraced the notion of public diplomacy, at least the
mid-twentieth century version, years before; in 1948, she had advocated people-to-people contact through letter-writing, supporting the effort to influence
the 1948 Italian elections via the "Letters to Italy" campaign in particular.
(One biographer claims Luce joined Joe Kennedy in helping to raise $2 million
in private funds that were then funneled to the DC in the 1948 election. If true,
presumably this was part of the CIA's covert operation.)[34]

Interviewed shortly before she left for Italy, Luce sounded an awful lot
like her female predecessors. "My job will be to represent *all* the American
people to *all* the Italian people," she said. "I shall try to travel throughout
Italy, seeing people of every region and of every class, trying to understand
them." When it came to her routine circle of acquaintance, she fell down in
this area. Partly it was a language issue. Luce did learn some Italian and soon
could deliver prepared (and rehearsed) remarks in the language, which
earned her considerable approval. But she was never fluent, and for conducting business she relied on an interpreter. And it owed in part to her partisanship and ideology; she was comfortable with those on the Italian right and
had nothing to do with their opposite numbers on the left. Thus, she spent
disproportionate time in the company of conservative businesspeople and
writers who could speak English. As we have seen, with this flaw she was in
good company, but her comprehension of the Italian scene would have been
stronger had she developed more diverse social ties.[35]

Nevertheless, Luce added people's diplomacy to her repertoire as well. An
ambassador, she remarked in 1955, is not a "glorified messenger boy" but
rather, "in the widest sense," a people-to-people representative. After three
years on the job, Luce had visited twenty-seven cities and traveled twenty-five
thousand miles inside Italy. Whether it was her swift visit to Salerno flood
victims, deliberately flying Linee Aeree Italiane as a show of confidence after
one of its airliners crashed at Idlewild, or personally introducing Romans on

the street to a visiting Joe DiMaggio, Luce made a fine goodwill ambassador with a keen eye for the endearing gesture. Visiting an agricultural project in southern Italy in 1953, Luce "astounded and delighted" her audience by climbing aboard a tractor and driving it. The Italian government certainly gave her credit for people's diplomacy, if in a predictably sexist manner. "If the woman, as ambassador, was quite capable of filling her difficult post," stated an official radio broadcast after her resignation in late 1956, "she was just as capable in the highest role of woman—that is, as a mother." Distributing gifts to the Italian poor, it suggested, was as important to her as any diplomatic meeting. "This is why her name is a beloved one in thousands and thousands of Italian families." Some elites objected to her outreach. "The poor classes," one Italian sniffed, "regard her as a sort of American Madonna." But there is no doubt that the ambassador's good works and kind acts, along with her beauty and her sex, all made her a huge celebrity. In a magazine poll, female Italian university students chose her as the "ideal woman," while a 1955 survey showed her to be by far the best known foreign ambassador in Italy. Some two hundred Italian families apparently named their daughters "Clare."[36]

Sexism

The sexism Luce faced assumed several different forms. Simplest was the crude joke on the street: "The Ambassador," some would quip, "doesn't tote a fountain pen"—in Italian, a double entendre for penis. More subtle, as seen with the previous female chiefs, was the diminution of her professional experience, especially neglect of her two terms in Congress. The headline above a two-page photo spread (which included two photos of the congresswoman) in *Oggi,* one of Italy's major illustrated weeklies, read, "The Most Attractive Woman Playwright of Modern Times Becomes Ambassador to Italy." Another manifestation was the patronizing attitude of the traditional male. In the Chamber of Deputies, when PCI chief Palmiro Togliatti declared Luce "an old lady" who "brings bad luck to everything she touches," Prime Minister Fanfani defended her. "Further, as a man," he said, "I must express my regret at the violation of the most elementary rules of chivalry." ("The only thing I resent," Luce commented later, "is that no one in the government denied that I was an old lady.") Another was sexist praise. "She's a woman, yes, very much a woman," one Italian official commented. "But with brains—the brains of a man." Another was the mockery of femininity, seen, for example, in the Monarchist newspaper *Il Candido,* which greeted her arrival with a political cartoon featuring the US embassy flying a flag trimmed in lace. Yet another was simple underestimation. "Our politicians expected an easy time," wrote one Italian journalist. "They thought her Ingrid [Bergman] looking for her [Roberto] Rossellini, and being Italian, everybody thought himself a Rossellini. They were disappointed when they found no Ingrid. . . . It took them quite a while to adjust to the mind of a man clothed in fragile femininity."[37]

Additional sexism, in the form of the belief that women were too "soft," remained a threat. Like other women, Luce may have tried to compensate in this regard. Of course, it is impossible to separate views one would have held regardless from those affected to create a reputation for toughness. In any case, Luce does not seem to have encountered much trouble here. Her reputed quick wit and sharp tongue and her staunch conservatism and anti-Communism no doubt helped.

Luce did not even share the predilection of most diplomats, of both sexes, for the pacific settlement of disputes—a clear contradiction, never resolved, of her belief in women's unique ability to promote peace. For it turns out the F-86 Sabre jet fighter miniature she kept on her embassy desk signified more than she may have let on. She privately had advocated preventive war against the Soviet Union as early as 1947. Similarly, as ambassador Luce was generally far too militant for Eisenhower's liking, alarming him and his administration with her belief that the time had come for open military confrontation with the Soviet Union. In mid-1954, Eisenhower asked Luce for her appraisal of the world situation. Her classified, thirty-seven-page response was titled "Russian Atomic Power and the Lost American Revolution." Several of its basic recommendations were either commonplace, such as maintaining nuclear superiority, or even progressive, such as ceasing US support for dictators. But another stands out: the "liberation" of China using South Korean and Republican Chinese ground forces and US tactical nuclear weapons. Luce assumed that overall US nuclear superiority would prevent World War III and that the USSR would be severely weakened by having to support China. But this was neither the first nor last time she almost casually advocated reckless military solutions to international problems. Perhaps we can see why one of the characters in her last play, *Slam the Door Softly* (1970), remarks, "The hand that cradles the rock has ruled the world."[38]

Did Her Sex Matter?

The issue of Luce's sex seems to have diminished to some extent, and this rather early in her ambassadorship; this is certainly the case in the realm of Italian public opinion, as seen in polls from late 1953 and early 1954. In one, Italians were asked for their views of Washington's decision to send a female ambassador: 40 percent had no opinion, 25 percent believed it didn't matter, 18 percent were opposed, and 17 percent approved—nothing for Luce to write home about, certainly, but not the sort of numbers one would expect given some of the initial reactions to her appointment. In another, half of those polled knew her by name—only 2 percent could identify her predecessor, Ellsworth Bunker—and more than half who knew of her approved of Eisenhower's having chosen a woman. These results suggest that Luce was at least good enough to put her in league with other early female diplomats who incrementally undermined sexist attitudes toward women's participation in foreign affairs. Nor was it long into her term when she remarked on how little her sex got in the way of day-to-day diplomacy with her counterparts. "After the first minute or two of 'gallantry,'" she wrote in June 1953, "we settle down to the business at hand, and the difference in sexes is soon forgotten."[39]

Then again, the issue could certainly arise behind her back. For starters, she clearly discombobulated some male colleagues. It should not be "disconcerting" that "the American Ambassador is a woman—and an excessively good-looking blonde at that," reported the newly arrived British ambassador in Rome, Sir Ashley Clarke, "—but I do find it slightly spooky." More gravely, at a dinner in Washington, DC, Prime Minister Scelba (1954–1955) told Secretary Dulles that he had never received a reply to his question as to US policy in case of an Italian civil war. Dulles's understanding was that Scelba had received a reply through Luce and the US chief of naval operations, but Scelba replied that he could not discuss such matters with a woman. After his term, which arguably Luce did much to lengthen with her support, Scelba still maintained that "a male ambassador would have been better." Publicly, at least, Luce tended to shrug it all off. At the end of her tenure, someone asked her whether she had found being a woman a disadvantage. "I couldn't possibly tell you," she replied. "I've never been a man." But at least in one sense, she reportedly used her sex to her advantage: C. D. Jackson noted that she liked to flirt with Eisenhower, and that the president's appointment secretary said she got more time with the president than other envoys. "Golden curls," he concluded, "have more leverage than striped pants."[40]

The Spouse Issue

Like the other female envoys, Luce faced the diplomatic spouse issue. The problem was especially acute for her, since she ran a huge embassy and staff in the capital city of a major US ally that was also a famous cultural center and tourist destination. Some tasks normally handled by an ambassador's wife, such as planning dinner menus, Luce sometimes performed herself. Because she was in Rome, Luce had to entertain far more than her share of American visitors, travelers and VIPs alike. One junketing congressman—off by only about two thousand years—asked Luce how the Italian nationalist hero Giuseppe Garibaldi got his elephants across the Alps. Her British counterpart claimed that this entertainment distraction, by forcing her to neglect her professional contacts, rendered her a mediocre colleague. Moreover, inundated with invitations for an average of forty cocktail parties, four dinners, and several luncheons each week, Luce concluded that every embassy should have two ambassadors, one for social affairs and one for official business. Her male counterparts would not have fully understood this complaint.[41]

The assistance offered by her "hostess" husband, for all the predictable jokes about the role reversal, varied in quality. Never known for his social grace—one woman recalled he "had the worst naturally bad manners of any man she'd ever met"—Harry certainly tried to be a solicitous host, and he often succeeded. But he also dumbfounded guests at one reception by interrupting another US ambassador's wife mid-story and ushering them all to the door because the clock had struck midnight. Clare had other good help, especially her social secretary Letitia Baldridge, whom Luce had told when hiring her, "Your job is to be my wife!" But the ambassador could not avoid handling many of the traditional spousal duties herself, and this no doubt compounded her exhaustion and fragile health.[42]

Luce and the FSOs

Luce complained at first about her Foreign Service Officers as Mesta and Anderson had, although on different grounds: she thought she and other Eisenhower appointees were "virtually prisoners" of a Rooseveltian diplomatic corps. This critique, expressed only in private, seems to have referred mainly to the FSOs' execution of information policies and political (dis)loyalty to the president. Her views probably changed, however; six months later Luce admitted that she had "a pretty good team" in Rome, whom she applauded in her efficiency reports and basically agreed with on policy. For their part, her FSOs warmed to her. "She has won over the staff one hundred percent," said Durbrow, "and it didn't take her long, either." Their boss was intelligent, sought their advice, and had a keen sense of humor. Of course, with her fame and influence, Luce occupied a separate category from the other female ambassadors, so perhaps her FSOs were bound to treat her better. Still, for whatever reasons, she generally enjoyed much fuller cooperation from her career diplomats than some of her counterparts did. And Luce became and remained, long after stepping down, a staunch advocate of the Foreign Service. At one point, despite her former card-carrying membership in the China lobby, she intervened personally to help secure the promotion of one of the "China Hands" whose career had been derailed by McCarthyism (and whom most other officials, including Secretary Dulles, had abandoned).[43]

Luce's Morale and Resignation, 1955–1956

Despite her successes, Luce at times could descend into gloominess. A measure of her disenchantment—along with ambition, feminism, fatigue, pessimism, and more than a little self-pity—is a reflection she jotted down circa 1955, which is worth quoting at length. Luce considered her political future and decided she enjoyed little support among various population groups. She believed it impossible for a woman, "however able, if she is also a Catholic, a Republican, and the wife of Henry Luce, to receive any wide measure of group support." Then, with typical incisiveness, she reflected on her ambassadorship.

> One undertakes a piece of work because (a) it leads to riches; (b) it leads to "recognition"; (c) it leads to solutions; (d) it is pleasurable.
>   (a) This job is not making me rich.
>   (b) The oohings and ahings of visitors to the Villa Taverna, and the people you sit next to at dinner would not constitute recognition in any man's book. Why should they in mine?
>   (c) Anyone who can solve the Italian question is welcome to it.

(d) It's no fun, and in exchange for its sapping my strength and exhausting me, I am faced with the happy prospect of going through an election in Italy in early '56, which may go badly. And another in the U.S. in late 1956 which may go worse—and my reward is to be a few compliments passed on to me by itinerant visitors to Taverna if I win—and plenty of insults and jibes printed in the press if I lose.

Leaving aside the absurdity regarding her remuneration, and the possibility that this meditation represented Luce at her most discouraged, it remains clear from this, and other sources, that she failed to find contentment in this profession, just as she had failed in all her others.[44]

By mid-1956, Luce was severely frustrated by the Italian situation. Her pressure tactics had succeeded in helping to prevent the opening to the left, but they had consistently failed to move successive Italian premiers to launch an all-out assault on the PCI. On top of this, her fatigue had worsened. To get through her eighteen-hour days, she had been relying on Benzedrine—indeed, on a dangerous cocktail of pharmaceuticals. By early 1955 she had developed severe health problems that required extended stays in the United States; these partly resulted from one of diplomatic history's more bizarre episodes. She usually took her breakfast in bed and then stayed there to work. She would complain that her coffee tasted like poison—and she could not have known that she was right. After intense investigation (and suspicions of a deliberate plot), the culprit was discovered: ancient paint dust, containing arsenate of lead, had been drifting down from her ceiling. Luce insisted the story be hushed up; she worried that the mere possibility of an assassination plot might lead to the fall of the Scelba government and new elections, and, of course, a Communist victory. In 1956, her health began to recover, but she was still tired of the ambassadorship.[45]

After several postponements, Luce delivered her resignation to the president at the White House shortly after his reelection in November 1956. At the meeting, which took twice as long as scheduled, she apparently again shared her beliefs that the world situation was in crisis (intensified by the recent Soviet crackdown on the Hungarian revolt and the lack of a US response—"our Munich," she called it), that the administration did not have a handle on it, and that the time had come for a military confrontation with the USSR. Eisenhower may have had some success at "talking her down," but Luce's extreme assessment so alarmed him that he immediately dashed off a letter to her husband—one so sensitive he asked Harry to destroy it after reading—expressing his concern and implying that Harry should help address her pessimism. According to Ike's appointment secretary, at the time of the meeting Clare appeared "on the verge of a nervous breakdown," which if true, may have been related to her exhaustion and despair over global politics. A bit later, she was well enough to return to Rome to say her farewells, and she received a fond send-off. The Italians bestowed upon her the Grand Star of the Order of Merit of the Italian Republic, making her the first woman so honored. Two days after Christmas 1956, over five hundred people gathered at the airport to say goodbye. As the TWA airliner's door closed, they sang "For She's a Jolly Good Fellow."[46]

Luce and Brazil

It was not long, however, before the restless Luce sought another post. Already in December 1956, she expressed to Dulles her interest in serving, after a vacation, as either ambassador to France or special ambassador to NATO. In May 1957, Dulles offered to deposit her in the dumping ground for women, the US delegation to the United Nations General Assembly, but she saw this as the indignity that it was and declined. In October, she aimed higher, apparently expressing interest only in the posts of disarmament negotiator, ambassador to NATO, or ambassador to Germany. Sherman Adams, Ike's chief of staff, just wanted to give her some position so he would no longer have to deal with her. Dulles believed the disarmament position the likeliest, and Luce "might have ideas as to how to carry on propaganda"—which is how Dulles viewed the value of arms control negotiations generally—but thought, "The Russians are not going to negotiate with her."[47]

In late 1958, Harry Luce—often the point of contact—informed Secretary Dulles that his wife would like another ambassadorship, perhaps in Spain. But Eisenhower liked the incumbent in Madrid. Moreover, the Spanish had made it clear they would not accept a female envoy, and any such opposition was disqualifying. In early January 1959, Cuba became a possibility, and Luce was interested—a fascinating "what if," considering that Fidel Castro's revolution had seized control in Havana just days before—but top State Department officials demurred, preferring to have a career diplomat on the scene at such a delicate moment. Dulles then proposed, through Harry, Brazil. The president, although, according to Dulles, for some reason "obviously not enthusiastic," reluctantly agreed. Dulles revealed his own mixed feelings when discussing the issue with Harry. According to his notes of the phone conversation, Dulles said we would not "want Mrs. Luce to become so excited about Brazilian prospects that she would try to get us to support everything that [Brazilian] President [Juscelino] Kubitschek wanted." When Mr. Luce posed the obvious rejoinder—Had that been a problem in Italy?—Dulles replied that the ambassador had made a large request but had been "a good soldier" when the request was turned down. One wonders, then, why Dulles even raised the issue—unless, of course, he did not fully trust Mrs. Luce, or he suspected her of suffering from terminal localitis and was deceitfully trying to use her husband to rein her in.[48]

Regardless, Dulles created the necessary opening. At first, Luce's confirmation was to have been pro forma, completed without even a hearing before the Senate Foreign Relations Committee. But then in early March 1959 the Latin American edition of *Time* ran a story on Bolivia that quoted an unnamed official at the US embassy in La Paz to the effect that US aid to the country had been wasted and the only solution was to "abolish Bolivia—let her neighbors divide up the country and its problems." Infuriated Bolivians attacked the US embassy and burned copies of the magazine along with the American flag. Some Americans began to question the wisdom of sending Luce, married to the offending press empire, to a neighboring country. Luce herself offered to withdraw, but the State Department told her to sit tight. Most important, Democratic senator and Foreign Relations Committee Latin American Subcommittee chair Wayne Morse, long an adversary of the Luces, seized on the controversy as a pretext to hold up the nomination. He could not bottle it up in committee, but he did help make the committee's hearing with her extremely contentious, and he delivered a three-hour diatribe against her on the Senate floor, in which he laid out her history of slash-and-burn partisanship and harsh attacks on Roosevelt. Here, arguably, the boomerang was returning. The debate was so bitter that, although the Senate voted to confirm her, 79–11, Harry Luce thought it would destroy her effectiveness as ambassador, and he publicly suggested she resign. She could have declined this odd advice, of course, and she could still easily have departed for Brazil, as she was ready to do. She had prepared assiduously and even graced the cover of Brazil's *Lady* magazine, sitting on her chaise lounge, a book titled *Brazil* prominently perched on her lap.[49]

Then, however, she unleashed her famous tongue again. "I am grateful for the overwhelming vote of confirmation in the Senate," she told a reporter. "My difficulties of course go some years back and began when Senator Morse was kicked in the head by a horse" (a reference to an actual 1951 incident). The story ran, and a major uproar ensued, especially in the Senate, where even some of her supporters objected and said they would have voted against her had she said such a thing earlier. At his press conference, Eisenhower was asked if Luce should withdraw, and he said no; she "operated very successfully" in Italy. But the next day, Luce set a modern diplomatic record by resigning a mere three days after having been confirmed. A Herblock cartoon depicted a horse explaining the confusions and contradictions of the affair to a bewildered passerby. "Anyhow," the horse summed it all up, "she's a very good diplomat, only she's not very diplomatic."[50]

But was this really, as Helen Lawrenson later wrote, "one wisecrack too many," one that "ruined her career"? Almost certainly not. It seems Luce had decided that she did not want the Brazil post after all. March 1959 was a time in Luce's life when she was beset by depression and indecision, as well as migraines and gastric issues; her marriage, always fraught, appeared near collapse. For these reasons, at this juncture she first took LSD, supplied by her therapist (Luce and her husband would both take the drug on multiple occasions, make notes on their experiences having taken it, and believe strongly in its benefits; *Time* and *Life* would devote extensive and favorable coverage to the drug, even after it had been endorsed by the 1960s' counterculture). A few months later, she credited LSD with having repaired her psyche, thus giving her the strength to hash out the terms that saved her marriage—and to walk away from the ambassadorship that she did not want. Along with Harry's public letter, her quip, which she insisted to the reporter was on the record, was her way to back out. Thus *The Ambassadorship That Wasn't* is much more about her indecisiveness, or chronic lack of direction, or willingness to change her mind, and much less about her undisciplined wit.[51]

It is of course speculation, but with the domestic political transition of 1960 Luce probably would have served less than two years in Rio de Janeiro. The Brazil post was also a step down in terms of prestige (a descending glass ceiling we have arguably seen already with Anderson and will again). Nevertheless, a second successful ambassadorship might have solidified her diplomatic credentials and perhaps paved the way for additional prominent public service. Moreover, as it was, this episode certainly did not bolster her reputation. Even if her cutting remark was merely a calculated way to engineer her withdrawal, it confirmed the well-established impression that, for all her talent, she could not control her tongue.

Later Years

By stepping down from the Brazil post, Luce more or less ended her political career. In the 1960s and 1970s, she reinvented herself yet again as a conservative ideologue and pundit. Occasionally, though, she was active on the fringes of foreign policymaking. For example, she was involved with anti-Castro Cuban exile groups, and thus she may have been a source for Senator Kenneth Keating's mysterious charges, leveled well before the 1962 Missile Crisis erupted, that the Soviets were deploying missiles in Cuba.[52]

Luce sponsored the de facto First Lady of South Vietnam, Madame Nhu (Trần Lê Xuân), during her 1963 US speaking tour. Earlier in the year, Nhu had infamously mocked the Buddhist monks in her homeland as having "barbecued" the self-immolated monk, Thích Quảng Đức. She had thereafter continued dispensing her vituperative and sometimes embarrassing rhetoric, often directed against the United States, and thus became a major source of tension between Washington and the regime in Saigon, led by her brother-in-law President Ngô Đình Diệm. Especially while she was in the United States, the problem, according to one US official, was "press magnification of quotable comments by a lady who is unfortunately too beautiful to ignore." Harry Luce's *Time* referred to Madame Nhu—and certainly many in the West saw her—as a "Dragon Lady," the archetypal Asian blend of female seduction and danger first appearing in the 1930s comic strip *Terry and the Pirates*. The good looks, the Catholicism, the acid tongue, even the militant anti-Communism—Ambassador Luce and Madame Nhu had much in common, and perhaps Luce saw in Nhu a kindred spirit. Shortly after the tour, and mere days after Nhu's husband and brother-in-law were assassinated in a military coup, Luce published a spirited if specious defense of Nhu in the *National Review*. She offered to "adopt" Nhu when the latter's father vowed to disown her after one of her offensive utterances. Later, Luce gave Nhu advice about her proposed memoirs. As beautiful, independent, outspoken women, they were also linked in the minds of some traditional nonfeminists, such as First Lady Jacqueline Kennedy. Why do "these women," she asked herself in a 1964 interview, "have this queer thing for power?" Nhu, and by extension Luce, struck her and her husband as embodying everything "unattractive in a woman." JFK theorized that they resented having to depend on men for their power and thus hated them. "I wouldn't be surprised," Ms. Kennedy whispered, "if they were lesbians."[53]

Luce considered a run for US Senate in New York on the Conservative Party ticket in 1964 but decided to move west with her husband when he retired that same year. After Harry died in 1967, she moved to Hawai'i and hosted a sort of salon for prominent political figures, such as Henry Kissinger and Ronald and Nancy Reagan, when they crossed the Pacific. Richard Nixon offered her a post as US member of the Executive Board of UNESCO, but she wanted to remain in Hawai'i and, at sixty-five, she felt too old and tired. She did go on to serve on the President's Foreign Intelligence Advisory Board under Presidents Nixon, Ford, and Reagan (1973–1977, 1981–1986) and in 1976 was a founding member of the second Committee on the Present Danger. In her last few years, Luce moved back to Washington, DC, where she died in 1987, of brain cancer, at the age of eighty-four.[54]

Assessments

Evaluations of Luce's performance were, and have been, mixed, although those given by FSOs were generally favorable. Looking back, six of nine low- to mid-level FSOs from the Rome embassy interviewed praised Luce. The dissenters criticized her as a figurehead due to absenteeism; a "cruel woman" (for publicly chastising a subordinate); and more an authoritarian than a team-player. The majority of this admittedly small sample hailed the ambassador as intelligent, "capable and tough," "assertive, incisive, and energetic," "charming . . . [but] made of flint, if not stainless steel," "intellectually curious," with a "steeltrap mind," and representing "the very definition of the word 'charisma.'" The criticisms, moreover, tended to be narrower in scope, the compliments broader.[55]

The Foreign Service inspection of the Rome embassy in 1955 was rather favorable. Morale was "reasonably good"; this is compared to 1952, when inspectors had found room for improvement. The disparities in privileges granted (the same issue Anderson encountered in Copenhagen), which had affected morale, had been corrected. Inspectors noted the rarity of cliques, and no staffers felt second-class. And, despite an "average" quality staff that cuts had reduced to an "absolute minimum," both the ambassador and the political section were lauded for their political reporting. Luce was praised as "highly respected" and for providing "outstanding" representation."[56]

Higher up the food chain, opinions were more varied. Not quite one year after her arrival in Italy, two assistant secretaries of state ranked Luce only "adequate" and "adequate or more than adequate," respectively, on the scale

"Outstanding-Good-Adequate-Inadequate." One British ambassador in Rome, Victor Mallet, although writing after only about three months' exposure to her, described Luce as "able and ambitious," with "a good deal of charm to mix with her not too profound intelligence." He believed the Italians would have preferred a man, but she might recover from "a rather bad start," clearly a reference to such incidents as the Milan speech. Mallet's successor, Ambassador Clarke, noted in mid-1954 the troubles Luce's inexperience caused her but found her an intelligent and stimulating partner. She was also being worn down by having to perform both ambassadorial and spousal duties. In 1955, Clarke wrote that in the intervening year, Luce had "grown in stature," although she was still "a little dramatic." His last report on her, a few months before she resigned, declared her still "a good colleague within the limits which her very busy life imposes."[57]

Chief *New York Times* foreign correspondent C. L. Sulzberger, who was prejudiced against Luce, wanted to visit Italy to test her fearful claims about Italian Communism. When he dined with her in March 1954, he was "appalled." Beneath her beauty, he found the "most arrogant conceit" and "ruthlessly hard-boiled self-assurance" he had ever seen. She seemed to think she could quickly manipulate anyone through flattery. She would fish for praise from subordinates like Durbrow, and they would dutifully supply it. The journalist wondered how she gathered information, since she talked nonstop and thus had no opportunity to listen.[58]

Luce believed she had performed fairly well. Around 1959–1960, shortly after avoiding Brazil, she placed a male ambassador at the center of her treatment for a television drama (never produced). "The Diplomat," as Luce envisioned it, appears to have been an overly earnest, pedantic vehicle for promoting the Foreign Service, a sort of *Dragnet* for envoys. The core of the plot was the title character promoting US interests "in a world of ignorant, foolish or inimical people." He handled these "with patient, tired good humor. And he does not always win." If this was autobiographical, even in part, it captures Luce's transition away from her well-known arrogance toward the modesty increasingly apparent as she reflected on her career. When asked in 1973 what her greatest achievement had been as ambassador, she replied, "That I didn't make anyone ashamed that a woman had been made Ambassador. And, then, Trieste. Unquestionably. . . . I think." She concluded, "I was a good Ambassador." On the wall of her drawing room in Hawai'i hung a portrait René Bouché had painted of Luce as ambassador, wearing a cape and her Italian Grand Star medal.[59]

On balance, Luce was justly proud; her ambassadorship should be acknowledged for both its contribution to gender advancement and its diplomatic substance. Luce still served early enough for a poor or mediocre performance on her part to have stymied progress. She was likely not the best of the early female envoys; she certainly had her share of flaws. She worried too much and talked too much; at times she represented the Italian government's positions too zealously. But she was also competent and hardworking. She kept her post for almost four years and was offered a second one. Compared to the other female ambassadors of her era, she also had the most challenging portfolio, and by successfully managing it she did her part to help erode male dominance of the diplomatic field. As for the diplomacy, it is true that Luce did not succeed in reshaping Italian politics as she had hoped, but she did win over a tough crowd, helped sustain a friendly relationship between Washington and Rome, played a major role in resolving the Trieste issue, and demonstrated some ability to adapt (despite her generally uncompromising views). Finally, while ambassador she did manage to keep in check the acid tongue so vital in building and sustaining her multifaceted career.

More broadly, Clare Boothe Luce's life did not want for variety, or for that matter, contradiction. "Living in a sense between eras, she was a feminist who nevertheless relied heavily on strong men," wrote *Time* editor Henry Grunwald. "Her versatility—journalist, playwright, politician, proselytizer"—he omitted *diplomat*—"meant that she had not pursued any one career to the fullest. But the mixture was stunning." When Luce looked back on her life, she had her regrets, despite her self-assurance, and chief among those were her career choices—or perhaps, her refusal or inability to choose a career—despite a successful ambassadorship lying prominently among them. "I would have liked to have been a good writer," she told an interviewer as she turned seventy, which she would have measured with a Nobel Prize. "That, I would have considered a success." No mention of the ambassadorship. She had aimed for the top. But she concluded, "I suppose . . . I suppose I aspired too high." Perhaps that's why she did not consider herself a success, at least not completely. At one point, she considered writing her memoirs and calling them "Confessions of an Unsuccessful Woman." Historians need not be quite so harsh.[60]

Frances E. Willis

Switzerland, 1953–1957, Norway, 1957–1961, and Ceylon, 1961–1964

The Minister left last night. I have assumed charge. Willis.
—cable from US legation Stockholm to State Department,
October 12, 1932

Who is Willis?
—Secretary of State Henry L. Stimson, after reading the cable

On the evening of July 21, 1955, Switzerland's President Max Petitpierre hosted a formal dinner party at the neoclassical Palais Eynard in Geneva. His esteemed guests included Soviet premier Nikolai Bulganin; British prime minister Anthony Eden; French prime minister Edgar Faure; and US president Dwight Eisenhower. They had come for a summit meeting, one that dominated international headlines—and small wonder. It had been ten years since the last such meeting, in the Berlin suburb of Potsdam, where the leaders of the victorious Grand Alliance held their last meeting of World War II. Now, that alliance having collapsed into bitter enmity, after the death of Josef Stalin East–West relations had nevertheless thawed sufficiently to permit this gathering. The dinner party was men only—forty of them—with one exception. The forty-first guest had a clutch in her hand: fifty-six-year-old Frances E. Willis, US ambassador to Switzerland. As the ranking US representative in the host country, she had been required by protocol to introduce Presidents Petitpierre and Eisenhower when the latter arrived at the airport five days earlier. And now, at the gala, wearing the one gown in the sea of tuxedos, Willis was translating for the Swiss and American leaders.[1]

In one sense, even if only for a fleeting moment, Willis's patience was now being rewarded. For the ambassadorship that brought her onto this stage was not a patronage appointment for political work in the United States but rather the result of a painstaking, twenty-five-year slog over formidable obstacles through the career Foreign Service, one that began with Willis's appointment as a lowly FSO-unclassified in a Chilean seaport. When someone remarked to Ambassador Willis that a "lot of women would like to be in your shoes," she replied, "It took me long enough to get into them!" That is, Willis was a pioneer of a type very different from Ruth Bryan Owen. And now she was afforded the chance to commit the ultimate gender intrusion, as the one woman allowed into the stag affair attended by the most powerful men on the planet.[2]

Yet the party also captures Willis's professional conditioning. Eight years later, when she was ambassador to Ceylon, an interviewer would ask her if she could recall any especially exciting moments in her career. She cited Geneva 1955, closing her eyes, in the words of the reporter, "as if recalling the intensely magnetic nature" of such an important gathering. And still, the relentlessly diplomatic professional she was, she could only bring herself to relate the banality that it had been "an exciting experience." So it was also in her private letter home and another interview about other vignettes from Geneva, such as conversing at lunch with Soviet marshal Georgy Zhukov, the great hero of the Great Patriotic War. In her retelling, the meal had entailed "animated conversation but nothing political," although in an interview she did allow that they discussed his daughters and horseback riding. Being allowed to sit with the US delegation at the very last meeting in the Palais des Nations was "all very interesting." We will probably never know what Willis really thought or felt about these moments. She kept no diary; she wrote no memoir; her many letters home now available to researchers are mostly circumspect. The professionalism that had facilitated her rise through the ranks to become the first female American chief of mission to emerge from the Foreign Service was the same trait that prevented her from revealing virtually anything about one of that career's obvious highpoints.[3]

Willis's Early Career

Willis was born in May 1899 in Metropolis, Illinois, but moved with her family to Memphis, Tennessee; Kenosha, Wisconsin; and finally Redlands, California. She graduated from Stanford University with a BA (1920) and a PhD

(1923), writing her dissertation on the Belgian parliamentary system. Teaching positions in political science at Goucher and Vassar Colleges followed, but Willis decided, "I ought to know more about government than I had learned from books." Also, she disliked what she saw as the isolationist direction of US foreign relations in the 1920s. Thus motivated, she took, and passed, the Foreign Service entrance examinations in 1927, becoming only the third woman to do so. Her high level of education and study abroad had no doubt equipped her well. Apparently she planned to spend only a few years as a Foreign Service Officer (FSO), but she would find the work simply too interesting to give up.[4]

During the first two decades of her career, however, and even before she was appointed, Willis frequently encountered the hostility toward women described in chapter 1, tempered by occasional support. Old Hand William Castle's account of a meeting of the five-member Foreign Service Personnel Board in May 1927 is worth quoting at length.

> There was only one bad row in the board and that was when I insisted on admitting a lady [Willis]. She was by far, at least in intellectual equipment, the best candidate we had examined and she was, furthermore, very presentable, obviously efficient and calm. [Wilbur H.] Carr and [Edward J.] Norton insisted on marking her way down because they do not want women in the Service. I pointed out that this seemed to me entirely dishonest, that, furthermore, it was breaking the law inasmuch as we were compelled to accept women if they came up to the standard. Carr said that they never did come up to the standard and that, therefore, we should always throw them down. I asked him whether he thought it was fair to let the regulations stand as they are, to let women spend a year or two studying for the Service when there was absolutely no chance of their getting in. He admitted that it was not fair, but that there were the higher interests of the Service to be considered. We had a pretty hot discussion about the matter and finally the Civil Service man, who had been inclined at first to agree with Carr and Norton, switched over and agreed with Joe [Grew, committee chair, now obviously more open to admitting women] and me so we won out.

That is how close Frances Willis came to remaining a college professor, despite having passed the entrance examinations and impressed in the interview. After she completed her training, department officials noticed that another class member, Paul Daniels, was smitten with Willis and had proposed marriage. He apparently wrote on his post preference form, "Wherever Frances Willis is posted." Department officials could have ignored this information, but they chose to act on it, taking the unusual step of assigning them both to the same post in Chile, obviously hoping they would marry so they could dismiss her from the service.[5]

Willis's first assignment was as an FSO-unclassified performing consular work in the city of Valparaíso (1928). She was allegedly asked what she would do when approached by a drunken sailor, swearing at her. "I'll learn a lot more words," she replied. Before too long, Willis began to stand out for her ability, not just her sex. A Foreign Service Inspector noted in July 1930 that she was the only one of the three FSOs present pulling her weight and commended her for her attitude and performance.[6]

From there her slow ascent through the ranks continued, first in the embassy in Stockholm, to which she was transferred in 1931. There, she found that one of the Old Hands' claims had merit: as she admitted to the British minister—who gratuitously described her as being "of the slightly masculine schoolmarm type"—her sex reduced her usefulness outside the legation by 100 percent. However, the US legation's small size gave Willis the opportunity for her first "first." In October 1932, with her superiors away, she became the first woman ever in the Foreign Service to serve as chargé d'affaires ad interim, which produced considerable publicity.[7]

In 1934, Willis was transferred to Belgium, where she served for six years under four different chiefs, including Old Hand Hugh Gibson. By 1940, despite having reached the rank of second secretary, after a dozen years and four promotions Willis still privately suspected that she was being given more than her share of the embassy busywork. As we have seen, the Brussels assignment placed her squarely in the path of the Blitzkrieg in 1940, and again she filled in as chargé, with such duties as filing a complaint with the German occupation authorities.[8]

From there it was on to Spain. Neutral, wartime Spain was a hotbed of intelligence activity on both sides, and the US embassy served as a listening post. Myriad issues arose that added to the responsibilities of American personnel—apparently including, after mid-January 1944, Frances Willis. She was assigned duties with "The Pond," a secret US intelligence agency (1942–1955) separate from the (CIA-precursor) Office of Strategic Services

and run by John "Frenchy" Grombach. It often relied on FSOs as case officers to handle intelligence jobs for the State and War Departments (and later,
the CIA). We do not know what Willis did in The Pond; her work probably
included some role in escorting downed American pilots and Free French
agents across Spain to Gibraltar, a task that entailed significant physical risk.
Her official FSO duties already included serving as courier with the diplo
matic pouch within Spain, so perhaps her assignment to The Pond made
sense. Regardless, we can assume her selection further attests to her competence and reliability.[9]

For roughly the first fifteen years of her career, two basic trends marked
Willis's path. First, her performance was good enough to warrant mostly
positive, sometimes glowing reviews from the chiefs of mission above her and
good enough to produce repeated, if slow, promotions. Second, however,
many of her evaluations were tempered either by criticism or faint praise, or,
in the case of the all-important final versions, were produced by anonymous
State Department evaluators whose summary evaluations graded her significantly more harshly than had the individual evaluations they summarized.
Her career was in serious danger of plateauing when, in 1944, she was
detailed to the Department in Washington and was named assistant to the
undersecretary of state. The undersecretary who chose her: none other than
the ultimate Old Hand, Joseph Grew, one who had helped admit her to the
service in 1927. Grew and his successor, Dean Acheson, found Willis an outstanding officer, and, with their clout, they reset her career on an upward
trajectory. She was now generally rated "excellent" in her evaluations, and she
was given much greater responsibility, first in the Division of Western European Affairs (1946–1947), then as a first secretary in a major embassy (London, 1947–1951). By 1950, her reputation was such that two chiefs requested
her to serve as their DCM; John Moors Cabot, who would later be sent to
Rio de Janeiro, when Clare Luce withdrew, won the contest and got Willis in
Helsinki. Shortly after arriving, she was promoted to Foreign Service Class I,
the highest FSO rank and the equivalent of major general in the US Army.[10]

Switzerland, 1953–1957

Willis's breakthrough to the top came in 1953. It had taken twenty-five years;
several male colleagues who entered the Foreign Service around the same
time as Willis had been named chiefs years before she was. Ellis Briggs, for

example, entered two years before Willis but landed his first ambassadorship nine years before she did. President Eisenhower chose Willis as ambassador to Switzerland, an interesting move, considering that Swiss women did not yet enjoy the right to vote (they would not win it at the federal level until 1971, due partly to the structural difficulty of amending the Swiss constitution). This drew the attention of many newspapers, including the *New York Post,* which, in its inimitable style, led with the headline "Lady Envoy to Vote-less Gals." But thereafter, Willis was not terribly well known, certainly compared to her contemporary, Clare Boothe Luce. In 1957, Willis appeared on *What's My Line?*—one would think this a sign, in the American 1950s, that she had arrived—but its panelists failed to guess her profession even without their usual blindfolds and even having been given Willis's name.[11]

The immediate American reaction to the announcement was mixed; women's groups applauded, while at least a few observers were opposed. The vice president of a Seattle bank protested in a letter to Eisenhower that the appointment was an insult to the Swiss, an act for which he could see no justification "except that it may gratify the malicious desires of a few meddling feminists in this country."[12]

Needless to say, Willis's appointment did not result from some great feminist project in the Eisenhower administration. Secretary of State Dulles would later appear proud of having appointed the first career ambassador who was a woman and indeed would call for more female ambassadors, but he chose Willis in spite of her sex and in spite of the disenfranchisement of Swiss women, not because of these factors. He calculated, correctly, that the Swiss would not formally object to a female envoy. Bern, the capital city, of course echoed with rumors of official dissatisfaction—some of them false, and, along with a leak about the selection itself, possibly intended to scuttle the nomination—but after hosting a political appointee, the Swiss were relatively satisfied to be receiving a professional. The Swiss minister in Washington reported collecting "excellent" reviews of her and praised her "character and intelligence, competence and simple ways." The Swiss foreign ministry thus recommended accepting her, which Bern did, followed by unanimous US Senate confirmation on July 20, 1953.[13]

Rather than a feminist plot, Willis's assignment to Bern should be seen as part of the pattern: this was now five out of six female chiefs assigned to northern and western European countries considered in Washington to be of low importance. It is true that almost all first ambassadorships for career

FSOs were not the most prestigious. Nevertheless, the Dulles who sang Willis's praises was the same Dulles who would later describe Bern to which he sent her as "a rather dull, sleepy place . . . out of the mainstream of current political events," the ambassadorship there "not much of a job."[14]

Predictions of widespread negative Swiss reaction to the appointment seem to have been unwarranted. One Swiss satirical magazine did paint it as a scheme to enfranchise Swiss women, and both sides in the nation's internal debate over women's suffrage made use of it. But when Willis presented her credentials in October, the subject did not arise at her forty-five-minute press conference after the ceremony (although it would on subsequent occasions). Coverage of the ceremony and the press conference were mostly friendly, the remainder being factual rather than negative. The Communist press ignored her presence, in marked contrast to Luce's reception by far left Italian press organs.[15]

When asked for any advice she could give to Swiss women seeking the vote, Willis demurred, saying she had no right to interfere in Switzerland's internal affairs. She did add that she personally disapproved of the Swiss policy, but her job was limited to representing her country. Reporters often sought her views on Swiss women's suffrage, she said in 1954, "but I have not been in the Foreign Service 27 years for nothing." She would answer that she wanted her Bern appointment to last, and the speediest way to end it "was to get mixed up in the internal politics of the country."[16]

Swiss Watches

Willis, however, could not help but become embroiled in the matter of Swiss timepieces. In July 1954, President Eisenhower approved a 50 percent increase in the duties on Swiss watches and watch movements. After World War II, Swiss watch movement exports to the United States had soared, their value amounting to over one-half of all Swiss exports to the United States and one-third of all Swiss watch movement exports. The US watch industry claimed it had suffered grave damage and for years lobbied the government, seeking protection. Eisenhower, in part buying exaggerated claims that preserving existing American watchmakers' jobs (and their skills) was necessary for national defense, obliged them.[17]

The Swiss reaction was swift. The legation in Washington declared the tariff hike "a serious blow" not only to Swiss–US relations but also "the very principle of freedom of trade." The latter point hinted at disgust, soon seen well beyond Switzerland, at Washington's apparent hypocrisy—extoling the sanctity of free commerce one moment, jacking tariffs the next. Swiss petitions circulated demanding official retaliation, and three thousand Swiss watchmakers launched a "Don't Buy American" week (although, lacking official support, such boycotts did not last).[18]

Willis obviously found herself in a difficult position. She had argued strongly to the president against the tariff increase, but now, like any good diplomat, she carefully explained the new policy to the angry Swiss. And yet, she also managed to maintain cordial relations with them throughout the episode. This was no doubt in part because, although she had failed to thwart the tariff increase in the first instance, she soon managed to help mollify Bern in the second. For American watchmakers did not rest on their laurels; they now sought imposition of import quotas on top of the higher tariff. Together with State Department officials and presidential advisor Nelson Rockefeller, Willis succeeded in blocking the move. The Swiss Foreign Office summed up its view publicly: "Ambassador Willis has judiciously discharged the function of a diplomat to act as a shock absorber." US officials too approved of their envoy's performance. An assistant secretary of state sent Dulles a memo, the sole purpose of which was to declare Willis an ambassador "par excellence," one who had "represented our Government under particularly trying circumstances with distinction."[19]

Likewise, her efforts in Bern overall earned rave reviews. "Miss Willis," in the words of a State Department evaluation (1954), "gets a very high rating from all sources"; another, sorting twenty-seven chiefs in Europe into the categories "outstanding," "good," "adequate," and "inadequate," listed Willis as "good." In mid-1955, she was appointed career minister, the equivalent of a three-star general and requiring Senate and presidential approval. Any misgivings Swiss officialdom had in 1953 seem to have dissipated by the time of her departure in 1957, for it is abundantly clear that the Swiss had come to appreciate her deeply and were genuinely disappointed to be losing her. All seven of Switzerland's ruling federal councilors attended her farewell luncheon, an unprecedented gesture.[20]

Norway, 1957–1961

By late 1956, Willis's stint in Bern was coming up on four years, a standard tour at the time. Dulles rejected the suggestion that Willis be considered for the ambassadorship to Poland. Poland, after all, lay behind the Iron Curtain, not in northern or western Europe. In early 1957, Willis was told she would be remaining in Bern. But then, the administration wanted a spot for a political appointee, former journalist Henry J. Taylor, a friend of the president. It suggested Norway, but he preferred Switzerland, so it solved the problem by bumping Willis to Norway. According to her DCM, Willis was furious, not because of the transfer but because of the reason behind it. Norway was a step up in terms of prestige, for it was a Cold War ally of considerable strategic importance to the United States, but it was deemed a secondary partner. Along with this lower status, moreover, Norway shared with the rest of Scandinavia a reputation for high levels of female inclusion and equality. With Owen, Harriman, and Anderson already having gone to the region, a small pattern was emerging. Eisenhower had merely confirmed it when, in a 1955 memo to Dulles, he discussed the possibility of placing another female ambassador "in the Scandinavian countries, or possibly in Belgium, or in any other place where we think a woman could appropriately serve." Shifting Willis to a post such as Norway, and not Poland, was thus entirely predictable.[21]

It did not hurt Willis that she was now the second American woman headed to Oslo, treading in the footsteps Florence Harriman had left twenty years earlier. Norway probably had a reputation by now; Finland and Austria sent their only female chiefs to Oslo as well—although Norway had not yet sent a woman of its own abroad.

Willis's time in Norway was relatively uneventful. In June 1959, the Americans' morale improved somewhat when they occupied the new, modernist, three-sided embassy chancery at Henrik Ibsen gate 48 designed by Finnish American architect Eero Saarinen. The following year, a press report had Willis snubbing the first deputy premier of the USSR, Anastas Mikoyan, at the opening of a Soviet exhibition in Oslo; fortunately, this was mistaken, and eyewitnesses could attest to the story's inaccuracy. Finally, Willis was appointed to serve as a representative on the US delegation to the United Nations for the last four months of 1960.[22]

Commensurate with Norway's greater importance in Washington, however, Willis faced a new set of responsibilities in Oslo. Like Denmark, Norway after World War II had gradually shed its traditional neutrality and joined NATO. Norway's political importance in the region expanded, since Denmark and Iceland followed its lead within the alliance. It too was strategically located, bordering on the Soviet Union in the far north and, in this thermonuclear age, lying directly astride the shortest path for bombers and missiles between the United States and the Soviet Union. Norway's roles in intelligence, reconnaissance, and naval affairs—the Soviet Navy was building up in the Barents Sea, and responsibility for matching it passed from the Royal Navy to the US Navy—all grew significantly in the late 1950s. Thus did Willis's mission include a Military Assistance Advisory Group, and her duties included liaising with NATO's Northern Command.[23]

Willis succeeded in promoting the growth of Norwegian confidence in the security provided by the western alliance. She recommended speedy conclusion of a bilateral agreement on a jointly financed shipbuilding program for the Royal Norwegian Navy, a recommendation followed within six months. More broadly and more subtly, Willis helped assuage Oslo's fears of being dragged into World War III, especially since the Eisenhower administration had significantly increased US reliance on the rapidly growing nuclear arsenal under its New Look doctrine. In short, Willis recognized Norway's growing importance in NATO and helped successfully manage that transition.[24]

Ceylon, 1961–1964

Willis served in Oslo until 1961, when John F. Kennedy sent her to her last posting, Ceylon (then still a British dominion, renamed Sri Lanka in 1972). She was sad to leave Oslo. But finally, at least, she was realizing a career-long dream of a posting in Asia.[25]

One of Willis's predecessors in Ceylon served as a painful reminder of the price the United States sometimes paid for allowing amateurs to serve as chiefs of mission. Maxwell Henry Gluck—self-made millionaire founder of the Darling Stores Corporation, Kentucky horse breeder, and heavy contributor to Eisenhower's campaigns—was nominated ambassador to Ceylon in 1957. His confirmation hearing could have gone better.

> J. William Fulbright: What are the problems in Ceylon you think you can deal with?
>
> Gluck: One of the problems are the people there. I believe I can—I think I can establish, unless we—again, unless I run into something that I have not run into before—a good relationship and good feeling toward the United States.

FULBRIGHT: Do you know our ambassador to India?

GLUCK: I know John Sherman Cooper, the previous ambassador.

FULBRIGHT: Do you know who the prime minister of India is?

GLUCK: Yes, but I can't pronounce his name.

FULBRIGHT: Do you know who the prime minister of Ceylon is?

GLUCK: His name is unfamiliar now, I cannot call it off.

(Ceylon's prime minister, S. W. R. D. Bandaranaike, reputedly responded that he did not know how to pronounce Gluck's name either.) Gluck gained such infamy that he later counted as one of Richard Hofstadter's poster children (or more precisely, "Exhibit C") in his indictment of *Anti-Intellectualism in American Life* (1963). Gluck lasted one year and sixteen days in his position. Ellis Briggs later lamented how often the State Department "condoned the dispatch abroad of ambassadors whose qualifications for diplomacy have approximated those of an amputee for ballet dancing." Even though two ambassadors came between Gluck and Willis, he still warranted mention in the Ceylonese press at the time of her appointment. The good news, if one can call it that, is that this sort of predecessor made it easy for Willis to shine.[26]

Consistent with the low priority Kennedy assigned such appointments, the appointment of Frances Willis as ambassador to Ceylon was the routine reassignment of a career diplomat from one secondary post to another, determined wholly within the State Department. This did represent a geographic first—the United States had never sent a woman to Asia—and Ceylon, with its strategic location and neutral status in the Cold War, was a country of moderate importance in Washington. However, for Willis if anything it was a step backward in terms of prestige. She, after all, in 1962 would be one of only seven diplomats honored with the rank of career ambassador, and yet, as one of her DCMs argued, Ceylon was an appropriate first post, not the capstone of a distinguished career. Moreover, it was no coincidence that Ceylon was the country led at the time by the world's first female prime minister, Sirimavo Bandaranaike, who came to power in 1960 after her husband's assassination. Just as presidents sent African American diplomats in this period almost exclusively to African and Caribbean nations, so did they send first Mesta, and now Willis, to countries led by women.[27]

Frances E. Willis, ambassador to Switzerland (1953–1957), Norway (1957–1961), and Ceylon (1961–1964) with President John F. Kennedy, 1961. Willis was the first woman ambassador to emerge from the career Foreign Service, a difficult journey that took twenty-five years. (Abbie Rowe, White House Photographs, John F. Kennedy Presidential Library and Museum)

Bandaranaike led a young nation, which had gained its independence from Great Britain only in 1948. Her government and its predecessors had pushed the country sharply to the left, including nationalization of several economic sectors. And with its ethnic tensions between Sinhalese and Tamils, its Buddhist majority, its underdeveloped economy, and its equatorial climate, Ceylon really was a long way from western Europe. When Ceylon welcomed John Glenn's *Friendship 7* spacecraft while on its "fourth orbit," a world tour, elephants unloaded it. Willis had to acquire an entirely new wardrobe, and her residence featured "a beautiful garden filled with exotic birds and an occasional monkey." This was a very different posting for her in many ways—and probably her toughest.[28]

The *Washington Post* declared it "especially fitting" to send a female ambassador to a female prime minister, and Bandaranaike expressed her "special pleasure" to the Americans over their appointment of a woman. But Willis's successor in Colombo recalled that the prime minister objected to it, thinking it "almost patronizing," which, of course, it was. And later, Willis did not believe the gender alignment had improved her access to the prime minister.[29]

Willis's habit was to try to learn at least some of the language of every host country to which she was assigned, and she decided to tackle Sinhala, with its fifty-four-character alphabet and high level of difficulty for westerners. She always believed, like the British ambassador in Copenhagen had, that one cannot fully understand a country without speaking its language. She was especially motivated in this case. "Maybe there is some post in the world where not a single American on the staff speaks the language," she had written privately when disdaining *The Ugly American* (Eugene Burdick and William Lederer's bestselling 1958 novel and harsh take-down of US blundering in the developing world, in her view a "grossly exaggerated . . . caricature"), "but I doubt it." To her horror, in Colombo she found one such embassy—in which no American could either speak or read the local language—and now it was hers. Typically, she resolved to do something about it herself.[30]

US–Ceylonese relations had hit a rough patch in the early 1960s; Ceylon's socialist government and its relatively close relations with Moscow and Beijing concerned Washington. The main problem on Willis's watch was Bandaranaike's expropriation of 108 gas stations owned by the American firms Caltex and Esso. Under Article 620(e) of the Foreign Assistance Act of 1962, aka the Hickenlooper Amendment, US aid was to be severed to any country that seized American-owned property absent fair or timely compensation, which in this case Ceylon had not provided. Willis tried to dissuade Washington from carrying out the suspension, but she did not succeed, although she did persuade the State Department to preserve funding for academic exchanges. In February 1963, she informed the Ceylonese of the cut off, which meant that twenty-eight US aid technicians were withdrawn and $3.9 million in loans and grants suspended.[31]

The reaction in Ceylon was fierce. "Ceylon is not prepared to dance to the tune of the capitalist countries to obtain aid!" Bandaranaike exclaimed. The extreme left organized a "Down with America" rally at Galle Face Green, where thousands of protesters held up such signs as "Willis Ain't Willing" and "Miss Willis Go, Compensation No." A coffin marked "Oil Companies" was carried to the beach and, after a monk performed a mock ritual, cast into the sea. Both Uncle Sam and "Auntie Willis" were burned in effigy. Yet Willis remained as cool and professional as ever. A State Department evaluation lauded her for "handling [a] difficult situation with great skill, even though she disagrees with the Department's policy line on aid to Ceylon."[32]

Serving in a less stable country in the developing world added another layer of difficulty to Willis's work—especially when compounded by the spouse issue. A visiting assistant secretary of state, Phillips Talbot, reported on a dinner party for eighteen Willis had arranged and now had to host in the middle of a power outage caused by a labor strike. First, Willis wondered whether she could claim a tax deduction for the business loss of over $6,000 (in today's dollars) worth of frozen food, which was now spoiled. Then, with guests cancelling, not keeping Willis informed as to their attendance, or showing up unannounced at the last minute, the "never-never-land atmosphere of Ceylon was reinforced." The ambassador admitted to Talbot that "she had never seen such a game of musical chairs at a dinner table—and all done by candlelight without fans or air conditioners. Ah, Ceylon!"[33]

It was from the Ceylon assignment that Willis finally retired in 1964, after thirty-seven years in the Foreign Service. In retirement, she performed contract work for the State Department (e.g., at the United Nations), lectured, and traveled. In 1974, she suffered a stroke and thereafter experienced worsening aphasia and memory loss. She died in her longtime hometown of Redlands, California, in 1983, at the age of eighty-four.[34]

Willis's Experiences as a Female Diplomat

Willis faced much of what one might expect for one of the few women in the career Foreign Service. First, and most obviously, she was treated differently because she was a woman, although throughout her career and even after her retirement, she steadfastly denied that the State Department discriminated against women. Willis's stock response when asked was, "I have been discriminated for—not against." Once she denied even seeing any discrimination. This was true, in one sense: some of the worst discrimination she underwent was carried out in her confidential evaluations, which she never saw. After another denial that Foreign Service women faced discrimination, she added that they "just don't last long enough to reach the top." Yes, but they failed to "last long enough" at least in part because of discrimination, especially in the form of the marriage ban. In a 1951 speech in Helsinki, she went even further, declaring, "Women will have to do a better job of staying in the Service if any is ever to reach the top." This comes perilously close to victim-blaming. In Switzerland, she even made the patently false claim that her promotions progressed just as those of her male colleagues had (and that is something she could verify, as she could note the relative progress of her peers). For example, at the very beginning of her career, she was promoted from FSO-unclassified (a probationary rank) to vice consul after three and a half years, whereas it normally took one year.[35]

She also denied that women were exiled to obscure posts, which in fact they usually were, depending on one's definition of *obscure*. The State Department and successive presidential administrations did not discriminate so much, of course, that they refused Willis ambassadorships; indeed, one should note that most Foreign Service men never receive an ambassadorship, much less three of them. But they did discriminate to the extent that they confined Willis to posts that were, in official Washington, not prestigious, desirable, or important—not even progressive steps up from one to the next.[36]

After retiring, Willis did awkwardly soften the old denials: there was no discrimination, "but there are plenty of prejudiced individuals." The question then becomes, at what point does the number of prejudiced individuals and their actions constitute discrimination? Publicly, Willis seems to have denied the existence of discrimination, either by unreasonably generalizing from a single case—her own—or by resorting to semantic evasion.[37]

More important, her personal correspondence, although by no means rife with tales of oppression, tells a story different from her public claims. Here we see, for example, after nearly a decade on the job, Willis noting that her superiors "are always prejudiced against me to begin with and it takes long hard work to break down the prejudice." Indeed, more openminded superiors warranted specific mention as such. When she arrived at her new post in Madrid in 1940, she wrote home about having been met by "that same unmistakable misgiving over having a woman on the staff under what I now find a somewhat sticky veneer of cordiality." Some of the prejudice came from women, in one case from the US ambassador's wife, who told Willis in "no uncertain terms" that she opposed the admission of women into the Foreign Service.[38]

Willis was also subjected to other treatment that her male colleagues were not, some arguably little more than a nuisance but noteworthy nonetheless. A female diplomat was rare enough that she was sometimes mistaken for a diplomat's wife. Similarly, Willis was saddled with additional concerns about appearances, especially to avoid suspicions of romantic involvement with male colleagues. Such appearances had incomparably graver implications for her than for the men, so she had to be especially careful.[39]

Moreover, on the job she feared that concerns about her safety during periods of international tension, for example, the Munich crisis of 1938, would lead to her transfer. To the contrary, Willis would have numerous opportunities to demonstrate her physical courage. As we have seen, she was on duty in Brussels on May 10, 1940, when the German Blitzkrieg swept through the Low Countries and bombs fell three hundred feet from the US embassy grounds. For two months, she and the rest of the staff remained in limbo, cut off from all contact with the outside world, before being allowed safe passage out, but she stoically stuck it out with the others. Moreover, a subordinate from the Ceylon embassy recalled years later that Willis won additional respect from her staff for her coolness during the Cuban missile crisis of 1962, a hectic, tense episode even for embassies far removed from the Caribbean.[40]

The novelty of her career ensured Willis a considerable amount of press coverage for a career diplomat, which, as with the other women, was sexist. This included photo captions describing her "primly snipping rosebushes" at her California home or adding a "Woman's Touch in Foreign Affairs"; interviewers asking for her reaction to Nikita Khrushchev in "purely feminine terms"—"how does he strike you as a man?"—or inquiring whether she could cook; publishing incessant references to her appearance, clothing, and furnishings; indeed, entire articles with headlines such as "SHE LIKES EMBASSY FIREPLACES AGLOW WITH HOMELIKE COZINESS." To be sure, much of this coverage appeared in the women's columns or society pages of newspapers, which by nature emphasized the domestic. And, Willis contributed to this problem with her typically guarded, stock answer when asked about her hobbies (even though she obviously had some, such as bridge, dancing, and classical music): "A well-run office" and a "well-kept house." Willis thus received more publicity than most other diplomats, but, as it did for her female colleagues, this represented a mixed blessing.[41]

How Did Willis Succeed?

How Willis succeeded—apart from the obvious, her superior performance—is an especially important question because, as stated, all five of the other female chiefs during her career were political appointees. We have seen the sexism they faced, but they entered the diplomatic world at the top. Willis, by contrast, had to work for a quarter-century to reach the ambassadorial level and then had to perform in order to stay there for eleven years, without the benefit of political clout or connections outside the State Department. She achieved so much for several reasons, some obvious, some not, some peculiar to women, some not.

Mentors

First, her career flourished with the help of influential mentors. Willis impressed at least some of the right people, including Joseph Grew and Hugh Gibson. Fortunately for her, Grew and Gibson, along with Norman Armour, were the Old Hands whom in early 1953 Secretary Dulles had asked to advise him on appointments. These "Three Wise Men" placed Willis on their list of recommendations for chiefs of mission, and Dulles acted. Whether he would have done so without their input is highly questionable.[42]

The existence of such mentors does not contradict the above portrait of discrimination; quite the opposite. For Willis was winning over a tough audience, most of all Gibson; especially since she rose through the ranks, she probably contributed even more than the other women to undermining the sexism so prevalent in the diplomatic world. Evidence of this exists from the very beginning of her career. In early 1931, FSO Edward Crocker received word that Willis would be joining him at the US legation in Stockholm. He wrote, "I am entirely against having women in the diplomatic service." One year later, he reported that Willis had arrived the previous week and had impressed everyone with her modesty and lack of affectation: "We are delighted to have her here." More important, both Grew and Gibson, quintessential Old Hands, had at first opposed admitting women into what at that time was a most exclusive club. But clearly, Willis was instrumental in changing Gibson's mind and in confirming to Grew the wisdom of his changing views. In 1944—three years before any member of Willis's 1927 Foreign Service class had made ambassador—Gibson wrote that she already should have been running an embassy. And Grew, asked about her nomination for the Bern post, replied that he thought "nobody could do a better job than she." Willis thus played a demonstrable role in undermining the sexist attitudes prevalent among the diplomatic elite.[43]

Remaining Single and the Spouse Issue

Second, Willis never married, which remained a condition of employment for female FSOs throughout the period of her service. She was engaged to be married when in her late teens, but her fiancé, an American airman in France during World War I, died in a train wreck just after the Armistice. Thereafter she remained single. "I just couldn't see having a husband trail around after me," she recalled in retirement. She enjoyed her life and work so much that she never missed marriage. In addition, Willis must have noticed the fate of most early female FSOs—marriage followed swiftly by resignation—and resolved to preserve her career.[44]

Of course, remaining unmarried denied Willis the many benefits of a Foreign Service spouse. She recognized the problem even before becoming an ambassador, when the need was less acute. "What I really needed was a 'wife,'" she remarked in 1953. Once in charge at Bern, Willis partly compensated by having her aging mother come to live in the embassy with her and fulfill many of the duties usually handled by a spouse (while also allowing Willis to care for her—which, however, presumably meant the net reduction in "workload" may have been minimal). But around the time her mother turned eighty-seven, in 1959, she could no longer assist as hostess (she died the following year), and so the spouse issue returned. Willis apparently relied on her DCM's wife a great deal. But with no spouse at home to receive diplomatic calls while she was at the embassy, she had to set aside one day per week to take care of that—and then, of course, work harder on official business the other days.[45]

Attention to Detail

A third explanation for Willis's survival is her career-long command of the diplomatic rule book. Looking back, colleagues agreed that since men were often seeking to trip her up, she decided early on to protect herself by learning State Department regulations better than anyone else—thus converting the disproportionate time she spent as an administrative officer into an asset—and adhering to them scrupulously. This attention to detail, thoroughness, and propriety helped build her reputation and aided her career. Whether its extent was necessary is of course unknowable, but its existence could only have helped her. For the extremely rare woman in a male-dominated organization, she was certainly not going to thrive as a sloppy maverick.[46]

As she gained seniority, however, Willis's precision evolved into an unwillingness to delegate—and when she did delegate, a tendency to micromanage—the greatest weaknesses in her managerial style. Thus she did not give new officers the benefit of the doubt; they had to prove themselves before she increased their responsibilities. She opened all of the classified incoming mail, and she "had to see every written word that left the embassy," one FSO remembered. Roy Melbourne, Willis's first DCM in Bern, recalls her public affairs officer saying that when the ambassador called him on the phone, he thought, "What have I done wrong now?" This accompanied Willis's enduring attachment to the rules. Her own desire to balance the table at embassy dinners led her to impose on some unlucky embassy couple: they were placed on standby in case another male or female was needed at the last minute (which would then leave the remaining partner in dinner limbo). Willis even insisted that the official US seal be affixed on the new Oslo embassy, in accordance with regulations—over the objections of architect Saarinen, who was trying to preserve the integrity of his design. In at least one case, her reputation as an administrative stickler made her the butt of jokes: the word around the Colombo embassy was that toilet paper in the restrooms was "two-ply and you have to sign the blue copy and send it to Frances."[47]

Some junior officers appreciated the close oversight because they were learning the ropes. But for senior staff, who already knew their jobs, she was a burden. Melbourne recounts his frustration that Willis failed to make use of his (considerable) expertise, although to her credit, when he called her on it after a particularly egregious episode, she apologized and their relationship improved significantly thereafter. Washington noticed the issue; a March 1963 evaluation concluded that, although "she has improved staff morale, there is some criticism over her inclination to exert too tight a rein on subordinates, especially her Agency for International Development Mission, while concerning herself unnecessarily in the details of operations." Obviously, the magnitude of the problem should not be exaggerated, considering how effective the embassies she ran clearly were. But from this angle, her reputation for industry assumes a new, less flattering cast: a good deal of it was effort she could have, and should have, left to staff. This was a minor, but nevertheless unfortunate byproduct of the perfectionism she used to protect herself.[48]

Low-Key Feminism

Fourth, and finally, Willis almost without exception refused to make her sex a public issue, complain about sexism, or promote openly the interests of women (this may help explain why she did not leave behind more indications of the discrimination she faced). It is safe to assume—not surprisingly, there is little direct evidence—that she did this deliberately, understanding that to challenge openly the male chauvinism and discrimination would be counter-productive, self-destructive, or both. Anyone in Willis's time and place unavoidably faced the classic dilemma of working inside the system or outside; she chose the former.

Self-Perception and "the Women's Issue"

This raises the key questions of how Willis understood herself as a woman in a male-dominated institution and how she handled "the women's issue." Posing these questions entails reliance, again, on incomplete or ambiguous evidence. In a rare statement of direct relevance, for example, made at the age of twenty-one, while she was in graduate school, Willis flatly denied that she was a feminist—but this came in the context of her frustration at not being taken seriously by a male classmate. This complexity, even apparent contradiction, marks her entire career, but the overarching reality becomes fairly clear in the form of two Frances Willises: the public Willis, who downplayed her sex and showed no interest in promoting women's equality; and the private Willis, who was highly aware of her gender identity and sought, in her own way, to promote women's equality.[49]

Usually, Willis avoided any public discussion of women's issues and, in fact, tried to avoid discussing the issue of women in the Foreign Service altogether—including during her many speeches before women's groups. She reportedly did not want to address the State Department's conference on "The Role of Women in U.S. Foreign Affairs" in May 1957 because she succeeded based on her ability, not her sex. She ultimately relented and took part—and in her introduction then still rejected the event's entire premise by announcing, "Today I am not going to speak to you as a group of women but as individual citizens." Even more telling, that same month she was asked to preview a draft list of questions an interviewer would pose. The only questions she excised were those that referred to her sex or to women in general.[50]

Even in retirement, Willis was loath to cooperate in accounts of her career, mainly because she objected to articles about women in the Foreign Service in principle (she would doubtless have disapproved of this chapter, if not this entire book). "I went into the Service as an officer," she wrote in 1968, "not as a woman." This more individualistic, less gender-conscious approach was, of course, not unique; most of the first women to enter the British Diplomatic Service (beginning only in 1946) shared it. This had always been her attitude, which she substantiated by citing a formative experience: when she entered the Foreign Service in 1927 as the only woman in her class, she was instantly the object of intense curiosity. After one week, one of the men admitted to her that some of them had had misgivings, "but he added, 'we don't object to you because you take it all as a matter of course.' And so I did for thirty-seven years." Willis hit upon this formula for success and stuck with it so long that it became automatic. But this was a calculated tactic born of necessity, the means toward an end that was, at least in part, feminist (in the sense of promoting women's equality). And despite Willis's avowed preference, those conservative means should not be allowed to obscure that progressive end. Of course, her insistence that she should be judged as an officer, and not as a woman, can itself be seen as feminist.[51]

Moreover, Willis was conscious of established gender roles and knew that she was stepping outside of them, both with her career in general and in individual instances. In her private correspondence she did note when she achieved one of her firsts for women, sometimes with evident pride, despite her subsequent claims to the contrary. Or consider the consciousness that could generate the following account early in her career. "I had such a good time with [a male guest] and some of my confreres" at a Stockholm function, she wrote in 1932, "that I . . . didn't have time to stand around with the women and criticize and admire what people had on." Fragmentary evidence, certainly, but again it suggests a gender awareness at odds with her public persona.[52]

Finally, hints that Willis consciously chose a subtle yet feminist approach emerge from one of her rare encounters with another female officer. FSO Margaret Joy Tibbetts, later another US ambassador to Norway (1964–1969), was assigned in 1949 to the embassy in London, where Willis was a first secretary and Tibbetts's senior. Willis "was very wary of me at first," Tibbetts recalled, "but when she saw that I wasn't going to do the sort of thing that she didn't think was right, she let me go pretty much on my own." Here, it seems that Willis feared that another woman might rock the boat in an assertively feminist way but was relieved to find that Tibbetts shared her views. Tibbetts continued that when she arrived in London, Willis asked her if she was interested in "the women's issue," and advised, "You did the most for women by becoming a competent officer." That Willis would ask the question, and follow with that suggestion in that context, strongly suggests that she had shrewdly chosen an overt/covert approach—nose-to-grindstone, gender-denying on the outside, yet fundamentally, consciously feminist on the inside—and insisted it was the way to go. The evidence is far from conclusive, but it points to Willis having played a role that was, on balance, consciously feminist.[53]

People's Diplomacy

Having been formally trained and indoctrinated in the ways of the Foreign Service, and having spent decades slowly rising within it, Willis did not place quite as much emphasis on people's diplomacy as her predecessors had. She still seems to have engaged in it significantly more than many male colleagues, both career and noncareer, certainly as much as her workaholic's schedule would permit. For example, Willis entertained people from all walks of life. "You can't restrict social activities to those in government only," she said while in Oslo. "It's my job to know the people of the country in general." She also traveled widely and got to know a wider range of people. For example, in Switzerland she paid courtesy calls on officials in cantonal capitals such as Lausanne—partly because Switzerland is a confederation, its twenty-two cantons relatively powerful and important—something ambassadors usually did not do. She also spoke widely and toured many sites, including the small establishments that produced the two-hundred-pound rounds of Swiss cheese. One indication of how a culture of ambassadorial public diplomacy had not yet fully emerged is that, in a national US radio broadcast in which she explained her job, Willis hastened to add that she spent most of her time not away from Bern, but rather in the office.[54]

Protocol

As we have seen, protocol usually caused trouble for female ambassadors, and Willis was no exception. The Swiss were somewhat relieved that Willis was single, obviating the need to accommodate her husband. Because German was one of the country's official languages, her title became a minor issue. *Auf Deutsch,* a male ambassador's title was *Herr Botschafter;* but for Willis, *Frau Botschafter* would not work, because that meant "wife of the ambassador." So instead they went with *Frau Botschafterin,* with the feminine noun ending. In a place like Norway, the related factors could compound, especially from the standpoint of the embassy protocol officer. "Protocol is challenging," one remembered, "when the chief of mission is a single woman, when there is a monarchy with a widower king, when the government is socialist-labor, and when there is abundant aquavit and cold weather." Even at this late date, twenty years after Harriman's presence, slip-ups could occur. After one formal dinner at the Royal Palace hosted by King Olav V, the men were ushered to one room for cigars and brandy, the women to another for coffee, according to long-standing tradition. Ambassador Willis was grouped with the women, but after an interval, the Chief of Protocol came and retrieved her and handed her off to the chamberlain, who then led her to the king, with whom she had a brief chat. More informally, Willis had her uses as a high-ranking (and single) female diplomat. In May 1954, Secretary Dulles was attending the Geneva Conference while Willis was away in Copenhagen. He called her back on a moment's notice, for which she had to take the redeye. One of the reasons: He was hosting a luncheon for the British and French foreign ministers and their wives, Ms. Dulles could not attend, and he needed someone to balance the table.[55]

Willis's Assertiveness

One possible mark against her at the time—although admirable in retrospect—was that Willis does not seem to have eased her ascent with undue deference, obsequiousness, or reticence when interacting with superiors or prominent figures. She was as likely to make wisecracks while showing Clare Boothe Luce around the US embassy compound in Brussels (1940) as she was with peers or subordinates, and she could give as good as she got. In Switzerland in early 1954, she dined with British World War II giant Field Marshal Bernard Montgomery. In her retelling, Monty baited her right away, making "some sweeping statements," one to the effect that "no soldier ever made a good politician or vice versa—it was obvious what he expected me to reply"—considering who had appointed her—"but I looked him in the eye and . . . said 'I cannot agree with you because after all, we began with General Washington.'"[56]

Partly this was her sense about just how far she could go, an awareness present well before she became an ambassador. "I have attended meetings where Frances, the only woman present, quietly and unobtrusively steered the proceedings and moved them along to useful conclusion," a colleague remembered. "Nothing pushy or manipulative, simply a deft touch, good humor, impressive competence and the authority that brings with it." As a chief, Willis could be assertive with foreign leaders; on one occasion, Prime Minister Bandaranaike kept the ambassador waiting so long beyond the time of an appointment, she simply left. She spoke up at meetings of US ambassadors in Europe, and one colleague recalls that the State Department never intimidated her; if she received instructions she found disagreeable, she did not hesitate to cable her objections back to Washington, resistance we have seen in the case of Ceylon. When a senior State Department advisor called Ambassador Willis to get the necessary Swiss permission for negotiations that were to begin on their soil the very next day, she delivered—and then added, by his account, "Don't you ever do that to me again!" This is the sort of reaction that risked triggering the classic double standard—suitably assertive coming from a man, unsuitably aggressive coming from a woman—and not what one might expect from a woman in the habit of maintaining a low profile.[57]

Assessments of Willis

Foreign Service Officers who worked under Willis occasionally criticized but usually praised their chief, "a wonderful woman," as one of them put it. Several noted the refusal to delegate and the exactitude; one called her a "very hard set lady," and another noted her sometimes "ploddy demeanor." But she was clearly a considerate boss, who publicly gave credit to subordinates for successes. She saw one departing junior FSO and his family off at the train station at the crack of dawn. She took an interest in the training and welfare of junior officers, to make sure they began their careers well (a fact noted by the Foreign Service Inspectors). In Bern, two bachelor officers on her staff shared living quarters and were always seen together. It is true that Willis had no known conflict with these officers, but still, rather than engaging in gay-baiting, as Mesta had, she simply called them in and suggested it was better that they not be seen together too often. Another admired her sharpness. "One of the genuine brains that I met in the Foreign Service," he said, one with "a great capacity for going to the heart of an issue." Finally, one noted her ability to straddle the gender divide: "She seems to manage at dinner parties to powder her nose with the women and figuratively to smoke cigars with the men."[58]

The Foreign Service Inspectors found the Bern embassy in 1955 to be "a smoothly and efficiently run organization" that could "serve as a model for small Embassies." Led by the ambassador, who traveled widely, the quality of representation was "very high." Willis, they added, "is admired and respected throughout the country and there is no doubt that she is among the most outstanding Chiefs of Mission in Switzerland." The Swiss watch issue required her to be "a sympathetic listener yet a strong supporter of U. S. policy." The inspectors heard admiration and praise for Willis in all social circles and all cities they visited. That the watch tariff increase had not provoked more anti-American sentiment, they concluded, was "largely due to her." They detected the delegation problem, noting that the DCM "did not have enough work to do, to put it bluntly," but since Willis was away at the time and they could not interview her, they pursued the issue no further than recommending merging the positions of DCM and chief political officer—an accommodation, not a solution. In 1959, however, the inspectors in Oslo may have found that Willis had eased up a bit, at least when it came to her deputy. They observed that although she monitored all of the embassy's functions, the ambassador delegated operational responsibility to her DCM.[59]

"A career diplomat, who combines professional ability with personal charm," the British ambassador began his 1954 summary. These had earned her admiration and respect among the Swiss even though they themselves offered few leadership opportunities to women. He found her a "frank and honest colleague." According to him, her assignment was a tough one, especially at that moment—doubtless a reference to the issue of Swiss watches— and she was "tackling her official duties as well as social obligations with admirable ability, fortitude and cheerfulness." The following year, he updated his evaluation simply, "I like and admire her more and more." Willis left an impression after she left Norway as well. When now-ambassador Tibbetts arrived in Oslo in 1964, Norwegian statesman Trygve Lie said to her, "You know, it came up in the cabinet, another woman." And he had commented, "Look, the last one was better than most of the men."[60]

Frances Willis was thus, by all accounts, an excellent envoy. And while compiling her impressive record, she also achieved many firsts, and not just the obvious and most important one of being the first female chief of mission to have emerged from the career Foreign Service. Willis was also one of the first two female diplomats (simultaneously) presented at the Court of St. James (1948); the first woman promoted to counselor and to FSO-1 (1951); the first woman promoted to career minister (1955); the first female chief of mission posted outside Europe (1961); and the first woman designated career ambassador (one of the State Department's highest honors, 1962).

Willis of course had her share of flaws, her refusal to delegate and her micromanagement chief among them. In terms of gender progress, she also deserves criticism for so categorically denying the existence of sex discrimination in the State Department—especially after she retired, when she no longer had to fear retaliation and could have made a real contribution to the Foreign Service reform efforts of the 1970s.

Nor were the contours of Willis's career or the factors in her success unique—her status as a professional diplomat among political appointees notwithstanding—whether the comparison is with women closer to the inside of the foreign relations establishment or with those farther to the outside. She confirms some of the patterns about women and foreign relations discerned by scholars such as Hoff and Morin, which include how male mentors were usually important; how these women usually demonstrated great courage; and, most obviously, how they all suffered sexism or discrimination.[61]

Willis developed the determination, skill, and coping strategies key to persist and ultimately thrive, in a diplomatic corps hostile to women that changed little over the course of her career. Nevertheless, she changed some men's minds about women in diplomacy. In addition, more so than the political appointees, Willis was also an inspiration, perhaps even a mentor, to other female professional diplomats (although of course as a career diplomat, she had far more opportunity for mentoring than her political-appointee counterparts). This constituted a sizable contribution in itself, considering that America in the 1950s, while not quite the misogynist prison camp of stereotype, was still not the most auspicious place for women seeking to break boundaries. Where the other female chiefs undermined sexism in diplomacy more generally and from the outside, Willis undermined it more specifically in the Foreign Service and Department of State, and she did so from within. In playing this role, she preferred to make her contributions indirectly, behind the scenes, more by example than by declaration, an impermeable professional shell all that was visible. But that does not render her contributions any less real. Considering the character of the Foreign Service at the time, there was probably no other way.[62]

Epilogue

1964–2018

It's just I never thought the secretary of state could be a man.
—a State Department official's nine-year-old son, upon learning
that Colin Powell was replacing Madeleine Albright, 2001

In February 2010, the fashion magazine *Marie Claire* ran a photo spread titled "Fashion: Women Run the World." A supposed "new era" at the United Nations—where still no woman has ever served as secretary general and gender equality targets for staffing have been repeatedly missed—inspired the editors to indulge "in a little fashion fantasy: Women run the world, and a new power dressing triumphs. All hail embellished suits, protocol-bending patterns, and radically feminine takes on classic jackets." In the third photo, striding purposefully down a corridor at the United Nations, were four young women, one wearing a Y and Kei jacket ($990), another toting a Michael Kors handbag ($2,495). "POWER SHIFT," read the caption. "All-female ambassadors stage a march of progress past portraits of former secretary-generals."[1]

Generally one should hesitate before turning to *Marie Claire* for evidence of how women are doing in the international realm. Yet in one sense, this piece reflects the limits of women's progress. In 2010, as in the *Ambassador's Ball in the Days to Come* of 1896, women dominated international relations only in the world of make-believe, indeed now not even to satirize their equality but rather to peddle phony feminism and costly couture. American women have indeed taken great strides in diplomacy over the last century, and since the first six female envoys discussed here—but it has taken a good long while, and the achievements have been incomplete. The positive trend may even have stalled. *Power drift* may more accurately describe the recent period than *power shift*.

The Big Six

The changes that have occurred have been gradual, uneven, woven from many strands. Some of the weavers were the early female chiefs of mission, the "Big Six." Neither female FSOs nor female chiefs became "normal" by the 1960s. But what might appear as stagnation during their time, when the appointments remained few in number and seemed confined to small European countries, in fact constituted gradual progress: ambassadorial rather than just ministerial appointments; a post in a major ally (Italy) rather than just minor allies or neutrals; a post in a Communist bloc country (Bulgaria); and a post in Asia (Ceylon). While this was about setting precedents rather than establishing norms, one by one, presidents lifted de facto restrictions on female assignments, all the more impressive since the overall number remained token. And they never regretted expanding these boundaries, however timidly and incrementally they may have gone about doing so.

These presidents—Roosevelt, Truman, Eisenhower, and Kennedy—were not feminists, to put it mildly. Although they all appointed women to government posts, including two in the cabinet, doing so was not a high priority for any of them, and the number of ambassadorial appointments per administration did not rise. Indeed, as we have seen, presidents made these moves mainly because they were lobbied, sometimes relentlessly. Without the push provided by such figures as Eleanor Roosevelt, Molly Dewson, India Edwards, and Hubert Humphrey, this story might have followed a very different path (although of course, once on the job, it was the Bix Six themselves who had to perform). But in this sense, it helped that the United States was a democracy. The relative responsiveness of the nation's system, especially the granting of women's suffrage in 1920, afforded a way for women to enter public life and thus its diplomatic corps. Moreover, that America is a highly imperfect democracy—one in which ambassadorships are distributed based on not only merit but also fundraising ability, political links, even celebrity—actually accelerated the process of inclusion. All five of the noncareer appointees had been active in politics beforehand, which gave them the necessary connections and experience to take and hold these positions. Conversely, had all US envoys been drawn exclusively from among the ranks of career FSOs, the date of the chief of mission breakthrough would have been deferred considerably.

Apart from most having (varied) political backgrounds, these women were not cut from the same cloth. Certainly they were all white and at least nominal Christians. But they varied greatly in educational levels (from finishing school, through some college, to a PhD); age at time of appointment (from forty to sixty-six); and wealth and social class (from modest means to both old and new wealth, although not all were constant—Luce with [extreme] upward mobility and Harriman downward).

Despite their different profiles, these women mostly came together to produce an unexpected bonus: people's diplomacy. On their own initiative, most if not all of these women engaged in it. Even Anderson in Bulgaria did, under the worst possible conditions. Did they practice people's diplomacy because they were women? Or because they were amateurs? This is unknowable, but it seems that the amateur women did it much more than the amateur men. Regardless, they were improvising, drawing on what they knew, whether it was retail politics—Owen's travels around Denmark approximated her trips through Florida's Fourth District—or, in the case of Mesta, experience as a Washington, DC, society hostess (among the other hats she had worn). On the flip side, these women were not constrained by lengthy acculturation in the ways of formal diplomacy. Thus, they were free to conceive of their roles in unconventional and even controversial ways, for example, as Owen and Mesta saw the minister's job as the promotion of the host country's interests as well as America's. But the women's improvisation and newness to the field led to innovation. Willis, the one career professional, engaged in people's diplomacy at least a bit less than the others (although still more than most male envoys at the time); perhaps the Foreign Service "trained out of her" much of any inclination toward people's diplomacy. The sample here is too small to make definitive generalizations, but one thing is clear: US representation in these countries had an added dimension. And whether the goal was simply closer bilateral relations or waging the Cold War successfully, winning goodwill through people's diplomacy—in countries that were mostly democracies, in which average people beyond the salons and smoking rooms had a voice—was a useful means of achieving it.

In this regard, paradoxically, all these women benefitted in some ways from their novelty or rarity. This piqued extraordinary interest among the public and the press in their host countries; they became well known, even celebrities. And with the possible exception of Willis in Ceylon—due to the policy she had been instructed to execute—in every case they enjoyed immense popularity, perhaps more than that of any foreign ambassador preceding them. That is, people paid them close attention and liked what they saw. It bears repeating that a popular ambassador is not necessarily a good ambassador, but a popular American ambassador can certainly enhance positive sentiment toward the United States, and she is certainly better positioned to excel at the representational aspect of her profession.

Since the 1960s, these representational activities have grown in importance as part of an ambassador's job. Before this, the relatively isolated ambassadors of twentieth-century professional diplomacy were repeatedly urged to "get out more," and most of the women described here—independently of each other—were doing so already. This trend would have occurred anyway, but it was cumulative, and several female ambassadors succeeded in part by contributing people's diplomacy to it.

All of these women were highly attuned to, and at least partly motivated by, their historic role. They feared letting other women down, worried about interrupting women's progress, or, on the positive side, happily took part in women's advancement or helping pave the way for other women in the future. Even Frances Willis, with her more circumspect approach, clothed in public denials of gender consciousness or of having experienced bias, nevertheless privately lamented the discrimination she repeatedly faced, took pride in the "firsts" she achieved as a woman, and advised at least one female colleague that her own emphasis on low-key competence was the best way to promote women's equality. All were feminists, although Perle Mesta, the only one to join the National Woman's Party, was uniquely outspoken. But this similarity should not surprise, because over the course of their particular third of a century, relatively little changed for women, both in American society and in the world of diplomacy.

But this does not mean nothing changed. Although it is of necessity anecdotal, the evidence overall suggests that all of these women, with the probable exception of Mesta, helped change men's minds about women in diplomacy. William Phillips grudgingly acknowledged the usefulness of Ruth Owen's more populist approach and her success within that context. Florence Harriman improved markedly in the eyes of her British counterpart over a span of eighteen months, changed some minds in Norway's ruling circles, and became a source of pride for President Roosevelt for her performance literally under fire—after he had assigned her to a country ostensibly safe and out of the way. Eugenie Anderson won the admiration of George Kennan, a man who, at least in earlier days, was a profound misogynist. On repeated occasions, Bulgarian apparatchiks learned the hard way how tough she could be. Clare Boothe Luce overcame the initial hostility of both her embassy subordinates and Italian foreign ministry officials alike. Old Hand Hugh Gibson, an early, staunch opponent of female diplomats, ended up lobbying for Frances Willis's appointment as ambassador because she had served under him in Brussels. Later, Willis struck Trygve Lie as not only competent but "better than most of the men." Indeed, that two of the chiefs, Mesta and Luce, enjoyed outsized political clout in Washington helped them overcome the opposition their appointments stirred up in Luxembourg and Italy. Sadly, powerful men are rarely so helpful to historians as to confide to their diaries, "Wow. Have I gotten the women-folk wrong all these years," or, alternatively, "The women have proven themselves for decades. But they still shouldn't be diplomats." But the available evidence certainly suggests that these women helped change the attitudes of those influential men—and in a period before the broader social context began pushing men in the same direction. Moreover, judging by how uniformly popular they were in their host countries, it stands to reason that they changed some minds there too.

The impact of these women should not be exaggerated. The lack of progress toward gender equality in diplomacy during their time suggests a narrative more of continuity than of change. Nevertheless, we should not underestimate what they were up against, either; they encountered numerous obstacles. Often, they had to combat or evade the career men's attempts to usurp their authority, dictate the terms of their ambassadorships, or confine them to prescribed roles. They ran their legations and embassies lacking the traditional spouse, all the while coping with double standards, sexist press coverage, and complexities of protocol, or outright insults involving it—often in the face of male indifference or hostility, both foreign and American.

Despite these, the Big Six made a significant contribution. Their performances were certainly of unequal quality; a healthy gap separates the records of Eugenie Anderson and Perle Mesta. But they all, even the latter, performed well enough for an experiment to continue, and then to cease being an experiment, and then to be expanded as presidents slowly removed restrictions on such appointments. They helped change the attitudes of the men around them—and above them. With their people's diplomacy, they enhanced America's ties with their host countries and anticipated the age of public diplomacy. And, by helping to set us in the right direction, toward a day when the diversity of America is truly reflected in its representatives abroad, they helped construct a "people's diplomacy" in more ways than one.

A Bit of the Way with LBJ

In early 1964, the year both Frances Willis and Eugenie Anderson stepped down as chiefs of mission, a new president seemed to take particular interest in hiring additional women. Lyndon Johnson had actually embarked on this journey just before Christmas 1963, shortly after succeeding to the presidency, when he had a brainstorm. "This is screwy, but can you hold on to your chair?" he asked Press Secretary Pierre Salinger on the phone. "Would it be just terrible to ask Miz Kennedy to be ambassador to Mexico?" Salinger responded tepidly about the former First Lady's potential interest, but Johnson was momentarily undeterred. "God, Almighty! It'd electrify the Western Hemisphere. She'd just walk out on that balcony and look down on them, and they'd just pee all over themselves, every day!" Yet his enthusiasm soon waned, and he never made the offer.[2]

Johnson then demonstrated far more personal interest in naming women to government posts in general, and ambassadorships in particular, than any of his predecessors had. In January 1964, he made front-page news with the announcement that he would hire fifty women for significant government posts in thirty days. As only he could, he then leaned on the bureaucracy, including Foggy Bottom, to make it happen. On January 20, he spoke on the telephone with Secretary of State Rusk about the possibility of appointing a woman as US ambassador to Finland.

> LBJ: I want to get some real outstanding woman [in] this country, pretty soon, so you think of that . . .
>
> RUSK: Uh huh.
>
> LBJ: . . . Somebody suggested the president of Bryn Mawr College, who's about fifty-odd, and they say she's exceptional, I've forgotten who it was [who said that], Rah-, uh, Ros Gilpatric today.
>
> RUSK: Uh huh, uh huh.
>
> LBJ: They say she's very scholarly, very able, uh [a] very persuasive person. And, uh, but I want to get that pretty soon before these women run me out.
>
> RUSK: Right, right.

It was a telling conversation (or monologue). The secretary of state, chief of what was still a thoroughly male-dominated institution, demonstrated with his unenthusiastic responses what a jarring departure the president's new-found interest was. To be sure, Johnson remained in most ways a profound male chauvinist. In late March 1964, for example, he discussed the possible candidate for a position with his assistant Ralph Dungan.

LBJ: How old is she?

DUNGAN: She's forty-seven, as I recall.

LBJ: That's a little old for me.

DUNGAN: [laughs] She's a spry forty-seven.

LBJ: Is she good-looking?

DUNGAN: Uh, no, she's, uh—

LBJ: Well I'll—be—damned.

Johnson named ten women to Senate-confirmed posts in his first thirteen months in office—the same number Kennedy had in three years. They included four chiefs of mission, double the number serving at one time of any previous president. But their assignments mostly had a comically familiar ring: the first three were Denmark (Katharine White), Norway (Margaret Tibbetts), and Luxembourg (Patricia Harris, the first African American female ambassador). The last was Nepal, to which LBJ dispatched Caroline Laise who, with her husband, Ellsworth Bunker (South Vietnam), formed the first American ambassadorial married couple. And Johnson's interest in appointing women waned fairly quickly. His explanation to Rusk—"before these women run me out"—was candid: his interest in the subject was almost entirely political, and it mostly vanished after the 1964 election.[3]

President Johnson's commitment was free to rise and fall because of an environment that, in some respects, had changed little. In the State Department and posts abroad, the token number of female chiefs and small number of female FSOs accorded with the indifferent tone LBJ had encountered with Secretary Rusk. Veteran ambassadors reflecting on diplomacy as a career, like Willard Beaulac, still believed diplomatic careers were not for women and expressed this view publicly. "The Foreign Service exists in order to do a job for the United States," he wrote in his 1964 book, "and in general the job can best be done by men." Relatively progressive senior officials, such as Assistant Secretary Lucius Battle, continued to concede only that "it would be perfectly all right to have a woman ambassador in just about any of the Scandinavian countries." Even more sobering was the trend in hiring (and promotion). Not only had the number of female FSOs stopped rising; it had begun to decline. The 336 female FSOs of 1960 shrank to 147 by 1970; that latter figure represented 5 percent of the total—the same percentage as in 1953—and women occupied only 2.5 percent of senior positions. Too few women were passing the entrance examinations, and those who did were denied the opportunities necessary for advancement; thus the increase of the 1950s was reversed by female retirees going unreplaced. This coincided with an upturn in the recruitment of male middle-class military veterans intended to address the elitist, gay stereotype so prevalent in the 1950s, and the trends may have been related. Regardless of motive, admitting and promoting women was scarcely more a priority in 1970 than it had been ten, or twenty, or even thirty years earlier.[4]

Major Change

Thereafter, substantial, if slow, progress occurred, mainly because women began taking matters into their own hands. Obviously the complex web of broader social developments beginning in the 1960s, in particular the advent of second-wave feminism, provided a crucial new context. But within the State Department and Foreign Service, women still had to act to bring about change. In 1970, a group of female FSOs founded the Women's Action Organization (WAO) to pressure the State Department into addressing the myriad inequalities women had been suffering ever since Lucile Atcherson joined the Foreign Service in 1922. Before too long, the WAO comprised over a thousand members and had secured several reforms, for example, an end to the marriage ban (1971), increased recruitment of women, and the dropping of references to sex and marital status in evaluations.[5]

The WAO was essentially a moderate organization, choosing to work within the department to change policy. Far more confrontational was one particular junior officer, Alison Palmer. Palmer joined the Foreign Service in 1960 (the undersecretary who administered the oath to her class of twenty-eight men and four women announced, "Gentlemen, I congratulate you; you are now Foreign Service Officers"). After several years' service, Palmer filed a formal complaint with the State Department's Equal Employment Opportunity (EEO) office claiming that she had been denied three assignments because of her sex. In the last case, Ethiopia, she was told openly, "The Ambassador there doesn't want you because you are a woman." The ambassador, Edward Korry, added in a message to the department, "the savages in Ethiopia would not be receptive to a woman, except maybe to her form." In 1971, the EEO found that discrimination existed in the State Department, and it ordered Palmer's promotion and the removal of restrictions on the assignment of officers. Her appeal to the Civil Service Board of Appeal seeking *retroactive* promotion and other remedies was denied, so in 1972 she filed a federal law suit under Title VII of the Civil Rights Act of 1964. She won this case in 1975, and she plowed the back pay she was awarded into a class action suit on behalf of all female FSOs the following year (a move over which WAO members split). During much of the legal process, Palmer encountered denials from colleagues and higher officials that any discrimination existed as well as the "loss" of documents, stonewalling, retaliation, and sexual harassment. Career FSO and Executive Secretary to the Secretary of State Lawrence Eagleburger—who would later graciously allow that one particular female ambassador put "a human face on diplomacy"—declared at one point, "We are going to GET Alison. I don't care how long it takes. We are going to get her."[6]

The State Department never did "get" Palmer; quite the contrary. It took *thirty-four years*, and many colleagues, including some women, remained hostile toward her even years later, but the several judgments and consent decrees culminating in termination of the suit in 2010 imposed crucial changes on the State Department and Foreign Service. These include an end to discrimination in the entrance examinations, hiring, assignments (e.g., underrepresentation in political and DCM positions, overrepresentation in consular positions), efficiency reports, promotions, and awards; back pay totaling over $1 million for women denied promotions; mandatory or improved EEO training for managers and other responsible officials; and creation of a Council for Equality in the Workplace. Along the way, in the "radical flank" dynamic seen in other, broader reform movements, Palmer's militancy may actually have strengthened the hand of the WAO, whose demands did not, in the words of Deputy Undersecretary for Management William Macomber, the State Department's point man on the issue from 1969 to 1973, include "any of them crazy, bra-burning kinds of things."

Regardless, Palmer's tenacity played a major role in dragging the Department of State closer to compliance with the Foreign Service Act of 1980, which demanded a diplomatic corps that is "truly representative of the American people throughout all levels of the Foreign Service." Recently, ambassadors such as Phyllis Oakley and Eileen Malloy have acknowledged the importance of Palmer and her co-litigants to their careers.[7]

Other women continued to get ahead by choosing the low-key approach, built on such tactics as patience and putting men at ease, preferred by Frances Willis. Jean Wilkowski, a DCM in the late 1960s and named the first female US ambassador to an African country (Zambia, 1972), objected when one of the feminist FSOs remarked, "Lady, you never would have gotten where you are today if it wasn't for our movement." Wilkowski believed neither that the issues were so clear-cut nor that the movement had directly affected her promotions. Madeleine Albright would share this approach and outlook.[8]

Meanwhile, throughout the 1970s and 1980s, women compiled an impressive string of additional "firsts." These include first female assistant secretary (public affairs, Carol Laise, 1973); first female Hispanic ambassador (Honduras, Mari-Luci Jaramillo, 1977); first female undersecretary (security assistance, science and technology, Lucy Benson, 1977); and first woman to head a geographic bureau (assistant secretary for European and Canadian affairs, Rozanne Ridgway, 1985).[9]

In 1981, President Ronald Reagan chose political scientist Jeane Kirkpatrick to be the first female US ambassador to the United Nations, a position with cabinet rank. Once during a meeting in the White House Situation Room, Kirkpatrick saw a mouse scurry across the floor. "I thought to myself that day," she later said, "that the mouse was really no stranger a creature to find in the Situation Room than I was." Having risen so high, Kirkpatrick perhaps understandably faced at least her share of sexism. After she took a hard line on an issue at one White House meeting, some of the men were overheard wondering whether "it was the wrong time of the month." Despite her cabinet rank, she was subordinate to Alexander Haig, Reagan's first secretary of state. "I don't know how anybody expects," he allegedly announced in a meeting, "that I will work with that bitch." His problem was solved when he resigned after eighteen months in office. One study, however, lists Kirkpatrick's sex as only one of several possible explanations for her relative lack of influence in the Reagan administration.[10]

Nothing has meant more, of course, than women breaking through to the top of the foreign policy establishment. This watershed occurred in 1997, when at the start of his second term President Bill Clinton named his UN ambassador, Madeleine K. Albright, to be his secretary of state. Albright's presence, along with that of a few other women she placed in senior positions, led to men at the State Department referring to "the chicks in charge" (although, tellingly, the vast majority of senior posts were still occupied by men). Albright did not find it easy. Toward the end of her tenure, she reflected that women faced enormous prejudice. "Women have to work twice as hard and run twice as fast. I've had to prove myself every single day," she said, a sentiment shared by many female diplomats. She also learned that men often did not know how to treat women as equals in terms of protocol; the secretary was often greeted by politicians and dignitaries—both American and foreign—with a kiss. This left Letitia Baldridge "speechless." "Someone of her rank and dignity," she commented, "should be greeted with a hand-shake—a double-handed handshake if you're a good friend."[11]

Albright was followed by the first African American to occupy the post, Colin Powell (2001–2005), and then by two more women: Condoleezza Rice (also the first African American woman in the position, 2005–2009), and Hillary Clinton (2009–2013). This breakthrough, indeed, this apparent nor-malization, has obviously been momentous, and not only because of its inspi-rational effect on American girls and women, inside and outside the Foreign Service. It has also sent ripples through world diplomacy. For example, within one year of Clinton's swearing in, twenty-five foreign countries had dis-patched female ambassadors to Washington, an all-time high and a five-fold increase over the late 1990s. Some of this "Hillary Effect" no doubt stemmed from the same crass, pandering impulse that helped direct Perle Mesta and Frances Willis to countries headed by women. But the result was also norm-setting, and sending a woman to Washington may have been a way for a country to signal its modernization and synchronization with the United States. One of these foreign envoys said that the cluster of three female secre-taries has "had a worldwide effect. . . . It's inspiring, motivating and certainly encouraging." At a Q and A with US troops stationed in Saudi Arabia, Sec-retary Albright was asked about how she was being received by leaders of countries with less equality for women. "Well, they're learning," she quipped.[12]

Albright and Clinton in particular used their positions to stress the inter-national importance of women's issues. This was no coincidence; the two worked closely together and agreed on the importance of this approach when Albright was secretary and Clinton was First Lady, the latter delivering her landmark "Women's Rights are Human Rights" speech at the Fourth World Conference on Women in Beijing in 1995. But as secretary, Clinton pursued it with greater vigor, elevating women's issues to a central place in US foreign policy. "The subjugation of women is a direct threat to the security of the United States," Clinton declared at the United Nations in 2010. "It is also a threat to the common security of our world, because the suffering and denial of the rights of women and the instability of nations go hand in hand." Nor was this mere assertion. Scholars have recently found that the best predictor of a state's peacefulness is not its level of wealth, democracy, or ethnoreligious identity but rather how well its women are treated.[13]

This major departure, what Valerie Hudson and Patricia Leidl have labeled "The Hillary Doctrine," manifested itself in several ways. Clinton drew attention to neglected global issues that disproportionately affect women and girls, for example, cookstove use (smoke from crude, poorly ventilated stoves is implicated in almost 2 million deaths per year, significantly contributes to climate change, and comes from burning wood that women and children must spend hours collecting, often in dangerous areas). The secretary almost always made a point during foreign visits of meeting leading women from local NGOs. She also took major steps to make her new priority the State Department's as well. For example, she created the Office of Global Women's Issues, headed by an ambassador at large. And, she ordered the integration of gender awareness into department training of new FSOs, strategy, and policy guidance, for example, instituting the first Quadrennial Diplomacy and Development Review (2010), to establish a four-year plan for the State Department and the US Agency for International Development; women and girls appeared 133 times in its 242 pages. This was all part of Clinton's larger strategy to link diplomacy and economic development to promote social stability. This sort of approach is often labeled "soft power," although Clinton called it "smart power." And the Big Six would have applauded her preferred means of doing so. "You've got to have government-to-government, government-to-people, and people-to-people contacts," she repeatedly declared, in the words of a senior assistant.[14]

For critics, however, this effort came at a price. It was led by a "feminist hawk," who had supported the 2003 Iraq War as a US senator and military intervention in Libya in 2011 as secretary (although, paradoxically, such

First Lady Michelle Obama and Secretary of State Hillary Rodham Clinton with International Women of Courage Award winners, 2012. Back row left is Melanne Verveer, the first US ambassador at large for Global Women's Issues, a position emblematic of Clinton's attempts to bring women's issues to the forefront of US foreign policy. Clinton was the third female secretary, but women have still fallen far short of achieving equality in American diplomacy. (US Department of State)

"toughness" may have facilitated her focus on smart power issues); whose activism raised the specter of "feminist imperialism"; and whose policies risked endangering the very women they were intended to empower, if and when US personnel departed, especially from countries like Afghanistan. Most importantly, the question remains: did Clinton's efforts to institutionalize such initiatives succeed? Already during her term signs appeared, for instance, that US officials on the ground in Iraq had clearly not bought into the agenda, and, in the words of Hudson and Leidl, that "gender programming had become a thoughtless box-checking exercise that did not, in the end, help women." And the Donald Trump administration has greatly deemphasized women's issues internationally; it waited more than two years before nominating someone, Kelley E. Currie, for the post of ambassador at large for Global Women's Issues. At minimum, it may take several consecutive secretaries placing equally strong emphasis on this agenda to bring about the necessary cultural changes among officials that would truly change policy in the field.[15]

Many female envoys report that they have found their sex in some ways advantageous. In her oral history that traced female ambassadors into the early 1990s, Ann Miller Morin found that many of the women could be blunt with male host-country officials, especially in developing countries, without giving offense. Some discovered that men could more easily ask women for assistance or advice without losing face. As we have seen with the early chiefs, some women continued to experience the upside to sexism (which, of course, is in no way mitigating): in their host countries, they have often been viewed as more caring, interested, and approachable. Sexism at the highest levels could also open some doors. In 1999, Vicki Huddleston was chosen to run the US Interests Section in Havana—the de facto US embassy, in the absence of formal diplomatic relations—in part due to her sex. "I knew," she wrote later, "that Castro preferred to deal with women." Moreover, some made use of the flip side of exclusion from male society: unlike their male counterparts, they could mix freely with the female population, an ability of incalculable importance.[16]

In the Obama administration, more female ambassadors served and represented a larger percentage of the total than ever before. The number remained in the single digits through the administration of Gerald Ford (1974–1977), and the percentage of ambassadors that is female was stuck in the single digits through that of Ronald Reagan (1981–1989). Steady increases in both numbers and percentages did not begin until the early 1990s, culminating in the Obama administration, during which the proportion of all ambassadorships given to women reached 32.6 percent (see table 1). These figures are impressive, considering that for all of US history, women have constituted only 9.3 percent of the 4,822 total chiefs of mission as of September 2018 (12.9 percent of 3,492 chiefs, if one begins counting in 1933). They also stand out in the international context. As of about 2014, among the fifty countries with the highest GDP, only four did as well as or better than the United States, and none reached a female ambassador rate of 50 percent (the four countries were Finland, 44 percent; Philippines, 41 percent; Sweden, 40 percent; and Norway, 33 percent). The global average was a disappointing 15 percent.[17]

The Limits

Nevertheless, celebration is far less warranted than the recent numbers, or the qualitative advances outlined above, would suggest. First and most obviously,

Table 1. Female US ambassadors appointed, by president (as of April 2015)

President	Number of female ambassadors	Total number of ambassadors	Female ambassadors as percentage of total
Obama w/nominated*	116	367	31.6
Obama	105	346	30.3
G. W. Bush	118	474	24.9
Clinton	78	420	18.6
G. H. W. Bush	22	213	10.3
Reagan	21	394	5.5
Carter	19	201	9.5
Ford	7	94	7.4
Nixon	5	242	2.1
Johnson	4	161	2.5
Kennedy	2	130	1.5
Eisenhower	4	228	1.8
Truman	2	192	1.0
Roosevelt	2	208	1.0
TOTAL	392	3,303	11.9

* The final Obama figures as of December 2016 are 139 total female ambassadors appointed, or 32.6 percent of his total (Ambassador Tracker [@Philip Arsenault], "Obama has appointed a record 139 female ambassadors, representing a record 32.6% of his ambassador appointments," Twitter, 12:45 P.M., December 10, 2016, https://twitter.com/PhilipArsenault/status/807687626526441473).

Source: Adapted from Ambassador Tracker (@Philip Arsenault), "@Diplopundit I've since updated the chart," Twitter, 4:55 P.M., April 14, 2015, https://twitter.com/PhilipArsenault/status/588128404614082560/photo/1.

32.6 percent is still well short of 51 percent (the proportion of the American population that is female). Second, the trend line has not consistently risen; indeed, in the first eighteen months of the Trump administration, the number of female ambassadors (confirmed and nominated) has declined to 26.1 percent (an even greater drop has been seen in the appointment of racial minorities). Third, the percentage of positions occupied by women declines in inverse relationship with seniority, a widely seen institutional phenomenon identified long ago as the "law of increasing disproportion." In 2016, women constituted 40 percent of Foreign Service Officers, but only 33 percent of US ambassadors, and only 31 percent of senior State Department officials. More specifically, although women occupied the top spot for twelve out of sixteen years between 1997 and 2013, their representation in the most senior positions has lagged. For example, several women have served as undersecretary for public diplomacy and public affairs, but only two as director of policy planning, one as deputy secretary (one of two second-rank deputy positions), and one as undersecretary for political affairs (the No. 4 position). And that one political undersecretary, Wendy Sherman, notes that the same holds true beyond Foggy Bottom: "A glance at the major foreign policy publications and the panelists at major conferences will show that our security and diplomacy leaders are still predominantly men."[18]

Fourth, the geographic distribution of female appointments greatly undermines the importance of the overall numbers. For example, the United States has sent more female chiefs—seven—to one country than to any other: Luxembourg. Incidentally, two of these envoys are notorious and do not go by the name Perle Mesta. One was Ruth Farkas, wife of a department-store magnate, who expressed interest in making a large donation to Richard Nixon's 1972 reelection campaign in exchange for an ambassadorship. She felt let down by the initial offer, reportedly responding to Nixon's personal attorney, "Isn't $250,000 an awful lot of money for Costa Rica?" The Farkases ending up shelling out $300,000 for Luxembourg. Although Farkas was neither wholly unqualified nor a poor performer once on the job, her appointment remains one of the more egregious cases of pay-to-play.[19]

Another was Cynthia Stroum, a venture capitalist and Democratic fundraiser appointed by Barack Obama. Stroum resigned in early 2011, after only a little more than one year on the job. A State Department inspector general's report—which former ambassador Dennis Jett described as perhaps "the worst report card ever given an embassy"—revealed her abuse of staff, misappropriation of funds, and obsession with renovations of the ambassador's residence. Some of her staff had requested transfers to the embassies in Kabul and Baghdad.[20]

Beyond Luxembourg, the distribution pattern is discouraging. As of early 2016, just behind the Grand Duchy—having received six female US ambassadors each—are Barbados, Kyrgyzstan, Malta, Micronesia, Nepal, Niger, Papua New Guinea, and the Solomon Islands. At the other end of the spectrum, twenty-seven countries have never received a female US ambassador, and those include nations far more central to US foreign policy:

Afghanistan, China, Germany, Iran, Israel, Saudi Arabia, and Turkey. Two countries to which the United States has sent the most ambassadors, seventy-four each, are also on that list: Russia and Spain. Only six American women have served in countries that along with the United States comprise the G-7, and only three of those in the twenty-first century. President Trump has appointed two additional women to G-7 countries: Kelly Knight Craft, the first female ambassador the United States has ever sent to Canada, and Jamie D. McCourt, ambassador to France. The rarity of women sent to these prestige posts—Brazilian female diplomats call such slots the "Elizabeth Arden Circuit"—may in part reflect the relative dearth of wealthy women, considering the enormous out-of-pocket costs of entertaining in capitals like London, Paris, and Rome (as ambassador to France in the 1990s, Pamela Harriman spent $10,000 to $15,000 of her own money per month on official entertainment). Yet in general, the United States unfortunately finds itself in good company: a recent study of thousands of ambassadorial appointments found that female ambassadors worldwide are less likely to be sent to countries of the highest economic and military status—just as they are less likely to be sent to violent or militarized countries, denying them the prestige that often comes from undertaking such assignments (consider again the fluke of Florence Harriman's assignment to "peaceful" Norway, and the effect on her reputation when war came and put her to the test). Overall, while much more widely dispersed geographically than the early female chiefs were, their successors do not yet enjoy equal access to more prestigious ambassadorial posts.[21]

Arguably (and ironically), the several top appointments to the United Nations also present a problem. Despite what might be suggested by the dismissal of Wonder Woman as the United Nations' honorary ambassador for the empowerment of women and girls in December 2016, we seem to be witnessing the continued feminization of US representation at the UN. Of course, women have recently occupied the ambassadorship, and that position is an important one. But it is nevertheless striking that since 2009, *only* women have done so—as of this writing, yet another woman, Kelly Knight Craft, has been nominated for the office, by an administration notable for the small number of women slotted into senior posts. As it did in its early days, the United Nations apparently continues to present—albeit, again, at the highest level—an opportunity to pad the number of female appointments while preserving more influential foreign policy positions in

Washington for men. And this, in turn, may represent only part of a larger, more disturbing possibility: that in US foreign relations, as force increasingly outweighs diplomacy, and in Washington, as the Pentagon exercises more influence than the State Department (while consuming *twelve times* what is spent on the latter and foreign assistance combined), the diplomacy can be safely ceded to women. This would cancel out or, at minimum compromise, much of the recent gender progress.[22]

Why Problems Persist

Apart from the self-evident, that the wider society has continued to exhibit considerable misogyny and gender discrimination, some specific factors help explain how elusive gender equality remains in the American diplomatic world of the early twenty-first century. First, for all the improvements it has undertaken, the State Department could be better equipped to ensure equality. For example, as of 2013, no single body within the department bore responsibility for gender issues, in contrast to the structure of many other institutions. Rather, that responsibility is shared among the Office of Civil Rights, the Family Liaison Office, a few divisions of Human Resources, and other offices.[23]

Second, the tension between career and family continues to plague the women far more than the men. Male and female FSOs experience the same rate of attrition, which has held steady at approximately 3.5 percent. Thus it is not that women leave the service; they remain, but they do not rise at the same rate, and it is clear that the issue of work-life balance helps explain why. This obviously is true throughout the private and public sectors, but apparently it has caused greater morale problems in the State Department than elsewhere in the federal government. One ambassador recalls how, as a junior FSO in the 1980s who had to extend her maternity leave, she learned later about back-channel communications concerning her "lack of seriousness" about her job. Another, Gina Abercrombie-Winstanley, who has also faced the double burden of being a woman and a racial minority, took a position in Saudi Arabia at a time when she had two small children; it was a major stepping stone in her career, but the severe emotional toll on her family lasted for years. A study of all 603 career US ambassadors between 1993 and 2008 found the women far more likely to be single, and far less likely to have children, than their male counterparts. A majority of the sixty participants in a 2015 Department focus group reported that women's advancement still suffers due to caregiver bias (just as a far larger survey by the Women's Foreign Policy Group had found in 1998). "I don't think I ever would have been secretary of state if I had stayed married," Madeleine Albright recalled. Even the most sanguine end up conceding the point. "With work-life balance, I tell people that you can have it all," said Roberta Jacobson, US ambassador to Mexico (2016–2018). "You just can't have it all at once." This, of course, begs the question. "When women can have both," as former ambassador Julia Chang Bloch said in 2004, "that's when women will have finally made it in diplomacy. Unfortunately, we still have a long way to go." And that is partly because work-life balance is also an issue for men, and the situations of each sex are of course connected. A better work-life balance for men, that is, more equitably sharing domestic responsibilities, would by definition expand opportunities for women.[24]

Third, gender bias and double standards in the broader culture persist in the diplomatic world as well. This can be true at the very top, if one counts the unwelcome backrub President George W. Bush gave to German chancellor Angela Merkel between sessions at the St. Petersburg G-8 summit in July 2006. Jeane Kirkpatrick had experienced the old sexual conundrum: if assertive, she said, a woman is seen as lecturing or "schoolmarmish" (a term the *Washington Post* also used to describe Madeleine Albright in 2000); if reticent, a woman is considered weak or a nonentity. The title of a paper written for the WAO in 1980 still captures the dilemma: "Nice Girl or Pushy Bitch: Two Roads to Nonpromotion." While perhaps somewhat milder or more subtle in recent years, this form of discrimination endures. When in the running for undersecretary of political affairs in 2011, Wendy Sherman had to struggle to overcome concerns—shared even by women above her, including Secretary Clinton, who had faced the same unfair criticism—that she was "not a team player," that is, too assertive, an accusation seldom thrown at men exhibiting precisely the same behavior. In 2015, one former ambassador described working on promotion panels and noting the gender contrast in evaluation files: women tended to be judged by their current status, men by their potential; women were called "good managers," and men were called "leaders." Simple bias still appears too. Samantha Power, Barack Obama's second ambassador to the United Nations, recounts a "disappointing" March 2016 debate in the Security Council on a resolution to address sexual exploitation and abuse by UN peacekeepers. The resolution passed, but for the first time Power felt "acutely aware" of being the only woman on the UNSC; her male colleagues, she sensed, acted as if her sex were the only explanation for her leading the charge on the issue. Several of them tried to weaken the resolution and afterward used the stereotypical loaded terms to describe her, such as "passionate" and "emotional."[25]

And then there are the routine indignities visited on even the most senior women, such as Condoleezza Rice, who as national security advisor and then secretary of state had to ward off the crush of one foreign leader; stare down the attempt of another, a "ladies' man" who had bragged to western diplomats that he could conquer any woman in two minutes, to get his way by charming her; and sit through an infuriating, condescending fifty-minute lecture by a (male) senior Chinese diplomat. All this is not to mention the issues of sexual harassment and sexual assault, which persist in the State Department and Foreign Service just as in most other institutions. More than 50 current and former female ambassadors, along with over 150 other women in the national security field, signed an open letter in November 2017 demanding an end to the sexual assault and harassment that either they or a colleague they knew had suffered.[26]

Fourth, sexist media coverage is harder to find, but it still exists. In 2002, Rice received the sort of treatment more typical of the 1950s. A symbol of women's progress as the first female national security advisor, Rice was subject of a *Time* cover story. And while it is true that a sidebar within, "All About Condoleezza," was devoted to her personal life, two of its items— "Pump Passion . . . she's been known to splurge on eight pairs of *Ferragamos* in a single spree," and "Brains—and Beauty . . . [she] favors *Yves Saint Laurent No. 10* lipstick in red"—are not of the sort one would find in an equivalent article if her name had been Connor Rice. "Rice manages to look perfectly put together almost always," read a profile after she was named secretary in 2005. "Bobby pins keep that modified 1960s flip hairdo in place." Sometimes it is the little things, more annoying than appalling, such as the online edition of the *Washington Post* relegating to its "Arts and Living" section a story about the huge uptick in female ambassadors sent to Washington, DC, during Clinton's tenure (2010, a throwback to the era when much of the discussion of female ambassadors appeared in the women's pages). And while perhaps a last vestige of earlier attitudes, and not at all reflective of the publication in general, in 2014 the *Foreign Service Journal* published an article on two-time ambassador Shirley Temple Black in which a career diplomat could still exclaim, "What an ornament she was for U.S. diplomacy!" Such public discussion is not nearly as bad as it was in the mid-twentieth century. But it still helps tilt the playing field against women.[27]

Some particularly unfortunate responses followed the United States' military intervention in Libya in 2011. This involved the admittedly unusual situation of three senior women on Obama's foreign policy team—Secretary Clinton, UN ambassador Susan Rice, and Samantha Power, then a senior member of the National Security Council staff—advocating military action, most senior men opposing it, and the women prevailing. Still, any chance that this circumstance might pass without comment, in the interest of mature, gender-neutral discussion commensurate with the normalization of senior female appointments, evaporated in a spate of multilayered sexism. "The girls took on the guys," said one reporter. Other commentators referred to the "girls" as "warrior women" and "Valkyries." (For good measure, Power's earlier arguments for humanitarian intervention were also, as later in 2016, described as "passionate.") Complicating factors, for example, that the final decision was made not by the women but by President Obama, that Obama did so not primarily because of the women's recommendation but because of the terms of engagement he settled upon, or that the interventionists did *not* exclusively consist of women, were ignored; the three women were just too useful to sexist axe-grinders. One commentator who opposed Operation Odyssey Dawn, Patrick Buchanan, referred to the "three sisters' war"; one politician who supported intervention but opposed the administration, Republican US senator Lindsey Graham, used the women to impugn the manliness of the president. "I thank God," he remarked, "for strong women in the Obama administration"—because, of course, the use of military force equals strength, and restraint equals weakness. Some image-conscious administration officials conceded the argument and rushed to downplay the women's role in the decision. The retrograde media and political environment surrounding the women despite the progress reflected in their influence was, in this case at least, palpable.[28]

The good news is that it has become more acceptable to push back against sexist coverage, at least if you are Secretary Clinton. In late 2010, she was interviewed before an audience in Kyrgyzstan.

Moderator 1: Okay. Which designers do you prefer?

Secretary Clinton: What designers of clothes?

MODERATOR 1: Yes.

SECRETARY CLINTON: Would you ever ask a man that question? (Laughter.) (Applause.)

MODERATOR 1: Probably not. Probably not. (Applause.)

MODERATOR 2: How many hours do you sleep?

SECRETARY CLINTON: That's my answer.

MODERATOR 1: Yeah, I got it. I got it. That was a tough one.

Somewhere, Madame Pandit was smiling—or frowning. At a press conference in the 1950s, a reporter asked her the color of her sari. She shot back, "Did you ask my predecessor the color of his tie?"[29]

In short, many of the problems female diplomats faced in the mid-twentieth century persist, to at least some degree. Some are remarkably familiar, such as the self-doubt most of the early chiefs felt, to which some today, such as Wendy Sherman, also admit—consistent with a tech-industry study showing that men typically apply for positions when they have 60 percent of the qualifications, yet women only apply when they have 100 percent. To survive in the bureaucracy, even relatively senior female diplomats, like women everywhere, will continue to have men steal their ideas, interrupt them when they are speaking, and mansplain issues to them, even if they have already made clear that they are more expert on the subject at hand. And for fear of being written off as "not a team player," or worse, they will be expected to tolerate such behavior. Other problems have diminished considerably. The professional environment today is not nearly so hostile, the patriarchy is not quite so dominant, and women are taken more seriously; exclusively male settings are not nearly so prevalent; marriage, spousal, and protocol issues are far less problematic; and, while it is unclear whether the number of women in the department and Foreign Service has reached the necessary critical mass, it is certainly easier for women to stick together, engage in mutual self-help, and provide the mentoring so crucial to women's advancement. With the exception of the career professional Frances Willis, the Big Six had no women around them to mentor, had they been so inclined. But as one of Secretary Clinton's male advisors points out, women should not have to rely only on each other.[30]

Still, while less acute than in the mid-twentieth century, structural, social, and cultural issues all remain to be addressed. Happily, new groups have arisen, such as Executive Women at State (founded in 2007), that are taking them on. They have their work cut out for them, but it is difficult to exaggerate the importance of their effort. For a diverse diplomatic corps is not only a moral imperative. It is also "important for the world to see the face of America," says former assistant secretary Linda Thomas-Greenfield. "They need to understand that we are a diverse society and that diversity is our strength." From a purely practical standpoint, it is the way to maximize our access to badly needed talent, and in certain negotiations, diversity "may enhance your ability to persuade," says one ambassador. A diverse officer pool generates leaders who in turn produce "more creative insights, proffer alternative solutions, and thus make better decisions," Susan Rice argued in 2016. It is not "just some feel-good project," journalist Nicholas Kralev adds. "It's the only way to ensure that the State Department is ready to challenge old modes of thinking and craft solutions that truly represent what today's America has to offer." Who represents us tells others—and reminds ourselves—who we are. Thus, for both moral and practical reasons, America should resume building on what Lucile Atcherson began back in 1922—and what the Big Six did beginning in 1933.[31]

Acknowledgments
and Permissions

Let me begin by taking my whack at the myth of solitary achievement—*no one* accomplishes anything entirely by herself. And when you take as long as I have to finish a book, you incur so many debts of gratitude that you cannot possibly repay them all. But I will try, with my apologies to any whom I have unjustly omitted.

First come the many academic friends and colleagues who have shared documents and ideas, commented on parts of or provided venues for developing this work, or otherwise provided help and encouragement. I'm grateful to, among others, Alessandro Brogi, Robert Dean, Betty Dessants, Mary Dupont, Brian Farrell, Catherine Forslund, Andy Fry, Petra Goedde, Kelly Gray, Ann Heiss, Jane Hunter, Charles Stuart Kennedy (and other oral history interviewers with the Association for Diplomatic Studies and Training), Ron Landa, Paul Lesch, Ralph Levering, Helen McCarthy, John McNay, Ann Miller Morin, Chester Pach, Andrew Rotter, Robert Shaffer, Glenda Sluga, Mark Stout, and Molly Wood.

My thanks also to the many, many unsung archivists and librarians without whom history writing would be impossible.

I am also grateful for assistance from Pennsylvania State University, the Minnesota Historical Society, and the European University Institute.

Radio host Ron Errett of 790 WPIC and podcaster Joe Coohill, aka Professor Buzzkill, have been incredibly kind and supportive in sharing their respective platforms with me and helping keep alive my love of history.

Presumably few academics can claim *two* mentors who have won the Pulitzer Prize, but I had the good fortune to begin my career under the guidance of John Gaddis and Marty Sherwin, and they both inspire me still.

Other friends—some in the biz, some not—have made these years a great pleasure, and I cannot thank them enough: Alan and Sherri Baumler,

Jim and Susan Bell, Lynn Botelho, John Gordon, Matt Grant, Tim Haggerty, Cate McClanahan, Sam Muir, and Rosalie Thomas.

Two relatives of the ambassadors I write about deserve special thanks. Eugenie Anderson's daughter, Johanna Ghei, and Francis Willis's nephew, Nick Willis, have both been most generous with their time and comments, and the latter's own book on his aunt is an indispensable resource.

When this book appears, I will have spent twenty years at Penn State Shenango, my wonderfully supportive academic home. I could not have completed it without the friendly support of three administrators in particular, Elaine Andrews, Jo Anne Carrick, and Fred Leeds. So many faculty and staff have made Shenango a place I love coming to every day, but in particular I thank Brandi Baros, Lisa Bertin, Steve Brewer, Claudia Brown, Madonna Brown, Louise Brydon, Jamie Calhoun, Matt Ciszek, Jammie Clark, Missa Eaton, Melissa Fowler, Stacy Gongloff, Matthew Goral, Chuck Greggs, Billie Jean Horvath, Liz Izenas, Erika Jones, Sandy Kimmel, Amy Petrucci-Effinite, Angela Pettitt, Kathy Mastrian, Catrina Messett, Julie Papadimas, Andy Puleo, Bruce Raynor, Greg Singer, Jane Williams, Jeanne Zingale, and Karen Zoccole.

Similarly, countless Shenango students have inspired me, but for becoming friends, serving as my research assistants, running the student clubs I sponsor, or keeping in touch long after they have moved on, I thank Heidi Ashcroft, Julie Babich, Ashley Balas, David Borton, Ann Churchman, Mikayla Cutshaw, Randy Ebert, Adrienne Elliott, Tonja Fleischer, Breanna Gassner, Holly Grande, Alaina Kress, Cyndi Marriotti, Christin Pyle, Steve Shook, Candice Strautnieks, Michelle Terzigni, Michele Truax-Ohl, Ariane Wagler, Genna Warner, Andrea Webster, Jessie Weller, and Shannon Whitaker.

Working with the University Press of Kentucky has been an honor and a pleasure; all institutions should be run by such friendly, efficient, and committed people. My thanks to Melissa Hammer, Erin Holman, Ila McEntire, Natalie O'Neal, and Jackie Wilson in particular. I also thank the two anonymous readers UPK chose; they provided invaluable suggestions for improving the manuscript.

My brothers—David, Erik, and Fletcher—have remained awesome despite our devolution through middle age. I hereby demand that they come out to Pittsburgh again for the next weekend get-together if they haven't already.

My wife, Soo, was here for the first book, and is still with me for the second. She has not only put up with me all these years, but she also bravely slogged through the manuscript and made it much better. For her patience, intelligence, wise counsel, and love, a million thank yous are not enough.

Finally, the dedication can only hint at how much I owe my parents. Mom and Dad: Thank you so much. I miss you.

Permissions

Chapter 2 is derived, in part, from an article published in *Diplomacy & Statecraft* 16 (March 2005): 57–72, available online at https://www.tandfonline.com/doi/abs/10.1080/09592290590916130.

Portions of chapter 5 appeared in a different form in Philip Nash, "Ambassador Eugenie Anderson," *Minnesota History* 59 (Summer 2005): 249–62, available online at http://collections.mnhs.org/MNHistoryMagazine/articles/59/v59i06p249-262.pdf, and appear here with permission of the Minnesota Historical Society.

Chapter 7 is derived, in part, from "'A Woman's Touch in Foreign Affairs'? The Career of Ambassador Frances E. Willis, "*Diplomacy & Statecraft* 13 (June 2002): 1–20, available online at https://www.tandfonline.com/doi/abs/10.1080/714000319.

Portions of the epilogue appeared in a different form in Philip Nash, "A Woman's Place Is in the Embassy: America's First Female Chiefs of Mission, 1933–64," in *Women, Diplomacy and International Politics since 1500*, ed. Glenda Sluga and Carolyn James (London: Routledge): 222–39, © Glenda Sluga and Carolyn James, reproduced with permission of the Licensor through PLSclear.

Notes

Abbreviations

AFN	Anderson Family Newsletters, CF, box 4, EMAP
ACMF	Anderson Copenhagen Miscellaneous Files, box 4, EMAP
AWF	Presidential Papers of Dwight D. Eisenhower (Ann Whitman File), DDEL
BFP	Bess Furman Papers, LC
BMF	Bulgaria Ministry Files, 1962–1965, EMAP
CCF	Copenhagen Correspondence Files, EMAP
CF	Copenhagen Files, EMAP
CMF	Correspondence and Miscellaneous Files, EMAP
COF	Copenhagen Office Files, CF, box 1, EMAP
CDF	Central Decimal File, RG 59, NARA
CBLP	Clare Boothe Luce Papers, LC
DDEL	Dwight D. Eisenhower Library, Abilene, KS
DOS	Department of State
EMAP	Eugenie Moore Anderson Papers, MHS
EMHP	Edward M. House Papers, Sterling Memorial Library, Yale University, New Haven
ERP	Eleanor Roosevelt Papers, FDRL
FAOHC	Foreign Affairs Oral History Collection, Association for Diplomatic Studies and Training, Arlington, VA, www.adst.org
FC	Family Correspondence, 1920–1966, boxes 3–13, FEWP
FDRL	Franklin D. Roosevelt Presidential Library, Hyde Park, NY
FEWP	Frances E. Willis Papers, HIA
FHP	Fannie Hurst Papers, Harry Ransom Center, University of Texas at Austin
FJHP	Florence Jaffray Harriman Papers, Manuscript Division, LC
FLB	Family Letters from Bulgaria, 1962, PC, BMF, box 11
FRUS	*Foreign Relations of the United States,* Washington, DC: GPO, 1934–1964.
FSIC	Foreign Service Inspection Corps
FSIR	Foreign Service Inspection Report
GCMS	General Correspondence and Memoranda Series, JFDP, DDEL.

GFKP	George F. Kennan Papers, SGML
GGAP	Garret G. Ackerson Jr. Papers, Lauinger Library, Georgetown University
HCHL	Herbert C. Hoover Presidential Library, West Branch, IA
HIA	Hoover Institution Archives, Stanford University, Stanford, CA
HL	Houghton Library, Harvard University, Cambridge, MA
HSCP	Hugh S. Cumming Papers, Alderman Library, University of Virginia
HSTP	Harry S. Truman Papers, HSTL
HSTL	Harry S. Truman Presidential Library, Independence, MO
IEP	India Edwards Papers, HSTL
JFKL	John F. Kennedy Presidential Library, Boston, MA
JFDP	John Foster Dulles Papers, DDEL
JPMP	J. Pierrepont Moffat Papers, HL
JPP	Jefferson Patterson Papers, Manuscript Division, LC
LBJL	Lyndon Baines Johnson Presidential Library, Austin, TX
LC	Library of Congress, Washington, DC
MHS	Minnesota Historical Society, St. Paul
MWDP	Mary W. Dewson Papers, FDRL
NA-UK	The National Archives, Kew, London, United Kingdom
NARA	National Archives and Records Administration, Archives II, College Park, MD
OCI	Office of the Chief Inspector
PACRF	Public Affairs Correspondence and Related Files, 1953–1968, CMF
PC	Personal Correspondence, BMF
PSF-FDRL	President's Secretary's File, FDRL
PSF-HSTL	President's Secretary's File, HSTL
RG	Record Group
RMP	Raymond Moley Papers, HIA
POF	President's Office File, FDRL
SGML	Seeley G. Mudd Library, Princeton University, Princeton, NJ
SL	Schlesinger Library, Harvard University, Cambridge, MA
SSM	Speeches and Speech Materials, boxes 11 and 12, EMAP
WPP	William Phillips Papers, MS Am 2232, HL
WRCP-HCHL	William R. Castle Jr. Papers, HCHL
WRCP-HL	William R. Castle Jr. Papers, HL
WJCP	Wilbur J. Carr Papers, Manuscript Division, LC

Prologue

1. Thomas W. Lippman, *Madeleine Albright and the New American Diplomacy* (Boulder, CO: Westview, 2000), 8.

2. E. Wilder Spaulding, *Ambassadors Ordinary and Extraordinary* (Washington, DC: Public Affairs Press, 1961), 180.

3. Glenda Sluga and Carolyn James, "Introduction: The Long International History of Women and Diplomacy," in *Women, Diplomacy and International Politics since 1500,* ed. Glenda Sluga and Carolyn James (Abingdon, UK: Routledge, 2016), 2.

4. Emily Rosenberg, "Gender," *Journal of American History* 77 (June 1990): 116–24. For similar misgivings, see Laura McEnaney, "Gender," in *Encyclopedia of American Foreign Policy,* vol. 2, ed. Alexander DeConde et al., 2nd ed. (New York: Charles Scribner's Sons, 2002), 124–25.

5. Megan Threlkeld, "Twenty Years of *Worlds of Women:* Leila Rupp's Impact on the History of U.S. Women's Internationalism," *History Compass* 15 (June 2017): https://onlinelibrary.wiley.com/doi/abs/10.1111/hic3.12381; Sluga and James, "Introduction," 11n7; Molly Wood, "Gender and American Foreign Relations," in *The Routledge History of Gender, War, and the U.S. Military,* ed. Kara D. Vuic (New York: Routledge, 2017), 210.

6. Joan Hoff-Wilson, "Conclusion: Of Mice and Men," in *Women and American Foreign Policy: Lobbyists, Critics, and Insiders,* ed. Edward P. Crapol, 2nd ed. (Wilmington, DE: Scholarly Resources, 1992), 177–79.

7. Alice Kessler-Harris, "Do We Still Need Women's History?" *Chronicle of Higher Education* 54 (December 7, 2007): B6.

8. Walter Monfried, "Uncle Sam's Diplomatic Nieces," *Milwaukee Journal,* August 9, 1954, 12.

1. The Patriarchs

Epigraph: Lillie de Hegermann-Lindencrone, *The Sunny Side of Diplomatic Life, 1875–1912* (New York: Harper & Brothers, 1914), ix.

1. Charles Dana Gibson, *An Ambassador's Ball in Days to Come, Life,* June 25, 1896, 514–15, also in Gibson, *Pictures of People* (New York: Russell & Son, 1896).

2. See Jane Hunter, *How Young Ladies Became Girls: The Victorian Origins of American Girlhood* (New Haven: Yale University Press, 2002), 389–92, and Martha Patterson, *Beyond the Gibson Girl: Reimagining the American New Woman, 1895–1915* (Urbana: University of Illinois Press, 2005), 28–31.

3. Gail Bederman, *Manliness and Civilization: A Cultural History of Gender and Race in the United States, 1880–1917* (Chicago: University of Chicago Press, 1995), 10–15.

4. Robert L. Beisner, *From the Old Diplomacy to the New, 1865–1900* (Arlington Heights, IL: AHM Publishing, 1975), 31; "Israeli Envoy Recalled Over Nude Exploit in El Salvador," *Washington Post,* March 13, 2007.

5. *The Memoirs of Cordell Hull,* 2 vols. (New York: Macmillan, 1948), 1:188–89.

6. Quoted in Spaulding, *Ambassadors Ordinary and Extraordinary,* 7–8.

7. Wilson quoted in Waldo H. Heinrichs, *American Ambassador: Joseph C. Grew and the Development of the United States Diplomatic Tradition* (New York: Oxford University Press, 1966), 123; Martin Weil, *A Pretty Good Club: The Founding Fathers of the U.S. Foreign Service* (New York: Norton, 1978), 15–23; C. Ben Wright, "George F. Kennan, Scholar-Diplomat: 1926–1946," (PhD diss., University of Wisconsin, 1972), 12; John L. Gaddis, *George F. Kennan: An American Life* (New York: Penguin, 2011), 37–41.

8. Sir Ernest Satow, *A Guide to Diplomatic Practice*, 2 vols. (London: Longmans Green, 1917), quoted in Robert D. Schulzinger, *The Making of the Diplomatic Mind: The Training, Outlook, and Style of United States Foreign Service Officers, 1908–1931* (Middletown, CT: Wesleyan University Press, 1975), 10–11; Charles W. Thayer, *Diplomat* (New York: Harper & Brothers, 1959), 88.

9. Hugh R. Wilson, *Diplomacy as a Career* (Cambridge, MA.: Riverside, 1941), 19; Bertram D. Hulen, *Inside the Department of State* (New York: Whittlesey House, 1939), 168–69.

10. *The Memoirs of Ambassador Henry T. Grady: From the Great War to the Cold War,* ed. John T. McNay (Columbia: University of Missouri Press, 2009), 26–27, see also 155–57; David Mayers, *FDR's Ambassadors and the Diplomacy of Crisis: From the Rise of Hitler to the End of World War II* (Cambridge: Cambridge University Press, 2013), 191–93; Lynne Olson, *Citizens of London: The Americans Who Stood With Britain in Its Darkest, Finest Hour* (New York: Random House, 2010), 23–26, 76–78.

11. Ellis O. Briggs, *Proud Servant: The Memoirs of a Career Ambassador* (Kent, OH: Kent State University Press, 1998), 15–16, 35, 192.

12. Heinrichs, *American Ambassador,* 14–16, 46–47.

13. Heinrichs, *American Ambassador,* 144–45, 192; Masanori Nakamura, *The Japanese Monarchy: Ambassador Joseph Grew and the Making of the "Symbol Emperor System"* (Armonk, NY: M. E. Sharpe, 1992), 56–58; John Thares Davidann, *Cultural Diplomacy in U.S.–Japanese Relations, 1919–1941* (New York: Palgrave Macmillan, 2007), 168–69.

14. John J. McCloy, "New Tasks for Diplomacy," *Life,* March 30, 1953, 90, 92; Kennedy to Willis, May 29, 1961, quoted in Nicholas J. Willis, *Francis Elizabeth Willis: Up the Foreign Service Ladder to the Summit—Despite the Limitations of Her Sex* (Carmel, CA: Nicholas J. Willis, 2013), 385–86.

15. Thayer, *Diplomat,* 217; William Phillips, *Ventures in Diplomacy* (Boston: Beacon, 1952), 463.

16. Thayer, *Diplomat,* 217–31; Heinrichs, *American Ambassador,* 161; Eric Clark, *Corps Diplomatique* (London: Allen Lane, 1973), 109–17, British protocol chief quoted on 110.

17. Graham H. Stuart, *American Diplomatic and Consular Practice,* 2nd ed. (New York: Appleton-Century-Crofts, 1952), 213.

18. Molly M. Wood, "Diplomatic Wives: The Politics of Domesticity and the 'Social Game' in the U.S. Foreign Service, 1905–1941," *Journal of Women's History* 17 (Summer 2005): 142–94; Molly M. Wood, "'Commanding Beauty' and 'Gentle

Charm': American Women and Gender in the Early Twentieth-Century Foreign Service," *Diplomatic History* 31 (June 2007): 505–30; Willard Beaulac, *Career Diplomat: A Career in the Foreign Service of the United States* (New York: Macmillan, 1964), 181.

19. Phillips, *Ventures in Diplomacy,* 463; Wood, "Diplomatic Wives," 150–56; Howard B. Schaffer, *Ellsworth Bunker: Global Troubleshooter, Vietnam Hawk* (Chapel Hill: University of North Carolina Press, 2003), 32; Spaulding, *Ambassadors Ordinary and Extraordinary,* 244–46.

20. Wood, "Diplomatic Wives," 151–52; Edward M. Bennett, "Joseph C. Grew: The Diplomacy of Pacification," in *Diplomats in Crisis: United States–Chinese–Japanese Relations, 1919–1941,* ed. Richard Dean Burns and Edward M. Bennett (Santa Barbara, CA: ABC-Clio, 1974), 66.

21. W. S. Gilbert, *Princess Ida,* in *The Savoy Operas,* 2 vols. (New York: Oxford University Press, 1962), 1:309–10; H. W. Brands, *Inside the Cold War: Loy Henderson and the Rise of the American Empire, 1918–1961* (New York: Oxford University Press, 1991), 37–38, 109–10; "Henderson, Loy W.—Ambassador to Iran," n.d. (1954), Evaluation of Chiefs of Mission (2), box 1, Personnel Series, Chief of Mission Subseries, JFDP.

22. Clark, *Corps Diplomatique,* 121; Wood, "Diplomatic Wives," 142; Henry S. Villard, *Affairs at State* (New York: Thomas Y. Crowell, 1965), 140; Jewell Fenzi, with Carl L. Nelson, *Married to the Foreign Service: An Oral History of the American Diplomatic Spouse* (New York: Twayne, 1994), 74.

23. Michael Kimmel, *Manhood in America: A Cultural History,* 2nd. ed. (New York: Oxford University Press, 2006), 92, 120–24; Lloyd C. Griscom, *Diplomatically Speaking* (Boston: Little, Brown, 1940), 222; E. Anthony Rotundo, *American Manhood: Transformations in Masculinity from the Revolution to the Modern Era* (New York: Basic Books, 1993), 227; Roosevelt quoted in Douglas Brinkley, *The Wilderness Warrior: Theodore Roosevelt and the Crusade for America* (New York: HarperCollins, 2009), 184.

24. Griscom, *Diplomatically Speaking,* 199–200; Thayer, *Diplomat,* 235.

25. Heinrichs, *American Ambassador,* 7–12; Warren F. Ilchman, *Professional Diplomacy in the United States, 1779–1939: A Study in Administrative History* (Chicago: University of Chicago Press, 1961), 87–88; "Hunting Decided Life Work of Ambassador to Japan," *Washington Post,* February 10, 1932, 4; Joseph C. Grew, *Turbulent Era: A Diplomatic Record of Forty Years, 1904–45,* 2 vols. (Boston: Houghton Mifflin, 1952), 1:13.

26. Ellis O. Briggs, *Shots Heard Round the World: An Ambassador's Hunting Adventures on Four Continents* (New York: Viking, 1957).

27. Albert D. Sears, "Diplomacy," *New York Times,* April 22, 1956, 245; Schulzinger, *Making of the Diplomatic Mind,* 10; Deane Heller and David Heller, *John Foster Dulles: Soldier for Peace* (New York: Holt, Rinehart & Winston, 1960); anonymous diplomat quoted in Thayer, *Diplomat,* 241. Malcolm Toon, US ambassador to the Soviet Union in the late 1970s, recalled having met an admiral who wanted to be an ambassador after he retired. Toon replied, "When I retir[e] from the

Foreign Service, I'd like to command an aircraft carrier. . . . The admiral said that was ridiculous because a naval command requires years of training and experience. I said, 'That's exactly how it is with an embassy'" (Beth Horning, "A Diplomat Lost, Then Found," *Tufts Magazine,* Fall 2017, 62–63).

28. Adams quoted in Spaulding, *Ambassadors Ordinary and Extraordinary,* 3–4, see also 18; *Sun* quoted in Eric Goldman, *The Crucial Decade—And After: America, 1945–1960* (New York: Vintage, 1960), 123.

29. Heinrichs, *American Ambassador,* 101; Drew Pearson and Robert S. Allen, *Washington Merry-Go-Round* (New York: Horace Liveright, 1931), 145; Waller quoted in *Distinguished Service: Lydia Chapin Kirk, Partner in Diplomacy,* ed. Roger Kirk (New York: Syracuse University Press, 2007), 141.

30. Arthur M. Schlesinger Jr., *The Vital Center: The Politics of Freedom* (Boston: Houghton Mifflin, 1949), 168, 166; I. F. Stone, quoted in Weil, *Pretty Good Club,* 145; "Career Diplomats," *Washington Post,* April 6, 1947, B4.

31. Alistair Cooke, *The American Home Front, 1941–1942* (New York: Atlantic Monthly Press, 2006), 32; Russell to Benton, "Public Opinion Survey on Stereotype of 'An American Diplomat,'" January 22, 1946, Stereotype of "An American Diplomat," 1946, attachment, box 11, Subject Files, 1945–52, Office of Public Affairs, Office of the Assistant Secretary of State for Public Affairs, Lot 54 D 202, Lot Files, RG 59, NARA.

32. Hester O'Neill, "Ingenuity and Courage Are Tools of Trade for Foreign Service Officers," *Christian Science Monitor,* February 20, 1950, 13; "Hull Lauds American Diplomats as Men Who Don't Wear Spats," *Los Angeles Times,* August 4, 1938, 7; Robert Young, "Cookie Pushers Resent the Tag, One of 'Em Says," *Chicago Daily Tribune,* December 10, 1952, B3.

33. Royal Typewriter Company advertisement, "No Sissies Wanted," *American Foreign Service Journal* 18 (April 1941): 233.

34. Thruston Morton to John Foster Dulles, "Confidential Evaluation of Chiefs of Mission and Recommended List of Posts Where a Change Seems Desirable," September 20, 1954, Tab Group III, Subject File (Strictly Confidential) Chiefs of Mission—Evaluation, box 2, Personnel Series, JFDP. *Miss Nancy,* a term originating in the nineteenth century, first referred to a straight man considered insufficiently manly, and then later also to a gay man (Rotundo, *American Manhood,* 278, 272).

35. K. A. Cuordileone, *Manhood and American Political Culture in the Cold War* (New York: Routledge, 2005), 58, 60; Barbara Epstein, "Anti-Communism, Homophobia, and the Construction of Masculinity in the Postwar U.S.," *Critical Sociology* 20 (1994): 21–44; David Oshinsky, *A Conspiracy So Immense: The World of Joe McCarthy* (New York: Oxford University Press, 2005), 108–12, McCarthy's latter (May 1950) speech quoted on 157; Jack Lait and Lee Mortimer, *Washington Confidential* (New York: Crown, 1951), 96–97; David K. Johnson, *The Lavender Scare: The Cold War Persecution of Gays and Lesbians in the Federal Government* (Chicago: University of Chicago Press, 2004), 76; Robert Dean, *Imperial Brotherhood: Gender and the Making of Cold War Foreign Policy* (Amherst: University of Massachusetts Press, 2001), 66.

36. Butler quoted in Goldman, *Crucial Decade,* 125; Cal Alley cartoon, *Attack,* in Dean, *Imperial Brotherhood,* 91, see also 89–92 on Acheson.

37. Westbrook Pegler, quoted in Johnson, *Lavender Scare,* 65, see also 68–69; Kalman Seigel, "Kennan Decries Witch Hunts As a Peril to Federal Service," *New York Times,* February 22, 1953, 1.

38. Talleyrand quoted in Charles W. Freeman Jr., ed., *The Diplomat's Dictionary* (Washington, DC: National Defense University Press, 1994), 81; Grenville Murray, *Embassies and Foreign Courts: A History of Diplomacy* (London: G. Routledge, 1855), 102.

39. Edward P. Crapol, "Lydia Maria Child: Abolitionist Critic of American Foreign Policy," Robert E. May, "'Plenipotentiary in Petticoats': Jane M. Cazneau and American Foreign Policy in the Mid-Nineteenth Century," Janet L. Coryell, "Duty and Delicacy: Anna Ella Carroll of Maryland," and John M. Craig, "Lucia True Ames Mead: American Publicist for Peace and Internationalism," all in Crapol, *Women and American Foreign Policy,* 1–18, 19–44, 45–65, and 67–90; Gregg Wolper, "Woodrow Wilson's New Diplomacy: Vira Whitehouse in Switzerland, 1918," *Prologue* 24 (Fall 1992): 227–39; Tibor Grant, "Against All Odds: Vira B. Whitehouse and Rosika Schwimmer in Switzerland, 1918," *American Studies International* 40 (February 2002): 34–51, esp. 35–43.

40. See especially Leila J. Rupp, *Worlds of Women: The Making of an International Women's Movement* (Princeton, NJ: Princeton University Press, 1997) and Harriet Hyman Alonso, *Peace as a Women's Issue: A History of the U.S. Movement for World Peace and Women's Rights* (Syracuse, NY: Syracuse University Press, 1993).

41. Bennie DeWhitt, "A Wider Sphere of Usefulness: Marilla Ricker's Quest for a Diplomatic Post," *Prologue* 5 (Winter 1973): 203–7; quotations from 204, and Frederick Van Dyne, *Our Foreign Service: The "A B C" of American Diplomacy,* (Rochester, NY: Lawyers Co-Operative Publishing Co., 1909), 75.

42. Kimmel, *Manhood in America,* 81, 85–86; George Chauncey, *Gay New York: Gender, Urban Culture, and the Making of the Gay Male World, 1890–1940* (New York: Basic Books, 1994), 111–26; Kevin P. Murphy, *Political Manhood: Red Bloods, Mollycoddles, and the Politics of Progressive Era Reform* (New York: Columbia University Press, 2008).

43. George F. Kennan, *Memoirs, 1925–1950* (New York: Pantheon, 1967), 13, 16; George F. Kennan, "Russia's International Position at the Close of the War with Germany," May 1945, appendix B of the same volume, 545.

44. George F. Kennan, "The Prerequisites: Notes on the Problems of the United States," 1938, folder 4, box 240, GFKP; Gaddis, *George F. Kennan,* 114–19, 290.

45. Carr quoted in Schulzinger, *Making of the Diplomatic Mind,* 51.

46. William R. Castle, Jr. diary, March 23, 1925, 91, MS Am(erican) 2021, WRCP-HL.

47. Van Dyne, *Our Foreign Service,* 75.

48. Dudley Harmon, "Women Left in Tests For Diplomatic Posts," *Washington Post,* October 19, 1936, X10; Spaulding, *Ambassadors Ordinary and Extraordinary,* 180.

49. Murray, *Embassies and Foreign Courts,* 102; Wilbur Carr Diary, January 22, 1925, May 3, 1926, in Diary 1925 and Diary 1926 (2), both in box 3, WJCP; Frank Costigliola, "'Unceasing Pressure for Penetration': Gender, Pathology, and Emotion in George Kennan's Formation of the Cold War," *Journal of American History* 83 (March 1997): 1309–39; and Frank Costigliola, "'I React Intensely to Everything': Russia and the Frustrated Emotions of George F. Kennan, 1933–1958," *Journal of American History* 102 (March 2016): 1075–1101.

50. Homer L. Calkin, *Women in the Department of State: Their Role in American Foreign Affairs* (Washington, DC: Department of State, 1978), 10. Unless otherwise noted, this account of Schwimmer's ministry is based on Grant, "Against All Odds," 43–47, and Peter Pastor, "The Diplomatic Fiasco of the Modern World's First Woman Ambassador, Róza Bédy-Schwimmer," *East European Quarterly* 8 (Fall 1974): 273–82.

51. David S. Patterson, *The Search for Negotiated Peace: Women's Activism and Citizen Diplomacy in World War I* (New York: Routledge, 2008), 38–39, 157–59; quotation from Pastor, "Diplomatic Fiasco," 278.

52. This account draws on Barbara E. Clements, *Bolshevik Feminist: The Life of Alexandra Kollontai* (Bloomington: Indiana University Press, 1979), esp. 221–24, 242–70; Cathy Porter, *Alexandra Kollontai: The Lonely Struggle of the Woman Who Defied Lenin* (New York: Dial Press, 1980), esp. 408–85; and Susanne Schattenberg, "Ein Diplomat in Kleid: Aleksandra Kollontaj und die sowietische Diplomatie," in *Das Geschlecht der Diplomatie: Geschlechterrollen in den Außenbeziehungen vom Spätmittelalter bis zum 20. Jahrhundert,* ed. Corina Bastian et al. (Cologne: Böhlau Verlag, 2014), 215–35.

53. Lindley to Chamberlain, January 10, 1925, enclosure, "Report on Heads of Foreign Missions at Norway," 24, FO 419/13, and Kerr to Simon, January 1, 1935, enclosure, "Report on Heads of Foreign Missions at Stockholm," 137, FO 419/29, both in NA-UK; Anthony F. Upton, *Finland, 1939–1940* (Newark: University of Delaware Press, 1974), 92–94, 97; Schattenberg, "Diplomat in Kleid," 221 (Kollontai quotation my translation); Kerr, quoted in Foreign and Commonwealth Office, *Women in Diplomacy: The FCO, 1782–1999* (London: Records & Historical Services, FCO, 1999), 9.

54. Barbara J. Harris, *Beyond Her Sphere: Women and the Professions in American History* (Westport, CT: Greenwood, 1978), 95–121; Ilchman, *Professional Diplomacy in the United States,* 169.

55. This account of Atcherson's career, unless otherwise noted, is based on Molly Wood, "Lucile Atcherson Curtis: The First Female Diplomat," *Foreign Service Journal* 90 (July–August 2013): 44–48; Molly Wood, "Wives, Clerks, and 'Lady Diplomats': The Gendered Politics of Diplomacy and Representation in the U.S. Foreign Service, 1900–1940," *European Journal of American Studies* 10 (March 2015): http://ejas.revues.org/10562; Calkin, *Women in the Department of State,* 58–78; and Marilyn S. Greenwald, *A Woman of the Times: Journalism, Feminism, and the Career of Charlotte Curtis* (Athens: Ohio University Press, 1999), 1–11.

56. Grew to Hugh Wilson, January 19, 1925, in Grew, *Turbulent Era,* 1:646–47. (Wilson suggested a separate branch for women; Grew opposed it.)

57. Robert Bliss to Atcherson, December 5, 1922, *The Text Message* (blog), http://blogs.archives.gov/TextMessage/2013/09/09/an-archives-filled-with-firsts/ (page discontinued as of March 21, 2019); Personnel Board quoted in Wood, "Lucile Atcherson Curtis," 47.

58. "O'Prune" [Gibson] to Grew, April 20, 1925, and "Winkie" [Grew] to "O'Prune," May 15, 1925, both in box 1, Hugh S. Gibson Papers, HIA; Gibson to Castle, July 15, 1925, quoted in Ilchman, *Professional Diplomacy in the United States,* 234; Gibson to Fred [Dolbeare?], August 1, October 26, 1926, Gibson to Castle, August 23, 1927, all in Atcherson (Miss Lucille) Inquiry, 1926–1927, box 1, as well as Marriner to Castle, January 14, 1927, and Castle to Marriner, February 2, 1927, both Switzerland 1927, box 14, all in WRCP-HCHL.

59. Albert Halstead, quoted in Ilchman, *Professional Diplomacy in the United States,* 234–35.

2. Ruth Bryan Owen

Epigraph: Constance Marshall, "Ruth Bryan Owen," *Woman's Journal,* January 1928, 10.

1. Sarah P. Vickers, *The Life of Ruth Bryan Owen: Florida's First Congresswoman and America's First Woman Diplomat* (Tallahassee, FL: Sentry, 2009), 129–30; "Mrs. Owen Hailed as Pioneer Woman Envoy by Mrs. Roosevelt and 800 at Dinner Here," *New York Times,* May 10, 1933, 15; "Speeches Given at Dinner for Ruth Bryan Owen," New York City, May 9, 1933 (sound recording), RXA 5649 A-13–15-B1–5, Recorded Sound Reference Center, LC.

2. "Mrs. Owen Hailed as Pioneer Woman"; "Speeches Given at Dinner for Ruth Bryan Owen."

3. Sally Vickers, "Ruth Bryan Owen: Florida's First Congresswoman and Lifetime Activist," in *Making Waves: Female Activists in Twentieth-Century Florida,* ed. Jack E. Davis and Kari Frederickson (Gainesville: University Press of Florida, 2003), 25–27; Michael Kazin, *A Godly Hero: The Life of William Jennings Bryan* (New York: Knopf, 2006), 170–71; Ann Miller Morin and Kristie Miller, "A Dame among the Danes," *Foreign Service Journal* 74 (January 1997): 41; Ruth Bryan Owen, "Diplomacy as a Career for Women," *Christian Science Monitor,* January 9, 1935, WM1; George Brown, "Ruth Bryan Owen Brings Rich Talent to Diplomacy," *Washington Herald,* April 23, 1933, D-8.

4. Vickers, "Ruth Bryan Owen," 27–33; Brooke Kroeger, *Fannie: The Talent for Success of Writer Fannie Hurst* (New York: Random House, 1999), 106; Rudd Brown, *Ruth Bryan Owen, Congresswoman and Diplomat: An Intimate Portrait* (North Charleston, SC: CreateSpace, 2014), 71.

5. Vickers, "Ruth Bryan Owen," 33–45; Kroeger, *Fannie,* 175.

6. Jo Freeman, *A Room at a Time: How Women Entered Party Politics* (Lanham, MD: Rowman & Littlefield, 2000), 172–73; Susan Ware, *Partner and I: Molly Dewson, Feminism, and New Deal Politics* (New Haven: Yale University Press, 1987), 171–72. Crushed by her defeat, Owen may have suffered a nervous breakdown (Brown, *Ruth Bryan Owen,* 120–21).

7. Susan Ware, *Beyond Suffrage: Women in the New Deal* (Cambridge, MA: Harvard University Press, 1981), 57–61; Jean Edward Smith, *FDR* (New York: Random House, 2007), 82–83; Frank Freidel, *Franklin D. Roosevelt: A Rendezvous with Destiny* (Boston: Little, Brown, 1990), 49–50.

8. Frank Freidel, *Franklin D. Roosevelt: Launching the New Deal* (Boston: Little, Brown, 1973), 138, 143–44; H. W. Brands, *Traitor to His Class: The Privileged Life and Radical Presidency of Franklin Delano Roosevelt* (New York: Anchor, 2008), 293; Raymond Moley, *The First New Deal* (New York: Harcourt, Brace & World, 1966), 73, 73n; Owen to Fannie Hurst, March 21, 1933, folder 1, box 194, FHP; Harold Horan, "Diplomatic Pouch," *Washington Post,* June 25, 1933, 7; Blanche Wiesen Cook, *Eleanor Roosevelt:* vol. 2 of 3, *1933–1938* (New York: Viking, 1999), 68–69; Ware, *Partner and I,* 186.

9. "Madame Minister," *Washington Post,* April 28, 1933, 6.

10. Brown, *Ruth Bryan Owen,* 121–22; Owen to House, September 30, 1932, House to Owen, October 5, 1932, Owen to House, October 31, 1932, all in folder 2928, box 84, EMHP; see also Owen to House, November 15, 1932, in the same folder.

11. Owen to House, April 6, 1933, box 84, folder 2929, EMHP; "Mrs. Owen to Be Envoy at Copenhagen; She Will Be First Woman Named Minister," *New York Times,* April 4, 1933, 9; Raymond Moley Diary, March 27, 1933, Folder Jan-Jl 1933, box 1, RMP.

12. Frederick W. Coleman diary, April 1, 1933, box 1, Frederick W. Coleman Diaries, HIA; "Ruth Bryan Owen Envoy to Denmark," *New York Times,* April 13, 1933, 3.

13. Coleman to Hull, April 8, 1933, 123 Owen, Ruth Bryan/2, CDF 1930–39; Grew to Owen, May 9, 1933, ser. 1, box 65, Joseph Grew Papers, MS Am 1687, HL; Moffat to Byington, March 14, 1933, 22:1931–33, JPMP, MS Am 1407, attachment.

14. Corinne Lowe, "Our First Woman Diplomat," *Pictorial Review* 35 (February 1934): 67.

15. Translations from *Extrabladet,* May 23, 1933, and *Berlingske Tidende,* May 23, 1933, both quoted in Calkin, *Women in the Department of State,* 162.

16. Ruth Bryan Owen, *Leaves from a Greenland Diary* (New York: Dodd, Mead, 1935), 4; Owen to Hurst, June 5, 1933, folder 1, and Owen to Hurst, January 30, 1934, folder 2, both box 194, FHP.

17. "America's First Woman Envoy Keeps Open House in Denmark," *Washington Post,* December 10, 1933, S8; "Danish New Year Levee a Triumph for Mrs. Owen," *New York Times,* January 2, 1934, 6; "OWEN: Inunguak—or America's Entertaining Envoy to Denmark," *Newsweek,* September 28, 1935, 22; Katherine

Smith manuscript, "My Life—Berlin, 1935–1939," n.d., Smith, Subject File, box 4, Truman Smith Papers, HCHL, 79.

18. "Mrs. Owen in Denmark," *New York Times,* April 5, 1933, 18; Sidney Hertzberg, "Mrs. Owen Winning Danish Good-Will," *New York Times,* January 21, 1934, 2; Wayne Francis Palmer, "Men of State," *New Outlook* 163 (May 1934): 37; "Diplomatic Pouch," *Washington Post,* April 16, 1933, 13; Danish newspaper quoted in "To Denmark & Iceland," *Time,* April 24, 1933, 13; "Mr. Roosevelt's New Deal for Women," *Literary Digest* 115 (April 15, 1933): 24; Owen to Cora [?], April 29, 1934, Ruth Bryan Owen Rohde Letters, SL.

19. Owen to F. Roosevelt, July 27, 1933, November 17, 1933, F. Roosevelt to Owen, December 7, 1933, all in Ruth Bryan Owen Rohde 1933–44, file 437, and Claude G. Bowers to F. Roosevelt, December 13, 1933, F. Roosevelt to Bowers, February 5, 1934, both in Claude G. Bowers, Spain 1933–38, file 303, all in POF.

20. Jussi M. Hanhimäki, *Scandinavia and the United States: An Insecure Friendship* (New York: Twayne, 1997), 5–6; Owen to Roosevelt, July 27, 1933, Ruth Bryan Owen Rohde 1933–44, file 437, POF; Owen to Hull, January 23, 1934, Sayre to Owen, May 7, 1934, Owen to Hull, June 13, 1934, "Memorandum by the Assistant Secretary of State (Grady)," November 28, 1934, all in *Foreign Relations of the United States (FRUS), 1934* (Washington, DC: GPO, 1951), 2:123–26; Hertzberg, "Mrs. Owen Winning Danish Good-Will."

21. "Denmark Is Proving Roosevelt Policies, Mrs. Owen Declares," *Christian Science Monitor,* November 21, 1934, 9; Owen-Steinhardt correspondence, July–October 1934, in folder M–O 1934, box 9, and Owen to Steinhardt, January 15, 1935, folder M–O 1935, box 12, both in Lawrence Steinhardt Papers, LC; "Mrs. Owen Honored by Florida College," *New York Times,* November 1, 1935, 26; "Danish Like Mrs. Owen, First Lady of U.S. Diplomacy," *Appleton (WI) Post-Crescent,* May 21, 1934.

22. Nicholas Cull, "Public Diplomacy: Taxonomies and Histories," *Annals of the American Academy of Political and Social Science* 616 (March 2008): 31–54.

23. "Mrs. Owen to Keep Beer," *New York Times,* April 16, 1933, 12; "The American Minister Visits to [sic] Widow of a Laborer," translation from unknown Danish newspaper, n.d., attached to Owen to Hull, June 26, 1933, 123 Owen, R. B./32, CDF 1930–39.

24. Bess Furman, *Washington By-Line: The Personal History of a Newspaper Woman* (New York: Knopf, 1949), 212; translation of Danish press accounts, May 2, 1936, attached to Owen to Hull, May 4, 1936, 123 Owen, Ruth Bryan/226, CDF 1930–39; Lowe, "Our First Woman Diplomat," 4.

25. Brown, *Ruth Bryan Owen,* 114; "Ruth B. Owen Visits Eskimos, Eats Caribou," *Washington Post,* August 11, 1934; Owen to Fannie Hurst, May 27, 1934, folder 2, box 194, FHP; Katherine Smith, "My Life," 80.

26. Jessie Hill to Hurst, June 27, 1935[?], attachment, "Ruth Bryan Owen," folder 2, box 194, FHP; Bjarne Rosing to Hull, November 5, 1934, 123 Owen, Ruth Bryan/135, CDF 1930–39.

27. "Better Understanding of Others Urged by Woman Envoy of U.S. to Denmark," *Christian Science Monitor,* October 1, 1934, 2; "America's First Woman Envoy Keeps Open House in Denmark."

28. Brown, *Ruth Bryan Owen,* 135; Lowe, "Our First Woman Diplomat," 4, 66; "America's First Woman Envoy Keeps Open House in Denmark"; Hubert Eaton to Hull, July 23, 1935, 123 Owen, Ruth Bryan/174, CDF 1930–39.

29. Owen, "Diplomacy as a Career for Women," WM2.

30. "Mrs. Owen Weds King's Aide Today," *Washington Star,* July 12, 1936; Harold Ickes, diary, July 10, 12, 1936 (microfilm), Harold Ickes Papers, LC, 1608, 1617–18; E. Roosevelt, "Women in Politics" [January–April, 1940], in *What I Hope to Leave Behind: The Essential Essays of Eleanor Roosevelt,* ed. Allida M. Black (Brooklyn, NY: Carlson Publishing, 1995), 253.

31. Owen to Furman, June 3, 1936, Owen, Ruth Bryan, General Correspondence, box 31, BFP; Kroeger, *Fannie,* 235; Morin and Miller, "Dame among the Danes," 43.

32. Dewson to E. Roosevelt, July 23, 1936, Owen, Ruth Bryan, 1936, General Correspondence Files, box 3, MWDP; Winship to Hull, July 16, 1936, 859.9111/141, and "Danish Press Comment on Mrs. Ruth Bryan Owen's Wedding," July 18, 1936, 123 Owen, Ruth Bryan, attachment, both in CDF 1930–1939; William Castle diary, HL, 388; Ickes diary, December 16, 1936, 1851.

33. Stephen Early to Roosevelt, August 27, 1936, Roosevelt to Early, August 28, 1936, and Early to Marvin McIntyre, August 29, 1936, all Ruth Bryan Owen Rohde 1933–44, file 437, POF; "Ruth Owen Quits Her Post as Envoy," *New York Times,* August 31, 1936, 1, 6; Owen to F. Roosevelt, contained in Owen to Hull, August 29, 1936, 123 Owen, Ruth Bryan, CDF 1930–1939.

34. Owen to Willis, September 13, 1936, Foreign Service, 1936, box 15, FEWP; Owen to Furman, June 17, 1936, Owen, Ruth Bryan, General Correspondence, box 31, BFP; "The Woman Diplomat," *New York Times,* September 1, 1936, 20; Wood, "'Commanding Beauty' and 'Gentle Charm,'" 526–27.

35. Ickes diary, December 16, 1936, 1851; Dewson to E. Roosevelt, July 18, 1936, ER 100 1936, Owen, Ruth Bryan, box 639, ERP; Owen to Dewson, September 8, 1936, Owen, Ruth Bryan, 1936, General Correspondence Files, box 3, MWDP; "Stateswoman's Shin," *Time,* October 5, 1936, 16.

36. Owen to Hurst, May 23, 1938, folder 2, box 194, FHP; "Woman Ambassador?" *Aspen Times,* May 26, 1938, 2; George Kennan, "Memoirs, Part II: 'Washington, 1937–1938,'" 1938, folder 3, box 240, GFKP, 7.

37. Kroeger, *Fannie,* 297; Owen to Furman, September 16, 1940, Owen, Ruth Bryan (2), box 31, General Correspondence, BFP.

38. Ruth Bryan Owen, *Look Forward, Warrior* (New York: Dodd, Mead, 1942); John Cudahy, "Ruth Bryan's Plan for New World Order," *Chicago Daily Tribune,* March 21, 1943, F11; Vickers, *Life of Ruth Bryan Owen,* 201–7.

39. Vickers, *Life of Ruth Bryan Owen,* 201–7; "Mrs. Rohde Re-Elected to Post," *New York Times,* December 15, 1948, 42; "Mrs. Rohde Urges Faith in U.N. Aims,"

New York Times, May 15, 1947, 29; "Mrs. Roosevelt Praises U.N. Mood," *New York Times,* September 21, 1949, 4; Peggy Frank, "The Incomparable India: A Profile of India Edwards," December 6, 1960, Edwards, India—Publicity, box 1, IEP; "New Institute to Aid U.N.," *New York Times,* December 8, 1952, 43.

40. Vickers, *Life of Ruth Bryan Owen,* 201 7; Owen to India Edwards, February 28, March 21, 1951, both in Correspondence, 1951, box 1, IEP.

41. Translations from *Extrabladet,* August 31, 1936, and *Børsen,* September 1, 1936, both in "Review of the Danish Press, August 15 to 31, 1936," attached to Winship to Hull, September 1, 1936, 859.9111/144, CDF 1930–39; "Denmark Honors Mrs. Rohde," *New York Times,* August 9, 1946, 15; "Denmark Honors Mrs. Rohde," *New York Times,* November 13, 1949, 32.

42. James McDonald diary, April 22, 1934, in *Advocate for the Doomed: The Diaries and Papers of James G. McDonald, 1932–1935,* ed. Richard Breitman, Barbara McDonald Stewart, and Severin Hochberg (Bloomington: University of Indiana Press, 2007), 369; Smith, "My Life," 78, 80.

43. Gurney to Simon, "Reports on Heads of Missions," January 1, 1935, 129, FO 419/29, NA-UK; Garret to Rhodita Ackerson, April 22, 1934, folder 8, box 2, GGAP.

44. Ackerson to Mother and Dad, April 23, 1934, folder 10; Ackerson to Rhodita Ackerson, April 29, 1934, folder 8; Ackerson to Family, May 8, 1934, folder 10; Ackerson to Mother and Dad, May 30, 1934, folder 10; Ackerson to Rhodita Ackerson, n.d. (c. June 3–July 24, 1934), folder 11; and Ackerson to Rhodita Ackerson, November 4, 1934, folder 9, all in box 2, GGAP.

45. Ackerson to Mother and Dad, December 16, 1934, folder 12, box 2, GGAP; Wilbur J. Carr, June 4, 1934 entry, Diary, 1934, box 5, WJCP; Kroeger, *Fannie,* 233; Brown, *Ruth Bryan Owen,* 136–37.

46. Carr, June 4, 1934, entry; Carr, "Interview with North Winship, Counselor at Copenhagen," May 13, 1935, May–July 1935, box 12, WJCP.

47. Winship to Moffat, December 4, 1934, vol. 7: N–Z, 1934, JPMP; Carr, "Interview with North Winship"; William Phillips diary, May 14, 1935, 823–24, folder 3, volume 7, WPP.

48. On Dodd, see Erik Larson, *In the Garden of Beasts: Love, Terror, and an American Family in Hitler's Berlin* (New York: Crown, 2011), esp. 216–17, 247–48, 255–58, 296, 342, 345–46.

49. Owen to E. Roosevelt, June 18, 1933, 100, O 1933, box 581, ERP; Owen to Hurst, July 10, 1933, folder 1, box 194, FHP; Lowe, "Our First Woman Diplomat," 4, 66; quotation from Owen to House, June 13, 1933, box 84, folder 2929, EMHP; Wilbur J. Carr, November 11, 1935, entry, Diary, 1935, box 5, WJCP.

50. Owen to Nancy Astor, February 9, 1934, courtesy Helen McCarthy; Helen McCarthy, *Women of the World: The Rise of the Female Diplomat* (London: Bloomsbury, 2014), 131.

51. William Phillips diary, May 14, 1935, October 3, 1934, 6:425, November 11, 1935, 7:1130, and April 27, 1936, 10:1470–71, all in folder 6, WPP.

52. Wilbur Carr, November 19, 1934, entry, Diary, 1934, box 5, WJCP.

53. Kroeger, *Fannie,* 216; Owen to Hurst, July 10, 1933; Hurst to Owen, September 21, 1933, folder 1, box 194, FHP.

54. F. Roosevelt to Owen, August 19, 1933, Ruth Bryan Owen Rohde 1933–1944, file 437, POF; Spaulding, *Ambassadors Ordinary and Extraordinary,* 183; "Woman Diplomat."

55. "A Woman Minister," *Washington Post,* April 26, 1933, 6.

3. Florence Jaffray Harriman

Epigraph: Maxine Davis, "'Just Like Daisy': The Extraordinary Mrs. J. Borden Harriman, American Minister to Norway," *Saturday Evening Post,* June 22, 1940, 82.

1. Quoted in Harriman, "Address by Mrs. Borden Harriman Before the Democratic Women's Luncheon Club, December 9, 1940," 4, Speeches and Articles about Norway, 1940–1943, box 24, FJHP.

2. Florence Harriman, *From Pinafores to Politics* (New York: Henry Holt, 1923), 16, 34; "Brides and Grooms," *New York Times,* November 14, 1889.

3. Johanna Neuman, *Gilded Suffragists: The New York Socialites Who Fought for Women's Right to Vote* (New York: Washington Mews, 2017), 5–22; Harriman quoted in Kristie Miller, "Harriman, Daisy," in *American National Biography,* ed. John A. Garraty and Mark C. Carnes, 24 vols. (New York: Oxford University Press, 1999), 10:140.

4. Kristie Miller, "'Eager and Anxious to Work': Daisy Harriman and the Presidential Election of 1912," in *We Have Come to Stay: American Women and Political Parties, 1880–1960,* ed. Melanie Gustafson et al. (Albuquerque: University of New Mexico Press, 1999), 65, 68–69, quotation at 73; Jo Freeman, *We Will Be Heard: Women's Struggles for Political Power in the United States* (Lanham, MD: Rowman & Littlefield, 2008), 51, 58–65; Susan Ware, "Harriman, Florence Jaffray Hurst," in *Notable American Women: The Modern Period,* ed. Barbara Sicherman and Carol Hurd Green (Cambridge, MA: Harvard University Press, 1980), 314.

5. Katie Louchheim, *By the Political Sea* (Garden City, NY: Doubleday, 1970), 61–62; Ware, *Beyond Suffrage,* 27.

6. Carolyn Bell Hughes, "Mercy Wore a Hat Pin," *(Washington Post) Potomac,* August 2, 1964, 25; Miller, "Harriman," 140.

7. Miller, "Harriman," 140; Ware, "Harriman," 314; *Bridging Two Eras: The Autobiography of Emily Newell Blair, 1877–1951,* ed. Virginia Jeans Laas (Columbia: University of Missouri Press, 1999), 236–39, 246–47; Arthur M. Schlesinger Jr., *A Life in the Twentieth Century: Innocent Beginnings, 1917–1950* (Boston: Houghton Mifflin, 2000), 386–87; Louchheim, *By the Political Sea,* 56; Florence Harriman, "Twenty Years a Hostess in the Washington Social Whirl," *American Magazine,* July 1936, 80.

8. Harriman, *From Pinafores to Politics,* 355–56; Harriman address, Pond's Radio, February 2, 1931, in *From Megaphones to Microphones: Speeches of American*

Women, 1920–1960, ed. Sandra J. Sarkela et al. (Westport, CT: Praeger, 2003), 70–71.

9. Ware, *Partner and I,* 166; Harriman to Moley, May 5, 1933, 72-2 Indexed Correspondence, H, I (108) 37–50, box 72, RMP; "President Confers with Mrs. Harriman," *New York Times,* August 23, 1933, 19; "The Reminiscences of Mrs. Florence Jaffray Harriman," April 1950, Columbia University Oral History Project, New York, 1972, 25–26; "Mrs. Harriman Hinted For Diplomatic Post," *Washington Post,* January 14, 1934, 1; "Mrs. Harriman May Be Envoy." *Los Angeles Times,* May 24, 1934, 8.

10. Molly Dewson to Eleanor Roosevelt, July 25, 1936, Roosevelt, Anna Eleanor, 1925–1936, General Correspondence Files, box 3, MWDP; Davis, "Just Like Daisy," 24; "Scoffs at Fears of Dictatorship," *New York Times,* March 3, 1937, 11; "24 Labor Rallies Back Court Plan," *New York Times,* April 20, 1937, 16.

11. Florence Harriman, *Mission to the North* (Philadelphia: J. B. Lippincott, 1941), 36; Harriman to Sumner Welles, March 31, 1938, Confidential Oslo Correspondence, 1937–1940, box 4, FJHP; see also "Mrs. J. B. Harriman Slated As U.S. Minister to Norway," *New York Times,* April 2, 1937, 1, 11.

12. Ware, *Partner and I,* 186, 191; Mary W. Dewson, "An Aid to the End," unpublished autobiography, 1949, 2 vols., 1:39, Mary W. Dewson Papers, SL; Philip V. Cannistraro, Edward D. Wynot Jr., and Theodore P. Kovaleff, introduction to *Poland and the Coming of the Second World War: The Diplomatic Papers of A. J. Drexel Biddle, Jr., United States Ambassador to Poland, 1937–1939,* ed. Philip V. Cannistraro, Edward D. Wynot Jr., and Theodore P. Kovaleff (Columbus: Ohio State University Press, 1976), 7; Florence Harriman, "Speech by Mrs. J. Borden Harriman—Phi Beta Kappa Dinner," n.d. (circa 1941), 1, Speeches and Articles about Norway, 1940–43, box 24, FJHP.

13. Hambro quoted in T. K. Derry, *A Short History of Norway,* 2nd ed. (London: Allen & Unwin, 1968), 235.

14. Sigmund Skard, *The United States in Norwegian History* (Westport, CT: Greenwood, 1976), 169–71; Wayne S. Cole, *Norway and the United States, 1905–1955: Two Democracies in Peace and War* (Ames: Iowa State University Press, 1989), 54–71.

15. Harriman, *Mission to the North,* 36–39; Douglas Craig, *Progressives at War: William G. McAdoo and Newton D. Baker, 1863–1941* (Baltimore: Johns Hopkins University Press, 2013), 68; "Mrs. Harriman Endorsed," *New York Times,* April 22, 1937, 15; "Mrs. Harriman Is Confirmed," *New York Times,* April 28, 1937, 16; US Congress, Senate, 75th Cong., 1st Sess., April 27, 1937, *Congressional Record,* 81:3867; "To Oslo," *Time,* April 12, 1937, 21.

16. "Oslo Ready for Mrs. Harriman," *New York Times,* April 4, 1937, 31; "Another Woman Minister," *New York Times,* April 3, 1937, 18; Harriman, *Mission to the North,* 64.

17. Gibson to Harriman, April 20, 1937, Norway Personal Correspondence, 1937–1940, box 2, and Phillips to Harriman, April 15, 1937, folder 8, Correspondence, n.d., box 30, both in FJHP; Harriman, *Mission to the North,* 38–39.

18. Harriman, typewritten notes, "Story in Detail," n.d., Writings, n.d., 2, box 32, FJHP.

19. "Dogs, Missing Bags Complicate Sailing of Mrs. J. B. Harriman," *Washington Post,* June 3, 1937, 11; Harriman to Hull, July 6, 1937, 123 Harriman, CDF 1930–1939, 4–5.

20. Harriman, *Mission to the North,* 50; Patterson to Carnell (mother), May 13, 16, and June 5, 1937, all in folder 8, box 21, JPP.

21. Patterson to Carnell, June 14, 1937, folder 8, box 21, Patterson, "Typed Excerpts," February 23, 1938, folder 3, box 39, JPP; Patterson to Carnell, January 8, 14, 1938, both folder 1, box 22, all in JPP; see also Patterson to Carnell, October 16, 1938, folder 2.

22. Patterson to Carnell, October 28, November 30, 1937, both in folder 8, box 21, and March 29, 1938, folder 1, box 22, Patterson, "Typed Excerpts," August 3, 1938, folder 3, box 39, and Patterson to Carnell, October 5, 1938, folder 2, box 22, all in JPP; Ralph F. de Bedts, *Ambassador Joseph Kennedy, 1938–1940: An Anatomy of Appeasement* (New York: Peter Lang, 1985), 243.

23. Harriman, Annual Efficiency Report on Jefferson Patterson, October 1, 1937, Confidential Oslo Correspondence, box 4, FJHP; Harriman to Welles, 2, December 15, 1938, folder 17, box 52, Sumner Welles Papers, FDRL.

24. Harriman to Hugh Cumming, January 11, 18, 1939, both Miscellaneous Oslo Correspondence, 1937–1940, box 9, Harriman to Cumming, August 24, 1939, C—Oslo Correspondence (General), 1937–1940, box 4, all in FJHP; Harriman to Cumming, March 5, 1940, 1940 Jan–June, Correspondence, box 8, HSCP.

25. Marquis W. Childs, *I Write from Washington* (New York: Harper & Bros., 1942), 146; Patterson, "Typed Excerpts," November 19, 1937, folder 2, box 39, JPP; Harriman, *Mission to the North,* 321–22.

26. Harriman, *Mission to the North,* 67.

27. "Norway Holds Enchantments for Visitors," *Chicago Daily Tribune,* August 29, 1937, F2; Harriman, *Mission to the North,* 95.

28. "Politics a Hobby to Mrs. Harriman," *New York Times,* April 24, 1937, sec. 6, 6; "Busy Grandmother," *Scholastic,* May 6, 1940, 16; "Woman Diplomat," *Newsweek,* June 2, 1941, 48; Davis, "Just Like Daisy," 24–25.

29. Harriman, *Mission to the North,* 89–90.

30. Harriman, *Mission to the North,* 43; Harriman to Hull, "Opening of the 87th Regular Storting," 3, January 21, 1938, 857.032/45, CDF 1930–1939.

31. Harriman, typewritten notes, "Story in Detail," 5–6.

32. Translation of Ulla Mayer, "Mrs. Borden Harriman, A Diplomat with Many Interests," *Morgenbladet,* June 29, 1937, 2, Interviews, 1937, box 6, FJHP.

33. E. Roosevelt to Harriman, August 25, 1940, fol 100 Har–Has 1940, box 716, ERP; Owen to Harriman, August 22, 1938, R—Oslo Correspondence (General) 1937–1940, box 7, FJHP.

34. Harriman to F. Roosevelt, December 5, 1939, and F. Roosevelt to Harriman, January 9, 1940, both "Confidential" Oslo Correspondence, 1937–1940, Cumming

to Harriman, December 12, 1939, and Harriman to Cumming, January 29, 1940, both C—Oslo Correspondence (General) 1937–40, all in box 3, FJHP.

35. Harriman, *Mission to the North,* 321, 91.

36. Harriman, *Mission to the North,* 211; "Mrs. Harriman a Weaver in Tribute to Norse Ways," *New York Times,* May 11, 1938, 20; Mary Hornaday, "Dear Madam Minister," *Christian Science Monitor Weekly Magazine,* July 6, 1938, 3; Paul Ford, "Private Lives," n.d. (c. 1944–1948), News Clippings, n.d., box 32, FJHP.

37. Harriman, *Mission to the North,* 165–74; Harriman to Hull, "The Minister's Trip to the Lofoten Fisheries," March 29, 1939, Norway: 1935–39, box 45, Diplomatic Correspondence, PSF-FDRL.

38. Harriman, *Mission to the North,* 219–20; translation of "Where a Woman Is Steering, It Is the Heart Which Determines the Course," *Alle Kvinner's Blad,* 43, October 1939, attached to Harriman to E. Roosevelt, October 26, 1939, 100 Harr–Harv, box 689, ERP.

39. Cole, *Norway and the United States,* 53; translation of article by Linken Smedal, *Urd,* October 21, 1939, in Scrapbook on Publicity, 1946, box 29, FJHP; Harriman, *Mission to the North,* 321. It was Biddle, and not Harriman, who would be named US minister to the Norwegian and other governments in exile in 1941.

40. Admiralty to ACOS, October 27, 1939, FO 371/23701, N 5807, NA-UK; J. Garry Clifford, "The Odyssey of *City of Flint,*" *American Neptune* 32 (April 1972): 101. The *City of Flint* had already rescued two hundred survivors of the SS *Athenia,* the first ship sunk in World War II.

41. Louchheim, *By the Political Sea,* 56; Harriman, *Mission to the North,* 230.

42. Harriman, *Mission to the North,* 232; Clifford, "*City of Flint,*" 111–15; Helen Essary, "Dear Washington," *Washington Times-Herald,* n.d. (c. January 30, 1940), Miscellaneous Oslo Correspondence, 1937–1940, box 9, FJHP.

43. Clifford, "*City of Flint,*" 111–15; Cole, *Norway and the United States,* 88; "Woman of the Month," *Independent Woman* 15 (May 1940): 128; Arthur Capper to Harriman, November 14, 1939, C—Oslo Correspondence (General), 1937–1940, box 4, FJHP.

44. Harriman to Hull, April 9, 1940, *FRUS, 1940,* 5 vols. (Washington, DC: GPO, 1959), 1:144; Cole, *Norway and the United States,* 94–98; Harriman, *Mission to the North,* 246–89; Harriman to F. Roosevelt, April 30, 1940, Norway 1940, box 45, Diplomatic Correspondence, PSF-FDRL.

45. Harriman, *Mission to the North,* 253, 269, 283–89; Sterling to Hull, April 13, 1940, 123 Harriman, Florence, CDF 1940–1944; J. Michael Cleverley, "The First American Official Killed in This War," *Foreign Service Journal,* December 2003, https://web.archive.org/web/20070713045256/http://www.afsa.org/fsj/dec03/cleverley.pdf.

46. Harriman, *Mission to the North,* 304; Greene to Cumming, August 19, 1940, 1940 Jul–Dec, Correspondence, box 8, HSCP; Harriman to F. Roosevelt, April 30, 1940.

47. "Transport Loading American Refugees," *New York Times,* August 14, 1940, 3; Breckinridge Long Diary, August 17–19, 1940, 153–55, box 5, Breckinridge Long Papers, LC; "U.S. Refugee Vessel Ends Perilous Trip; Royal Party Lands," *New York Times,* August 29, 1940, 1–2; *Paramount News* 41(1), August 29, 1940, PN 41.1, pt. 4, Motion Picture, Sound and Video Records Section, Special Media Archives Services Division, NARA.

48. "'Daisy' Harriman Outruns Bombs," *Life,* May 13, 1940, 33; Schoenfeld to Hull, August 6, 1940, 124.57/61, CDF 1940–1944; Castle diary, September 7, 1940, MS Am 2021, Diary Jul–Dec 1940, Vol. 40, WRCP-HL, 321; Greene to Harriman, n.d. (c. July 21, 1940), Personal Miscellaneous Correspondence, 1940–1947, box 2, FJHP; Hull to Harriman (c/o American legation Stockholm), April 15, 1940, 123 Harriman, Florence, CDF 1940–1944; Davis, "Just Like Daisy," 82; Dewson, "An Aid to the End," 1:39; Ware, *Partner and I,* 191.

49. Harriman to F. Roosevelt and Harriman to Hull, both November 29, 1940, 123 Harriman, Florence, CDF 1940–1944; F. Roosevelt to Harriman, February 4, 1941, Roosevelt, Franklin Delano, 1940–1949, box 18, FJHP.

50. Monica McCall to Harriman, April 21, 1944, "About Book 'Mission to the North,'" 1941–1944, box 16, FJHP; "W. C. Bullitt Refutes Lindbergh Statement," *New York Times,* January 26, 1941, 4; "Lend-Lease Bill," Hearings Before the Committee on Foreign Affairs, House of Representatives, 76th Cong., 1st Sess., on HR 1776, January 25, 1941 (Washington, DC: GPO, 1941), 659, 660; Harriman address [May 7,] 1941, in Sarkela, *Megaphones to Microphones,* 218.

51. Lise Namikas, "The Committee to Defend America and the Debate between Internationalists and Interventionists," *Historian* 61 (Summer 1999): 858–63; Press Release, Royal Norwegian Embassy, "Mrs. J. Borden Harriman Receives Norse Decoration at Embassy Reception," August 3, 1942, Norway, 1940–1948, box 17, FJHP; Robert A. Divine, *Second Chance: The Triumph of Internationalism in America During World War II* (New York: Atheneum, 1971), 30, 35, 64, 86–87, 167, 212; Steven Casey, "The Campaign to Sell a Harsh Peace for Germany to the American Public, 1944–1948," *History* 90 (January 2005): 62–92; "May Appoint Mrs. Harriman," *New York Times,* March 26, 1941, 27.

52. Philco advertisement, *Ladies Home Journal,* October 1950.

53. Harriman to Herbert Swope, December 28, 1938, S—General Oslo Correspondence, 1937–1040, box 8, FJHP.

54. Spaulding, *Ambassadors Ordinary and Extraordinary,* 180.

55. Dormer to Eden, January 1, 1938, enclosure, "Report on Heads of Foreign Missions Accredited to Norway," 4, FO 419/32, Dormer to Halifax, July 1, 1939, FO 371/23671, enclosure, "Report on Heads of Foreign Missions Accredited to Norway," 4, both in NA-UK.

56. Harriman, "Address Before the Democratic Women's Luncheon Club," 4.

57. "Woman of the Month," 128; Review of *Mission to the North, Spectator* (London), December 19, 1941, 585–86.

4. Perle S. Mesta

Epigraph: W. J. Taylor-Whitehead, *Luxembourg: Land of Legends* (London: Constable, 1951), vii.

1. This introduction draws upon Perle Mesta, with Robert Cahn, *Perle: My Story* (New York: McGraw-Hill, 1960), 2–4. "Mrs. Mesta Enjoys Merman Musical," *New York Times*, October 26, 1950, 13; and Paul Lesch, *Playing Her Part: Perle Mesta in Luxembourg* (Luxembourg: American Chamber of Commerce in Luxembourg, 2001), 41–50.

2. "Widow from Oklahoma," *Time*, March 14, 1949, 27; Mesta, *Perle*, 76–79, 97–98; Freeman, *Room at a Time*, 133, 207–08; Eulalie McDowell, "Two-Party Gal," *Collier's*, June 12, 1948, 96.

3. Mesta, *Perle*, 79–82; Hope Ridings Miller to Belmont Faires, March 5, 1986, in *Perle Mesta: Patriot, Diplomat, Philanthropist, 1890–1975* (Oklahoma City: State of Oklahoma, Office of the Governor, 1986); "Mesta, Hon. Perle," Social Office File, HSTL.

4. Marjorie Williams, *The Woman at the Washington Zoo: Writings on Politics, Family, and Fate* (New York: PublicAffairs, 2005), 16–17; James J. Kenneally, *A Compassionate Conservative: A Political Biography of Joseph W. Martin, Jr., Speaker of the House of Representatives* (Lanham, MD: Lexington Books, 2003), 68–69; Amanda Smith, *Newspaper Titan: The Infamous Life and Monumental Times of Cissy Patterson* (New York: Knopf, 2011), 418, 424; Mesta to Pollitzer, December 21, 1946, folder 8, box 51, National Woman's Party Papers, LC.

5. Robert G. Nixon, interview by Jerry N. Hess, OH No. 265, vol. 4: 598–602, October 29, 1970, HSTL; Edwin Young, "Perle Mesta Cover," February 26, 1949, and Alyce Moran, "Mesta Cover VII: For President and Country," February 28, 1949, both in Dispatches from *Time* Magazine Correspondents: First Ser., 1942–1955 (MS Am 2090), reel 86, No. 508, 2, 9, HL; Margaret Truman, *Bess W. Truman* (New York: Macmillan, 1986), 248; "Widow from Oklahoma."

6. Georgia Cook Morgan, "India Edwards: Distaff Politician of the Truman Era," *Missouri Historical Review* 78 (April 1984): 293–310; India Edwards, *Pulling No Punches: Memoirs of a Woman in Politics* (New York: G. P. Putnam's Sons, 1977), 171–73, 187; Edwards to Acheson, February 4, 1949, 121.41, CDF 1945–1949.

7. E. Roosevelt to Acheson, February 2, 1949, and Acheson to E. Roosevelt, February 17, 1949, both quoted in Calkin, *Women in the Department of State,* 119–20; Robert L. Beisner, *Dean Acheson: A Life in the Cold War* (New York: Oxford University Press, 2006), 114.

8. Susan M. Hartmann, *The Home Front and Beyond: American Women in the 1940s* (Boston: Twayne, 1982), 154–55; Edwards, *Pulling No Punches,* 8; Harry S. Truman, "The President's News Conference, February 13, 1947," online by Gerhard Peters and John T. Woolley, *The American Presidency Project,* https://www

.presidency.ucsb.edu/node/232672; Lenore Bradley, "The Uphill Climb: Women in the Truman Administration," *Whistle Stop: Harry S. Truman Library Institute Newsletter* 23 (1994): 5; Leila J. Rupp and Verta Taylor, *Survival in the Doldrums: The American Women's Rights Movement, 1945 to the 1960s* (New York: Oxford University Press, 1987), 65.

9. Hartmann, *Home Front and Beyond*, 56, 148–57; Calkin, *Women in the Department of State*, 95–117; [Harold Nicholson], "Women in the Foreign Service," *American Foreign Service Journal* 19 (May 1942): 261, 291; Edwin C. Wilson remarks, Commencement Exercises, American College for Girls, June 13, 1946, folder 2, box 1, Edwin C. Wilson Papers, Mandeville Special Collections Library, University of California San Diego; "Hot Words Hurled in UNO Committee," *New York Times,* January 25, 1946, 3.

10. Nancy E. McGlen and Meredith Reid Sarkees, *Women in Foreign Policy: The Insiders* (New York: Routledge, 1993), 34.

11. Memorandum of Conversation, March 1, 1949, box 1, Summaries of the Secretary's Daily Meetings, 1949–52, General Records of the Office of the Executive Secretariat, Lot Files, Entry 393, Lot 58D609, RG 59, NARA; Acheson, Memorandum of Conference with the President, "Appointment of Ambassadors," March 24, 1949, 3, Acheson, Memorandum of Conference with the President, "Ambassadorial List," March 31, 1949, 2, both 1949, box 1, Memorandums of Conversations with the President, 1949–52, General Records of the Office of the Executive Secretariat, Lot Files, RG 59, NARA; see also Acheson, Memorandum of Conference with the President, April 21, 1949, 1, 121.4, CDF 1945–1949.

12. Mesta, *Perle,* 127–28, 130.

13. Mesta, *Perle,* 130–32; Lesch, *Playing Her Part,* 28; Henry Wales, "Envoy Looks on Social Events as World Cure," *Chicago Daily Tribune,* August 24, 1949, B9; Martha Gellhorn, "Party Girl in Paradise," *Saturday Evening Post,* January 7, 1950, 76; "Mrs. Mesta Says Intuition Helps a Woman Diplomat," *New York Times,* December 18, 1950, 26; "An Oyster for Perle," *Time,* July 4, 1949, 6.

14. *Congressional Record—Senate,* July 5, 1949, 81st Cong., 1st Sess., 8823–31; Mesta, *Perle,* 134; "Barkley and Acheson Attend New Minister to Luxembourg at Ceremony in Presence of Many of the Capital's Notables," *New York Times,* July 9, 1949, 6.

15. Cynthia Harrison, *On Account of Sex: The Politics of Women's Issues, 1945–1968* (Berkeley: University of California Press, 1988), 54–55; *Meet the Press,* transcript, December 10, 1949, 5, television transcripts, Edwards, India 12/10/49, box 203, Lawrence Spivak Papers, LC; C. David Heymann, *The Georgetown Ladies' Social Club: Power, Passion, and Politics in the Nation's Capital* (New York: Atria, 2003), 38.

16. Robert Murphy, *Diplomat among Warriors* (Garden City, NY: Doubleday, 1964), 326.

17. Donald A. Kruse, interview by Charles S. Kennedy, March 17, 1997, 11, FAOHC, http://www.adst.org/OH%20TOCs/Kruse,%20Donald%20A.toc.pdf; Seymour Freidin and William Richardson, "Our Tiniest Ally," *Collier's,* June 7, 1952, 50.

18. Le Gallais dispatches quoted in Lesch, *Playing Her Part*, 26–27, 92.

19. Lucius D. Battle, interview by Dayton Mak, July 10, 1991, 55, FAOHC, http://www.adst.org/OH%20TOCs/Battle,%20Lucius%202Dtoc.pdf.

20. Lesch, *Call Her Madam* (Luxembourg: Samsa Film, 1998); Daniel Schorr, *Staying Tuned: A Life in Journalism* (New York: Simon & Schuster, 2001), 33.

21. C. L. Sulzberger, *A Long Row of Candles: Memoirs & Diaries, 1934–1954* (New York: Macmillan, 1969), 483; E. Roosevelt, "The Real Perle Mesta," *Flair*, October 1950, 31, 110.

22. Westbrook Pegler, "Fair Enough," *Washington Times-Herald*, February 25, 1953; Daniel Schorr to Tilly Schorr, September 11, 1952, folder 15, box 4, Daniel Schorr Papers, LC.

23. Bech and Spaak quoted in Murphy, *Diplomat among Warriors*, 326.

24. Murphy, draft, "Murphy Memoirs," folder 3, and Dwyer to Gibbs, May 10, 1963, folder 11, both box 154, as well as Murphy to Gibbs, June 13, 1963, folder 3, box 155, all Robert D. Murphy Papers, HIA.

25. Gellhorn, "Party Girl in Paradise," 78; Eric Kocher, *Foreign Intrigue: The Making and Unmaking of a Foreign Service Officer* (Far Hills, NJ: New Horizon Press, 1990), 65.

26. Various press summaries and translations from the US embassies in The Hague, Copenhagen, and Oslo, 1950–1951, found in 123 Mesta, CDF 1950–1954.

27. "Perle Mesta: New-Type Diplomat," *U.S. News and World Report*, December 23, 1949, 27; Lesch, *Playing Her Part*, 32; John Stanton, "Mrs. Mesta's Grand Entry," *Life*, September 12, 1949, 36.

28. "Glittering Jobs for Mrs. Mesta," *U.S. News and World Report*, July 1, 1949, 44; David Perlman, "Perle Mesta Makes Good," *Los Angeles Times*, January 29, 1950, G9; "Small Package," *Time*, September 5, 1949, 26; Mesta, Interview by William Bradford Huie and Henry Haslett, *Longines Chronoscope*, August 18, 1952, 200 (R)-LW-130, RG 200, NARA; "Mrs. Mesta Puts Diplomacy Before Dinners Because She 'Loves' Her Role as U.S. Envoy," *New York Times*, April 8, 1950, 15; see also, for example, "Perle's Progress," *Chicago Daily Tribune*, April 14, 1953, 20.

29. Stanton, "Mrs. Mesta's Grand Entry," 26; "What's a Woman Do?" *Life*, May 18, 1953, 59.

30. "Chafing-Dish Diplomacy," and Al Hirschfeld cartoon, both *Collier's*, October 15, 1949, 82; photograph in Mesta, *Perle*.

31. Scott to Byington, February 21, 1951, 123 Mesta, CDF 1950–1954; Perkins to Acheson, June 20, 1952, Secretary's Appointments, November 1950–October 1952, 2, box 22, Misc. Records, 1947–1952, Records of the Executive Secretariat (Dean Acheson), Lot Files, RG 59, NARA; anonymous officials quoted in Anatole Visson, "Perle's New Oyster—II," June 24, 1949, Dispatches from *Time* Magazine Correspondents: 1st ser., reel 90, No. 528 and "An Oyster for Perle," 7; Moose to Wailes, November 21, 1951, box 527, FSIC, OCI, FSIRs, 1950–1959, Lot Files, RG 59, NARA; Castle Diary, November 16, 1950, 198–99, reel 11, WRCP-HCHL.

32. David K. E. Bruce Diary entries, July 10, August 14, 1952, July 1, 1952–September 30, 1952, both in folder 1 of 2, box 1, October 20, 1952, October 1, 1952–December 31, 1952, folder 1 of 3, box 1, March 3, 1953, folder January 1, 1953–March 31, 1953, box 2, all Diaries of David K. E. Bruce, 1949–1974, Lot 64 D 327, RG 59, NARA.

33. Memorandum of Conversation, April 21, 1950, 611.50A94/4–2150, CDF 1950–1954; Mesta, *Perle,* 163.

34. West to Kirk, June 13, 1949, folder 090 Awards, Decorations, box 7, Lux, US Legation and Embassy Luxembourg, Classified General Records, 1944–1962, RG 84, NARA; Mesta, *Perle,* 142–46.

35. Mesta, *Perle,* 144–45; Perlman, "Perle Mesta Makes Good," G9; Kocher, *Foreign Intrigue,* 59–71.

36. Kocher, *Foreign Intrigue,* 59, 69–70; Andre Claude, interview in Lesch, *Call Her Madam.*

37. Moose to Wailes, November 20, 1951, and Moose, "Foreign Service Inspection Report," November 15, 1951, Section 3—Personnel, Inspector's Comment, 6/b, 2/b, both box 527, FSIC, OCI, FSIRs, 1950–1959, Lot Files, RG 59, NARA; Allchin to Morrison, "Luxembourg: Heads of Foreign Missions," March 12, 1951, in "Further Correspondence Respecting Belgium and Luxembourg," part 5, 60, January to December 1951, FO 466/5, NA-UK; Paulette Hilgert-Wagner, interview in Lesch, *Call Her Madam.*

38. Mesta, "Report on the Foreign Service Personnel of the American Legation in Luxembourg," n. d., attached to Truman to Mesta, August 11, 1952, box 182, PSF-HSTL.

39. Alonzo L. Hamby, *Man of the People: A Life of Harry S. Truman* (New York: Oxford University Press, 1995), 314, 409; Truman to David H. Morgan, January 28, 1952, in *Off the Record: The Private Papers of Harry S. Truman,* ed. Robert H. Ferrell (New York: Harper & Row, 1980), 234–35; Truman to Acheson, August 11, 1952, August 1952, box 71, Memoranda of Conversation, Dean G. Acheson Papers, HSTL.

40. *Congressional Record—Senate,* July 5, 1949, 8831; George L. West, interview by Charles S. Kennedy, February 9, 1990, 21–22, FAOHC, http://www.adst.org/OH%20TOCs/West,%20George%20L.TOC.pdf; Betty Beale, "Exclusively Yours," *Washington Star,* January 31, 1954; Wailes to Moose, December 4, 1951, box 527, FSIC, OCI, FSIRs, 1950–59, Lot Files, RG 59, NARA.

41. Daniel Schorr, "Ambassadress Extraordinary," *Daily Mail,* October 5, 1949.

42. David Lardner, "Letter from Luxembourg," *New Yorker,* October 21, 1944, reprinted in *The* New Yorker *Book of War Pieces* (New York: Reynal & Hitchcock, 1947), 402; "Perle Mesta: New-Type Diplomat," 26.

43. Mesta, *Perle,* 147; Perlman, "Perle Mesta Makes Good," G13.

44. Perlman, "Perle Mesta Makes Good," G12.

45. Mesta, *Perle,* 163–64, 174; Marie McNair, "Parties Secondary with Mrs. Mesta," *Washington Post,* April 7, 1950, B2; Allchin to Younger, "Luxembourg: Heads of Foreign Missions," July 10, 1950; Allchin to Morrison, "Luxembourg:

Heads of Foreign Missions," March 12, 1951; *Longines Chronoscope,* August 18, 1952; Murphy, *Diplomat among Warriors,* 326.

46. Mesta to Acheson, September 23, 1949 and Acheson to Mesta, October 13, 1949, both 102.21/9–2249, CDF 1945–1949; Rosemary L. Ginn, interview by Ann M. Morin, October 28, 1997, 69, FAOHC, http://www.adst.org/OH%20TOCs /Ginn,%20Rosemary%20L.toc.pdf; Murphy, *Diplomat among Warriors,* 326–27; "Luxembourg Insists Mrs. Mesta's House Is Haunted by Nazi Ghosts," *Los Angeles Times,* September 12, 1949, 19.

47. Mesta, *Perle,* 174; "Perle Loves It!" *Washington Post,* August 11, 1950, C3.

48. Mesta, *Perle,* 176.

49. Lucy Key Miller, "Front Views and Profiles," *Chicago Daily Tribune,* November 9, 1951, B6; Herter to McFall, August 18, 1952, and McFall to Herter, August 25, 1952, both 123 Mesta, CDF 1950–1954.

50. Lewis, "Madame Minister," 27; Schorr, "Ambassadress Extraordinary"; Henry McLemore, "The Lighter Side," *Los Angeles Times,* July 21, 1950, B18.

51. Mesta, *Perle,* 150, 153–54, 157–58; Volney Hurd, "Mrs. Mesta's Gracious Touch," *Christian Science Monitor,* October 17, 1951, 9; Lesch, *Playing Her Part,* 56; John Dolibois, *Pattern of Circles: An Ambassador's Story* (Kent, OH: Kent State University Press, 1989), 242.

52. Moose, "Foreign Service Inspection Report," 29.

53. Edward M. Rowell, interview by Charles S. Kennedy, September 19, 1995, 202–3, FAOHC, http://www.adst.org/OH%20TOCs/Rowell,%20Edward%20M. toc.pdf.

54. Truman to Mesta, July 21, 1950; see also Truman to Mesta, August 25, 29, and September 15, 1950, all Chron Name File, Mesta, George Mrs., box 290, Chronological File (Blues), PSF-HSTL.

55. Mesta to Eisenhower, January 12, 1953, and Eisenhower to Mesta, February 9, 1953, both in Personnel Matters 1953–1954 (2), box 6, Subject Series, JFDP; James Bonbright, interview by Peter Jessup, February 26, 1986, 125–26 FAOHC, http://www.loc.gov/resource/mfdip.2004bon01/#seq-1; Eisenhower to Mesta, April 10, 1953, in *The Papers of Dwight David Eisenhower: The Presidency: The Middle Way,* ed. Louis Galambos and Daun Van Ee (Baltimore: Johns Hopkins University Press, 1996), 14:167, 167n3; "Mrs. Mesta's Term Will End on April 13," *Washington Post,* March 28, 1953, 7.

56. Lesch, *Playing Her Part,* 88–89.

57. Alfred Cheval, "Perle Mesta Packs Up to Leave Luxembourg," *Los Angeles Times,* April 12, 1953, 36; Ketcham to Department of State, April 15, 1953, and attachment (translated newspaper excerpts, among them one from *Revue,* April 2, 1953, from which the quotation is taken), 123 Mesta, CDF 1950–1954.

58. Bohlen to Smith, June 6, 1953, 123 Mesta, CDF 1950–1954; *New York Times,* July 21, 1955, 1, 6; Mesta, *Perle,* 188–99, 204–8; Reinhardt to Dulles, July 20, 1955, 751G.00/7–2055, CDF 1955–1959.

59. Oshinsky, *Conspiracy So Immense,* 417; Mesta, *Perle,* 7.

60. Robert Fritts, interview by Charles S. Kennedy, September 8, 1999, 23, FAOHC, https://www.adst.org/OH%20TOCs/Fritts,%20Robert%20E.toc.pdf.

61. Castle Diary, October 23, 1953, 183, reel 11, WRCP-HCHL; Henry L. Kimelman, interview by Charles S. Kennedy, October 29, 1993, FAOHC, 10, http://adst.org/wp-content/uploads/2013/12/Kimelman-Henry-L-.toc_.pdf.

62. *United States of America v. John Doe,* Deposition of Richard M. Nixon, June 23, 1975, Nixon Grand Jury Records, *Records of the Watergate Special Prosecution Force, 1971–1977,* 25–26, US Government Information website, http://www.gpo.gov/fdsys/pkg/GPO-NARA-WSPF-NIXON-GRAND-JURY-RECORDS/content-detail.html. "Mesta wasn't sent to Luxembourg because she had big bosoms," Nixon added. "Pearl Mesta went to Luxembourg because she made a good [financial] contribution."

63. Freidin and Richardson, "Our Tiniest Ally," 49; Harry C. Barteau, *Historical Dictionary of Luxembourg* (Lanham, MD: Scarecrow, 1996), 135.

64. Hurd, "Mrs. Mesta's Gracious Touch," 9; Merman quoted in Bob Thomas, *I Got Rhythm! The Ethel Merman Story* (New York: G. P. Putnam's Sons, 1985), 109. Merman said this in response to Mesta singing an Irving Berlin tune at a party where she and Merman first met. "If Perle's going into my racket," Merman added, to Margaret Truman, "I may ask your dad for a diplomatic job."

5. Eugenie M. Anderson

Epigraph: Ernest Leiser, "Denmark's American Sweetheart," *Saturday Evening Post,* May 5, 1951, 123.

1. Eugenie Moore Anderson, oral history, conducted by Leila Johnson, May 7–July 8, 1971, 117, MHS; Isobel Gale, "Danes Know and Like Ambassador Anderson," *Minneapolis Star,* November 15, 1950, 41; Anderson to Max Kampelman, July 1, 1950, Eugenie Anderson, 1949–54, box 22, Max M. Kampelman Papers, MHS; Anderson, family newsletter, July 8, 1950, 7–11, and William Roll to Department of State, July 21, 1950 (which includes the text of Anderson's July 4 speech and a partial text of the *Berlingske Tidende* July 5 editorial), both in ACMF.

2. On Anderson, see also John Pederson, "'A Lioness for Denmark?'—Eugenie Anderson and Danish American Relations, 1949–1953," in *Danish–North American Relations since World War II,* ed. Peter L. Peterson (Ames, IA: Danish American Heritage Society, 2004): 45–57.

3. Anderson oral history, 6–7, 29, MHS; Johanna Ghei, interview by Philip Nash, June 19, 2007; Leland Stowe, "U.S. Diplomacy's First Lady—Mrs. Eugenie Anderson" (article manuscript), 5, October 1964, Biographical Sheets, Subject Files, BMF, box 25, EMAP; Sally Luther, "America's First 'Madam Ambassador,'" *Minneapolis Tribune,* October 16, 1949, Women's News, 1; Bob Daily, "The Music Major Who Became America's First Woman Ambassador," *Carleton Voice* 48, Winter 1982, 16.

4. Margaret Crimmins, ". . . One Woman's View," *St. Paul Pioneer Press*, July 8, 1962, Women's Section, 3; Anderson oral history, 32–33, MHS; Anderson to Mrs. Russell B. Hawkins, September 8, 1952, CCF, CF, 1949–1953, H 1952, box 2.

5. Anderson oral history, 38–40, MHS; Clarissa Start, "Madam Ambassador," *St. Louis Post-Dispatch*, October 23, 1949; Marjorie Bingham, "Keeping at It: Minnesota Women," in *Minnesota in a Century of Change*, ed. Clifford E. Clark Jr. (St. Paul: Minnesota Historical Society Press, 1989), 451–52; Barbara Stuhler, *Ten Men of Minnesota and American Foreign Policy, 1898–1968*, (St. Paul: Minnesota Historical Society, 1973), 2–3, 10–11.

6. Anderson oral history, 37–38, 41–44, MHS; "DFL Committeewoman Has No Time for Bach Now," *Minneapolis Star*, March 17, 1949, 22.

7. Anderson oral history, 47, MHS; Anderson to Hubert Humphrey, July 31, 1945, Personal Correspondence, Ai–Ap, General Correspondence: June–Dec. 1945, A–G, Mayoralty Files, box 1, Hubert H. Humphrey Papers, MHS.

8. John Earl Haynes, *Dubious Alliance: The Making of Minnesota's DFL Party* (Minneapolis: University of Minnesota Press, 1984), 125–43; Peggy Lamson, *Few Are Chosen: American Women in Political Life Today* (Boston: Houghton Mifflin, 1968), 168; Anderson oral history, 58–59, MHS.

9. Haynes, *Dubious Alliance*, 138–40; Lamson, *Few Are Chosen*, 170; Charles Lloyd Garretson III, *Hubert H. Humphrey: The Politics of Joy* (New Brunswick, NJ: Transaction, 1993), 99n37; Anderson, interview conducted by Peggy Lamson, n.d. (c. 1967), box 1, MC-183, Peggy Lamson Papers, SL, 9.

10. Steven M. Gillon, *Politics and Vision: The ADA and American Liberalism, 1947–1985* (New York: Oxford University Press, 1987), 47–50; Sean J. Savage, *Truman and the Democratic Party* (Lexington: University Press of Kentucky, 1997), 134–35; Carl Solberg, *Hubert Humphrey: A Biography* (New York: Norton, 1984), 11–19; see also Jennifer A. Delton, *Making Minnesota Liberal: Civil Rights and the Transformation of the Democratic Party* (Minneapolis: University of Minnesota Press, 2000), esp. 129–59, and "Updated Memo by EA Written about Events at Phila Convention of 1948," n.d., Eugenie Anderson report on Democratic National Convention, 1948, box 27, EMAP.

11. Anderson oral history, 74, MHS.

12. Edwards, *Pulling No Punches*, 177–79; Anderson to Dorothy Jacobson, February 2, 1949, Anderson to Orville Freeman, February 2, 1949, and Arthur Schlesinger to Anderson, January 19, 1949, all Correspondence Regarding Ambassadorial Appointment, Jan.–Sept. 1949, COF; Anderson oral history, 78, MHS.

13. Anderson to Max Kampelman, May 7, 1949, Correspondence Regarding Ambassadorial Appointment, Jan.–Sept. 1949, COF.

14. "DFL Committeewoman Has No Time for Bach Now," *Minneapolis Star*, March 17, 1949, 22; Anderson, "Mrs. Ambassador," outline, parts 1: 2, and 3:29–30, n.d. (c. 1954), Personal and Miscellaneous Files, box 16, EMAP; Anderson to India Edwards, February 28, 1949, Correspondence Regarding Ambassadorial

Appointment, Jan.–Sept. 1949; *New York Post,* October 28, 1949; Anderson, interview by Lamson, 13–14.

15. Lamson, *Few Are Chosen,* 174–75; M. W. Halloran, "Patronage and Bonds Keep Politics Stewing," *Minneapolis Tribune,* July 31, 1949, Upper Midwest sec., 4 (see also Leonard Lyons, "The Lyons Den," *New York Post,* February 2, 1950); Anderson to Hubert Humphrey, July 29, 1949, COF; Anderson oral history, 80, MHS; Anderson, "Mrs. Ambassador," outline, part 1:3; *Congressional Record— Senate,* October 19, 1949, 81st Cong., 1st Sess., 14985–87; "The Pride of Red Wing," *Time,* October 24, 1949, 25.

16. "Warning to an Ambassador: Dear Madame Eugenie Anderson," translation of *Information* article, n.d. (December 22, 1949), in Anderson, "Mrs. Ambassador," draft chapter 4, 2–7, 7–10; Anderson oral history, 93, 104–5, MHS.

17. Stowe, "U.S. Diplomacy's First Lady," 6; "Woman Ambassador Starts Danish Lessons," *Minneapolis Star,* October 13, 1949; Anderson to Department of State, January 9, 1950, 123 Anderson, Eugenie, CDF 1950–1954; Anderson, "Mrs. Ambassador," draft chapter 4, 20.

18. Anderson oral history, 101–2, MHS; Bill White, "Eugenie Anderson Cover," May 26, 1952, Dispatches from *Time* Magazine Correspondents: First ser., reel 125, No. 698, 3.

19. "Cokes and *Smörgåsbord,*" *Time,* February 6, 1950, 18; Anderson, family newsletters, December 31, 1949, and January 8, 1950, AFN: March 1950; "Mrs. Anderson Invites Laborers to Dine at Villa," *Washington Post,* January 22, 1950, C4.

20. Anderson, "Mrs. Ambassador," outline, part 3:29 and draft chapter 12, 15–16; Anderson, family newsletter, January 22, 1950, AFN: 1949–March 1950; Leland Stowe, "Eugenie Anderson Shows the Flag," *Reader's Digest,* March 1965, 176.

21. Anderson, "Mrs. Ambassador," draft chapter 11, 4, outline, part 1:20, and draft chapter 4, 33–34; Anderson oral history, 105, 114–16, MHS; Anderson, "Address . . . on Mother's Day, May 14, 1950," Speech Texts, 1948–1953, SSM, box 11.

22. A. W. G. Randall to Eden, "Denmark before and after the Second World War," November 3, 1952, in "Further Correspondence Respecting Denmark," part 6, January to December 1952, 26–27, FO 471/6, NA-UK.

23. Anderson, family newsletter, November 25, 1950, 5, AFN: August, 1950– December, 1950, box 45; Anderson to Edwards, May 9, 1950, CCF, 1949–53, box 2.

24. Anderson, "Mrs. Ambassador," outline, part 3:1–4; Anderson, "The Negro in America Today," January 16, 1952, Speech Texts, 1952, SSM, box 12.

25. Edward Sparks to Secretary of State, November 18, September 14, 1949, both 123 Anderson, CDF 1945–1949; Leiser, "Denmark's American Sweetheart," 31, 123; Si Freidin, "Woman Ambassador Pleases Danish People," *Denver Post,* April 18, 1951.

26. Pernille Lind Olsen, "Bodil Begtrup (1903–1987)," *KVINFO,* 2003, http:// www.kvinfo.dk/side/171/bio/32/.

27. Brooks McClure to William Roll, May 12, 1952, M, CCF, CF, box 3. (This details the investigation by eight *Time* reporters for a story on the ambassador that

never ran, presumably because they found too little damning information. See Anderson to Edwards, June 12, 1952, Edwards, India, CCF, CF, box 2.) Anderson, family newsletter, February 4, 1951, ACMF; Letter to the editor, *Minneapolis Tribune,* March 9, 1958, 3E; Lawrence W. Taylor, "Foreign Service Inspection Report—Copenhagen," November 9, 1951, box 526, FSIC, OCI, FSIRs, 1950–59, Lot 56D725, RG 59, NARA.

28. Anderson, family newsletter, May 7, 1950, AFN: April, 1950–July, 1950; Anderson, "Mrs. Ambassador," draft chapter 11, 6–10; Kristin Midtgaard, "National Security and the Choice of International Humanitarian Aid: Denmark and the Korean War, 1950–1953," *Journal of Cold War Studies* 13 (Spring 2011): 148–74; Anderson, "Mrs. Ambassador," draft chapter 12, 28–29.

29. Leiser, "Denmark's American Sweetheart"; "Woman Liberal Is Named Envoy," unknown newspaper, October 13, 1949, folder 2415, box 1701, Official File, HSTP, HSTL; Sally Luther, "Ambassador Anderson Steps from Housewife Role with Minimum Fanfare," *Christian Science Monitor,* October 25, 1949, 4; *New York Post,* October 28, 1949; "Ambassador Eugenie," *Pathfinder,* November 2, 1949, 36; *Minneapolis Tribune Picture* magazine, March 19, 1950, cover; "U.S. Ambassadors," *Time,* December 31, 1951, 14–15; Christine Sadler, "Women Keep Fires High for New Deal," *Washington Post,* July 21, 1952.

30. Anderson, family newsletter, February 25, 1951, 7–8, AFN: 1951; Anderson, "Mrs. Ambassador," outline, part 2:12.

31. Anderson oral history, 99–100, MHS; "Eugenie in Center of Blue Cheese Dispute," *St. Paul Pioneer Press,* November 11, 1951; Anderson, "Mrs. Ambassador," draft chapter 4, 9–10; Anderson, family newsletter, April 9, 1950, AFN: April, 1950–July, 1950; Anderson, "Mrs. Ambassador," outline, part 1:19–22; Sam Yates to Department of State, March 4, 1950, 123 Anderson, Eugenie, CDF 1950–1954; Anderson, interview by Lamson, 14.

32. White, "Eugenie Anderson Cover," 1–2; Stowe, "U.S. Diplomacy's First Lady," 17.

33. "American Foreign Service Inspection Report, Part I, Personnel," (Inspector's Comments), October 31, 1949, Copenhagen 1949, box 35, FSIRs, Inspection Reports, 1936–1964, Master Locator Record (MLR) 5449, RG 59, NARA; Lyon to Anderson, December 14, 1949, CCF, CF, 1949–1953, L 1950–1951, box 3; Anderson oral history, 112–13, MHS; Anne Crolius to Anderson, October 11, 1950, Ch–Cy, CCF, box 2; Anderson, family newsletter, May 21, 1950, 8–9, AFN: April 1950–July 1950, box 4.

34. Anderson oral history, 82, MHS; White, "Eugenie Anderson Cover," 6–7; Anderson 1962 quoted in Mary Dupont, *Mrs. Ambassador: The Life and Politics of Eugenie Anderson* (St. Paul: Minnesota Historical Society Press, 2019), 6; Fred Neumeier, "'Her Excellency' Eugenie Returns Home in Triumph," *St. Paul Pioneer Press,* October 22, 1951, 1, 2; "Mrs. Ambassador Meets the Press," transcript of Danish State Radio House interview, April 20, 1950, Speech Texts, 1948–1951, 2–3, SSM, box 11.

35. Anderson, "Mrs. Ambassador," draft chapter 11, 5–6.

36. Anderson, "Mrs. Ambassador," draft chapter 12, 22; Anderson, Lamson interview, 18–19.

37. Anderson oral history, 124–28, quotation at 124, MHS; Anderson to Acheson, "Rank of U.S. Woman Ambassador to Denmark," January 19, 1953, 123 Anderson, Eugenie, CDF 1950–1954.

38. Anderson oral history, 124–28, MHS; Anderson, memorandum, March 14, 1952, CCF, CF, box 4; Anderson to Acheson, "Rank of U.S. Woman Ambassador"; Anderson to Edwards, June 12, 1952, 2.

39. Truman to Anderson, April 24, 1956, PACRF, 1953–1968, box 9.

40. Anderson to Acheson, No. 679, January 19, 1953, 123 Anderson, Eugenie, CDF 1950–1954; Anderson, "Mrs. Ambassador," outline, part 3:31–33.

41. Anderson oral history, 144–61, MHS; John B. Martin, *Adlai Stevenson and the World: The Life of Adlai E. Stevenson* (Garden City, NY: Doubleday, 1977), 399–402.

42. Humphrey to Anderson, May 28, 1952, and Anderson to Humphrey, May 29, 1952, both Humphrey, Sen. Hubert H., and Anderson to Jacobsons, J, all CCF, CF, box 2; Albert Eisele, *Almost to the Presidency: A Biography of Two American Politicians* (Blue Earth, MN: Piper, 1972), 126–27; Lamson, *Few Are Chosen,* 180–81; Anderson oral history, 162–68, MHS.

43. "Woman Ex-Envoy Bids For Minn. Senate Seat," *New York Herald Tribune,* April 27, 1958; "Thye Leads 4 DFL Prospects for Senator," *Minneapolis Tribune,* February 2, 1958, Upper Midwest. sec. 1; "DFL Leaders Remember Eugenie Anderson," *Minneapolis Star Tribune,* April 5, 1997, A16; Anderson oral history, 164–68, MHS; Eisele, *Almost to the Presidency,* 127.

44. Harrison, *On Account of Sex,* 73–81; Office of the White House Press Secretary, "Remarks of the President to a Delegation of Women Assigned to Missions of the United Nations—Rose Garden," December 11, 1961, John F. Kennedy Presidential Library and Museum Archives, http://www.jfklibrary.org/Asset-Viewer/Archives/JFKPOF-036-029.aspx.

45. Dean, *Imperial Brotherhood,* 169–243; Arthur M. Schlesinger Jr., *A Thousand Days: John F. Kennedy in the White House* (Boston: Houghton Mifflin, 1965), 406, 407; Peter Collier and David Horowitz, *The Kennedys: An American Drama* (New York: Summit, 1984), 264; "Meeting on Europe and General Diplomatic Matters," July 30, 1962, in *The Presidential Recordings: John F. Kennedy: The Great Crises,* vol. 1 of 3, *July 30–August 1962,* ed. Timothy Naftali (New York: Norton, 2001), 46–50.

46. Adlai Stevenson, "Telephone Conversation with President Elect John F. Kennedy, January 13, 1961," in *The Papers of Adlai Stevenson:* vol. 7 of 8, *Continuing Education and the Unfinished Business of American Society, 1957–1961,* ed. Walter Johnson (Boston: Little, Brown, 1977), 615; Humphrey to Anderson, February 9, 1961, Anderson, E–L, Control Files: 1961, A–Cha, Senatorial Files, 1949–1964, box 1, Humphrey Papers; Freeman to Anderson, March 6, 1962, Freeman, Orville,

PACRF, box 6; Anderson, oral history interview by Larry J. Hackman, March 11, 1973, 20, JFKL.

47. Anderson to Edwards, March 25, 1962, Edwards, India, CMF, box 6; Anderson, Remarks at Farewell Dinner, Red Wing, July 1, 1962, 15, 21–23, Speech Texts, 1954–1964, SSM, box 12.

48. Andrei Pantev, "The Historic Road of the Third Bulgarian State," in *Bulgaria in a Time of Change: Economic and Political Dimensions,* ed. Iliana Zloch-Christy (Aldershot: Avebury, 1996), 19; Department of State, untitled report, March 15, 1963, Weekly Report on DCM Positions—Posts Being Considered, box 195, Office of the Director General, Senior Officer Files Maintained in the Personnel Operations Division, Lot 65D355, RG 59, NARA; Donald C. Tice, interview by Charles S. Kennedy, February 10, 1997, 22, FAOHC, http://adst.org/wp-content/uploads/2013/12/Tice-Donald-C.toc_.pdf. The United States had severed diplomatic relations with Bulgaria in 1950 and only restored them in 1959.

49. Anderson, notes on visit to White House, May 22, 1962, personal notes on meeting with President John F. Kennedy before leaving for Bulgaria, May 1962, 1–2, Personal and Miscellaneous Files, box 27, EMAP.

50. Lamson, *Few Are Chosen,* 182; Anderson oral history, 195, MHS; Anderson, family newsletter, October 1, 1962, FLB.

51. David Binder, "Bulgaria and U.S. Moving to Amity," *New York Times,* July 22, 1963, 2; Neil Hurley, "Blue-Eyed and Faithful, the Minister's a Doll," *International Commerce,* October 26, 1964; Betty O'Regan, "Grandmother Tackles Diplomacy," *Washington Star,* August 11, 1964; Graham Hovey, "The Little Woman From Red Wing Just Won't Be Pushed Around," *Minneapolis Tribune,* July 30, 1963, 2; W. D. Friedenberg, "U.S. Envoy Is the Belle of the Balkans," *Washington Daily News,* December 14, 1963, 17; Anderson oral history, 246, MHS; Anderson oral history, 30–31, JFKL; Lamson, *Few Are Chosen,* 185–86; Nicholas G. Andrews, interview by Charles S. Kennedy, April 12, 1990, 16, FAOHC, http://www.adst.org/OH%20TOCs/Andrews,%20Nicholas%20G.toc.pdf. For Anderson's July 4 address, see DOS Press Release, "American Minister Speaks on Bulgarian Television and Radio," July 3, 1963, Speech Texts 1954–1964, SSM, box 12.

52. Anderson oral history, 278–79, MHS; Anderson, family newsletter, October 13, 1962, FLB. Anderson worried that the Bulgarian security police were somehow fishing the paper scraps out of the sewers.

53. Isabelle Shelton, "Twist Stirs Bulgarians," *Washington Star,* June 9, 1963, D2; Mary Neuburger, "*Kebabche,* Caviar, or Hot Dogs? Consuming the Cold War at the Plovdiv Fair, 1947–72," *Journal of Contemporary History* 47 (January 2012): 48–68; Zhivkov quoted in Walter Hixson, *Parting the Curtain: Propaganda, Culture, and the Cold War, 1945–1961* (New York: St. Martin's, 1997), 231; Anderson family newsletter, September 17, 1962, Sofia 1962, Re: Plovdiv Fair, Subject Files, BMF, box 25 (the fullest account of this episode); Anderson to Department of State, October 16, 1962, 869.191-PL/10–1662, CDF 1960–1963; Anderson to Kennedy, October 10, 1962, K, PC, box 10; Lamson, *Few Are Chosen,* 183–85.

54. Anderson, family newsletters, July 18, 1963, 7, and July 24, 1963, 2, both FLB; Graham Hovey, "Eugenie 'Firsts' Surprise Bulgaria," *Minneapolis Star Tribune,* July 7, 1963, 7; Anderson to Department of State, "Plastics USA Exhibit," 1–2, August 12, 1963, CUL 8 Exhibit & Display Program, Plastics USA, box 1, Bulgaria, Sofia Legation, Classified General Records, 1963, MLR 2183B, RG 84, and English Translations of Bulgarian Visitor Comments, Plastics USA, July 10, 1963, U.S. Plastics Exhibition: Sofia, Bulgaria July 7–17, 1963 (English translations), box 10, Comment Books and Lists of Visitors Related to U.S. Exhibits in the USSR, Rumania, and Bulgaria, Office of Exhibits, RG 306, both in NARA.

55. Loyal Gould, "Eugenie Too Much for Bulgarian Reds," *Minneapolis Star,* December 12, 1962, 20C; Hovey, "Little Woman From Red Wing," 2; Paul Underwood, "Chinese Attacks Moscow on Cuba," *New York Times,* November 9, 1962, 1; "Good for Eugenie!" *Washington Star,* November 11, 1962. Undiplomatic speech by the Bulgarian prime minister would trigger a similar protest by Anderson two years later (David Binder, "Envoy Walks Out as Bulgar Premier Assails U.S.," *New York Times,* September 9, 1964, 14).

56. Anderson oral history, 276, MHS; Johnson to Rusk, December 27, 1963, POL–3 Bul, Subject-Numeric File 1963, RG 59, NARA; David Binder, "Sofia Mob Stones the U.S. Legation Over Spy Charges," *New York Times,* December 28, 1963, 1.

57. Anderson oral history, 278, 289–91, MHS; "Minister EUGENIE MOORE ANDERSON," n.d. (March 1963), State, Chiefs of Mission Review 3/63, box 88A, Departments and Agencies, President's Office File, JFKL; Kennan to Rusk, July 23, 1963, PER Anderson, Eugenie, Subject-Numeric File 1963. Chiefs of mission were not supposed to comment on each other's performance.

58. John Macy, Memorandum for Record, "Eugenie Anderson," July 24, 1965, Anderson, Mrs. Eugenie, John W. Macy Jr. Papers, LBJL; Anderson oral history, 292–343, MHS; Daily, "Music Major," 17; Peg Meier, "A Woman—And Diplomat—of Substance," *Minneapolis Star Tribune,* April 5, 1997, A16.

59. Dupont, *Mrs. Ambassador,* 193–95, 206–13; Anderson oral history, 346–53, MHS; Anderson, Memorandum for the President, "Vietnam," December 7, 1967, Travel Program File, Vietnam Trip, 1967, Political Party Activities, 1958–1970, Political Party Activities, 1945–1970, box 14, EMAP; Lori Sturdevant, "Longtime DFLer Eugenie Anderson Endorses Boschwitz," *Minneapolis Star Tribune,* October 28, 1984, B1, B8.

60. Anderson oral history, 297–314, MHS; Anderson to Freeman, "Major Foreign Policy Speech in Boston on Sept. 19," September 12, 1968, Hubert Humphrey Campaign, 1968, box 14, EMAP.

61. Lamson, *Few Are Chosen,* 193–94.

62. Acheson to Humphrey, September 10, 1953, Acheson, Dean, box 10, EMAP (read at banquet honoring Anderson), 2. Acheson later told India Edwards that Anderson "was one of the two best political diplomatic appointments that President Truman ever made." The other was David Bruce (Edwards, *Pulling No Punches,* 178).

6. Clare Boothe Luce

Epigraph: "Mrs. Luce's Successor," *Washington Post,* May 7, 1959, A20.

1. This introduction draws on Sylvia Jukes Morris, *Price of Fame: The Honorable Clare Boothe Luce* (New York: Random House, 2014), 341–43; Ralph G. Martin, *Henry and Clare: An Intimate Portrait of the Luces* (New York: G. P. Putnam's Sons, 1991), 311–12; Alden Hatch, *Ambassador Extraordinary: Clare Boothe Luce* (New York: Henry Holt, 1955), 207, 216–18; and Clare Boothe Luce to Jackson, June 18, 1953, *FRUS, 1952–1954,* Western Europe and Canada, volume 6, part 2, https://history.state.gov/historicaldocuments/frus1952–54v06p2/d744.

2. Newspaper excerpt translations in MSA/USIS, "Italian Press Highlights," No. 229, May 30–31, June 1, 1953, see also MSA/USIS, "Italian Press Trends," No. 82, May 31, 1953, both in Strictly Confidential—L (4), box 2, GCMS.

3. "Mrs. Luce Boning Up for Duty," *Washington Post,* March 19, 1953, 27; Mario Del Pero, "The United States and 'Psychological Warfare' in Italy, 1948–1955," *Journal of American History* 87 (March 2001): 1319n36. In a poll of Italians that fall, fewer than 2 percent of respondents believed that Luce's comment or indeed foreign meddling generally had played a role in the DC's loss of votes (Cantril to Coates, December 2, 1953, 765.00/12–253, attachment, 13, CDF 1950–1954).

4. Carolyn Kraus, "Power, Resistance, and the Writings of Female Illegitimacy: Eva Peron, Clare Boothe Luce, and Flore Triotan," *Journal of Research in Gender Studies* 1 (2011): 9–42; Digby Diehl, "Q&A: Clare Boothe Luce," *Los Angeles Times,* May 13, 1972, 127; Sylvia Jukes Morris, *Rage for Fame: The Ascent of Clare Boothe Luce* (New York: Random House, 1997).

5. Luce and Marquis Childs, "Madame Minister" (unpublished draft, 1939), folder 3, box 334, CBLP; Luce and Marquis Childs, "Madame Minister"—typescript—with revisions and corrections, box 2, Marquis Childs Papers, Special Collections, University of Iowa, Iowa City; Mark Fearnow, *Clare Boothe Luce: A Research and Production Sourcebook* (Westport, CT: Greenwood, 1995), 38–42. It not known whether Florence Harriman, serving in Oslo at the time, inspired the play.

6. Morris, *Rage for Fame,* 161–325.

7. W. A. Swanberg, *Luce and His Empire* (New York: Scribner's, 1972), 221; Carol Kelly-Gangi, ed., *A Woman's Book of Inspiration* (New York: Fall River, 2017), 54; Morris, *Rage for Fame,* 329. Luce was also called "The Delicate Monster" and "that lovely asp" (Helen Lawrenson, *Stranger at the Party* [New York: Random House], 98; Cissy Patterson quoted in Smith, *Newspaper Titan,* 397).

8. Clare Boothe Luce, interview by Ann M. Morin, June 19, 1986, 22, FAOHC, http://www.adst.org/OH%20TOCs/Luce,%20Clare%20Boothe.toc.pdf; Willis, *Frances Elizabeth Willis,* 187–99; Clare Boothe [Luce], *Europe in the Spring* (New York: Knopf, 1940); Morris, *Rage for Fame,* 369–88, 396–97.

9. Morris, *Rage for Fame,* 398–401; Stephen Shadegg, *Clare Boothe Luce: A Biography* (New York: Simon & Schuster, 1972), 119–23; David Selznick to Luce, November 21, 1941, folder 4, Correspondence 1941, A–Z, box 757, CBLP.

10. Lawrenson, *Stranger at the Party,* 121; Alan Brinkley, *The Publisher: Henry Luce and His American Century* (New York: Vintage, 2010), 305–6; Luce, "America in the Post-War Air World," delivered February 9, 1943, *Vital Speeches of the Day,* March 15, 1943, 331–36; Jennet Conant, *The Irregulars: Roald Dahl and the British Spy Ring in Wartime Washington* (New York: Simon & Schuster, 2008), 115–22, 189–90.

11. Luce, "A Greater and Freer America," delivered June 27, 1944, *Vital Speeches of the Day,* July 15, 1944, 586–88; Shadegg, *Clare Boothe Luce,* 194; "Notes and Comment," in "The Talk of the Town," *New Yorker,* July 8, 1944, 13. Luce's friend and colleague Joe Martin probably helped draft the speech (Kenneally, *Compassionate Conservative,* 110).

12. Edwards, *Pulling No Punches,* 87, 171–81.

13. Shadegg, *Clare Boothe Luce,* 207–11; Martha W. Lear, "On Harry, and Henry and Ike and Mr. Shaw," *New York Times Magazine,* April 22, 1973, 50; Henry Grunwald, *One Man's America: A Journalist's Search for the Heart of His Country* (New York: Doubleday, 1997), 151.

14. Morris, *Price of Fame,* 294–306; Eisenhower Diary entries, September 27, November 25, 1949, and March 22, 1950, *The Eisenhower Diaries,* ed. Robert H. Ferrell (New York: Norton, 1981), 163, 166, 173; Brinkley, *Publisher,* 370–73; Beverly Smith Jr., "Things They Wish They Hadn't Said," *Saturday Evening Post,* September 19, 1959, 140–41.

15. Harrison, *On Account of Sex,* 58–62; Dwight D. Eisenhower, remarks at Portland, Oregon, October 7, 1952, in "Campaign Statements of Dwight D. Eisenhower: A Reference Index," 278, DDEL.

16. Morris, *Price of Fame,* 307–10.

17. Maree-Anne Reid, "'Kiss the Boys Goodbye': Clare Boothe Luce's Appointment as United States Ambassador to Italy," *Australasian Journal of American Studies* 16, no. 2 (1997): 45–67; Swanberg, *Luce and His Empire,* 343; Elbridge Durbrow, interview by John T. Mason Jr., No. 3, June 4, 1981, Columbia Center for Oral History, box 68, Elbridge Durbrow Papers, HIA; Shadegg, *Clare Boothe Luce,* 231–34; John Foster Dulles to Eisenhower, December 27, 1952, Dulles, John F. Prior Inauguration, box 1, Dulles-Herter Series, AWF; Luce diary, January 22, 1953, folder 10, box 56, CBLP; "Where Must We Seat Mrs. Luce? Rome Is Asking," *Chicago Daily Tribune,* February 9, 1953, 4; Mario Del Pero, "American Pressures and Their Containment in Italy during the Ambassadorship of Clare Boothe Luce, 1953–1956," *Diplomatic History* 28 (June 2004): 415.

18. H. Luce to Dulles, February 3, 1953, Luce, Henry R. 1953, box 72, reel 27, John Foster Dulles Papers, SGML; Dozier to H. Luce, January 24, 1953, folder 19, box 739, CBLP; see also Hatch, *Ambassador Extraordinary,* 204–6.

19. Luce, "Victory Is a Woman," *Woman's Home Companion,* November 1943, 122; "Women Diplomats—take 1," n.d. (c. 1943–1945), folder 11, Congressional File, Subject File, Women, box 600, and Luce, untitled draft speech on women and the peacemaking to come, n.d. (circa 1944), folder 29, Speeches, box 677, both in CBLP.

20. Luce to Frances Bolton, March 14, 1953, folder 1311, box 74, Frances P. Bolton Papers, Western Reserve Historical Society, Cleveland; Cynthia Lowry, "Something New Has Been Added," *Washington Post,* March 8, 1953, S11.

21. Durbrow to Luce, March 11, 1953, and Luce to Durbrow, March 20, 1953, both in folder 7, box 634, CBLP; Durbrow, interview by John T. Mason Jr., 169.

22. "Benvenuta," *Time,* May 4, 1953, 38.

23. Alessandro Brogi, "Ambassador Clare Boothe Luce and the Evolution of Psychological Warfare in Italy," *Cold War History* 12 (May 2012): 270–73; NSC 5411/2, "U.S. Policy toward Italy," April 15, 1954, esp. 7–9, Italy (5), box 5, Disaster File, NSC Staff Papers, White House Office, DDEL.

24. "Italian Reds Chant Derision of Clare Luce," *Chicago Daily Tribune,* January 27, 1954, 4.

25. Luce to Jackson, June 30, 1953, Luce, Henry R. & Clare, 1953, box 70, C. D. Jackson Papers, DDEL.

26. Roberto G. Rabel, *Between East and West: Trieste, The United States, and the Cold War, 1941–1954* (Durham, NC: Duke University Press, 1988), 147–49, 157–62; Memorandum of Conversation, Eisenhower and President Giovanni Gronchi, February 28, 1956, Italy (6), box 33, International Series, AWF; Hatch, *Ambassador Extraordinary,* 231–32; C. L. Sulzberger, *The Last of the Giants: Memoirs and Diaries, 1954–1963* (New York: Macmillan, 1970), 284; Murphy, *Diplomat among Warriors,* 422–24; Morris, *Price of Power,* 399–400; "The President's News Conference of April 29, 1959," *Public Papers of the Presidents: Dwight D. Eisenhower, 1959* (Washington, DC: GPO, 1960), 344; Luce, draft memo to Dulles, n.d., folder 2, box 633, CBLP; Guidotti quoted in Sulzberger, *A Long Row of Candles,* 983.

27. Eisenhower to Luce, November 7, 1953, *FRUS, 1952–1954,* Western Europe and Canada, volume 6, part 2, https://history.state.gov/historicaldocuments/frus1952–54v06p2/d754#fn:1.3.2.7.4.48.4.6; Morris, *Price of Fame,* 391; Merchant to Undersecretary, March 16, 1955, Aid 1954–1955, box 20, Subject Files Relating to Italian Affairs, 1944–56, Lot Files, Lot 58D357, RG 59, NARA.

28. Luce diary, March 13, 1953, folder 10, box 56, CBLP; Luce to Jackson, September 7, 1953, and Luce to Dulles, March 18, 1954, both in Letters 1953, box 1, Classified Records of Clare Boothe Luce, 1953–1956, MLR 2783, RG 84, NARA.

29. Del Pero, "United States and 'Psychological Warfare' in Italy," 1330; Sulzberger, *Long Row of Candles,* 980; Claire Sterling and Max Ascoli, "The Lady of Villa Taverna," *Reporter,* February 23, 1956, 14.

30. Sterling and Ascoli, "Lady of Villa Taverna," 13.

31. Randall B. Woods, *Shadow Warrior: William Egan Colby and the CIA* (New York: Basic Books, 2013), 95–103, 108–10.

32. Allesandro Brogi, *Confronting America: The Cold War between the United States and the Communists in France and Italy* (Chapel Hill: University of North Carolina Press, 2011), 185, 222; Brogi, "Ambassador Clare Boothe Luce," 281–85.

33. Sulzberger, *Long Row of Candles,* 916; Luce, Memorandum of Conversation, July 20, 1953, 1, Memoranda of Conversations '53, box 4, Italy, Rome Embassy,

Records of Clare Boothe Luce, 1955–57, Lot 64F26, MLR 2783A, RG 84, NARA.

34. Luce, "Ambassador Luce: Paper for American Assembly" (undelivered), April 28, 1956, folder 13, box 687, CBLP, 35; Clare Boothe Luce, "Your Letters May Win the Peace," *Look*, November 23, 1948, 128; Shadegg, *Clare Boothe Luce*, 224–25; Tim Weiner, *Legacy of Ashes: The History of the CIA* (New York: Doubleday, 2007), 26–27.

35. Luce quoted in Gretta Palmer, "The Lady and the Lion . . . in One," *Catholic Digest*, April 1953, 57; Sulzberger, *Long Row of Candles*, 977; Sterling and Ascoli, "Lady of Villa Taverna," 19.

36. Luce, "Luce Tells Diplomats Role Abroad," *Washington Post*, March 25, 1955, 6; Luce, "Ambassador Luce: Paper for American Assembly," 21–22; Shadegg, *Clare Boothe Luce*, 257–58; Katie Louchheim, "Clare Boothe Luce Orders Political Cake, Eats It, Too," *Washington Post*, July 12, 1953, S1; US Embassy Rome to DOS, "Official Italian Radio Broadcast on Ambassador Luce's Resignation," attachment, "Script of the RAI English Language Broadcast," November 20, 1956, folder 7, box 642, CBLP; "Madam Ambassador Clare Boothe Luce: Her Versatile and Crowded Years," *Newsweek*, January 24, 1955, 28; John W. Jones to Burke Elbrick, November 28, 1956, box 3, folder 910.02 Italy—Luce (Ambassador)—1957, MLR 3092, Bureau of European Affairs, Office of West European Affairs, Decimal Files Related to Italy and Austria, 1953–1958, Lot Files, RG 59, NARA; "Mrs. Luce Is Girls' 'Ideal,' Boys for Gina," *New York Herald Tribune*, November 17, 1956; Spaulding, *Ambassadors Ordinary and Extraordinary*, 200.

37. Morris, *Price of Fame*, 315; "Italians Are Given Full View of Envoy," *Washington Post*, March 24, 1953, 15; William Attwood, "Mrs. Ambassador," *Look*, May 18, 1954, 133, 131; "Premier Leaps to Defense of U.S. Envoy Luce," *Chicago Daily Tribune*, January 30, 1954, 6; Hatch, *Ambassador Extraordinary*, 217; Indro Montanelli of the *Corriere della Sera*, quoted in Hatch, *Ambassador Extraordinary*, 215.

38. Helen Lawrenson, "The Woman," *Esquire*, August 1974, 152, 154; August 10, 1954, *The Diary of James C. Hagerty: Eisenhower at Mid-Course, 1954–1955*, ed. Robert Ferrell (Bloomington: Indiana University Press, 1983), 114; Luce, "Russian Atomic Power and the Lost American Revolution," August 21, 1954, esp. 30–31, Luce, Henry R. & Clare, 1954 (2), box 70, C. D. Jackson Papers; *Slam the Door Softly* quoted in "Clare Boothe Luce Shared Billing with Women's Lib," *New York Times*, June 28, 1971, 26.

39. Henry Gaggiottini, "Anti-U.S. Stories Add Flame to 'Cold War,'" *Chicago Daily Tribune*, January 31, 1954, 6; Attwood, "Mrs. Ambassador," 133; Luce to Edward Bernays, June 5, 1953, folder 18, Correspondence 1953, A–H, box 763, CBLP.

40. Ashley Clarke to Geoffrey Harrison, November 23, 1953, 2, FO 371/107389, NA-UK; Dulles, "Memorandum of Conversation with Prime Minister Scelba at Dinner, March 28, 1955," March 29, 1955, Strictly Confidential—L (3), box 2, GCMS; Sterling and Ascoli, "Lady of Villa Taverna," 16; [?] Steele to [?] Williamson,

"Mrs. Luce—II," November 24, 1956, Dispatches from *Time* Magazine Correspondents: Second Ser., 1956–1968 (MS Am 2090.1), folder 1956 Nov. 23–29, box 75, HL; C. D. Jackson Diary, December 31, 1953, quoted in Evan Thomas, *Ike's Bluff: President Eisenhower's Secret Battle to Save the World* (Boston: Little, Brown, 2012), 410.

41. "Madam Ambassador Clare Boothe Luce," 35; Sterling and Ascoli, "Lady of Villa Taverna," 12; Mallet to Salisbury, July 20, 1953, 44, FO 482/7, NA-UK; "Busy Clare Says Embassy Needs Helper," *Washington Post,* January 28, 1955, 57.

42. Woman quoted in Loudon Wainwright, *The Great American Magazine: An Inside History of* Life (New York: Knopf, 1986), 53; Sulzberger, *Long Row of Candles,* 979; Hedley Donovan, *Right Places, Right Times: Forty Years in Journalism Not Counting My Paper Route* (New York: Henry Holt, 1989), 260–61; Letitia Baldridge, *A Lady, First: My Life in the Kennedy White House and the American Embassies of Paris and Rome* (New York: Viking, 2001), 89–90.

43. Luce to Joe Martin, July 27, 1953, and Luce to Joe Martin, January 19, 1954, both in folder 8, box 605, and Luce, various efficiency reports, n.d. (c. 1955), folder 9, box 635, all in CBLP; Martin, *Henry and Clare,* 317; E. J. Kahn Jr., *The China Hands: America's Foreign Service and What Befell Them* (New York: Viking, 1975), 17–20.

44. Luce, memorandum, "Group Support of CBL as a Public Figure," 6–7, n.d. (ca. 1955), folder 2, box 633, CBLP.

45. Leopoldo Nuti, "The United States, Italy, and the Opening to the Left, 1953–1963," *Journal of Cold War Studies* 4 (Summer 2002): 41; M. B. Rosenbluth to Luce, June 14, 1954, folder 8, Correspondence 1954 M–Z, box 764, CBLP; Morris, *Price of Fame,* 385, 406–7; Paul D. McCusker, interview by Charles S. Kennedy, October 14, 1991, 6, FAOHC, http://www.adst.org/OH%20TOCs/McCusker,%20 Paul%20D.toc.pdf; Shadegg, *Clare Boothe Luce,* 262–65; Martin, *Henry and Clare,* 331–34.

46. Morris, *Price of Fame,* 432–36; Eisenhower to H. Luce, November 19, 1956 and H. Luce to Eisenhower, November 20, 1956, both Luce, Henry (1), box 25, Administration Series, and Ann Whitman Diary, November 19, 1956, Nov. '56 Diary ACW (1), box 8, Ann Whitman Diary Series, both in AWF; "Italy Honors U.S. Envoy," *New York Times,* December 19, 1956, 15.

47. Dulles, "Telephone Call from Governor Adams," December 17, 1956, (Personnel Matters) 1955–1957 (4) and Dulles, "Memorandum of Conversation with Mr. and Mrs. Luce . . . December 31, 1956," January 2, 1957 (Personnel Matters) 1955–1957 (3), both box 6, Subject Series, JFDP; Morris, *Price of Fame,* 441; MTC, Sherman Adams to Dulles, October 29, 1957, Memoranda Tel Conv.—W.H. Sept. 2, 1957 to Dec. 26, 1957 (2), box 12, Telephone Conversation Series, JFDP.

48. Dulles, Memorandum of Conversation, October 13, 1958, and Dulles, Memorandum of Conversation with Mr. Henry R. Luce, January 19, 1959, both in DDRS Online, Document Nos. CK3100198245, CK3100182740; Memoranda of Telephone Conversations, H. Luce to Dulles, January 12, 1959, Dulles to Loy

Henderson, January 12, 1959, Dulles to Christian A. Herter, January 12, 1959, Christian A. Herter to Dulles, January 13, 1959, Dulles to H. Luce, January 13, 1959, all memoranda of telephone conversations—Gen. Jan 4, 1959 to May 8, 1959 (3), box 9, Telephone Conversation Series; Christian A. Herter, "Telephone Calls . . . January 12, 1959," CAH Telephone Calls, January 1, 1959, to April 27, 1959 (3), box 12, Christian A. Herter Papers, DDEL.

49. John F. Kennedy to Luce, March 5, 1959, folder 1, box 209, CBLP; Martin, *Henry and Clare,* 349–52; Christian A. Herter, "Telephone Conversation with Mrs. Clare Boothe Luce," March 3, 1959, CAH Telephone Calls, January 1, 1959 to April 27, 1959 (2), box 12, Herter Papers; US Senate, Committee on Foreign Relations, *The Nomination of Clare Boothe Luce to be Ambassador to Brazil, April 15, 1959* (Washington, DC: GPO, 1959); *Lady,* May 1959, cover, folder 2, box 646, CBLP.

50. "The President's News Conference of April 29, 1959," 344; "Quick Action by Mrs. Luce Sets Record," *Chicago Daily Tribune,* May 2, 1959, 3; Herbert Block cartoon, n.d. (circa early May 1959), folder 2, Public Service, Subject File, Ambassador to Brazil, Political Cartoons, box 649, CBLP.

51. Lawrenson, *Stranger at the Party,* 127; Martin, *Henry and Clare,* 351–52; Stephen Siff, "Henry Luce's Strange Trip: Coverage of LSD in *Time* and *Life,* 1954–68," *Journalism History* 34 (Fall 2008): 129.

52. Brinkley, *Publisher,* 389; Max Holland, "A Luce Connection: Senator Keating, William Pawley, and the Cuban Missile Crisis," *Journal of Cold War Studies* 1 (Fall 1999): 139–67.

53. Heather Marie Stur, *Beyond Combat: Women and Gender in the Vietnam War Era* (Cambridge: Cambridge University Press, 2011), 17–38; Harlan Cleveland quoted in Howard Jones, *Death of a Generation: How the Assassinations of Diem and JFK Prolonged the Vietnam War* (New York: Oxford University Press, 2003), 385; Luce, "The Lady *Is* for Burning: The Seven Deadly Sins of Madame Nhu," *National Review,* November 5, 1963, 395–99; Robert E. Herzstein, *Henry R. Luce,* Time, *and the American Crusade in Asia* (New York: Cambridge University Press, 2005), 217; Jaqueline Kennedy, interview by Arthur M. Schlesinger Jr., Spring 1964, in *Jacqueline Kennedy: Historic Conversations on Life With John F. Kennedy,* ed. Michael Beschloss (New York: Hyperion, 2011), 305–6.

54. Morris, *Price of Fame,* 566; see also David W. Eyre, *Clare: The Honolulu Years* (Honolulu: Mutual Publishing, 2007).

55. William J. Crockett, interview by Thomas Stern, June 20, 1990, 16–17, FAOHC, https://www.adst.org/OH%20TOCs/Crockett,%20William%20J.1990.toc.pdf; James B. Engle, interview by Charles S. Kennedy, August 1, 1988, 4, FAOHC, https://www.adst.org/OH%20TOCs/Engle,%20James%20Bruce.toc.pdf; Norman W. Getsinger, interview by Charles S. Kennedy, January 19, 2000, 21–24, FAOHC, https://www.adst.org/OH%20TOCs/Getsinger,%20Norman%20W.toc.pdf; William C. Harrop, interview by Charles S. Kennedy, August 24, 1993, 10, 13, FAOHC, https://www.adst.org/OH%20TOCs/Harrop,%20William%20C.toc.pdf; Paul D. McCusker, interview by Charles S. Kennedy, October 14, 1991, 6, FAOHC,

https://www.adst.org/OH%20TOCs/McCusker,%20Paul%20D.toc.pdf; Wells Stabler, interview by Charles S. Kennedy, February 28, 1991, 54–57, FAOHC, https://www.adst.org/OH%20TOCs/Stabler,%20Wells.toc.pdf; Thomas Stern, interview by Charles S. Kennedy, May 16, 1993, 8, FAOHC, https://www.adst.org/OH%20TOCs/Stern,%20Thomas.toc.pdf; Horace G. Torbert, interview by Charles S. Kennedy, August 31, 1988, 11, FAOHC, https://www.adst.org/OH%20TOCs/Torbert,%20Horace%20G.toc.pdf; August Velletri, interview by Charles S. Kennedy, February 12, 1993, 6, FAOHC, https://www.adst.org/OH%20TOCs/Velletri,%20August.toc.pdf.

56. "Inspection Report to the Department," November 22, 1955, Rome (folder 1), 1955, and "Statements to Facilitate Inspection: Part 5, Administration, (b) Personnel," September 1, 1952, Rome, 1952, 1953, both box 99, Foreign Service Inspection Reports, Inspection Reports, 1936–1964, MLR 5449, RG 59, NARA.

57. Livingston Merchant to Dulles, March 12, 1954, and Thruston Morton to Dulles, "Group II continued—Posts at which no change seems necessary," September 20, 1954, Tab II, both Evaluation of Chiefs of Mission (3), box 1, Personnel Series, JFDP; Mallet to Salisbury, July 20, 1953, 44; Clarke to Eden, July 20, 1954, 39, FO 482/8, Clarke to Macmillan, June 17, 1955, 6. FO 482/9, and Clarke to Lloyd, June 19, 1956, 5–6, FO 482/10, all in NA-UK.

58. Sulzberger, *Long Row of Candles,* 964, 974–77.

59. Luce, "The Diplomat," n.d. (circa 1959–1960), folder 3, box 327, CBLP; Lear, "On Harry," 56. The series *Passport to Danger* had already appeared on television (1954–1958); it starred Caesar Romero as a diplomatic courier and spy.

60. Grunwald, *One Man's America,* 574; Sally Quinn, "'I Suppose I Aspired Too High,'" *Washington Post,* April 29, 1973, F1; Lear, "On Harry," 56.

7. Frances E. Willis

Epigraph: Willis to Henry Stimson, October 12, 1932, reprinted in Calkin, *Women in the Department of State,* 168; "Career Woman," *Time,* July 20, 1953, 12.

1. Willis, *Frances Elizabeth Willis,* 322–24.

2. Louchheim, *By the Political Sea,* 236.

3. Roshan Peiris, "The Unflappable Miss Willis," *Ceylon Observer,* August 11, 1963, 10; Willis, *Frances Elizabeth Willis,* 324; Selwa Roosevelt, "Diplomatically Speaking," *Washington Star,* September 14, 1955.

4. Willis, "When the Russian Ambassador Couldn't Speak Norwegian and the American Could—and other recollections of a Career Diplomat," (Stanford) *Alumni Almanac* 9 (February 1971): 3; "'The Best' Diplomat," (San Bernardino, CA) *Sun-Telegram,* May 5, 1957; Rene Kuhn Bryant, "Woman Ambassador Sets a Pattern," *Tallahassee Democrat,* February 26, 1958, 6.

5. Castle diary, May 19, 1927, 108–9, reel 2, WRCP-HCHL; James C. H. Bonbright, interview by Peter Jessup, February 29, 1986, 36, FAOHC, http://www

.adst.org/OH%20TOCs/Bonbright,%20James%20Cowles%20Hart.toc.pdf; Willis, *Frances Elizabeth Willis,* 61.

6. William C. Trimble, interview by Charles S. Kennedy, February 24, 1990, 6, FAOHC, http://www.adst.org/OH%20TOCs/Trimble,%20William%20C.toc. pdf; George Messersmith to Carl F. Deichman, July 1, 1930, 1, Valparaiso, Chile Nov. 1930, Inspection Reports on Foreign Service Posts, 1906–39, box 168, CDF 1930–1939.

7. McCarthy, *Women of the World,* 144; Willis to Stimson, October 12, 1932; "Career Woman," 12.

8. Willis to Mother and Caroline, April 12, 1940, Apr. 1940, FC, box 7; Willis, *Frances Elizabeth Willis,* 173–77.

9. Mark Stout, "The Pond: Running Agents for State, War, and the CIA," *Studies in Intelligence* 48, no. 3 (2004): https://www.cia.gov/library/center-for-the-study-of-intelligence/csi-publications/csi-studies/studies/vol48no3/article07.html; George Strong to MILATTACHE AMEMBASSY Madrid, Spain, January 12, 1944 and Hohenthal to Military Intelligence Division, January 14, 1944, both courtesy Mark Stout; Findlay Burns, interview by Ann M. Morin, November 22, 1985, courtesy Morin.

10. Willis, *Frances Elizabeth Willis,* 105–282; Elbridge Durbrow to Willis, September 26, 1950, folder 1, Foreign Service 1950, box 17, FEWP.

11. Thomas Harris, "Lady Envoy to Voteless Gals," *New York Post,* August 2, 1953; "What's My Line?—Eddie and Marilyn Cantor; Martin Gabel [panel]," YouTube video, 25:35, from *What's My Line,* televised by CBS on June 2, 1957, posted by "What's My Line," January 12, 2014, https://www.youtube.com /watch?v=sAmSL6_EQu4.

12. R. C. MacDonald to Eisenhower, April 16, 1953, 9-B-Switzerland, Endorsement, Willis, Frances Elizabeth (Dr.), box 203, General File, White House Central File, DDEL.

13. Remarks by Secretary Dulles before Girls Nation, State Dept. Auditorium, July 12, 1956, Subject File: Dulles, John F., 19–10 Amb to Switzerland, box 19, FEWP; "Envoy to Norway Sworn In," *New York Times,* May 24, 1957, 4; "Woman Slated as Envoy to Bern Despite Anti-Feminist Swiss View," *New York Times,* April 15, 1953, 1; Livingston Merchant to Walter B. Smith, April 15, 1953, Switzerland, 1950–1955, 2 of 2, box 28, Miscellaneous Office Files, Assistant Secretary for European Affairs, 1943–1957, Lot Files, Lot 59D233, MLR 1274, RG 59, NARA; Swiss Foreign Ministry, "Agrément pour un ambassadeur des Etats-Unis d'Amerique en Suisse," June 26, 1953, DODIS, Diplomatische Dokumente der Schweiz, http://dodis.ch/9446.

14. Dulles, "Memorandum of Conversation with Henry J. Taylor," February 22, 1957, Memos of Conversation—General—T through Z, box 1, GCMS; Dulles, "Telephone Call to Henry Taylor," February 21, 1957, T (1), box 10, Personnel Series, JFDP.

15. Howard Donovan to Department of State, "Swiss Comment about Appointment of a Woman Ambassador," August 7, 1953, and Willis to Department of State,

"Arrival and Presentation of Credentials," October 12, 1953, both 123 Willis, Frances E., CDF 1950–1954; A. P. Vos to Willis, October 15, 1953, folder 11, Amb. to Switzerland, Clippings 1953, box 20, FEWP.

16. "Die amerikanische Botschafterin über schweizerische Lebensart," *Der Bund* (Bern), May 1, 1957, 1; Willis, "Text of CBS Coast to Coast Broadcast," 3–4, December 17, 1954, folder 3, Amb. to Switzerland, Speeches and Writings, 1954, box 18, FEWP.

17. Percy W. Bidwell, *What the Tariff Means to American Industries* (New York: Harper & Brothers, 1956), 88–129; Paul Erdman, *Swiss-American Economic Relations: Their Evolution in an Era of Crises* (Basel: Kyklos-Verlag, 1959), 122–25, 141–47.

18. Charles E. Egan, "President Raises Duty on Watches; Swiss Indignant," *New York Times*, July 28, 1954, 1; "Swiss Retaliate," *New York Times*, August 16, 1954, 24; Bidwell, *What the Tariff Means*, 91.

19. Stephen Benedict, "Memorandum for Mrs. Whitman," July 14, 1954, ACW Diary July 1954 (4), box 2, AWF; Willis, *Frances Elizabeth Willis*, 308–15, Swiss Foreign Office quoted at 311; Samuel C. Waugh to Dulles, November 16, 1954, 123 Willis, Frances E., CDF 1950–1954.

20. Thruston Morton to Dulles, "Group II continued—Posts at which no change seems necessary," September 20, 1954, and Livingston Merchant to Dulles, March 12, 1954, both Tab II, Evaluation of Chiefs of Mission (3), box 1, Personnel Series, JFDP; Willis, *Frances Elizabeth Willis*, 325; Morin, interview with Melbourne. The Merchant memo ranked only five envoys "outstanding."

21. Memorandum of Conversation, December 18, 1956, (Personnel Matters) 1955–1957 (4), box 6, Subject Series, JFDP; William L. Blue, interview by Ann M. Morin, April 8, 1985, courtesy Morin; Eisenhower to Dulles, March 23, 1955, Name File (Strictly Confidential) [A–B] (1), box 1, Personnel Series, JFDP.

22. Willis, *Frances Elizabeth Willis*, 339–69.

23. Mats R. Berdal, *The United States, Norway and the Cold War, 1954–60* (Basingstoke, Hampshire: Macmillan, 1997), 129, 134.

24. Willis to DOS, "Norway and U.S. Leadership," July 29, 1960, *FRUS, 1958–1960, Western Europe*, vol. 7, part 2, https://history.state.gov/historicaldocuments/frus1958–60v07p2/d301; Rolf Tamnes, *The United States and the Cold War In the High North* (Aldershot, UK: Dartmouth, 1991), 160.

25. Willis to Family, March 8, 1961, Mar. 1961, FC, box 13.

26. Richard Hofstadter, *Anti-Intellectualism in American Life* (New York: Vintage, 1963), 10–11; "Knight of the Bald Iggle," *Time*, August 12, 1957, 18; Briggs, *Proud Servant*, 267–68; Isabelle Shelton, "U.S. Woman Envoy," *Washington Star*, February 24, 1961.

27. Melbourne, interview by Morin; Michael L. Krenn, *Black Diplomacy: African-Americans and the State Department, 1945–1969* (Armonk, NY: M. E. Sharpe, 1999).

28. Leo LeClaire, interview by Ann M. Morin, May 29, 1985, courtesy Morin; Mildred Schroeder, "It's Always Ladies Day in Ceylon," *San Francisco Examiner*, May 3, 1963, 27.

29. "Woman Named New Ambassador to Ceylon," *Washington Post*, March 1, 1961, D3; Roger Jones to Willis, February 23, 1961, 123 Willis, Frances E., CDF 1960–1963; Cecil B. Lyon, interview by John Rovey, October 26, 1988, 90, FAOHC, http://www.adst.org/OH%20TOCs/Lyon,%20Cecil%20B.toc.pdf; Harold G. Josif, interview by Charles S. Kennedy, October 4, 1999, 41, FAOHC, http://www.adst.org/OH%20TOCs/Josif,%20Harold%20A.toc.pdf.

30. Willis, *Frances Elizabeth Willis*, 344; Willis to Family, January 25, 1959, Jan. 1959, FC, box 13. The Foreign Service Institute language difficulty rankings for English-speakers place Sinhala in category 4 on a scale from easiest (1, e.g., Spanish) to toughest (5, e.g., Arabic).

31. Willis to Phillips Talbot, December 20, 1962, Ceylon, 1962, box 20, National Security File, JFKL; Kenneth J. Vandevelde, "Reassessing the Hickenlooper Amendment," *Virginia Journal of International Law* 29 (Fall 1988): 145–46; Willis, *Frances Elizabeth Willis*, 398.

32. "Police Okay Anti-U.S. March," *Ceylon Observer*, February 15, 1963, 1; "Monk Performs Mock Ritual—At Anti-US Rally," *Ceylon Daily Mirror*, February 18, 1963, 3; *Observer* (London), February 24, 1963, 38; Willis to Department of State, February 18, 1963, POL 25–3 Ceylon, box 3857, Subj-Num File 1963, RG 59, NARA; Department of State, "Ambassador FRANCES E. WILLIS," n.d. (March 1963), State, Chiefs of Mission Review 3/63, box 88A, Departments and Agencies, President's Office File, JFKL.

33. Phillips Talbot to James P. Grant and Turner Cameron, March 9, 1964, POL–Political Affairs and Relations, January–March 1964, box 1, Bureau of Near Eastern and South Asian Affairs, Office of Country Director for India, Ceylon, Nepal & Maldives, Records Relating to Ceylon, 1964, Lot Files, RG 59, NARA.

34. Willis, *Frances Elizabeth Willis*, 411–37.

35. "Miss Willis Wins Senate Approval," *New York Times*, July 21, 1953, 6; Mary F. Harvey, "Ambassador Frances Willis: 'Determination to Make It Work' Cause of U.N.'s Growth in Strength," *Quincy Patriot Ledger*, October 24, 1960, 8; Nadine Ullmann, "Ex-Teacher Climbs Diplomatic Ladder," *Newsday*, November 29, 1960, 39; "Miss F. E. Willis präsentiert sich der Oeffentlichkeit," *Die Tat* (Zürich), October 11, 1953; Willis, "Women of the United States," Helsinki, April [19], 1951, folder 2, Foreign Service 1951, box 17, FEWP, 9; Willis, *Frances Elizabeth Willis*, 444.

36. Ullmann, "Ex-Teacher Climbs Diplomatic Ladder," 39.

37. Joellyn Kapp, "The Stanford Woman Speaks," (Stanford) *Alumni Almanac* 7 (January 1968): 6, Post Retirement, Clippings 1968, box 38, FEWP.

38. Willis to Family, n.d., July 1937, Willis to Family, February 6, 1938, Feb. 1938, both in FC, box 6 (see also Willis to Family, August 8, 1932, Aug. 1932, FC, box 4), Willis to Mother and Caroline, August 4, 1940, Aug. 1940, FC, box 7, and Willis to Family, n.d., July 1937, FC, box 6. The lack of discrimination in her letters, of course, says more about the nature of her correspondence—largely unrevealing from the historian's standpoint—than about her experiences.

39. Willis to Family, April 23, 1932, Apr. 1932, and Willis to Family, n.d., June 1932, both FC, box 4.

40. Willis to Mother, September 30, 1938, Sept. 1938, FC, box 6; LeClaire, interview by Morin.

41. *Time,* September 14, 1953, 54; *US News and World Report,* April 19, 1957, 18; Harvey, "Ambassador Frances Willis"; Harris, "Lady Envoy to Voteless Gals"; "She Likes Embassy Fireplaces Aglow with Homelike Coziness," unknown newspaper, Greensboro, NC, n.d. (ca. January 7, 1960), Amb to Norway, Clippings 1960, box 23, FEWP; "Den nye amerikanske ambassadør gleder seg til å komme til Oslo," April 10, 1957, *Aftenposten* (Oslo).

42. Dulles to Eisenhower, January 27, 1953, Personnel Matters 1953–1954 (2), box 6, Subject Series, JFDP; Willis to Hugh Gibson, May 19, 1953, Correspondence, Willis, Frances E., 1953–54, box 65, Hugh S. Gibson Papers, HIA.

43. Edward Crocker to Mother, January 5, 1931, and February 11, 1932, both in Lispenard Green, *A Foreign Service Marriage* (Washington, DC: Lispenard Green, 1985), 297, 312; Gibson quoted in Val Paraiso, "Where There's a WILLIS There's a Way," *Foreign Service Journal* 46 (February 1969): 26; Grew quoted in "Career Woman."

44. Willis, *Frances Elizabeth Willis,* 145–56; Willis quoted in Ruth Austen, "The Unretiring Ambassador," *Press* (Riverside, CA), January 8, 1974, A-12.

45. Willis quoted in Isabelle Shelton, "Francis Willis Here; Swearing-In Monday," *Washington Star,* August 7, 1953; Willis, *Frances Elizabeth Willis,* 301; Fisher Howe, interview by Charles S. Kennedy, October 13, 1999, 36-37, FAOHC, http://www.adst.org/OH%20TOCs/Howe,%20Fisher.toc.pdf; Henry J. Willis (Willis's brother), "A Chronicle," n.d. (ca. 1985), courtesy Ann M. Morin, 7–8.

46. Roy M. Melbourne, *Conflict and Crises: A Foreign Service Story,* rev. ed. (Lanham, MD: University Press of America, 1997), 162; Melbourne, interview by Morin; Burns, interview by Morin; Edward Keller, interview by Ann M. Morin, July 31, 1985, and Douglas Henderson to Jean Wilkowski, June 18, 1985, both courtesy Ann M. Morin.

47. Walter A. Lundy, interview by Raymond Ewing, September 23, 2005, 8, FAOHC, http://www.adst.org/OH%20TOCs/Lundy,%20Walter%20A..toc.pdf; William L. Blue, interview by Charles S. Kennedy, April 11, 1991, 15-16, FAOHC, http://www.adst.org/OH%20TOCs/Blue,%20William%20L.toc.pdf; Melbourne, *Conflict and Crises,* 162, 164; Thomas Linthicum and Henry Stebbins, "Inspection Report to the Department," October 14, 1955, box 534, Foreign Service Inspection Corps, Office of the Chief Inspector, Foreign Service Inspection Reports, 1950–1959, part D, 2–3, Lot 56D275, RG 59, NARA; LeClaire, interview by Morin.

48. Fidel, interview by Wilkowski; Melbourne, interview by Morin; Howe, interview by Kennedy; Martha A. Rau, interview by Pam Stratton, September 13, 1997, 9–10, FAOHC, http://www.adst.org/OH%20TOCs/Rau,%20Martha%20A.toc.pdf; "Ambassador FRANCES E. WILLIS," n.d. (March 1963).

49. Willis to Mother, March [15?], 1921, Mar. 1921, FC, box 3.

50. Betty Beale, "Oil Heiress Here; Miss Willis Balks," *Washington Star,* May 12, 1957; Willis, Speech at Department Conference, May 17, 1957, 1, Amb to Norway, Speeches & Writings 1957, box 21, and Catherine Marceron to Simone Poulain, May 13, 1957, and Arlene Stern to Simone Poulain, n.d., both in Amb to Norway, Subject File, Memoranda 1957, box 22, all in FEWP.

51. Willis to Myrtle Thorne, October 22, 1968, courtesy Ann M. Morin; Helen McCarthy, "Gendering Diplomatic History: Women in the British Diplomatic Service, circa 1919–1972," in Sluga and James, *Women, Diplomacy, and International Politics,* 177–78; more broadly on the British women, see McCarthy, *Women of the World.*

52. Willis to Family, November 27, 1932, Nov. 1932, FC, box 4.

53. Ann M. Morin, *Her Excellency: An Oral History of American Women Ambassadors* (New York: Twayne, 1995), 52, 54.

54. Lenore Brundige, "Ambassador's Life in Oslo Is Seven-Day-a-Week Job," *Pittsburgh Press,* August 13, 1959; Willis to Department of State, "Official Visit to Lausanne," February 5, 1954, 123 Willis, Frances E., CDF 1950–1954; Willis, "Text of CBS Coast to Coast Broadcast," 2.

55. "Miss Willis und das Protokol," *Die Tat* (Zürich), July 16, 1953; Ethel Van Degrift, "Swiss Tongues Tied on How to Address Frances E. Willis," *Los Angeles Times,* June 30, 1954, part 3, 2; Harry A. Cahill, interview by Charles S. Kennedy, July 29, 1993, 6, FAOHC, http://www.adst.org/OH%20TOCs/Cahill,%20 Harry%20A.toc.pdf; Willis to Family, February 7, 1959, Feb. 1959, and Willis to Enid and Henry, May 9, 1954, May 1954, both in FC, box 13.

56. [Luce], *Europe in the Spring,* 228–29; see also 222–23; Willis to Enid and Henry, February 7, 1954, Feb. 1954, FC, box 13.

57. William B. Dunham, "How Did You Get Here from There? Memoir of a Diplomatic Career," 1999, 51, FAOHC, http://www.adst.org/OH%20TOCs /Dunham,%20William%20B.TOC.pdf; LeClaire, interview by Morin; "Verbatim Minutes of the Western European Chiefs of Mission Conference, Paris, May 6, 1957," and "Northern European Chiefs of Mission Conference, London, September 19–21, 1957: Summary of Proceedings," both in *FRUS, 1955–1957, Western European Security and Integration,* vol. 4, https://history.state.gov/historicaldocuments /frus1955–57v04/d249, https://history.state.gov/historicaldocuments/frus1955–57v04 /d252; Allen Fidel, interview by Jean Wilkowski, February 11, 1985, courtesy Morin; Gerard C. Smith, *Disarming Diplomat: The Memoirs of Gerard C. Smith, Arms Control Negotiator* (Lanham, MD: Madison Books, 1996), 46.

58. George G. B. Griffin, interview by Charles S. Kennedy, April 30, 2002, 18, FAOHC, http://www.adst.org/OH%20TOCs/Griffin,%20George%20G.B.toc.pdf; John L. DeOrnellas, interview by Charles S. Kennedy, December 13, 2002, 22, FAOHC, http://www.adst.org/OH%20TOCs/Deornellas,%20John%20L.toc.pdf; Joseph A. Mendenhall, interview by Horace Torbert, February 11, 1991, 13, FAOHC, http://www.adst.org/OH%20TOCs/Medanhall,%20Joseph%20A.toc.pdf; Keller, interview by Morin; Linthicum and Stebbins, "Inspection Report to the Department:

Bern," part A, 3; Fidel, interview by Wilkowski; Harry I. Odell, interview by Peter Moffat, April 17, 2000, 11, FAOHC, http://www.adst.org/OH%20TOCs/ODELL, %20HARRY%20I.toc.pdf; Henry S. Bradsher, "They Handle High Government Posts in Ceylon," *State* (Columbia, SC), October 29, 1963, 11A.

59. Linthicum and Stebbins, "Inspection Report to the Department: Bern," part A, 1, 4–5, and part D, 2–3; Earl T. Crain and Kyle B. Mitchell, "Inspector's Report to Department," August 22, 1959, part A, 1, Oslo 1959, box 85, Foreign Service Inspection Reports, Inspection Reports, 1936–1964, MLR 5449, RG 59, NARA. Inspection reports on the Colombo embassy c. 1961–64 were not available at the time of this writing.

60. Sir Lionel Lamb to Anthony Eden, September 10, 1954, 20, FO 500/7, and Sir Lionel Lamb to Harold Macmillan, September 22, 1955, 4, FO 500/8, both in NA-UK; Morin, *Her Excellency*, 58.

61. Hoff-Wilson, "Conclusion," 182–84; Morin, *Her Excellency*, 264–65, 269–70.

62. Those inspired by Willis include other pioneer female diplomats such as Tibbetts and Constance Ray Harvey; see Morin, *Her Excellency*, 28, 52, 54, 58, and Melbourne, interview by Morin.

Epilogue

Epigraph: Quoted in Madeleine K. Albright, with Bill Woodward, *Madam Secretary: A Memoir* (New York: Miramax, 2003), 508.

1. "Fashion: Women Run the World," *Marie Claire*, February 2010, http://www.marieclaire.com/fashion/trends/articles/fashion-un (page discontinued as of April 15, 2019).

2. Telephone conversation #683, sound recording, LBJ and PIERRE SALINGER, December 23, 1963, time unknown, Recordings and Transcripts of Telephone Conversations and Meetings, LBJL, https://www.discoverlbj.org/item/tel-00683.

3. Harrison, *On Account of Sex*, 174–75; Telephone conversation #1447, sound recording, LBJ and DEAN RUSK, January 20, 1964, 9:25 P.M., Recordings and Transcripts of Telephone Conversations and Meetings, LBJL, https://www.discoverlbj.org/item/tel-01447; Johnson conversation, "Saturday, March 28, 1964, Ralph Dungan, 2:05 P.M.," in *Taking Charge: The Johnson White House Tapes, 1963–1964*, ed. Michael Beschloss (New York: Simon & Schuster, 1997), 301; Susan M. Hartmann, "Women's Issues and the Johnson Administration," in *The Johnson Years*: vol. 3, *LBJ at Home and Abroad*, ed. in Robert A. Divine (Lawrence: University Press of Kansas, 1994), 56, 59. See also "Editorial Note," *FRUS, 1964–1968*, vol. 33, https://history.state.gov/historicaldocuments/frus1964-68v33/d3. The president of Bryn Mawr to whom Johnson referred was Katherine E. McBride, who led the college from 1942 to 1970.

4. Beaulac, *Career Diplomat,* 51, also 51–52, 62–63; George Ball, TelCon with Lucius Battle, January 26, 1964, folder 24, box 158, George W. Ball Papers, SGML; Calkin, *Women in the Department of State,* 127–29; (the 2.5 percent figure includes women in *all* major Foreign Service personnel systems, not just FSOs, so the percentage of female FSOs was considerably lower); Beatrice L. McKenzie, "Alison Palmer's Fight for Sex and Gender Equity in the Twentieth-Century United States Foreign Service," in *Gender and Diplomacy,* ed. Jennifer A. Cassidy (London: Routledge, 2017), 44n7; Beatrice L. McKenzie, "The Problem of Women in the Department: Sex and Gender Discrimination in the 1960s United States Foreign Diplomatic Service," *European Journal of American Studies* 10, no. 1 (2015): para. 15, https://ejas.revues.org/10589; Barbara J. Good, "Women in the Foreign Service: A Quiet Revolution," *Foreign Service Journal* 58 (January 1981): 47–50, 67.

5. Calkin, *Women in the Department of State,* 131–57; McKenzie, "Problem of Women in the Department"; Good, "Women in the Foreign Service."

6. Alison Palmer, *Diplomat and Priest: One Woman's Challenge to State and Church* (North Charleston, SC: CreateSpace, 2015), 44–147, 288–99; McGlen and Sarkees, *Women in Foreign Policy,* 116; Morin, *Her Excellency,* 211.

7. Macomber quoted in Calkin, *Women in the Department of State,* 157; "Cracking the Glass Ceiling: A Conversation with Foreign Service Pioneers Who Overcame Challenges and Rose to the Top," Association for Diplomatic Studies and Training website, March 30, 2015, http://adst.org/wp-content/uploads/2013/12/Womens-Issues-Cracking-the-Glass-Ceiling.pdf; for a sample of officials' retrospective views on the Palmer case, see "The Palmer Case and the Changing Role of Women in the Foreign Service," n.d., *Moments in Diplomatic History,* Association for Diplomatic Studies and Training, http://adst.org/the-palmer-case-and-the-changing-role-of-women-in-the-foreign-service/. Palmer had retired from the Foreign Service in 1981.

8. Jean M. Wilkowski, *Abroad for Her Country: Tales of a Pioneer Woman Ambassador in the U.S. Foreign Service* (Notre Dame, IN: University of Notre Dame Press, 2008), 228. "Some who have been successful in invading the virtually all-male 'room at the top,'" one of the WAO's leaders wrote in 1981, noting the lack of senior women in the organization, "often help perpetuate male-dictated attitudes" (Good, "Women in the Foreign Service," 50).

9. For a thorough list of women's firsts, see Sylvia Bashevkin, "The Taking of Foggy Bottom? Representation in US Diplomacy," in *Gendering Diplomacy and International Negotiation,* ed. Karin Aggestam and Ann E. Towns (London: Palgrave Macmillan, 2018), 49.

10. Kirkpatrick quoted in McGlen and Sarkees, *Women in Foreign Policy,* 54; Helene von Damm, *At Reagan's Side: Twenty Years in the Political Mainstream* (New York: Doubleday, 1989), 266; Haig quoted in Peter Collier, *Political Woman: The Big Little Life of Jeane Kirkpatrick* (New York: Encounter Books, 2012), 118; Judith Ewell, "Barely in the Inner Circle: Jeane Kirkpatrick," in Crapol, *Women and American Foreign Policy,* 166–68.

11. Donna Miles, "Honoring State's Women," *State,* March 1999, www.state. gov/documents/organization/191091.pdf; Robin Wright, "Madeleine Albright: Reflections on a Historic Tenure at the State Department," *Los Angeles Times,* December 24, 2000, M3; Caroline Hwang, "The Power Kiss: Pro or Con?" *Glamour,* August 1997, 115.

12. Albright, *Madam Secretary,* 510–11; Mary Jordan, "'Hillary Effect' cited for increase in female ambassadors to U.S.," *Washington Post,* January 11, 2010, A1; Lippman, *Madeleine Albright,* 35. However, the percentage of foreign ambassadors in Washington, DC, who are women has declined since the "Hillary Effect" (Rebecca Turkington, "What Happened to Washington's Women Ambassadors?" Georgetown Institute for Women, Peace, and Security, September 5, 2017, https:// giwps.georgetown.edu/what-happened-to-washingtons-women-ambassadors-2/).

13. Albright, *Madam Secretary,* 340–41; Hillary Clinton, "Address to the United Nations Commission on the Status of Women," March 12, 2010, *American Rhetoric: Online Speech Bank,* http://www.americanrhetoric.com/speeches/hillaryclintonun-commissiononwomen.htm; Valerie Hudson, "What Sex Means for World Peace," *Foreign Policy,* April 24, 2012, http://foreignpolicy.com/2012/04/24/what-sex-means-for-world-peace/. (For the full statement of this argument, see Valerie Hudson et al., *Sex and World Peace* [New York: Columbia University Press, 2012]).

14. Valerie M. Hudson and Patricia Leidl, *The Hillary Doctrine: Sex and American Foreign Policy* (New York: Columbia University Press, 2015), 52–63; Steven Lee Myers, "Last Tour of the Rock-Star Diplomat," *New York Times Magazine,* July 1, 2012, 18–19; Hillary Clinton, *Hard Choices* (New York: Simon & Schuster, 2014), 560–89; Michael Hirsh, "The Clinton Legacy," *Foreign Affairs* 92 (May/June 2013): 85.

15. Hudson and Leidl, *Hillary Doctrine,* 49, 52–63; Gayle Lemmon, "The Hillary Doctrine," *Newsweek,* March 6, 2011, http://www.newsweek.com/hillary-doctrine-66105; Colum Lynch and Robbie Gramer, "At the U.N., America Turns Back the Clock on Women's Rights," *Foreign Policy,* March 14, 2019, https:// foreignpolicy.com/2019/03/14/at-united-nations-women-rights-gender-health-trump-diplomacy/.

16. Morin, *Her Excellency,* 272–73; Vicki Huddleston, *Our Woman in Havana: A Diplomat's Chronicle of America's Long Struggle With Castro's Cuba* (New York: Overlook, 2018), 56.

17. Ann Towns and Brigitta Niklasson, "Gender, International Status, and Ambassador Appointments," *Foreign Policy Analysis* 13 (July 2017): 521. In this study, only the highest-GDP countries were examined, because they dispatch the vast majority of all ambassadors and thus yield the most significant statistics (527–28).

18. Robert D. Putnam, *The Comparative Study of Political Elites* (Englewood Cliffs, NJ: Prentice-Hall, 1976), 33; Andrea Strano, "Foreign Service Women Today: The Palmer Case and Beyond," *Foreign Service Journal* 93 (March 2016): 24–28; Wendy Sherman, *Not for the Faint of Heart: Lessons in Courage, Power, and Persistence* (New York: PublicAffairs, 2018), 77.

19. Dennis C. Jett, *American Ambassadors: The Past, Present, and Future of America's Diplomats* (New York: Palgrave Macmillan, 2014), 81–82; see also Morin, *Her Excellency*, 75–88, 286n4.

20. US Department of State, Office of Inspector General, "Report of Inspection: Embassy Luxembourg, Luxembourg," Report No. ISP-I-11–17A, January 2011, https://www.stateoig.gov/system/files/156129.pdf; Jett, *American Ambassadors*, 135–38.

21. Hani Zainulbhai, "Few American Women Have Broken the Glass Ceiling of Diplomacy," July 22, 2016, *Fact Tank: News in the Numbers*, Pew Research Center, http://www.pewresearch.org/fact-tank/2016/07/22/few-american-women-have-broken-the-glass-ceiling-of-diplomacy/; Towns and Niklasson, "Gender, International Status, and Ambassador Appointments," esp. 529–38; Rogerio de Souza Farias and Gessica Fernanda do Carmo, "Brazilian Female Diplomats and the Struggle for Gender Equality," in Aggestam and Towns, *Gendering Diplomacy and International Negotiation*, 115; Sally Bedell Smith, *Reflected Glory: The Life of Pamela Churchill Harriman* (New York: Simon & Schuster, 1996), 398; Brigitta Niklasson and Ann Towns, "Gender, Status, and Ambassador Appointments to Militarized and Violent Countries," in Cassidy, *Gender and Diplomacy*, 100–119. The G-7 consists of Canada, France, Germany, Great Britain, Italy, Japan, and the United States.

22. "Wonder Woman Is Dumped as an Honorary UN Ambassador after Uproar over Her 'Skimpy Costumes, Big Breasts and White Skin,'" *Daily Mail*, December 13, 2016, http://www.dailymail.co.uk/news/article-4029466/Wonder-Woman-dumped-special-UN-ambassador-uproar.html#ixzz4m03tW6JZ; Bashevkin, "Taking of Foggy Bottom?" 59. As of this writing, a man, Jonathan Cohen, is acting US ambassador to the UN.

23. Margot Carrington, "How Are FS Women at State Faring?" *Foreign Service Journal* 90 (May 2013): 44.

24. Strano, "Foreign Service Women Today"; Carrington, "How Are FS Women at State Faring?" 45; Leslie Bassett, "Making It Work: Conversations with Female Ambassadors," *Foreign Service Journal* 94 (July–August 2017): 44–48; Costel Calin and Kevin Buterbaugh, "Male versus Female Career Ambassadors: Is the US Foreign Service Still Biased?" *Foreign Policy Analysis* 15 (April 2019): 216–19; "State of the Secretary," *New York Times Magazine*, April 23, 2006, 21; Heather Stevenson, "In the Wings: Roberta Jacobson Is Ready to Lead in Mexico—If Congress Lets Her," *Fletcher Magazine*, Spring 2016, 11; Julia Chang Bloch, "Women and Diplomacy," based on a speech delivered July 15, 2004, *American Ambassadors Review*, Fall 2004, https://www.americanambassadors.org/publications/ambassadors-review/fall-2004/women-and-diplomacy; see also Ann-Marie Slaughter's famous exposition, "Why Women Still Can't Have It All," *Atlantic*, July–August 2012, https://www.theatlantic.com/magazine/archive/2012/07/why-women-still-cant-have-it-all/309020/.

25. McGlen and Sarkees, *Women in Foreign Policy*, 59; John Lancaster, "No Clout Where It Counts," *Washington Post*, April 17, 2000, 6; Lois W. Roth, "Nice

Girl or Pushy Bitch: Two Roads to Nonpromotion," Women's Action Organization Occasional Paper, February 1980, available online at the Lois Roth Endowment website, https://rothendowment.org/wp-content/uploads/2014/12/Lois-Roth-1980-WAO-article.pdf; Sherman, *Not for the Faint of Heart*, 82–84; "Cracking the Glass Ceiling"; UN News Centre, "A Conversation with Female Ambassadors about the UN Security Council," *UN News: Global Perspectives, Human Stories,* March 17, 2016, http://www.un.org/apps/news/story.asp?NewsID=53474#.

26. Marcus Mabry, *Twice as Good: Condoleezza Rice and Her Path to Power* (New York: Modern Times, 2007), 260–63; Rosa Brooks, "#MeToo Is All Too Common in National Security," *Foreign Policy,* November 29, 2017, http://foreign-policy.com/2017/11/29/metoo-is-all-too-common-in-national-security-pentagon-state-department-sexual-harassment/; Maya Rhodan, "'We, Too, Are Survivors.' 223 Women in National Security Sign Open Letter on Sexual Harassment," *Time,* December 1, 2017, http://time.com/5039104/we-too-are-survivors-223-women-in-national-security-sign-open-letter-on-sexual-harassment/.

27. Evan Thomas, "The Quiet Power of Condi Rice," *Time,* December 16, 2002, 30; Anne Gearan, "Rice's Travels Keeping Her Diplomacy in Motion," *USA Today,* April 25, 2005, 6A; Jodi Jacobson, "Dramatic Rise in Women Ambassadors, and How the Washington Post Treats the Story," *Rewire.News,* January 11, 2010, https://rewire.news/article/2010/01/11/dramatic-rise-women-ambassadors-and-how-wash-ington-post-treats-story/; Ted Wilkinson, "Shirley Temple Black: A Natural Diplomat," *Foreign Service Journal* 91 (June 2014): 93.

28. Bob Dreyfuss, "Obama's Women Pushed War against Libya," *US Wars and Military Action* (blog), *Nation,* March 19, 2011, https://www.thenation.com/article/obamas-women-advisers-pushed-war-against-libya/; Maureen Dowd, "Fight of the Valkyries," *New York Times,* March 22, 2011, A27; Tony Allen-Mills, "Obama Pushed to War by Fight of the Valkyries," *London Sunday Times,* March 27, 2011, 16; Frederic Wehrey, *The Burning Shores: Inside the Battle for the New Libya* (New York: Farrar, Straus & Giroux, 2018), 40–43.

29. "Townterview Hosted by KTR," Bishkek, Kyrgyzstan, December 2, 2010, *Diplomacy in Action,* US Department of State, https://2009–2017.state.gov/secretary/20092013clinton/rm/2010/12/152294.htm; Anne Guthrie, *Madame Ambassador: The Life of Vijaya Lakshmi Pandit* (New York: Harcourt, Brace & World, 1962), 153.

30. Sherman, *Not for the Faint of Heart,* 75–78; Jake Sullivan, "I Was Hillary Clinton's Chief Foreign-Policy Advisor. And I Have a #MeToo Mea Culpa," *Foreign Policy,* December 8, 2017, https://foreignpolicy.com/2017/12/08/foreign-policy-hillary-clinton-jake-sullivan-me-too-mea-culpa/.

31. Susan Stevenson, "Executive Women @ State: Breaking Barriers," *Foreign Service Journal* 92 (June 2015): 44; *To the Contrary: A Discussion of Issue from Diverse Perspectives,* transcript, November 14, 2014, https://www-tc.pbs.org/to-the-contrary/content_documents/15/TotheContrary-2014–11–14.pdf; Robbie Gramer and Jefcoate O'Donnell, "White and Male: Trump's Ambassadors Don't Look Like the

Rest of America," *Foreign Policy*, September 17, 2018, https://foreignpolicy.com /2018/09/17/white-male-trump-ambassadors-dont-look-like-america-us-state-department/; Nicholas Kralev, "The State Department Has a Diversity Problem," *Foreign Policy*, May 22, 2016, http://foreignpolicy.com/2016/05/22/state-department -race-gender-diversity-susan-rice-kerry/.

Bibliography

Manuscripts

Acheson, Dean G. Papers. Harry S. Truman Presidential Library, Independence, MO.

Ackerson, Garrett G., Jr. Papers. Lauinger Library, Georgetown University, Washington, DC.

Anderson, Eugenie Moore. Papers. Minnesota Historical Society, St. Paul.

Bolton, Francis P. Papers. Western Reserve Historical Society, Cleveland, OH.

Ball, George W. Papers. Seeley G. Mudd Library, Princeton University, Princeton, NJ.

Carr, Wilbur J. Papers. Manuscript Division, Library of Congress, Washington, DC.

Castle, William R., Jr. Papers. Herbert C. Hoover Presidential Library, West Branch, IA.

———. ———. Houghton Library, Harvard University, Cambridge, MA.

Childs, Marquis. Papers. Special Collections, University of Iowa, Iowa City.

Coleman, Frederick W. B. Diaries. Hoover Institution Archives, Stanford University, Stanford, CA.

Columbia University Oral History Project. Columbia University, New York.

Cumming, Hugh S. Papers. Alderman Library, University of Virginia, Charlottesville.

Dewson, Mary W. Papers. Franklin D. Roosevelt Presidential Library, Hyde Park, NY.

———. ———. Schlesinger Library, Harvard University, Cambridge, MA.

Dulles, John Foster. Papers. Dwight D. Eisenhower Presidential Library, Abilene, KS.

———. ———. Seeley G. Mudd Library, Princeton University, Princeton, NJ.

Durbrow, Elbridge. Papers. Hoover Institution Archives, Stanford University, Stanford, CA.

Edwards, India. Papers. Harry S. Truman Presidential Library, Independence, MO.

Eisenhower, Dwight D. Presidential Papers (Ann Whitman File). Dwight D. Eisenhower Presidential Library, Abilene, KS.

Foreign Affairs Oral History Program. Association for Diplomatic Studies and Training, NFATC / Foreign Service Institute, Arlington, VA.

Foreign Office Records. National Archives, United Kingdom, Kew, London.

Furman, Bess. Papers. Manuscript Division, Library of Congress, Washington, DC.

Gibson, Hugh S. Papers. Hoover Institution Archives, Stanford University, Stanford, CA.

Grew, Joseph. Papers. Houghton Library. Harvard University, Cambridge, MA.

Harriman, Florence Jaffray. Papers. Manuscript Division, Library of Congress, Washington, DC.

Herter, Christian A. Papers. Dwight D. Eisenhower Presidential Library, Abilene, KS.

House, Edward M. Papers. Sterling Memorial Library, Yale University, New Haven, CT.

Humphrey, Hubert H. Papers. Minnesota Historical Society, St. Paul.

Hurst, Fannie. Papers. Harry Ransom Center, University of Texas, Austin.

Ickes, Harold. Papers. Manuscript Division, Library of Congress, Washington, DC.

Jackson, C. D. Papers. Dwight D. Eisenhower Presidential Library, Abilene, KS.

Kampelman, Max. Papers. Minnesota Historical Society, St. Paul.

Kennan, George F. Papers. Seeley G. Mudd Library, Princeton University, Princeton, NJ.

Lamson, Peggy. Papers. Schlesinger Library, Harvard University, Cambridge, MA.

Long, Breckinridge. Papers. Manuscript Division, Library of Congress, Washington, DC.

Luce, Clare Boothe. Papers. Manuscript Division, Library of Congress, Washington, DC.

Macy, John W., Jr. Papers. Lyndon B. Johnson Presidential Library, Austin, TX.

Moffatt, J. Pierrepont. Papers. Houghton Library, Harvard University, Cambridge, MA.

Moley, Raymond. Papers. Hoover Institution Archives, Stanford University, Stanford, CA.

Murphy, Robert D. Papers. Hoover Institution Archives, Stanford University, Stanford, CA.

National Security Files. John F. Kennedy Presidential Library, Boston.

National Woman's Party. Papers. Manuscript Division, Library of Congress, Washington, DC.

Oral Histories. Harry S. Truman Presidential Library, Independence, MO.

———. John F. Kennedy Presidential Library, Boston.

Patterson, Jefferson. Papers. Manuscript Division, Library of Congress, Washington, DC.

Phillips, William. Papers. Houghton Library. Harvard University, Cambridge, MA.

President's Office Files. Franklin D. Roosevelt Presidential Library, Hyde Park, NY.

———. John F. Kennedy Presidential Library, Boston.

President's Secretary's Files. Franklin D. Roosevelt Presidential Library, Hyde Park, NY.

———. Harry S. Truman Presidential Library, Independence, MO.

Record Group 59, Records of the Department of State. National Archives and Records Administration, Archives II, College Park, MD.

Record Group 84, Records of Foreign Service Posts of the Department of State. National Archives and Records Administration, Archives II, College Park, MD.

Record Group 200, National Archives Gift Collection. National Archives and Records Administration, Archives II, College Park, MD.

Record Group 306, Records of the United States Information Agency. National Archives and Records Administration, Archives II, College Park, MD.

Recordings and Transcripts of Telephone Conversations and Meetings. Lyndon B. Johnson Presidential Library, Austin, TX.

Rohde, Ruth Bryan Owen. Letters. Schlesinger Library, Harvard University, Cambridge, MA.

Roosevelt, Eleanor. Papers. Franklin D. Roosevelt Presidential Library, Hyde Park, NY.

Schorr, Daniel. Papers. Manuscript Division, Library of Congress, Washington, DC.

Smith, Truman. Papers. Herbert C. Hoover Presidential Library, West Branch, IA.

Sound Recordings. Recorded Sound Conference Center, Library of Congress, Washington, DC.

Spivak, Lawrence. Papers. Manuscript Division, Library of Congress, Washington, DC.

Time Magazine Correspondents. Dispatches. Houghton Library, Harvard University, Cambridge, MA.

Truman, Harry S. Papers. Harry S. Truman Presidential Library, Independence, MO.

Welles, B. Sumner. Papers. Franklin D. Roosevelt Presidential Library, Hyde Park, NY.

White House Central File. Dwight D. Eisenhower Presidential Library, Abilene, KS.

White House Office Files. Dwight D. Eisenhower Presidential Library, Abilene, KS.

Willis, Frances E. Papers. Hoover Institution Archives, Stanford University, Stanford, CA.

Wilson, Edwin C. Papers. Mandeville Special Collections Library, University of California, San Diego,

Published Primary Sources

Beschloss, Michael, ed. *Taking Charge: The Johnson White House Tapes, 1963–1964.* New York: Simon & Schuster, 1997.

Declassified Documents Reference System (DDRS Online). https://www.gale.com/c/us-declassified-documents-online.

Diplomatische Dokumente der Schweiz. https://www.dodis.ch/en/home.

Eisenhower Dwight David. *The Eisenhower Diaries.* Edited by Robert H. Farrell. New York: Norton, 1981.

———. *The Papers of Dwight David Eisenhower: The Presidency: The Middle Way.* Vol. 14. Edited by Louis Galambos and Daun Van Ee. Baltimore: Johns Hopkins University Press, 1996.

Foreign Relations of the United States. Washington, DC: GPO, 1934–1964.

Hagerty, James C. *The Diary of James C. Hagerty: Eisenhower at Mid-Course, 1954–1955.* Edited by Robert H. Ferrell. Bloomington: Indiana University Press, 1983.

Kennedy, John F. *The Presidential Recordings: John F. Kennedy: The Great Crises.* Vol. 1 of 3, *July 30–August 1962.* Edited by Timothy Naftali. New York: Norton, 2001.

Public Papers of the Presidents: Dwight D. Eisenhower, 1959. Washington, DC: GPO, 1960.

Roosevelt, Eleanor. *What I Hope to Leave Behind: The Essential Essays of Eleanor Roosevelt.* Edited by Allida M. Black. Brooklyn, NY: Carlson Publishing, 1995.

Sarkela, Sandra J., Susan M. Ross, and Margaret A. Lowe, eds. *From Megaphones to Microphones: Speeches of American Women, 1920–1960.* Westport, CT: Praeger, 2003.

Stevenson, Adlai. *The Papers of Adlai Stevenson.* Vol. 7 of 8, *Continuing Education and the Unfinished Business of American Society, 1957–1961.* Boston: Little, Brown, 1977.

Secondary Sources

Aggestam, Karin, and Ann E. Towns, eds. *Gendering Diplomacy and International Negotiation,* London: Palgrave Macmillan, 2018.

Albright, Madeleine K., with Bill Woodward. *Madam Secretary: A Memoir.* New York: Miramax, 2003.

Alonso, Harriet Hyman. *Peace as a Women's Issue: A History of the U.S. Movement for World Peace and Women's Rights.* Syracuse, NY: Syracuse University Press, 1993.

Baldridge, Letitia. *A Lady, First: My Life in the Kennedy White House and the American Embassies of Paris and Rome.* New York: Viking, 2001.

Barteau, Harry C. *Historical Dictionary of Luxembourg.* Lanham, MD: Scarecrow, 1996.

Bashevkin, Sylvia. "The Taking of Foggy Bottom? Representation in US Diplomacy." In Aggestam and Towns, *Gendering Diplomacy and International Negotiation,* 45–63.

Bax, Emily. *Miss Bax of the Embassy.* Boston: Houghton Mifflin, 1939.

Beaulac, Willard. *Career Diplomat: A Career in the Foreign Service of the United States.* New York: Macmillan, 1964.

Bederman, Gail. *Manliness and Civilization: A Cultural History of Gender and Race in the United States, 1880–1917.* Chicago: University of Chicago Press, 1995.

Beisner, Robert L. *Dean Acheson: A Life in the Cold War.* New York: Oxford University Press, 2006.

———. *From the Old Diplomacy to the New, 1865–1900.* Arlington Heights, IL: AHM Publishing, 1975.

Bennett, Edward M. "Joseph C. Grew: The Diplomacy of Pacification." In *Diplomats in Crisis: United States–Chinese–Japanese Relations, 1919–1941.* Edited by Richard Dean Burns and Edward M. Bennett, 65–89. Santa Barbara, CA: ABC-Clio, 1974.

Berdal, Mats R. *The United States, Norway and the Cold War, 1954–60.* Basingstoke, Hampshire: Macmillan, 1997.

Biddle, A. J. Drexel, Jr. *Poland and the Coming of the Second World War: The Diplomatic Papers of A. J. Drexel Biddle, Jr., United States Ambassador to Poland, 1937–1939.* Edited by Philip V. Cannistraro, Edward D. Wynot Jr., and Theodore P. Kovaleff. Columbus: Ohio State University Press, 1976.

Bidwell, Percy W. *What the Tariff Means to American Industries.* New York: Harper & Brothers, 1956.

Bingham, Marjorie. "Keeping at It: Minnesota Women." In *Minnesota in a Century of Change*. Edited by Clifford E. Clark Jr., 433–72. St. Paul: Minnesota Historical Society Press, 1989.

Blair, Emily Newell. *Bridging Two Eras: The Autobiography of Emily Newell Blair, 1877–1951*. Edited by Virginia Jeans Laas. Columbia, MO: University of Missouri Press, 1999.

Bloch, Julia Chang. "Women and Diplomacy," based on a speech delivered July 15, 2004. *American Ambassadors Review*, Fall 2004, https://www.americanambassadors.org/publications/ambassadors-review/fall-2004/women-and-diplomacy.

Bradley, Lenore. "The Uphill Climb: Women in the Truman Administration." *Whistle Stop: Harry S. Truman Library Institute Newsletter* 23 (1994): 1–5.

Brands, H. W. *Inside the Cold War: Loy Henderson and the Rise of the American Empire, 1918–1961*. New York: Oxford University Press, 1991.

———. *Traitor to His Class: The Privileged Life and Radical Presidency of Franklin Delano Roosevelt*. New York: Anchor, 2008.

Briggs, Ellis O. *Proud Servant: The Memoirs of a Career Ambassador*. Kent, OH: Kent State University Press, 1998.

———. *Shots Heard Round the World: An Ambassador's Hunting Adventures on Four Continents*. New York: Viking, 1957.

Brinkley, Alan. *The Publisher: Henry Luce and His American Century*. New York: Vintage, 2010.

Brinkley, Douglas. *The Wilderness Warrior: Theodore Roosevelt and the Crusade for America*. New York: HarperCollins, 2009.

Brogi, Alessandro. "Ambassador Clare Boothe Luce and the Evolution of Psychological Warfare in Italy." *Cold War History* 12 (May 2012): 269–94.

———. *Confronting America: The Cold War between the United States and the Communists in France and Italy*. Chapel Hill: University of North Carolina Press, 2011.

Brown, Rudd. *Ruth Bryan Owen, Congresswoman and Diplomat: An Intimate Portrait*. North Charleston, SC: CreateSpace, 2014.

Calin, Costel and Kevin Buterbaugh. "Male versus Female Career Ambassadors: Is the US Foreign Service Still Biased?" *Foreign Policy Analysis* 15 (April 2019): 205–23.

Calkin, Homer L. *Women in the Department of State: Their Role in American Foreign Affairs*. Washington, DC: Department of State, 1978.

Casey, Steven. "The Campaign to Sell a Harsh Peace for Germany to the American Public, 1944–1948." *History* 90 (January 2005): 62–92.

Cassidy, Jennifer A., ed. *Gender and Diplomacy*. London: Routledge, 2017.

Chauncey, George. *Gay New York: Gender, Urban Culture, and the Making of the Gay Male World, 1890–1940*. New York: Basic Books, 1994.

Childs, Marquis W. *I Write from Washington*. New York: Harper & Bros., 1942.

Clark, Eric. *Corps Diplomatique*. London: Allen Lane, 1973.

Clements, Barbara E. *Bolshevik Feminist: The Life of Alexandra Kollontai*. Bloomington: Indiana University Press, 1979.

Clifford, J. Garry. "The Odyssey of *City of Flint*." *American Neptune* 32 (April 1972): 100–116.

Clinton, Hillary. *Hard Choices*. New York: Simon & Schuster, 2014.

Cole, Wayne S. *Norway and the United States, 1905–1955: Two Democracies in Peace and War*. Ames: Iowa State University Press, 1989.

Collier, Peter. *Political Woman: The Big Little Life of Jeane Kirkpatrick*. New York: Encounter Books, 2012.

Collier, Peter, and David Horowitz. *The Kennedys: An American Drama*. New York: Summit, 1984.

Conant, Jennet. *The Irregulars: Roald Dahl and the British Spy Ring in Wartime Washington*. New York: Simon & Schuster, 2008.

Cook, Blanche Wiesen. *Eleanor Roosevelt*. Vol. 2 of 3, *1933–1938*. New York: Viking, 1999.

Cooke, Alistair. *The American Home Front, 1941–1942*. New York: Atlantic Monthly Press, 2006.

Costigliola, Frank. "'I React Intensely to Everything': Russia and the Frustrated Emotions of George F. Kennan, 1933–1958." *Journal of American History* 102 (March 2016): 1075–101.

———. "'Unceasing Pressure for Penetration': Gender, Pathology, and Emotion in George Kennan's Formation of the Cold War." *Journal of American History* 83 (March 1997): 1309–39.

Craig, Douglas. *Progressives at War: William G. McAdoo and Newton D. Baker, 1863–1941*. Baltimore: Johns Hopkins University Press, 2013.

Crapol, Edward P., ed. *Women and American Foreign Policy: Lobbyists, Critics, and Insiders*. 2nd ed. Wilmington, DE: Scholarly Resources, 1992.

Cull, Nicholas. "Public Diplomacy: Taxonomies and Histories." *Annals of the American Academy of Political and Social Science* 616 (March 2008): 31–54.

Cuordileone, K. A. *Manhood and American Political Culture in the Cold War*. New York: Routledge, 2005.

Davidann, John Thares. *Cultural Diplomacy in U.S.–Japanese Relations, 1919–1941*. New York: Palgrave Macmillan, 2007.

de Bedts, Ralph F. *Ambassador Joseph Kennedy, 1938–1940: An Anatomy of Appeasement*. New York: Peter Lang, 1985.

de Souza Farias, Rogerio, and Gessica Fernanda do Carmo. "Brazilian Female Diplomats and the Struggle for Gender Equality." In Aggestam and Towns, *Gendering Diplomacy and International Negotiation*, 107–24.

Dean, Robert. *Imperial Brotherhood: Gender and the Making of Cold War Foreign Policy*. Amherst: University of Massachusetts Press, 2001.

Del Pero, Mario. "American Pressures and Their Containment in Italy during the Ambassadorship of Clare Boothe Luce, 1953–1956." *Diplomatic History* 28 (June 2004): 407–39.

———. "The United States and 'Psychological Warfare' in Italy, 1948–1955." *Journal of American History* 87 (March 2001): 1304–34.

Delton, Jennifer A. *Making Minnesota Liberal: Civil Rights and the Transformation of the Democratic Party.* Minneapolis: University of Minnesota Press, 2000.

Derry, T. K. *A Short History of Norway.* 2nd ed. London: Allen & Unwin, 1968.

DeWhitt, Bennie. "A Wider Sphere of Usefulness: Marilla Ricker's Quest for a Diplomatic Post." *Prologue* 5 (Winter 1973): 203–7.

Divine, Robert A. *Second Chance: The Triumph of Internationalism in America during World War II.* New York: Atheneum, 1971.

Dolibois, John. *Pattern of Circles: An Ambassador's Story.* Kent, OH: Kent State University Press, 1989.

Donovan, Hedley. *Right Places, Right Times: Forty Years in Journalism Not Counting My Paper Route.* New York: Henry Holt, 1989.

Dupont, Mary. *Mrs. Ambassador: The Life and Politics of Eugenie Anderson.* St. Paul: Minnesota Historical Society Press, 2019.

Edwards, India. *Pulling No Punches: Memoirs of a Woman in Politics.* New York: G. P. Putnam's Sons, 1977.

Eisele, Albert. *Almost to the Presidency: A Biography of Two American Politicians.* Blue Earth, MN: Piper, 1972.

Epstein, Barbara. "Anti-Communism, Homophobia, and the Construction of Masculinity in the Postwar U.S." *Critical Sociology* 20 (1994): 21–44.

Erdman, Paul. *Swiss–American Economic Relations: Their Evolution in an Era of Crises.* Basel: Kyklos-Verlag, 1959.

Ewell, Judith. "Barely in the Inner Circle: Jeane Kirkpatrick." In Crapol, *Women and American Foreign Policy,* 153–71.

Eyre, David W. *Clare: The Honolulu Years.* Honolulu: Mutual Publishing, 2007.

Fearnow, Mark. *Clare Boothe Luce: A Research and Production Sourcebook.* Westport, CT: Greenwood, 1995.

Fenzi, Jewell, with Carl L. Nelson. *Married to the Foreign Service: An Oral History of the American Diplomatic Spouse.* New York: Twayne, 1994.

Foreign and Commonwealth Office. *Women in Diplomacy: The FCO, 1782–1999.* London: Records & Historical Services, FCO, 1999.

Freeman, Charles W., Jr., ed. *The Diplomat's Dictionary.* Washington, DC: National Defense University Press, 1994.

Freeman, Jo. *A Room at a Time: How Women Entered Party Politics.* Lanham, MD: Rowman & Littlefield, 2000.

———. *We Will Be Heard: Women's Struggles for Political Power in the United States.* Lanham, MD: Rowman & Littlefield, 2008.

Freidel, Frank. *Franklin D. Roosevelt: Launching the New Deal.* Boston: Little, Brown, 1973.

———. *Franklin D. Roosevelt: A Rendezvous with Destiny.* Boston: Little, Brown, 1990.

Furman, Bess. *Washington By-Line: The Personal History of a Newspaper Woman.* New York: Knopf, 1949.

Gaddis, John L. *George F. Kennan: An American Life.* New York: Penguin, 2011.

Garretson, Charles Lloyd, III. *Hubert H. Humphrey: The Politics of Joy.* New Brunswick, NJ: Transaction, 1993.

Gibson, Charles Dana. *Pictures of People.* New York: Russell & Son, 1896.

Gilbert, W. S. *The Savoy Operas.* 2 vols. New York: Oxford University Press, 1962.

Gillon, Steven M. *Politics and Vision: The ADA and American Liberalism, 1947–1985.* New York: Oxford University Press, 1987.

Goldman, Eric. *The Crucial Decade—And After: America, 1945–1960.* New York: Vintage, 1960.

Grady, Henry T. *The Memoirs of Ambassador Henry T. Grady: From the Great War to the Cold War.* Edited by John T. McNay. Columbia: University of Missouri Press, 2009.

Grant, Tibor. "Against All Odds: Vira B. Whitehouse and Rosika Schwimmer in Switzerland, 1918." *American Studies International* 40 (February 2002): 34–51.

Green, Lispenard. *A Foreign Service Marriage.* Washington, DC: Lispenard Green, 1985.

Greenwald, Marilyn S. *A Woman of the* Times*: Journalism, Feminism, and the Career of Charlotte Curtis.* Athens: Ohio University Press, 1999.

Grew, Joseph C. *Turbulent Era: A Diplomatic Record of Forty Years, 1904–45.* 2 vols. Boston: Houghton Mifflin, 1952.

Griscom, Lloyd C. *Diplomatically Speaking.* Boston: Little, Brown, 1940.

Grunwald, Henry. *One Man's America: A Journalist's Search for the Heart of His Country.* New York: Doubleday, 1997.

Guthrie, Anne. *Madame Ambassador: The Life of Vijaya Lakshmi Pandit.* New York: Harcourt, Brace & World, 1962.

Hamby, Alonzo L. *Man of the People: A Life of Harry S. Truman.* New York: Oxford University Press, 1995.

Hanhimäki, Jussi M. *Scandinavia and the United States: An Insecure Friendship.* New York: Twayne, 1997.

Harriman, Florence. *From Pinafores to Politics.* New York: Henry Holt, 1923.

———. *Mission to the North.* Philadelphia: J. B. Lippincott, 1941.

Harris, Barbara J. *Beyond Her Sphere: Women and the Professions in American History.* Westport, CT: Greenwood, 1978.

Harrison, Cynthia. *On Account of Sex: The Politics of Women's Issues, 1945–1968.* Berkeley: University of California Press, 1988.

Hartmann, Susan M. *The Home Front and Beyond: American Women in the 1940s.* Boston: Twayne, 1982.

———. "Women's Issues and the Johnson Administration." In *The Johnson Years.* Vol. 3 of 3, *LBJ at Home and Abroad.* Edited by Robert A. Divine, 53–81. Lawrence: University Press of Kansas, 1994.

Hatch, Alden. *Ambassador Extraordinary: Clare Boothe Luce.* New York: Henry Holt, 1955.

Haynes, John Earl. *Dubious Alliance: The Making of Minnesota's DFL Party.* Minneapolis: University of Minnesota Press, 1984.

Hegermann-Lindencrone, Lillie de. *The Sunny Side of Diplomatic Life, 1875–1912.* New York: Harper & Brothers, 1914.

Heinrichs, Waldo H. *American Ambassador: Joseph C. Grew and the Development of the United States Diplomatic Tradition.* New York: Oxford University Press, 1966.

Heller, Deane, and David Heller. *John Foster Dulles: Soldier for Peace.* New York: Holt, Rinehart & Winston, 1960.

Herzstein, Robert E. *Henry R. Luce, Time, and the American Crusade in Asia.* New York: Cambridge University Press, 2005.

Heymann, C. David. *The Georgetown Ladies' Social Club: Power, Passion, and Politics in the Nation's Capital.* New York: Atria, 2003.

Hixson, Walter. *Parting the Curtain: Propaganda, Culture, and the Cold War, 1945–1961.* New York: St. Martin's, 1997.

Hoff-Wilson, Joan. "Conclusion: Of Mice and Men." In Crapol, *Women and American Foreign Policy,* 173–88.

Hofstadter, Richard. *Anti-Intellectualism in American Life.* New York: Vintage, 1963.

Holland, Max. "A Luce Connection: Senator Keating, William Pawley, and the Cuban Missile Crisis." *Journal of Cold War Studies* 1 (Fall 1999): 139–67.

Huddleston, Vicki. *Our Woman in Havana: A Diplomat's Chronicle of America's Long Struggle with Castro's Cuba.* New York: Overlook, 2018.

Hudson, Valerie M., and Patricia Leidl. *The Hillary Doctrine: Sex and American Foreign Policy.* New York: Columbia University Press, 2015.

Hudson, Valerie M., Bonnie Ballif-Spanvill, Mary Caprioli, and Chad F. Emmett. *Sex and World Peace.* New York: Columbia University Press, 2012.

Hulen, Bertram D. *Inside the Department of State.* New York: Whittlesey House, 1939.

Hull, Cordell. *The Memoirs of Cordell Hull.* 2 vols. New York: Macmillan, 1948.

Hunter, Jane. *How Young Ladies Became Girls: The Victorian Origins of American Girlhood.* New Haven: Yale University Press, 2002.

Ilchman, Warren F. *Professional Diplomacy in the United States, 1779–1939: A Study in Administrative History.* Chicago: University of Chicago Press, 1961.

Jett, Dennis C. *American Ambassadors: The Past, Present, and Future of America's Diplomats.* New York: Palgrave Macmillan, 2014.

Johnson, David K. *The Lavender Scare: The Cold War Persecution of Gays and Lesbians in the Federal Government.* Chicago: University of Chicago Press, 2004.

Jones, Howard. *Death of a Generation: How the Assassinations of Diem and JFK Prolonged the Vietnam War.* New York: Oxford University Press, 2003.

Kahn, E. J., Jr. *The China Hands: America's Foreign Service and What Befell Them.* New York: Viking, 1975.

Kazin, Michael. *A Godly Hero: The Life of William Jennings Bryan.* New York: Knopf, 2006.

Kelly-Gangi, Carol, ed. *A Woman's Book of Inspiration.* New York: Fall River, 2017.

Kennan, George F. *Memoirs, 1925–1950.* New York: Pantheon, 1967.

Kenneally, James J. *A Compassionate Conservative: A Political Biography of Joseph W. Martin, Jr., Speaker of the House of Representatives.* Lanham, MD: Lexington Books, 2003.

Kennedy, Jaqueline. *Jacqueline Kennedy: Historic Conversations on Life with John F. Kennedy.* Edited by Michael Beschloss. New York: Hyperion, 2011.

Kessler-Harris, Alice. "Do We Still Need Women's History?" *Chronicle of Higher Education* 54 (December 7, 2007): B6.

Kimmel, Michael. *Manhood in America: A Cultural History.* 2nd ed. New York: Oxford University Press, 2006.

Kirk, Lydia Chapin. *Distinguished Service: Lydia Chapin Kirk, Partner in Diplomacy.* Edited by Roger Kirk. New York: Syracuse University Press, 2007.

Kocher, Eric. *Foreign Intrigue: The Making and Unmaking of a Foreign Service Officer.* Far Hills, NJ: New Horizon Press, 1990.

Kraus, Carolyn. "Power, Resistance, and the Writings of Female Illegitimacy: Eva Peron, Clare Boothe Luce, and Flore Tristan." *Journal of Research in Gender Studies* 1 (2011): 9–42.

Krenn, Michael L. *Black Diplomacy: African-Americans and the State Department, 1945–1969.* Armonk, NY: M. E. Sharpe, 1999.

Kroeger, Brooke. *Fannie: The Talent for Success of Writer Fannie Hurst.* New York: Random House, 1999.

Lait, Jack, and Lee Mortimer. *Washington Confidential.* New York: Crown, 1951.

Lamson, Peggy. *Few Are Chosen: American Women in Political Life Today.* Boston: Houghton Mifflin, 1968.

Larson, Erik. *In the Garden of Beasts: Love, Terror, and an American Family in Hitler's Berlin.* New York: Crown, 2011.

Lawrenson, Helen. *Stranger at the Party.* New York: Random House.

Lesch, Paul. *Playing Her Part: Perle Mesta in Luxembourg.* Luxembourg: American Chamber of Commerce in Luxembourg, 2001.

Lippmann, Thomas W. *Madeleine Albright and the New American Diplomacy.* Boulder, CO: Westview, 2000.

Louchheim, Katie. *By the Political Sea.* Garden City, NY: Doubleday, 1970.

[Luce], Clare Boothe. *Europe in the Spring.* New York: Knopf, 1940.

Mabry, Marcus. *Twice as Good: Condoleezza Rice and Her Path to Power.* New York: Modern Times, 2007.

Martin, John B. *Adlai Stevenson and the World: The Life of Adlai E. Stevenson.* Garden City, NY: Doubleday, 1977.

Martin, Ralph G. *Henry and Clare: An Intimate Portrait of the Luces.* New York: G. P. Putnam's Sons, 1991.

Mayers, David. *FDR's Ambassadors and the Diplomacy of Crisis: From the Rise of Hitler to the End of World War II.* Cambridge: Cambridge University Press, 2013.

McCarthy, Helen. "Gendering Diplomatic History: Women in the British Diplomatic Service, circa 1919–1972." In Sluga and James, *Women, Diplomacy, and International Politics,* 167–81.

―――. *Women of the World: The Rise of the Female Diplomat.* London: Bloomsbury, 2014.

McDonald, James G. *Advocate for the Doomed: The Diaries and Papers of James G. McDonald, 1932–1935.* Edited by Richard Breitman, Barbara McDonald Stewart, and Severin Hochberg. Bloomington: University of Indiana Press, 2007.

McEnaney, Laura. "Gender." In *Encyclopedia of American Foreign Policy,* Vol. 2 of 3. Edited by Alexander DeConde, Richard Dean Burns, and Frederik Logevall, 123–34. 2nd ed. New York: Charles Scribner's Sons, 2002.

McGlen, Nancy E., and Meredith Reid Sarkees. *Women in Foreign Policy: The Insiders.* New York: Routledge, 1993.

McKenzie, Beatrice L. "Alison Palmer's Fight for Sex and Gender Equity in the Twentieth-Century United States Foreign Service." In Cassidy, *Gender and Diplomacy,* 32–47.

―――. "The Problem of Women in the Department: Sex and Gender Discrimination in the 1960s United States Foreign Diplomatic Service." *European Journal of American Studies* 10, no. 1 (2015): https://ejas.revues.org/10589.

Melbourne, Roy M. *Conflict and Crises: A Foreign Service Story.* Rev. ed. Lanham, MD: University Press of America, 1997.

Mesta, Perle, with Robert Cahn. *Perle: My Story.* New York: McGraw-Hill, 1960.

Midtgaard, Kristin. "National Security and the Choice of International Humanitarian Aid: Denmark and the Korean War, 1950–1953." *Journal of Cold War Studies* 13 (Spring 2011): 148–74.

Miller, Kristie. "'Eager and Anxious to Work': Daisy Harriman and the Presidential Election of 1912." In *We Have Come to Stay: American Women and Political Parties, 1880–1960.* Edited by Melanie Gustafson, Kristie Miller, and Elisabeth I. Perry, 65–76. Albuquerque: University of New Mexico Press, 1999.

―――. "Harriman, Daisy." *American National Biography.* Vol 10 of 24. Edited by John A. Garraty and Mark C. Carnes, 140. New York: Oxford University Press, 1999.

Moley, Raymond. *The First New Deal.* New York: Harcourt, Brace & World, 1966.

Morgan, Georgia Cook. "India Edwards: Distaff Politician of the Truman Era." *Missouri Historical Review* 78 (April 1984): 293–310.

Morin, Ann M. *Her Excellency: An Oral History of American Women Ambassadors.* New York: Twayne, 1995.

Morris, Sylvia Jukes. *Price of Fame: The Honorable Clare Boothe Luce.* New York: Random House, 2014.

―――. *Rage for Fame: The Ascent of Clare Boothe Luce.* New York: Random House, 1997.

Murphy, Kevin P. *Political Manhood: Red Bloods, Mollycoddles, and the Politics of Progressive Era Reform.* New York: Columbia University Press, 2008.

Murphy, Robert D. *Diplomat among Warriors.* Garden City, NY: Doubleday, 1964.

Murray, Grenville. *Embassies and Foreign Courts: A History of Diplomacy.* London: G. Routledge, 1855.

Nakamura, Masanori. *The Japanese Monarchy: Ambassador Joseph Grew and the Making of the "Symbol Emperor System."* Armonk, NY: M. E. Sharpe, 1992.

Namikas, Lise. "The Committee to Defend America and the Debate between Internationalists and Interventionists." *Historian* 61 (Summer 1999): 843–63.

The New Yorker Book of War Pieces. New York: Reynal & Hitchcock, 1947.

Neuberger, Mary. "*Kebabche,* Caviar, or Hot Dogs? Consuming the Cold War at the Plovdiv Fair, 1947–72." *Journal of Contemporary History* 47 (January 2012): 48–68.

Neuman, Johanna. *Gilded Suffragists: The New York Socialites Who Fought for Women's Right to Vote.* New York: Washington Mews, 2017.

Niklasson, Brigitta, and Ann Towns. "Gender, Status, and Ambassador Appointments to Militarized and Violent Countries." In Cassidy, *Gender and Diplomacy,* 100–119.

Nuti, Leopoldo. "The United States, Italy, and the Opening to the Left, 1953–1963." *Journal of Cold War Studies* 4 (Summer 2002): 36–55.

Olson, Lynne. *Citizens of London: The Americans Who Stood With Britain in Its Darkest, Finest Hour.* New York: Random House, 2010.

Oshinsky, David. *A Conspiracy So Immense: The World of Joe McCarthy.* New York: Oxford University Press, 2005.

Owen, Ruth Bryan. *Leaves from a Greenland Diary.* New York: Dodd, Mead, 1935.

———. *Look Forward, Warrior.* New York: Dodd, Mead & Co., 1942.

Palmer, Alison. *Diplomat and Priest: One Woman's Challenge to State and Church.* North Charleston, SC: CreateSpace, 2015.

Pantev, Andrei. "The Historic Road of the Third Bulgarian State." In *Bulgaria in a Time of Change: Economic and Political Dimensions.* Edited by Iliana Zloch-Christy, 7–22. Aldershot, UK: Avebury, 1996.

Pastor, Peter. "The Diplomatic Fiasco of the Modern World's First Woman Ambassador, Róza Bédy-Schwimmer." *East European Quarterly* 8 (Fall 1974): 273–82.

Patterson, David S. *The Search for Negotiated Peace: Women's Activism and Citizen Diplomacy in World War I.* New York: Routledge, 2008.

Patterson, Martha. *Beyond the Gibson Girl: Reimagining the American New Woman, 1895–1915.* Urbana: University of Illinois Press, 2005.

Pearson, Drew, and Robert S. Allen. *Washington Merry-Go-Round.* New York: Horace Liveright, 1931.

Pederson, John. "'A Lioness for Denmark?'—Eugenie Anderson and Danish American Relations, 1949–1953." In *Danish–North American Relations since World War II.* Edited by Peter L. Peterson, 45–57. Ames, IA: Danish American Heritage Society, 2004.

Perle Mesta: Patriot, Diplomat, Philanthropist, 1890–1975. Oklahoma City: State of Oklahoma, Office of the Governor, 1986.

Phillips, William. *Ventures in Diplomacy.* Boston: Beacon, 1952.

Porter, Cathy. *Alexandra Kollontai: The Lonely Struggle of the Woman Who Defied Lenin.* New York: Dial, 1980.

Putnam, Robert D. *The Comparative Study of Political Elites.* Englewood Cliffs, NJ: Prentice-Hall, 1976.

Rabel, Roberto G. *Between East and West: Trieste, The United States, and the Cold War, 1941–1954.* Durham, NC: Duke University Press, 1988.

Reid, Maree-Anne. "'Kiss the Boys Goodbye': Clare Boothe Luce's Appointment as United States Ambassador to Italy." *Australasian Journal of American Studies* 16, no. 2 (1997): 45–67.

Rosenberg, Emily. "Gender," *Journal of American History* 77 (June 1990): 116–24.

Roth, Lois W. "Nice Girl or Pushy Bitch: Two Roads to Nonpromotion." Women's Action Organization Occasional Paper, February 1980, available online at the Lois Roth Endowment website, https://rothendowment.org/wp-content/up-loads/2014/12/Lois-Roth-1980-WAO-article.pdf.

Rotundo, E. Anthony. *American Manhood: Transformations in Masculinity from the Revolution to the Modern Era.* New York: Basic Books, 1993.

Rupp, Leila J. *Worlds of Women: The Making of an International Women's Movement.* Princeton, NJ: Princeton University Press, 1997.

Rupp, Leila J., and Verta Taylor. *Survival in the Doldrums: The American Women's Rights Movement, 1945 to the 1960s.* New York: Oxford University Press, 1987.

Savage, Sean J. *Truman and the Democratic Party.* Lexington: University Press of Kentucky, 1997.

Schaffer, Howard B. *Ellsworth Bunker: Global Troubleshooter, Vietnam Hawk.* Chapel Hill: University of North Carolina Press, 2003.

Schattenberg, Susanne. "Ein Diplomat in Kleid: Aleksandra Kollontaj und die sowjetische Diplomatie." In *Das Geschlecht der Diplomatie: Geschlechterrollen in den Außenbeziehungen vom Spätmittelalter bis zum 20. Jahrhundert.* Edited by Corina Bastian, Eva Kathrin Dade, Hillard von Thiessen, and Christian Windler, 215–35. Cologne: Böhlau Verlag, 2014.

Schlesinger, Arthur M., Jr. *A Life in the Twentieth Century: Innocent Beginnings, 1917–1950.* Boston: Houghton Mifflin, 2000.

———. *A Thousand Days: John F. Kennedy in the White House.* Boston: Houghton Mifflin, 1965.

———. *The Vital Center: The Politics of Freedom.* Boston: Houghton Mifflin, 1949.

Schorr, Daniel. *Staying Tuned: A Life in Journalism.* New York: Simon & Schuster, 2001.

Schulzinger, Robert D. *The Making of the Diplomatic Mind: The Training, Outlook, and Style of United States Foreign Service Officers, 1908–1931.* Middletown, CT: Wesleyan University Press, 1975.

Shadegg, Stephen. *Clare Boothe Luce: A Biography.* New York: Simon & Schuster, 1972.

Sherman, Wendy. *Not for the Faint of Heart: Lessons in Courage, Power, and Persistence.* New York: PublicAffairs, 2018.

Siff, Stephen. "Henry Luce's Strange Trip: Coverage of LSD in *Time* and *Life*, 1954–68." *Journalism History* 34 (Fall 2008): 126–34.

Skard, Sigmund. *The United States in Norwegian History.* Westport, CT: Greenwood, 1976.

Sluga, Glenda, and Carolyn James. "Introduction: The Long International History of Women and Diplomacy." In Sluga and James, *Women, Diplomacy, and International Politics,* 1–12.

———, eds. *Women, Diplomacy, and International Politics since 1500.* Abingdon, UK: Routledge, 2016.

Smith, Amanda. *Newspaper Titan: The Infamous Life and Monumental Times of Cissy Patterson.* New York: Knopf, 2011.

Smith, Gerard C. *Disarming Diplomat: The Memoirs of Gerard C. Smith, Arms Control Negotiator.* Lanham, MD: Madison Books, 1996.

Smith, Jean Edward. *FDR.* New York: Random House, 2007.

Smith, Sally Bedell. *Reflected Glory: The Life of Pamela Churchill Harriman.* New York: Simon & Schuster, 1996.

Solberg, Carl. *Hubert Humphrey: A Biography.* New York: Norton, 1984.

Spaulding, E. Wilder. *Ambassadors Ordinary and Extraordinary.* Washington, DC: Public Affairs Press, 1961.

Stout, Mark. "The Pond: Running Agents for State, War, and the CIA," *Studies in Intelligence* 48, no. 3 (2004): https://www.cia.gov/library/center-for-the-study-of-intelligence/csi-publications/csi-studies/studies/vol48no3/article07.html.

Stuart, Graham H. *American Diplomatic and Consular Practice.* 2nd ed. New York: Appleton-Century-Crofts, 1952.

Stuhler, Barbara. *Ten Men of Minnesota and American Foreign Policy, 1898–1968.* St. Paul: Minnesota Historical Society, 1973.

Stur, Heather Marie. *Beyond Combat: Women and Gender in the Vietnam War Era.* Cambridge: Cambridge University Press, 2011.

Sulzberger, C. L. *The Last of the Giants: Memoirs and Diaries, 1954–1963.* New York: Macmillan, 1970.

———. *A Long Row of Candles: Memoirs and Diaries, 1934–1954.* New York: Macmillan, 1969.

Swanberg, W. A. *Luce and His Empire.* New York: Scribner's, 1972.

Tamnes, Rolf. *The United States and the Cold War In the High North.* Aldershot, UK: Dartmouth, 1991.

Taylor-Whitehead, W. J. *Luxembourg: Land of Legends.* London: Constable, 1951.

Thayer, Charles W. *Diplomat.* New York: Harper & Brothers, 1959.

Thomas, Bob. *I Got Rhythm! The Ethel Merman Story.* New York: G. P. Putnam's Sons, 1985.

Thomas, Evan. *Ike's Bluff: President Eisenhower's Secret Battle to Save the World.* Boston: Little, Brown, 2012.

Threlkeld, Megan. "Twenty Years of *Worlds of Women:* Leila Rupp's Impact on the History of U.S. Women's Internationalism." *History Compass* 15 (June 2017): https://onlinelibrary.wiley.com/doi/abs/10.1111/hic3.12381.

Towns, Ann, and Brigitta Niklasson. "Gender, International Status, and Ambassador Appointments." *Foreign Policy Analysis* 13 (July 2017): 521–40.

Truman, Margaret. *Bess W. Truman.* New York: Macmillan, 1986.

Turkington, Rebecca. "What Happened to Washington's Women Ambassadors?" Georgetown Institute for Women, Peace, and Security. September 5, 2017. https://giwps.georgetown.edu/what-happened-to-washingtons-women-ambassadors-2/.

UN News Centre. "A Conversation with Female Ambassadors about the UN Security Council." *UN News: Global Perspectives, Human Stories,* March 17, 2016. http://www.un.org/apps/news/story.asp?NewsID=53474#.

Upton, Anthony F. *Finland, 1939–1940.* Newark: University of Delaware Press, 1974.

Van Dyne, Frederick. *Our Foreign Service: The "A B C" of American Diplomacy.* Rochester, NY: Lawyers Co-Operative Publishing Co., 1909.

Vandevelde, Kenneth J. "Reassessing the Hickenlooper Amendment." *Virginia Journal of International Law* 29 (Fall 1988): 115–68.

Vickers, Sally. "Ruth Bryan Owen: Florida's First Congresswoman and Lifetime Activist." In *Making Waves: Female Activists in Twentieth-Century Florida.* Edited by Jack E. Davis and Kari Frederickson, 23–55. Gainesville: University Press of Florida, 2003.

Vickers, Sarah P. *The Life of Ruth Bryan Owen: Florida's First Congresswoman and America's First Woman Diplomat.* Tallahassee, FL: Sentry, 2009.

Villard, Henry S. *Affairs at State.* New York: Thomas Y. Crowell, 1965.

von Damm, Helene. *At Reagan's Side: Twenty Years in the Political Mainstream.* New York: Doubleday, 1989.

Wainwright, Loudon. *The Great American Magazine: An Inside History of* Life. New York: Knopf, 1986.

Ware, Susan. *Beyond Suffrage: Women in the New Deal.* Cambridge, MA: Harvard University Press, 1981.

———. "Harriman, Florence Jaffray Hurst." In *Notable American Women: The Modern Period.* Edited by Barbara Sicherman and Carol Hurd Green, 314. Cambridge, MA: Harvard University Press, 1980.

———. *Partner and I: Molly Dewson, Feminism, and New Deal Politics.* New Haven: Yale University Press, 1987.

Wehrey, Frederic. *The Burning Shores: Inside the Battle for the New Libya.* New York: Farrar, Straus & Giroux, 2018.

Weil, Martin. *A Pretty Good Club: The Founding Fathers of the U.S. Foreign Service.* New York: Norton, 1978.

Weiner, Tim. *Legacy of Ashes: The History of the CIA.* New York: Doubleday, 2007.

Wilkowski, Jean M. *Abroad for Her Country: Tales of a Pioneer Woman Ambassador in the U.S. Foreign Service.* Notre Dame, IN: University of Notre Dame Press, 2008.

Williams, Marjorie. *The Woman at the Washington Zoo: Writings on Politics, Family, and Fate.* New York: Public Affairs, 2005.

Willis, Nicholas J. *Frances Elizabeth Willis: Up the Foreign Service Ladder to the Summit—Despite the Limitations of Her Sex.* Carmel, CA: Nicholas J. Willis, 2013.

Wilson, Hugh R. *Diplomacy as a Career.* Cambridge, MA: Riverside, 1941.

Wolper, Gregg. "Woodrow Wilson's New Diplomacy: Vira Whitehouse in Switzerland, 1918." *Prologue* 24 (Fall 1992): 227–39.

Wood, Molly M. "'Commanding Beauty' and 'Gentle Charm': American Women and Gender in the Early Twentieth-Century Foreign Service." *Diplomatic History* 31 (June 2007): 505–30.

———. "Diplomatic Wives: The Politics of Domesticity and the 'Social Game' in the U.S. Foreign Service, 1905–1941." *Journal of Women's History* 17 (Summer 2005): 142–94.

———. "Gender and American Foreign Relations" In *The Routledge History of Gender, War, and the U.S. Military.* Edited by Kara D. Vuic, 202–14. New York: Routledge, 2017.

———. "Wives, Clerks, and 'Lady Diplomats': The Gendered Politics of Diplomacy and Representation in the U.S. Foreign Service, 1900–1940." *European Journal of American Studies* 10 (March 2015): http://ejas.revues.org/10562.

Woods, Randall B. *Shadow Warrior: William Egan Colby and the CIA.* New York: Basic Books, 2013.

Wright, C. Ben. "George F. Kennan, Scholar-Diplomat: 1926–1946." PhD diss., University of Wisconsin, 1972.

Zainulbhai, Hani. "Few American Women Have Broken the Glass Ceiling of Diplomacy." *Fact Tank: News in the Numbers,* Pew Research Center, July 22, 2016, http://www.pewresearch.org/fact-tank/2016/07/22/few-american-women-have-broken-the-glass-ceiling-of-diplomacy/.

Index

Studies in Conflict, Diplomacy, and Peace

Series Editors: George C. Herring, Andrew L. Johns, and
Kathryn C. Statler

This series focuses on key moments of conflict, diplomacy, and peace from the eighteenth century to the present to explore their wider significance in the development of US foreign relations. The series editors welcome new research in the form of original monographs, interpretive studies, biographies, and anthologies from historians, political scientists, journalists, and policymakers. A primary goal of the series is to examine the United States' engagement with the world, its evolving role in the international arena, and the ways in which the state, nonstate actors, individuals, and ideas have shaped and continue to influence history, both at home and abroad.

Advisory Board Members

David Anderson, California State University, Monterey Bay
Laura Belmonte, Oklahoma State University
Robert Brigham, Vassar College
Paul Chamberlin, University of Kentucky
Jessica Chapman, Williams College
Frank Costigliola, University of Connecticut
Michael C. Desch, University of Notre Dame
Kurk Dorsey, University of New Hampshire
John Ernst, Morehead State University
Joseph A. Fry, University of Nevada, Las Vegas
Ann Heiss, Kent State University
Sheyda Jahanbani, University of Kansas
Mark Lawrence, University of Texas
Mitchell Lerner, Ohio State University
Kyle Longley, Arizona State University
Robert McMahon, Ohio State University
Michaela Hoenicke Moore, University of Iowa
Lien-Hang T. Nguyen, University of Kentucky
Jason Parker, Texas A&M University
Andrew Preston, Cambridge University
Thomas Schwartz, Vanderbilt University
Salim Yaqub, University of California, Santa Barbara

Books in the Series

Truman, Congress, and Korea: The Politics of America's First Undeclared War
Larry Blomstedt

The Legacy of J. William Fulbright: Policy, Power, and Ideology
Edited by Alessandro Brogi, Giles Scott-Smith, and David J. Snyder

The Gulf: The Bush Presidencies and the Middle East
Michael F. Cairo

Reagan and the World: Leadership and National Security, 1981–1989
Edited by Bradley Lynn Coleman and Kyle Longley

American Justice in Taiwan: The 1957 Riots and Cold War Foreign Policy
Stephen G. Craft

Diplomatic Games: Sport, Statecraft, and International Relations since 1945
Edited by Heather L. Dichter and Andrew L. Johns

Nothing Less Than War: A New History of America's Entry into World War I
Justus D. Doenecke

Aid under Fire: Nation Building and the Vietnam War
Jessica Elkind

Enemies to Allies: Cold War Germany and American Memory
Brian C. Etheridge

Grounded: The Case for Abolishing the United States Air Force
Robert M. Farley

Foreign Friends: Syngman Rhee, American Exceptionalism, and the Division of Korea
David P. Fields

The Myth of Triumphalism: Rethinking President Reagan's Cold War Legacy
Beth A. Fischer

The American South and the Vietnam War: Belligerence, Protest, and Agony in Dixie
Joseph A. Fry

Lincoln, Seward, and US Foreign Relations in the Civil War Era
Joseph A. Fry

Obama at War: Congress and the Imperial Presidency
Ryan C. Hendrickson

The Cold War at Home and Abroad: Domestic Politics and US Foreign Policy since 1945
Edited by Andrew L. Johns and Mitchell B. Lerner

US Presidential Elections and Foreign Policy: Candidates, Campaigns, and Global Politics from FDR to Bill Clinton
Edited by Andrew Johnstone and Andrew Priest

Paving the Way for Reagan: The Influence of Conservative Media on US Foreign Policy
Laurence R. Jurdem

The Conversion of Senator Arthur H. Vandenberg: From Isolation to International Engagement
Lawrence S. Kaplan

Harold Stassen: Eisenhower, the Cold War, and the Pursuit of Nuclear Disarmament
Lawrence S. Kaplan

JFK and de Gaulle: How America and France Failed in Vietnam, 1961–1963
Sean J. McLaughlin

Nixon's Back Channel to Moscow: Confidential Diplomacy and Détente
Richard A. Moss

Breaking Protocol: America's First Female Ambassadors, 1933–1964
Philip Nash

Peacemakers: American Leadership and the End of Genocide in the Balkans
James W. Pardew

The Currents of War: A New History of American-Japanese Relations, 1899–1941
Sidney Pash

Eisenhower and Cambodia: Diplomacy, Covert Action, and the Origins of the Second Indochina War
William J. Rust

So Much to Lose: John F. Kennedy and American Policy in Laos
William J. Rust

Foreign Policy at the Periphery: The Shifting Margins of US International Relations since World War II
Edited by Bevan Sewell and Maria Ryan

Lincoln Gordon: Architect of Cold War Foreign Policy
Bruce L. R. Smith

Thomas C. Mann: President Johnson, the Cold War, and the Restructuring of Latin American Foreign Policy
Thomas Tunstall Allcock